Reason and Tradition in Indian Thought

An Essay on the Nature of Indian Philosophical Thinking

JITENDRA NATH MOHANTY

CLARENDON PRESS · OXFORD

This book has been printed digitally and produced in a standard specification in order to ensure its continuing availability

OXFORD
UNIVERSITY PRESS

Great Clarendon Street, Oxford OX2 6DP

Oxford University Press is a department of the University of Oxford. It furthers the University's objective of excellence in research, scholarship, and education by publishing worldwide in

Oxford New York

Auckland Bangkok Buenos Aires Cape Town Chennai Dar es Salaam Delhi Hong Kong Istanbul Karachi Kolkata Kuala Lumpur Madrid Melbourne Mexico City Mumbai Nairobi São Paulo Shanghai Singapore Taipei Tokyo Toronto

with an associated company in Berlin

Oxford is a registered trade mark of Oxford University Press in the UK and in certain other countries

Published in the United States by Oxford University Press Inc., New York

Reprinted 2002

ISBN 0-19-823960-2

Dedicated to the inspiring and humbling
memories of the late Mahāmahopādhyāya Pandit Yogendra Nath
Tarkavedāntatīrtha and the late Pandit Ananta Kumar Tarkatīrtha,
my preceptors in Vedānta and Nyāya respectively. If this book has
any worth, I owe it to them. All its defects are mine.
As incomparable scholars and teachers they impressed upon me the
greatness of the Sanskrit philosophical tradition.

PREFACE

I started writing this book during the terms I spent as a Visiting Fellow at All Souls College, Oxford, while studying the Sanskrit material used in this work, and thinking about the problems discussed began some thirty years ago when I was teaching at the University of Calcutta. The Bodleian Library provided excellent opportunities to fill gaps in my researches. This led to the idea of a much extended project requiring another volume beyond this. While the present volume deals with what may be called 'theoretical reason', the second volume, which I hope to complete in a year's time, will be devoted to exploring practical and aesthetic reason in Indian thought, completing the Kantian-sounding division between morality, art, and religion.

Some parts of this volume had appeared as articles in *Philosophy, East and West* and the *Journal of Indian Philosophy*. Chapter 1 is a slightly altered version of my contribution to Rama Rao Pappu and R. Puligandla (eds.), *Indian Philosophy: Past and Future* (Delhi, 1982). The discussions on sentential meaning versus word meaning, in Chapter 3, were first presented in a seminar on Theory of Meaning at the Jadavpur University in 1982. The various remarks on *śabdapramāṇa* were first gathered together in my 1986 Presidential Address to the Indian Philosophical Congress; since then I have profited from numerous discussions, in Calcutta, and in Oxford, of the views expressed in it. Over a long period of time, I have raised various issues about Indian theories of meaning, and these have stimulated much controversy from which I, most of all, have profited. Remarks on the general nature of the *pramāṇa–prameya* theory were first presented at the University of Hawaii on the occasion of the celebrations of the fiftieth anniversary of the Philosophy Department; an earlier version of these remarks has appeared in *Philosophy East and West.*

Many people have taken my ideas seriously enough to criticize them. I have learned from all of them. I must make special mention of the late Kalidas Bhattacharya, Sibajiban Bhattacharya, Bimal Matilal, Eliot Deutsch, Karl Potter, Mark Siderits, Pradyot Mukhopadhyaya, Tara Chatterjee, Arindam Chakrabarty, Lawr-

ence Davis, and Anindita Balslev. From each of these, some of them former students, I have always learned something valuable.

Whatever I know of Indian philosophy, I have learned from my two great teachers: Mahāmahopadhyāya Pandit Yogendra Nath Tarkavedāntatīrtha and Pandit Ananta Kumar Tarkatīrtha. With the former I studied Vedānta, with the latter Navya-Nyāya. This volume is dedicated to their memories as a humble token of gratitude.

Nadia Kravchenko prepared the word-processed manuscript with considerable patience, for which she has earned my gratitude.

J.N.M.

CONTENTS

INTRODUCTION 1

1. INDIAN PHILOSOPHY: BETWEEN TRADITION AND MODERNITY 7
   Indian Philosophy 7
   Tradition and Modernity 11
   Some Features of the *Darśanas* 17

2. CONSCIOUSNESS AND KNOWLEDGE 26
   Introduction 26
   The Issues 32
   Is Consciousness Formed or Formless? 34
   Is Consciousness a Substance, a Quality, or an Act? 41
   Is Consciousness Intentional? 42
   Is Consciousness Self-Manifesting? 46
   Consciousness as Transcendental: Résumé 50

3. LANGUAGE AND MEANING 54
   Introduction 54
   Word-Meaning (Padārtha) 55
   Sentence-Meaning (Vākyārtha) 67
   Linguistic Understanding (Śābdabodha) 83
   A Résumé 88
   Meaning Intention? 89
   Language and the Ineffable 93
   Identity Sentences (*Sāmānadhikaraṇyavākyāni*) 95

4. THE NATURE OF INDIAN LOGIC 100
   Anumāna 100
   The Inferential Process 101
   The Structure of Inferential Cognition 103
   Attempt at an Interpretation 106
   A Résumé 131

5. INDIAN THEORIES OF TRUTH: THEIR COMMON FRAMEWORK 133
   Cognitions as bearers of Truth 134

Truth-Determination: Intrinsic (*Svataḥ*) or Extrinsic (*Parataḥ*)? 138
Some Definitions of 'Truth' 144

6. THE CONCEPT OF BEING AND THE ONTOLOGIES 150
Preliminary Remarks 150
Terminology 153
Is Beingness a Universal? 154
Existence: Neither a Universal nor a Real Predicate 158
Sattā as the Universal Substance 161
Résumé and Further Issues 165
Pluralism versus Monism: A Study in Contrasts 170

7. TIME, HISTORY, MAN, AND NATURE 184
An Excursus into the Concept of Time 184
History 187
Man, Subject and Person 192
The Concept of Nature 205
Science and Metaphysics 222

8. REMARKS ON THE *PRAMĀṆA THEORY* 227
General Observations on the *Pramāṇa–Prameya* Theory 227
The Foundational Nature of Consciousness 236
The Primacy of Perception 238
Memory and Historical Knowledge 241
Mathematics 243
Pramāṇas in Law and Medicine 247
The theory of *Śabdapramāṇa* 249
Theory of Action 259

9. THE NATURE OF INDIAN PHILOSOPHICAL THINKING 269
Empiricism, Rationalism, and Ultimate 'Grounding' 269
Philosophy as Interpretation of Tradition: Can it Also Be a Critic? 272
Philosophy as a Historical Inquiry and as a Science 276
Metaphilosophical Thinking: Theory, Practice, and Mystical Experience 277
Are Indian and Western Philosophies radically different? 282

INDEX 301

Introduction

These chapters had their origin in various attempts to isolate the distinctive features, if any, of Indian philosophy, especially as compared with Western philosophy. I began to think about Indian logical theories, epistemologies, semantic theories, and ontologies, these being the areas in which my original training and competence lay. But in the course of my investigation, it became increasingly clear to me that in order to be able to grasp what the Indian mode of thinking was, one had to go beyond the philosophies and to take a look at the Indian positive sciences as well. Historiography, positive law, and medicine were important areas, as was much of Hindu mathematics. Since my concern in this work is with the general mode of thinking, I have had to abstract from the detailed content of the theories. I have looked at their methodological (formal and contentual) commitments and also at their broad categorial concepts such as 'body', 'action', 'property', and 'law'. The same is also true of my concern with the philosophical theories in the more restricted sense. As far as it was possible for me, I have not dealt with the substance of their doctrines and have restricted myself to what appeared to me to be the deeper underlying structures. The book makes, and in my view needs to make, no claims to exhaustiveness. My purpose would be achieved if it succeeded only in revealing some of the parameters within which Indian philosophers have thought.

In dealing with fundamental distinctions between Indian and Western thought, my predecessors and some of my contemporaries have used clichés which I have found unhelpful and quite often positively misleading. In my view, one can no longer use such opposites as spiritual–non-spiritual intuition–intellect, logical–non-logical in philosophy when one is comparing philosophical worlds. These distinctions cut across the Indian–Western dichotomy. There are materialistic Indian systems, as there are Western philosophies which rely on logic and intellect or which reject intellectual methods for some sort of intuitive mode of deriving knowledge. Neither is the alleged religious context of Indian philosophy the decisive point, for, first, this context is not absent in much of classical Western thought and, secondly, it is

only a source of concerns rather than of justification of the positions taken. This is indeed as it should be, for one prime concern of philosophy is reflection on one's own culture, which indeed for the ancient Hindus as much as for Western thinkers contained a large religious component. As a matter of fact, what has impressed more impartial observers is the fact that in both traditions, Indian and Western, we find not only such a wide spectrum of philosophical views as baffles any attempt at generalization in terms of handy clichés, but also that there are large measures of correspondence between the types of philosophy on both sides. It is this phenomenon that has given rise to serious interest in comparative philosophy. But comparative philosophy, as soon as it overcomes the easy temptation to build contrasts in terms of clichés, falls into the other equally tempting extreme of correlating theories from one side to theories on the other. While it is on the whole a correct methodological assumption that the human mind functions on the whole, at a basic level, in the same way, and also that the very idea of categorizing philosophical thinking according to its geographical and national origins jars with the basic rationality of philosophy, these beliefs, if pressed too far, may mislead by making us insensitive to the different ways in which that common mode of functioning expresses itself.

Those who, like the present author, have spent large parts of their lives studying Sanskrit philosophical texts in traditional seats of Sanskrit learning under Sanskrit scholars who knew neither Western philosophy nor even any Western language cannot but be impressed by both the radical difference and the remarkable affinities between what goes on in that intellectual world and what goes on in the Western philosophical world. Having spent equally long periods of time in the study of Western logic, semantics, epistemologies, and metaphysics, I found myself in a position in which the more difficult and perplexing task, I felt, was not to capture the common features which were rather superficial, but to conceptualize and articulate the deep and significant differences should there be any, after the clichés had been exposed as empty. This book reflects that concern.

In the long run, the concern is: given the fact that philosophical thinking is a rational activity and that the Indian philosophers were as rational as any in the Western tradition, shall we say that they all share and exemplify one common conception of rationality?

Or, do they operate with a conception of rationality that is very different from their Western counterparts? By implication, it should be obvious that I am rejecting the understandings of those who turn to Indian thinking as an escape from the drab rationality of Western thinking. (I have noticed the same sort of exasperation in many Indian spiritual seekers with the rationality of the traditional philosophies of India.) No, philosophy in India was a supremely rational and critical enterprise. But how does one go about determining the nature of the underlying conception of rationality? Any such conception must have at least the following components: a theory of logic or of valid inference, an account of what should count as evidence for or against conclusions, a conception of what it is to know something, and a theory of action, specifically of moral action. But all of these involve semantical theories: how to construe the meanings of sentences constituting a rational–theoretical discourse and what makes sentences true if they are theoretical and obligatory if they are practical. It is then to these topics that the essays in this and the next volume are devoted. No attempt has been made to support a preconceived thesis. I have let each essay speak for itself, with the hope that at the end something of a rather loosely unified point of view will have emerged.

There is one strategy which I have at many places employed, which needs some explanation. I have looked for concepts and concerns, distinctions and directions of inquiry that abound and in fact determine much of Western thought but are absent in Indian thought. These 'lacks', as I have called them, are then used not to evaluate and judge but to understand. Why is it, I often asked myself long before this book came to be written, that Indian philosophers showed no great concern with history, or with mathematics? Indeed, it is not historical answers that I have been looking for, but rather conceptual and structural ones. Likewise how remarkable, I wondered, that the Indian logics and epistemologies, for all their sophistication, never came to distinguish between analytic and synthetic truths, or between necessary and contingent truths? Or did they? In either case, where should one look for their concepts of the modalities? These putative absences point, according to my methodological hypothesis, to some deep structures of Indian thought. They are not deficiencies, they are absences only in the context of comparative philosophy. But

here comparative philosophy shows itself to be positively useful and philosophically instructive.

In some matters, we can only speak of 'more or less', not of absolute distinctions. We can only say of a certain concept that it never quite occupied the centre of attention in one tradition in a manner in which it did in another tradition. To take one example, I have suggested the hypothesis that whereas in Indian thought the concept of the *subject* as the neutral disinterested knower occupies a decisive role, in Western thought the concept of the *person* as the active agent is more important, so much so that where the other concept emerges in either tradition, it is assimilated to the dominant concept. Here we find degrees of emphasis, centrality, and primacy, not absolute presence or total absence.

Each such finding is instructive and useful for systematic philosophizing. There is an attitude towards philosophy, closely connected with, though not logically implied by a historicist attitude, that I reject as perverse. Since all philosophical concepts arose within a particular culture at a certain point of time and so were absent prior to that, the historicist is often led to think that all philosophy is historical reflection, from which he draws the further conclusion that the course of history would render most, perhaps all our present concerns outdated. I think this is mistaken. There is both a historical and a supra-historical aspect to philosophy. I would say the same of cultural relativism. Not all philosophical concerns are culture-bound. Some transcend culture, and our goal, as philosophers, is to move from the one to the other level, and eventually to be able to relate them satisfactorily.

In this book, I have written about some fragments of Indian philosophy of classical times, the source material mostly dating from the beginnings of the Christian era up to the great logical period of the Navya-Nyāya. But I have not played the role of a neutral expositor. I have taken sides, expressed preferences, suggested new directions and often radical departures. In other words, I have played the role of a critical philosopher reflecting upon his own tradition. I have never been convinced that everything that concerned the Indian philosophers of the past should be relevant to us today. There must be many things there that are for us dead and only of antiquarian interest, some again whose interest is only cultural but not philosophical. The problems which I have dealt with are some of those which, in my view, are

living, and can provide the foothold for new creative thinking in self-conscious continuity with that tradition.

In doing all this, one of course interprets. Every interpreter intends to give *the* meaning of a text, but so also does every other. It is only a sign of philosophical naïvety to claim that there is just one privileged sense of a text or of a tradition, and that the author of the text or the ancients had it. One forgets that the author is also an interpreter of his own text, and that temporal proximity has nothing to do with authentic interpretation. There is no privileged access. This realization opens up the space within which such a work as this could be possible.

At the end of this introduction, a few words about the structure of the book. To a not too careful reader it may appear as though I have chosen a few disconnected topics and problems for study, that what is lacking is a structure. However, that is not so. Theoretical reason, as I see it, is best manifested in the way our beliefs are appraised as true, in the way our theories about what *is*, i.e. our sciences and ontologies, are substantiated. The larger theory within Indian philosophy which examines this procedure is the so-called *pramāṇa* theory. As I see it, the basis of all 'means of true cognition' (*pramāṇas*), of all evidencing, is consciousness. Hence, we begin by considering the theory of consciousness (Chapter 2). Beliefs and theories are expressed in language: they have to be understood before they are established as true or false: hence the need for a theory of meaning as a part of one's overall philosophy of language (Chapter 3). It is by one or more of these *pramāṇas* that truth is established. Although the list of *pramāṇas* varies from system to system, perception, inference, and language (*śabda*) are the most important of them. I do not deal with perception at any length, but only draw attention to its primacy in Chapter 7. In the same chapter, cases are made for recognizing memory, history, and mathematics as independent *pramāṇas*. *Pramāṇas* lead to the establishment (*siddhi*) of beliefs (or theories) as true: Chapter 5 brings out the underlying concepts of truth (*pramāṇa*). Once truth is established, the result is a determination of what *is*: Chapter 6 discusses the concept of 'being' and the dominant ontologies (of Sāṃkhya and Vaiśeṣika). Finally, metaphilosophical questions are raised in the concluding pages (Chapter 9) regarding the nature of philosophical thinking—questions which were anticipated in the introductory remarks of

Chapter 1, and amplified throughout the work, and finally gathered together in the concluding pages.

A personal confession: I have been a student of phenomenology (especially Husserlian phenomenology) and of Navya-Nyāya; it is in these two fields that I have published most. Readers of this work on Indian thought who are familiar with my earlier publications would expect me to be giving a phenomenological reading of Indian logic and epistemology. I make no such attempt consciously. Yet, as far I am concerned—and my earlier publications have made this point from various angles—good phenomenology and good analysis are inseparable: Husserl himself so well exemplifies both. In my view, the best of Indian philosophy is both phenomenological and analytical: it is both analysis of ordinary usage (*lokavyavahāra*) and description of how things are presented to the testimony of consciousness (*pratiti-sākṣikaḥ*). I have accordingly used methodological and contentual resources of both the phenomenological and analytical traditions to understand and interpret Indian thought: but underlying them all there is a conception of transcendental, but yet hermeneutic phenomenology that is operative but not thematized.

1

Indian Philosophy: Between Tradition and Modernity

INDIAN PHILOSOPHY

Anyone who asks 'What is Indian philosophy? What is "Indian" about it?' has already situated himself outside the tradition that we call Indian. None of the philosophers who shaped that tradition, and with whose writings we are acquainted, ever asked such a question. They lived and thought within that tradition which today, by the very questions we are asking, we are categorizing. Through this act of categorization, a rupture occurred. Or, rather, it is only such a rupture that could make such categorization possible.

To ask 'What is Indian philosophy?' is also, by posing that question, to contrast it with non-Indian philosophy. Unless one transcends the tradition, one cannot, and need not, ask such a question. Yet, unless one understands the tradition from within, one cannot answer it. We are thus confronted by a paradox, a paradox which we need not resolve, but, by nature of what we, the modern Indian philosophers, are, we have to live with. We cannot escape this tragedy.

And yet what sort of concept is the concept of 'Indian philosophy?' The fact that this inquiry is now taking place in the English language, making use of the Western concept of *philosophia*, cannot be totally ignored. Is it not the case, as Western thinkers have time and again insisted, that the concept of philosophy, not merely as the love of wisdom, but also as the first science, marks 'the *telos* which was inborn in European humanity at the birth of Greek philosophy'?[1] On the other hand, if philosophy is the highest and purest form of rational inquiry, is it at all permissible to speak of 'European rationality'? Does not an adjective such as 'European' impose a limitation which destroys the very sense of 'rationality'? If rationality is a universal, not

limited by geographical regions, historical epochs, or cultural relativities, then philosophy as the purest form of rational inquiry must be, in its very conception, capable of being a universal pursuit of mankind. Such a claim to universality is perfectly compatible with a great diversity of internal differentiation. European philosophy itself is not a homogeneous domain, but, rather, contains methodological, substantive, and metaphilosophical differences of every imaginable degree. It is, therefore, possible to speak of an overarching sense of rationality and so of 'philosophy' which will contain, within it, internal differentiations such as Indian *darśana* and Greek *philosophia*.

But Greek *philosophia* is love of wisdom, an *eros* which by its nature generates ceaseless inquiry and search aiming at wisdom. Indian *darśana* is systematic elaboration of truth, or an aspect of it, which has already been grasped; it is not search for truth but exposition of it, intellectual vindication, conceptual fixation, and clarification of what has been received. In *philosophia*, the individual thinker, captivated by the love of wisdom, plays the decisive role. In a *darśana*, the individual thinker, great or small, plays a subordinate role, he does not found a system but carries its explication forward. The *darśana* is a perception of truth, or a possibility of its perception, which antedates any individual thinker or expositor. Criticism, clarificatory-explicative as well as destructive, is either intrasystemic or intersystemic. Common to both the *philosophia* tradition and the *darśana* tradition is critical thinking, thinking which looks for evidence—empirical and rational—justifying cognitive claims, and elaborates principles of such justification, logic in the one case and the science of the means of true cognition (*pramāṇa-śāstra*) in the other; and which, using the tools thereby made available, reflects on the nature of what is, resulting in ontology in the one case and science of the objects of true cognition (*prameya-śāstra*) in the other.

The concept 'Indian philosophy' owes the other half of its problematic character to the difficulty of ascertaining what is in general meant by 'Indian' and what is meant by it in our specific context. If it is to a geographical region that we are referring, it is well known that political vicissitudes do not permit us to delimit that region in a historically invariant manner. Even when one speaks of 'Indian philosophy today', do we mean philosophical works written by Indians or works on Indian philosophy written by

anyone, Indian or non-Indian? (One may have to extend the scope of 'Indian' to 'Indian by descent' for obvious reasons.) But today Indians write on Western philosophy as much as non-Indians write on Indian philosophy. Authorship cannot be used to delimit Indian philosophy.

A more promising attempt would be the following: we start by ostensively listing the core source material in the various *darśanas*, and then extend the scope of 'Indain philosophy' to include any philosophical work which self-consciously takes up that core tradition, and perceives itself as continuing the discussion of the themes, issues, and problems formulated in, and arising out of, that tradition, no matter in what language and irrespective of the geographical and socio-political loyalty of the author. Note that this account makes use of the idea of self-consciously taking up and continuing a tradition. A tradition does not function, maintain itself, and grow by way of external causality. It is true that a tradition consists, in large measure, of sedimented meanings which need to be rescued from anonymity, reactivated, and appropriated; but that is not incompatible with saying that a tradition is a tradition for one only in so far as it is self-consciously taken up by the latter. To say the latter is *not* to say that for one who self-consciously takes up, lives, and continues a tradition, all elements of that tradition are transparent, or that large areas are not either anonymous or obscure or ambiguous. The process of living within a tradition is also a continuing process of interpreting it and interpreting oneself in the light of it. Most of us, naïvely participating, accept, in the measure suited to our understanding, some handed-down interpretation or other. The task of philosophy is to overcome the naïvety of this acceptance. But are we not talking now, not of Indian tradition in general, but of the tradition of the Indian *darśanas*? This already belongs to a higher level of self-conscious and reflective acceptance and participation, not in the sense that the participator distinguishes it from non-Indian traditions (he, in fact, in the past knew very little, if any, of them), but in the sense that he knows, justifies, and plays the rules of the game as laid down, developed, and professionally practised through the centuries.

Against the explication of 'Indian philosophy' suggested above, two criticisms may be made. In the first place, it may be pointed out that it makes Indian philosophy into an open-ended contex-

ture, in the sense that anything would count as belonging to its scope if it only self-consciously pursued, extended, and perceived itself as continuing the thoughts of the core tradition. And, secondly, one may want to argue that restricting the tradition to themes, issues, and problems is tantamount to denying that system-centred nature of the *darśana* tradition which was brought out earlier. To reply briefly: it would be unilluminating to restrict the tradition to the texts,[2] for, first, we do not know how narrowly circumscribed that core corpus has to be. Assuming that we have a core corpus, we still have the problem of identifying what the texts say apart from the interpretations which have historically unfolded. The orthodoxy of returning to the texts themselves is laudable, but the confidence that one can capture the sense of the texts independently of interpreting them is a sign of either dogmatism or naïvety. Our only access to the texts is through interpretations, and the sense of the texts may well be said to have unfolded through such interpretations.[3] Orthodoxy may go along with this, and yet want to close the acceptable interpretations at some point. But again such a move is arbitrary. Why close the acceptable Vedic interpretation with Sayana, and why not admit Sri Aurobindo and Dayananda? Admitting then the normative role that the return to the core texts should play, it is nevertheless desirable to leave room for creative possibilities of interpretation.

As regards the systemic nature of the *darśanas*: it is again true that the *darśanas* are systems, but it would be a mistake to suppose that they were closed, absolutely self-justifying systems. The basic conceptual framework for each *darśana* received some defence within it, as well as by way of intersystem dialogues and disputations, but the defence of a conceptual framework—the list of types of entity denoted by words (*padārthas*) and the list of means of true cognition (*pramāṇas*)—could not be radical[4] when carried out from within, for such a defence has to use the *pramāṇas* as formulated within that framework. The defence is rather *ex post facto*, a defence of what has been received. One may at this point genuinely ask whether a radical justification of a system is at all possible. With the Mādhyamikas one may reply in the negative; with Husserl one may want to shun philosophical system and do a different sort of philosophy aiming at radical self-reflection and self-criticism. It is in view of such possibilities, one ancient and the other contemporary, and it is also in view of

the inevitable weakening of belief in language as a means of true cognition (*śabdapramāṇa*), the source of the basic conceptual framework in each case, that today, in the global philosophical situation in which we, the Indian philosophers, find ourselves, it may be necessary to salvage, in the face of decay of the systems, the themes, issues, and problems and to go on from there.

TRADITION AND MODERNITY

Considerations such as these lead us to reflect on the concepts of 'tradition' and 'modernity' and on the situation in which the Indian philosophers find themselves today. There is a simple chronological sense which trivializes the deeper issues—the sense according to which in every age the latest to arrive on the scene is the modern while the old, that which is past but stored in memory, is the tradition. Such a shifting distinction is taken care of by the flow of time, as the present recedes into the past, the latest to arrive becomes old and vanishes into the dimness of recollection. Our problem is not simply the formal problem of temporality. 'Modernity' has a specific sense here, and, in the Indian context, tradition has a special role. Both need to be looked into.

I think it is important to distinguish between tradition and orthodoxy. Orthodoxy consists in fossilizing tradition into a lifeless, unchanging structure. Tradition, as distinguished from orthodoxy, is a living process of creation and preservation of significations. When a tradition is alive, it continues to grow, to create, and to respond to new situations and challenges. When it is no longer alive, it requires an orthodoxy to preserve its purity against possible distortions and desanctifications. A living tradition is ambiguous in the sense that it allows for growth and development in many different ways. It is false to oppose tradition to freedom of rational criticism, for rational criticism takes place, not within a vacuum but from within a tradition. What we are trying to capture, then, is not the opposition orthodoxy–modernity, but tradition–modernity.

If modernity means outright rejection of tradition, then of course there is no promise of fruitful dialogue and mediation. In so far as philosophy is concerned, modernity in this sense would amount to courting every modern fad or style, school or

movement. But such an attitude, quite apart from whether it is genuinely philosophical or Indian or both, can only exhaust itself in chasing after the most recent, the ultramodern for its own sake, i.e. just because it is the most recent. It is to that extent self-defeating and self-destroying.

There are two other, more promising ways of understanding 'modernity'. The first of these is that modernity consists in addressing oneself to what is contemporaneous. This is a fundamentally different attitude from that dismissed in the preceding paragraph. More responsible, it is not excited by the newest, but is challenged by the contemporary ongoing dialogue. That makes it more philosophical. Philosophical thinking, in an important respect, is a dialogue, and even when it is monological, the monologue consists in appropriating and internalizing a possible dialogical situation. But with whom can I converse, who can ask me questions, challenge my convictions, question my arguments, excepting one who is a contemporary? While this appears to me unexceptionable, I must add, however, that it does not exclude tradition from being a dialogical partner. My tradition *can* be contemporaneous with me. What is more, this is particularly true of the situation of an Indian philosopher. A living tradition, to the extent it is living, challenges the thinker. The Indian tradition is contemporaneous with the Indian philosopher; for one thing, it offers the most important challenge to him, a challenge to understand, interpret, and communicate with it. In the recent past, philosophers in India assumed a false, unphilosophical role in relation to their tradition, namely the role of interpreting that tradition to the West, to the so-called modern world. This is unphilosophical, for it is not the task of philosophy to interpret something *to* some audience. The philosopher interprets the text, such interpretation being the way his thinking answers the questions and the challenge the text offers to him, or rather the meeting of his questioning and the text's. What is more, in the special circumstance of the Indian context, the tradition permeates the life-world in which the philosopher finds himself; it in fact constitutes his life-world—not merely the subject-matter for scholarly research. Promising as it is, the notion of contemporaneity, then, succeeds in mediating between tradition and modernity, and reveals that opposition to be not after all an unbridgeable gulf and our situation not to demand a choice.

The other promising clue lies in the idea of criticism. The modern spirit is the critical spirit. Tradition demands respect and conformity. In view of the wide appeal of this way of formulating the contrast, it may be worth while to look deeper into its validity and limitations in the Indian context. To be fair to Indian philosophical thinking, we need to reformulate the contrast thus: it is not true that Indian tradition knows of no critical thinking. What is at stake *vis-à-vis* modernity is whether there are universal norms of criticism—logical, epistemological, or axiological—which can be applied indifferently to any mode of thinking.

The traditionalist may argue that, in truth, any critical norm should be internal to a tradition, so that although it can and should be relentlessly applied within that tradition it cannot coherently be used to question the basic framework of that tradition itself. In the context of Indian philosophical tradition, for example, it is misconceived to apply the norms derived from formal logic, or epistemological norms derived from either the empiricism or the rationalism of the Western tradition. According to the fundamental framework of a large segment of that tradition, scriptural texts are epistemologically stronger than either the purely logical considerations or sensuous evidence. Furthermore, the 'logical' itself is conceived as ancillary to and parasitical upon the perceptual and the scriptural, so that the tradition did not recognize the autonomy of the logical, be it in the sense of an autonomous, self-subsistent mode of being or in the sense of having an autonomous type of truth such as formal validity or analyticity. With the subordination of the logical to the perceptual and of the perceptual to the scriptural texts, the framework rules out any purely formal–logical or sensualistic, empirical criticism from within, and of course criticism from without is in any case inadmissible.

Against this powerful self-defence and also self-interpretation of the tradition, one may point out that it operates with too rigid a conception of the tradition to begin with, one which transforms a given tradition into a self-sufficient whole, a windowless monad. But such a view flies in the face of the historical growth, not merely of ideas within a tradition, but also of its own supposedly basic framework. There is no a priori reason against—and some empirical evidence in favour of—interaction with alien traditions as a factor contributing to that historical growth. Consider, for

example, the orthodox philosophical systems (*āstika darśanas*, excluding the *nāstika* ones, for the sake of simplicity alone) which define the range of variations within the tradition of Indian philosophy, and therefore also the invariant conceptual, logical, and epistemological framework for those variations. Neither these *darśanas* nor their basic frameworks were there in the scriptural literature. They were latter-day developments, and their expositors and advocates found for them footholds within the scriptures. To suppose that only these systems, and no others, could have developed within that tradition, that any other would have been basically incompatible with it, would be to insist on the possibility of an a priori deduction of those systems, which is an unsubstantiated and unsubstantiable claim. In fact, each *darśana* has grown and developed far beyond what was anticipated by the early masters.

Faced with such a challenge, the traditionalist will no doubt fall back on what is indeed a valid point: through all the variations in systematic discourse, the basic questions continued to be the same while only the answers differed. There also persists a unique style of philosophizing. The *darśanas* derived their fundamental concepts, if not doctrines, from the pre-systematic texts—concepts such as nature (*prakṛti*), action (*karma*), self (*ātman*), liberation (*mokṣa*), quality (*guṇa*)—and were elaborating the secret intentions of those texts (or at least thought themselves to be doing so). The validity of this last contention should be considered together with what is seemingly its counterpoint: many thinkers from within the tradition proved revolutionaries by challenging the basic framework (if there was one). Gautama, the Buddha, challenged the *ātman* tradition, Nāgārjuna challenged the metaphysical–epistemological framework, Raghunātha Śiromaṇi the inherited Vaiśeṣika categorial scheme from within, Vācaspati and Vijñānabhikṣu earned the title 'independent of all systems' (*Sarvatantrasvatantra*) by cutting across party lines and by seeking to reconcile systems, which certainly is hardly consistent with the traditional either/or conception of the *darśanas*. When a culture is living, it does not take refuge in the name of 'tradition' but indulges in adventures of thinking; when it is dead or dying, the idea of protecting a tradition from corruption poses itself as a vital concern.

While recognizing the uniqueness of the style and, in some

cases, of the content of philosophizing that went on in the Indian tradition, we still need to reject the attempt to fossilize that tradition into such a self-sufficient, autonomous whole as to render it immune to radical (as distinguished from internal) criticism. For, whereas in the context of other sorts of system (mathematical, and even cultural) genuine criticism is internal, it appears to be repugnant to the spirit of philosophy to limit criticism to the internal standards of a system. Radical questioning—i.e. questioning of the basic presuppositions including historical—cultural accomplishments—is intrinsic to philosophizing. Thus, there is, in the very nature of philosophizing, a universality which one ignores if one restricts it to the parameters of the *darśana* tradition, as much as if one restricts it, as many Western thinkers tend to do, to those of the *philosophia* tradition.

One may want to argue, in response to the above contention, that such universality is very nearly achieved in abstract sciences such as formal logic, but even there a logical or mathematical system is conventionally founded and admits of alternatives. Where thought is not empty or formal, when one thinks about oneself and one's world, one's aim shall be, not the abstract universality which is present in all content and so in the empty region of content-in-general, but the concrete universality which seeks the universal in the concrete and the particular: that precisely is assured by a well-founded tradition. It provides the content within which thought should search for the universal. Where indeed has philosophical thought been able to transcend the bounds of tradition? Is not European philosophy, despite all claims to the contrary, despite all claims to new breakthroughs, innovations, 'deconstructions', and 'constructions', still within the horizon which opened up with the Greeks and was subsequently determined by Christianity and the rise of modern science—all three of them historically based traditions?

I agree that there is a difference between philosophical thinking concerned with oneself and one's world and the abstract thinking expressed in the formal sciences, so that the former, as concrete reflection, cannot start with, or even aim at, the empty universality of the latter. Nevertheless, two remarks may be in order: one with regard to formal–logical thinking and the other with regard to concrete philosophizing. As to the former, although it is true that there are alternative systems of logic, yet a logical system is not all

arbitrary and the different alternative systems are not such that they bear no relation to each other. In fact, one may very well ask, why are they logics? In so far as they are logics, they share certain common features and satisfy certain common requirements. If this is true, what we learn is that the contention that even in formal systems there is no common norm, and that all norms are internal to a system, is not tenable. As to concrete philosophizing, although here thought moves within the horizon defined by a tradition, no tradition can, with finality, set limits to the reaches of critical–philosophical thinking. It is precisely the greatness of a living and developing tradition that it can turn its reflective glance on itself. Both in the self-reflection of a tradition, and in an individual's reflection upon his own prejudices, transcendence is achieved, without which philosophy would remain immanent criticism of culture. Neither the *darśana* tradition nor the *philosophia* tradition limit philosophy to this fate.

If the foregoing reflections have aimed at the thesis that tradition and modernity are not irreconcilably opposed to each other, that is because Indian philosophical tradition, with its emphasis on *pramāṇa*, contains enough of the critical spirit, and also because no responsible modernism could avoid taking seriously that alone on which it can build.

In the context of Indian philosophy, the relation to tradition today is all the more complex. This may be shown by bringing in the concept of the Indian life-world.[5] There is no doubt that that life-world is traditional; the beliefs, perceptions, and practices which constitute it are rooted in structures of meaning established long ago. The relation of the *darśanas* to this life-world has never been investigated, but it would seem that the law of determination holds good here as everywhere else: systematic philosophical thinking does not determine, but rather idealizes[6] the perceptions and beliefs constitutive of life-world. Life-world, on the other hand, under-determines the systems. Given this law of determination, we need only to recognize that a radical transformation is taking place in that life-world—a transformation whose relation to the underlying meaning-structures is, to be sure, uncertain. This transformation consists in part in the introduction of Western technology, and in part in the injection of political, economic, and social ideologies from the West. While the rural, agricultural, traditional base remains unchanged, a technology grafted on it is

not only bringing about vast changes but inevitably generating tensions in value and meaning systems. The political–democratic ideology, the consumption-orientated economy, and ideas of social egalitarianism are in conflict with the hierarchical, caste- and class-ridden, subsistence-orientated structures. The large question to which the Indian philosophers today cannot but respond is, can such a transformation of their own life-world leave them untouched? Should it not demand a re-examination of the traditional modes of thinking, if not to reject them, surely to reinterpret them, if necessary, from the vantage point of the present situation. Such a reinterpretation may be serious or trivial. It is serious when it is accompanied by competence in traditional learning and guided by genuinely philosophical motivations.

SOME FEATURES OF THE DARŚANAS

Genuinely philosophical motivations can arise from out of the philosophical situation we inherit, not from the life-worldly situation in which we find ourselves. To understand the philosophical situation we inherit, we need to ask about the essence of Indian philosophy, an essence in which not merely its Indianness but also its being philosophy is preserved. As most textbooks of Indian philosophy will show, our predecessors, during the first half of this century, understood this essence to lie in the spiritual–practical intention of the *darśanas*. Our generation does not share this understanding of the philosophical tradition, and rightly so. For, in the first place, it is not as though Western philosophy, in its beginning, did not have a spiritual–practical goal in view.[7] In the second place, the characterization in terms of a spiritual–practical goal by itself does scant justice to the purely theoretical issues and discussions which so dominate the *darśanas* that even the idea of a spiritual–practical goal itself receives purely theoretical treatment. Moreover, locating such an intention in the essence of Indian philosophy helps us little to understand the logical structure of the thinking which constitutes it. In the absence of such a global feature, and in view of the fact that the Indian philosophical world presents a bewildering variety of views, theories, and concerns, the best we can do is put forward less ambitious hypotheses and try them out to see if they work. I propose here, for my limited

purpose and within the limits of this chapter, several such hypotheses:

One may distinguish between two conceptions of philosophy. Philosophy may be regarded as a science, as an objective body of knowledge about the nature of things, statable in objectively true sentences. Or, philosophy may be regarded as man's historically developing self- and world-understanding. Only in the latter sense does philosophy have a history. In fact, in this sense, philosophy is historical enterprise rooted in the alleged historicity of man's understanding of himself and his world, which itself is historical–cultural. Indian philosophy, we may begin by noting, understands itself to be philosophy in the first sense. It is a body of knowledge about the nature of things. But this is a self-understanding that it shares with ancient Greek thought as well. Historicism is a specifically modern concept, coming to its own somewhere around the birth of Hegel's 1807 *Phenomenology*.

Since Aristotle defined metaphysics as the science of being *qua* being, Western thought has kept philosophy and science apart. If the sciences were gradually emancipated from philosophy, that was a destiny foreshadowed in the origins of philosophy as metaphysics. Indian philosophy does not, in that manner, separate itself from the sciences. It is true that the period of the *darśanas* preceded the rise of experimental science in the modern sense of the term. It is also true that European science was, in its Aristotelian phase, speculative natural philosophy. But a distinction between metaphysics and physics did not, in the Indian tradition, anticipate the clear-cut distinction of today. The Nyāya-Vaiśeṣika and the Sāṃkhya remained scientific, and dealt not only with being *qua* being, but with beings in their various regional aspects as well. This closeness to natural, empirical science had its salutary as well as controversial effect. It kept philosophy closer to experience, but it also led to an almost unlimited use of causal enquiry. The causal question was asked, even within epistemological and logical discourse.

The Judaeo-Christian tradition is supposed to have brought to the Western tradition two major components which superseded some earlier strands of thought in antiquity. These are: the idea of creation out of nothing and the conception of a linear temporal order. The former, seemingly only of theological relevance, has been of decisive influence in all aspects of thinking. Consider, for

example, one such consequence: the idea of pure possibilities as prior to the actual world, a thought which itself has determined Western logics and metaphysics. The latter component, seemingly secular, is really of theological origin. One needed a unique point of origin and an eschatological world-view in order to make sense of a unique, linear time, and both were allegedly supplied by Judaeo-Christian thought. Now, Indian thought certainly lacks the first component, though whether it lacks the second, i.e. a conception of linear time, will be discussed later in this work. How these alleged omissions have influenced the Indian mode of thinking overall is a question that needs to be pursued at many levels, something that need not be done here.

Next, I want to emphasize a nexus of moves which, at a deep level, characterize Indian philosophical thinking. Each of these requires a degree of elaboration and textual support which I cannot give within the limits of the present chapter. But even at the risk of appearing to be dogmatic, I propose to state them in order to draw attention to their nearly pervasive presence.

1. Consider, first, the concept of definition (*lakṣaṇa*). It is highly extensional. A definition does not seek to articulate the essence of the definiendum, but rather aims at uniquely identifying it. Any expression which succeeds in unique identification, which does not over-extend or under-extend, i.e. avoids both *ati-vyāpti* and *a-vyāpti*, is a good definition, even if the properties in terms of which the definition is constructed are accidents (*upalakṣaṇa*) and so neither genus nor differentium.

2. This extensional concept of definition fits well with an overall denotative, referential theory of meaning, so that a (Fregean) concept of sense as distinguished from reference is almost lacking in Indian thought. Three remarkable theories hover on the horizon suggesting a theory that is not referential, the theory of *sphoṭa*, the theory of *apoha*, and the grammarian's device of self-reference, but none is fully intensional (Chapter 3).

3. This extensionalism in theories of definition and meaning is combined with an intensional feature: analysis of a sentence in terms of the cognition (*jñāna*) that is expressed in it. This intensional feature goes well with the overall extensionalism because the cognition that is expressed is not a sense, but an event (property, act, or substantial modification, depending upon which system one happens to be talking about) belonging to someone's

self (*ātman*) (Chapter 2). Consequently, Indian logic is a logic of cognitions—in spite of its preoccupation with sentences and sentential contexts.

4. A logic of cognitions, in so far as it is concerned with cognitions (which are events), affiliates itself to psychology of a sort, but in so far as it is logic gives universal rules of the occurrence or non-occurrence of cognitive events of other types. Thus although logic and psychology are not distinguished, we have neither psychologism not logicism, but an almost unique way out (Chapter 4).

5. In the absence of formalization, a conception of purely formal validity as contradistinguished from material truth never emerged. As is well known, an inference is tested for its conformity to rules which include what could be called formal and non-formal requirements, but since the latter distinction was not made, the best we can say is that an inference was regarded as true if the conditions for its occurrence as a cognitive event were given (see (4) above) and if the state of affairs is as one infers it to be (Chapter 4).

6. The concept of truth is so formulated that it does not leave room for a further differentiation into necessary and contingent truth, or into analytic and synthetic truth. There is a most fascinating but enormously complex set of features centring around and connected with the role of the modal concepts in Indian thought. The basic extensionalism and non-essentialism suggest that the modal concepts should be absent as well, and, in fact, this appears to be the case. The Indian philosopher is not concerned with bare possibilities, with counter factual conditionals (the Nyāya looks upon arguments which make use of counterfactuals (*tarka*) as invalid (*a-pramā*)), with possible worlds, but rather with what allegedly is the case. Everything can be doubted, provided the appropriate causal conditions of the cognitive event called doubt (*samśaya*) are present.[8] But this possibility of doubt does not constitute pure possibilities, it constitutes what may at most be called 'motivated' possibilities.[9] But this theory of doubt does rule out of existence a class of truths that are indubitable and so necessary in the modal sense.[10] At the same time, a universal scepticism is ruled out on grounds of contradicting day-to-day practical life. While such a fallibilism clearly characterizes Nyāya-

Vaiśeṣika logic and epistemology, it is not otherwise in Vedānta in so far as empirical knowledge is concerned (Chapter 5).[11]

7. Although asserting causal relations in conceptual matters is hazardous, one may, without taking considerable risk, say that features (1)–(6) are closely connected with the fact that none of the Indian epistemologies recognized mathematical knowledge as a type of knowledge that is *sui generis*. One often finds amongst possible candidates to the status of an irreducible type of true cognition (*pramāṇa*) what is called *sambhava* (or, the possible). Examples given of this mode of knowing are generally arithmetical truths. All epistemologists who mention it reduce it to the standard form of inference, and so deny to it the status of an irreducible type of knowledge. In effect, mathematical knowledge played no role in the Indian epistemologies, not to speak of the paradigmatic position it occupied in the thought of the Greek rationalists. It may be noted that when the Nyāya logicians did find a place for numbers in their ontology, the resulting conception of number was a curious blend of intensional features, in so far as number was regarded as a *guṇa* or quality, and extensional features, in so far as this quality has a peculiar relation of *paryāpti*, i.e. the relation of extensionally belonging to all members of a class[12] (Chapter 7).

8. If mathematical knowledge was not a *pramāṇa*, neither was history. Again, we find, in the literature, the claim of tradition (*aitihya*) to be a *pramāṇa* set aside by reducing it to either word-generated cognition (*śabda*) or inference, or both (Chapter 6).[13]

9. Possibly connected with the non-recognition of historical knowledge as an irreducible mode of true cognition (*pramāṇa*) is the status of memory in the epistemologies. Memory was excluded from the scope of true cognition (*pramā*) either because it is not an original mode of knowledge but is rather parasitical upon past knowledge, or because what it apprehends, namely the past, is no more (Chapter 7.)[14]

In (1) to (9), I have drawn attention to several features of Indian philosophical tradition, which have been—by way of comparison with the Western tradition—described as 'lacks'. This locution is certainly misleading, particularly because talk of 'lack' carries the sense of deficiency. My purpose, on the contrary, has been to

bring into clear relief the nature of Indian philosophical thinking. Here we find a mode of thinking that cuts across many of the dichotomies that have presented themselves to Western thought as though they were jointly exhaustive and mutually exclusive. These are: rationalism and empiricism, logicism and psychologism, extensionalism and intensionalism, causal and descriptive enquiries, logical thinking and the ineffability theses. Some of these dichotomies are being challenged in contemporary Western thought, both analytic and phenomenological. It is exciting to find that Indian philosophers have totally bypassed these restrictive options. In the present philosophical context, that by itself is instructive and promising. It holds out the promise, not merely of studying Indian thought from the point of view of the Western philosophies, but also, by reversing that strategy, of critically studying the Western philosophies from the vantage-points of the typically Indian modes of thinking.

A task which the Indian philosopher of today has to face, which our immediate predecessors either overlooked or took for granted, is to decide what is living and what is dead in Indian philosophy. It is true that philosophical problems have many lives and some are known to have arisen from their graves. But there is also no doubt that today, with the natural sciences separated from their ancestry, it is no longer feasible to think of the sciences as belonging to philosophy, however one may otherwise want to understand the relations between the sciences and philosophy. Consequently, a large part of Indian philosophical literature, the part dealing with atomic theory, theories of physical composition and chemical reaction, and the classification of living beings, to mention some from a host of themes, should be excised and relegated to the study of the history of science.

To give another example, possibly a more controversial one: the theory of language (*śabda*) as a means of true cognition (*pramāṇa*), indeed as the one mode of knowing which can override all others, needs to be looked at afresh. It is here that tradition and modernity come headlong into conflict. Even if it is true that the life-world does not fully determine philosophical problems, it nevertheless appears that for a people whose faith in the infallibility of the scriptures is considerably weakened (or, if it continues to survive unscathed, it is on the defensive against the onslaughts of science, technology, and modern social and political

ideas), *śabdapramāṇa* can no longer provide the theoretical basis for a satisfactory philosophy. But that is not to reject language (*śabda*) altogether as a means of true cognition (*pramāṇa*). What is necessary is to re-examine the priorities and relative strengths and weaknesses. To be sure, no other age since antiquity has been, on sheer theoretical grounds, more amenable to the idea of recognizing the centrality of linguisitc texts in a culture's self-understanding and of language in cognitive, moral, and religious lives. But one also needs to recall the distinction between understanding a sentence *p* and knowing that *p*,[15] the different ways in which language is central to cognitive enterprise and to moral and religious life, and the problems connected with the notions of a text and its interpretations.[16] These methodological insights would, I believe, rehabilitate the tradition's self-understanding, without attempting to return to that naïve use of *śabdapramāṇa* to which a return is just impossible (Chapter 7).

Finally, it is also necessary to recognize those areas in which the Indian philosophical tradition made achievements on which we can continue to build. A tentative list of these would be: theories of consciousness, large parts of theory of knowledge and logic, spiritual psychology in the sense of descriptive psychology of mental functions, and grammar, syntax, semantics, and phenomenology, of language. These, and the specific themes coming under each, provide opportunities both for fruitful encounter between Indian and Western thinking, and for creative thinking for the Indian philosopher from within the tradition.

It is also necessary to bring to our consciousness the themes and concepts which, though richly available in the larger body of texts in the tradition, failed to come to the forefront in the classical *darśanas*. If there are such themes and such concepts, rescuing them form their philosophical anonymity could provide a strategy for gaining a new look at the tradition itself. Two examples might be the concepts of body and action. In the *darśanas* (excepting possibly the Sāṃkhya-Yoga), the human body is but a thing, physico-chemical and living; but in the large mass of Vedic literature as well as in the literature of the Yoga, body is talked about as symbolizing cosmic and subjective principles, as occupying the ambiguous middle region between nature and freedom. Likewise with the concept of action: the domination of the concept of (the law of) *karma*, and an overriding interest in the role of

action *vis-à-vis* knowledge as a means to salvation, did not permit the full development of a theory of action itself, although all its elements were present before the Hindu mind. To attempt such a theory, one needs to consider not merely the logical, epistemological, and psychological sources in the *darśanas*, but also the semantic discussion of imperative sentences, as well as legal literature on the permissible and the not permissible.

Not surprisingly, there are inevitably many problems of great philosophical importance which the Indian philosophical tradition did *not* concern itself with at all. Not all of these can be illuminated from sources within the tradition. In such cases, the Indian philosopher, without abandoning his Indianness, may, and in fact is bound to, go beyond the resources available from within. In an enterprise such as this, he will be a direct participant in a larger dialogue with a larger philosophical community. Indirectly, any philosopher—even the Indian philosopher when he is engaged in interpreting and creatively developing his tradition—in so far as he is philosophizing, is participating in, and contributing to, a larger global tradition.

In conclusion, I should add that it is for the individual thinker to make his own decision on how he shall resolve the tension between his sense of modernity and his sense of tradition. No authentic thinker can follow, or give, a general recipe. Decisions and commitments are made by individuals. They should be made with an openness to creative dialogue and with a sensitivity to the contemporaneity of both tradition and the chronologically contemporary. What is essential is to generate the dialogue.

NOTES AND REFERENCES

1. E. Husserl, *The Crisis of European Sciences and Transcendental Phenomenology*, ed. and trans. David Carr (Evanston, Ill.: Northwestern University Press, 1970), 15.
2. For the problems concerning the idea of the text, see M. Foucault, *Archaeology of Knowledge*, ed. and trans. A. H. Sheridan Smith (New York: Harper Colophon Books, 1972).
3. Here Hans-Georg Gadamer's idea of 'effective historical consciousness' is useful. See Gadamer, *Truth and Method* (New York: Seabury Press, 1975).

4. For a more detailed treatment of this, see ch. 6.
5. For the concept of 'life-world', see Husserl, *The Crisis of European Sciences*. For problems in this concept, see J. N. Mohanty, ' "Life-World" and "A Priori" in Husserl's Later Thought', *Analecta Husserliana*, 3 (1974), 46–65, and David Carr, 'Husserl's Problematic Concept of the Life-World', *American Philosophical Quarterly*, 7 (1970), 331–39.
6. Husserl introduced this concept in *The Crisis of European Sciences* in connection with his account of Galilean physics.
7. See J. Habermas, *Knowledge and Human Interest* (Boston, Mass.: Beacon, 1971).
8. See J. N. Mohanty, 'Nyāya Theory of Doubt', *Visva Bharati Journal of Philosophy*, 3 (1966), 15–35; repr. in my *Phenomenology and Ontology* (the Hague: Martinus Nijhoff, 1970).
9. I take this idea of 'motivated possibility' from Husserl.
10. A full substantiation of this would need a discussion of the nature of *vyāpti*. In my view, '*vyāpti*' should be understood extensionally, with the possible exception of the Buddhist understanding of a subclass of *vyāpti* in terms of (partial) identity (*tādātmya*).
11. Also for limitations to this fallibilism, see ch. 5.
12. See D. C. Guha, *Navya-Nyāya System of Logic* (Varanasi: Bharatiya Vidya Prakasan, 1968), esp. ch. 7 on 'Paryāpti'.
13. Again any hasty explanation of *why* this is so should be suspected. Possible explanations are: a general belief in the unreality of time (but not all *darśanas* regard time as unreal), a conception of time as cyclic (not all emphasize it; the Greeks nevertheless concerned themselves with history: there can be a philosophy of history compatible with the conception of cyclic time as asserting not recurrent events, but only recurrent patterns), a conception of spirit or consciousness as non-intentional and non-temporal, and the dominance of the ahistorical, individualistic concept of *karma*. Some of these are briefly discussed in J. N. Mohanty, 'Philosophy of History and its Presuppositions', in T. M. P. Mahadevan and Grace E. Cairns (eds.), *Contemporary Indian Philosophers of History* (Calcutta: World Press, 1977). Also see ch. 6.
14. See J. N. Mohanty, *Gaṅgeśa's Theory of Truth* (Santiniketan: Centre of Advanced Study in Philosophy, 1966), Introduction, pp. 39–40, esp. n. 33.
15. See J. N . Mohanty, 'Language and Reality' in *Phenomenology and Ontology*.
16. For this refer to the works of Gadamer, Ricœur, Derrida, and Foucault.

2

Consciousness and Knowledge

INTRODUCTION

Philosophical reflection has to begin with the data of experience. A major part of these data is constituted by the way we ordinarily talk about ourselves and about our world. Such common linguistic usage (*lokavyavahāra*), though not the final court of appeal for philosophical theories, is certainly a sure starting-point, if supplemented by the reports of introspection of ordinary men about their own experiences (*loka-pratīti*)). Let us then begin with some judgements we make about ourselves:

I see this blue jar.

I hear a loud noise.

I know him.

I desire happiness.

I hate to be deceived.

In each of these statements, a state of consciousness is ascribed to that which is designated by 'I'. However, any attempt to analyse these statements is faced with serious difficulties. For a satisfactory analysis of them, we need to answer the following questions:

1. What is the thing designated by 'I' to whom the states of consciousness such as seeing, hearing, knowing, desiring, hating are ascribed?

2. How are the states of consciousness which are ascribed to the thing designated by 'I' related to that thing? Are they related as qualities to a substance or as states to that of which they are states, or as actions are related to an agent?

3. How do I come to make the above statements, if and when I make them? It is on the basis of outer perception that I can say 'Here is a blue jar'. But what sort of experience underlies and makes possible the statement 'I see this blue jar'?

Question (3) owes its difficulty to the fact that properties very different from states of consciousness are also ascribed to the thing designated by 'I' Consider the statements:

I weigh 130 pounds.

I am thin.

I am blind.

I am deaf.

I am fair.

Any answer to the first question then has to keep in mind this possibility and must say whether both states of consciousness and bodily states (as well as other physical properties) are ascribed to one and the same thing or not. In other words, does the word 'I' designate any one thing when used by any one speaker, or does it stand, in each case, for two or more utterly different things?

In the broad spectrum of views arising out of Indian speculations on this problem, the Cārvāka view that the 'I' in all these instances stands for one sort of thing, namely the body, stands at one end, while at the other end there is what may be called the Buddhist no-entity theory according to which the 'I' does not stand for any entity at all. In between these two extremes, there are, broadly speaking, two significant varieties of dualism: one of these holds the near-Cartesian view that physical properties are ascribed to the body and states of consciousness to the self (*ātmā*), which is a substance distinct from the body and its sense-organs as also from what may be roughly called the mind. For the other, the 'I' is not ambiguous as it is for the first view, but rather stands for a complex formed out of two heterogeneous things: consciousness on the one hand and mind on the other. While this complex is the thing of which conscious states are directly predicated, physical states are only indirectly predicated of it—they are directly predicated of the body. The former view is defended, in spite of the other differences between them, by philosophers of both the Nyāya-Vaiśeṣika and Mīmāmsā schools; the latter by the Vedānta of Śaṃkara.

That physical states like 'weighing 130 pounds' and even properties like deafness or blindness are predicates of the body need not be disputed. But the thesis that states of consciousness

also are ascribed to the body would seem to be highly disputable, in view of the fact that states of consciousness like knowing, desiring, loving, and hating apparently possess properties which are not normally said to belong to the body. States of consciousness for one thing are intentional, i.e. they are *of* an object, they are directed towards some object or other in a manner in which no bodily state can be so directed. The body as a material object would seem to be non-intentional. Although it may respond to stimuli when acted upon by them, it does not refer to, is not directed towards, or is not *of* anything. Now there is a conception of body widely prevalent in modern phenomenological literature according to which the body is intentionally directed towards the world, but whether the classical Indian philosophies ever held such a view about body is a matter which will not be discussed here. At this point I do not wish to assume that they in fact did have such a concept of the body. With a non-intentional physicalistic conception of the body, the thesis that states of consciousness are ascribed to the body cannot but be highly vulnerable.

The other feature which states of consciousness have is that they are not possible objects of the cognitions mediated by the outer sense-organs, i.e. of the visual, auditory, tactual, olfactory, and taste senses. They are objects rather of inner perception. The body, however, is perceived by means of the outer senses. Again, as before, a subjectivistic conception of the body, of the felt or lived body as distinguished from the observed body, may obviate this objection against making states of consciousness properties of the body, but once again, as before, such a subjectivistic conception of the body may seem to be foreign to most classical Indian philosophies. Given the non-intentional, physicalistic conception of the body, the Cārvāka thesis, then, that states of consciousness are ascribed to the body cannot but be rejected. The body is an 'It', at most a 'mine', but not an 'I'. It is a this (*idaṃ*); the 'I' is not a this (*anidaṃ*). One could make an even stronger point: a body is someone's body, the body of one who calls himself 'I'. And I call myself 'I' independently of identifying a body as mine. On the contrary, identifying a body as mine, should its need ever arise, would presuppose the sense of 'I' as possible, independent of that identification. The relation of this body which I hav to 'I' is contingent: I could have possibly a very different body. From all this it would appear to follow that the 'I' does not

stand for my body. States of consciousness, then, are not ascribed to the body.[1]

A variation on the Cārvāka thesis that states of consciousness are ascribed to the body seeks to improve upon the simpler view as stated and criticized above by, first, ascribing each conscious state to some sense-organ or other, and then finding unification of conscious states, in so far as they belong to the same person, in the unitary structure of the body. According to this variant position, visual consciousness belongs to the eyes, auditory consciousness to the ears, and so on. These states of consciousness, though each belongs to a sense-organ, all belong to the same subject in the sense that these sense-organs are unified in the structure of one and the same body. But this view is no better than the one just discarded. Visual sensation, which may be in a sense located in the visual sense-organ (although that is a very misleading locution), does not as such amount to visual consciousness. One's eyes may be physically receiving sensory stimuli and so, by definition, have the appropriate sensations, but if one is preoccupied one may not be experiencing a consciousness of them. Likewise with the other senses. In all cases, having an appropriate sensation is a matter of the appropriate sense-organ being appropriately stimulated, but having a state of consciousness is something more than that. From the fact that sensations are located in the body, it does not follow that states of consciousness are also located in it.[2]

At the other end of the spectrum of views we are considering is the Buddhist no-ownership theory according to which there is no substantival I which could 'own' or be the substratum of the different states of consciousness. There is, rather, one series of changing states which are not to be construed as modifications of one unchanging substance. There are visual, auditory, tactual, olfactory, and taste sensations; there are feelings, desires, and volitions; there are conceptions; there are also moments of awareness and even 'I'-feelings. These form a complex series in which the various elements are intricately intertwined, as are the strands of a rope, thereby giving rise—owing to a tendency to hypostatize entities—to the conception of a permanent ego-substance as the 'owner' of these states. The 'I' is really a series. To say that I am having a thought now is to say that a thought-event is a member of the series which constitutes (my) sense of 'I'.

One difficulty of this theory, as should be immediately obvious and as was pointed out by most anti-Buddhist philosophers, is that it fails to account for the unity of self-consciousness and for experiences such as memory and recognition. If every perception, every state of consciousness, is its own subject—which is what the theory amounts to, since on this theory every state of consciousness is also self-intimating—then it follows that two or more different states cannot be ascribed, except erroneously, to the same subject. There being no identical subject of experiences, one necessary condition of the possibility for memory and recognition would remain unsatisfied: this condition being that the present recollection and the past experience to which it relates should 'belong' to the same subject. I cannot recollect your experiences. I cannot recognize a person whom you have seen, not I. This sort of transcendental argument, it may be replied, assumes that memory and recognition are, at least in some cases, veridical and the Buddhist may very well question this assumption itself, thereby wanting to render the transcendental argument ineffective *ab initio*. The Buddhist may then contend that although ordinary experience is based on the claim of memory to be valid, in reality, from the metaphysical point of view, it is based on ignorance; so also is recognition. In both cases we are mistaking similarity and membership of a series as identity. Both fail to take note of discontinuity and surreptitiously substitute for it continuity. In the face of such a challenge, the Hindu philosophers argue that the radicality of this thesis (which holds not merely that memory and recognition are sometimes deceptive, but that they are, as a matter of principle, always deceptive) would vitiate all ordinary experience including perception, for perception, as a matter of essential necessity, is a possible basis for memory and recognition. In other words what is now perceived may be recollected and recognized as the same. Such a scepticism, instead of answering the question we set out to answer, would destroy the foundations on which that question was based. Furthermore, recognition of an external object may err; similarity may in fact be mistaken for sameness. But how can similarity be mistaken for sameness, if there is no non-illusory application for the concept of sameness? How can the judgement 'This is the same as that' be mistaken, if sometimes a judgement of that form is not true? Coming back now to the sense of 'I' how could my sense of self-identity be mistaken when even

the possibility for its correct application is ruled out? As Śaṃkara argued, no one ever raises the doubt 'Do I exist?' No one is bothered by the doubt 'Am I the same person or not?'.[3] One may concede that one's personality, character, self-image may radically change over time, but even in such cases an external observer would want to say, if he followed the route taken by that change, that they are but succeeding states of one and the same self, and, in principle, it is possible for the person himself to say 'I have changed a great deal', which implies that he is still the same I.

For the Hindu thinkers, the identity of the I is a condition of the possibility of knowledge, of social life and moral relationships, of suffering and enjoyment, of spiritual bondage and release from that bondage, or ignorance and illumination.

Since we are, in this work, concerned primarily with the principles of reasoning, evidence, and rationality, and they are all grounded in the evidence of consciousness, we begin by considering the nature of consciousness. As remarked earlier, even if we set aside the materialist view that conscious states are properties of the body understood physicalistically and non-intentionally and the Buddhist view that there is neither a permanent substratum of the states of consciousness nor a permanent principle for awareness, all that is required is that states of consciousness are not properties of the body and that there is some core of identity in the midst of the fleeting states. But these two requirements are compatible with a wide variety of philosophical positions about self and consciousness.

My concern is with what is needed to sustain the possibility of knowledge and morality. I will proceed with a provisional hypothesis: namely, that for purposes of knowing we need an identity of *subject* and for purposes of morality an identity of *person*. We leave open the question whether we are not referring to one and the same entity under different descriptions. The usefulness of this provisional hypothesis is that it will enable us to understand much Indian speculation on knowledge and morality without eventually being compelled to accept that distinction. Furthermore, whatever else may characterize a subject and a person, he must be conscious. The subject *qua* subject must, in addition to being a conscious being, be a knower (*jñātā*)—one who knows, i.e. perceives, infers, understands texts, and also knows that he knows. The person, whatever else he may be,

must, *qua* a person, in addition to being a conscious being, be an agent (*kàrtā*)—one who acts and also enjoys or suffers (*bhoktā*) the consequences of his actions, who strives for the desirable goals of life such as material well-being, physical pleasures, greater righteousness, and spiritual freedom. It is obvious that the two, the subject and the person, cannot be entirely distinct entities, for no other reason than that knowledge is inextricably linked with action. But these are complications to which I will return at a later stage in this work.

For the present, in this book, which is devoted to cognition, we may begin by looking at the nature of consciousness and knowledge. In a work that is to follow, I plan to look at the concepts of action and morality. It is only then that we shall be in a position to return to the relation between cognition and action, and so between subject and person.

THE ISSUES

A fully developed cognitive state, besides being a state of consciousness, is expressed in a sentence or sentential-complex, and claims to be true of its subject. The mere consciousness of an object, what one may want to call 'awareness', is not, as such, knowledge of that object. There is a mode of consciousness which one may call 'thinking of', which is not yet knowing. One may think of unicorns, without knowing any. But knowing in the fully developed sense implies thinking, or its correlate, understanding. One cannot be said to know that *S* is *P* unless one understands what is meant by '*S* is *P*'. On the other hand, merely to understand the meaning of the sentence '*S* is *P*' is not *eo ipso* to know anything excepting that it means such and such, which is a rather degenerate sense of 'knowing'. In view of these distinctions, one may want to say that a fully developed knowledge involves (1) consciousness of something (2) understanding of the senses of the words and the sentence in which the cognitive state is expressed, and (3) a truth-claim to the effect that the thing is as it is thought to be. In addition, the knowledge must be of some specific cognitive sort: it must be, for example, either perceptual or inferential. In this chapter I will be concerned with (1), in the next two chapters with (2) and (3) respectively.

The Sanskrit word for consciousness is *cit*, *caitanya*, that for knowledge is *jñāna*. They are often used synonymously, for deeply metaphysical reasons. For our purpose, we shall use *jñāna* when a state of consciousness claims to be true of its object. In the absence of such a claim, or as abstracted from such a claim, we shall use *cit*. By making this terminological stipulation, we shall not feel committed to any of the deeper metaphysical positions.

What then is the nature of consciousness? While all Indian philosophers agreed that consciousness, when it has an object, performs the function of revealing, manifesting, illuminating it, they differed widely over what consciousness itself is, and in their answers to the various standard disputational issues. There was near unanimity, however, on one thing: consciousness is the ultimate source of the guarantee that anything exists, or is thus. You cannot say that something exists, and is thus, without making use of the testimony of (your) consciousness at some level. If asked to justify your ontological claim, you may first fall back on evidence at your disposal: perceptual evidence, grounds for legitimizing your inference if you have made one, or reports of reliable persons. But each of these must be presented to your consciousness. In the absence of your consciousness, you cannot assert anything; nothing can be said by you to be or to be thus and not thus. If you are a realist in your ontology, you may still have your world, but you cannot posit it, assert its existence, determine its nature. There would be 'darkness of the world' (*jagadāndhyaprasanga*). That knowledge is a mode of consciousness, or at least presupposes it, was widely recognized. Note that this priority is only epistemic or evidential priority. It may be that once this much is granted, the thesis that consciousness is also ontologically prior will soon follow. But that step was not taken by all.

But even granting that consciousness, like light, reveals all things upon which it is focused (note that the metaphor of light is widely used, in this connection, in Indian philosophical writings), one may still ask the following questions about its nature:

(*a*) Is consciousness formed (*sākāra*) or formless (*nirākāra*)?
(*b*) Is consciousness a substance (*dravya*), a quality (*guṇa*), or an action (*karma*)?
(*c*) Is consciousness always, essentially, of an object (*saviṣaya*) or is it essentially objectless (*nirviṣaya*)?

(*d*) Is consciousness self-revealing (*svaprakāśa*) or revealed by another (*paraprakāśa*)?

These are all traditional disputational issues over which schools of Hindu and Buddhist philosophers argued through the centuries, each one refining his arguments and strengthening his theses as the controversies continued to develop. We shall, for our purpose, single out some main threads of this discussion with a view to highlighting the nature and limitations of the controversies. At the end, I will suggest a position which incorporates the insights gained from Indian thought on these matters, but constructively goes beyond it in many ways. We shall also see, as we proceed, that answers to these questions were used in support of the ontological decisions that were made in connection with the realism–idealism controversy. In fact, as I will argue in Chapter 6, the relation between epistemology and ontology was much more complicated than the above remark may suggest.

IS CONSCIOUSNESS FORMED OR FORMLESS?

Let me begin with the first of the above questions: does consciousness have a form of its own, or is it formless? *ākāra*—which is translated here as 'form' but could also be rendered as 'shape'—is a function of the structural arrangement of the parts of a thing. Material things which are made up of parts are, in this sense, formed or *sākāra*. It is in this sense that the Nyāya and the Mīmāmsā realists deny any form to consciousness. Since, in their view, consciousness is not a substance (*dravya*) but rather a quality (*guṇa*) or an action (*karma*) (we are now touching upon the question (1)) it must be without parts. In the Nyāya ontology, only a substance can be made up of parts, a quality and an action cannot. The Buddhists who oppose this view and hold that consciousness is always formed (*sākāra*) have in their minds, curiously enough, the instantaneous event of conscious*ing*, which, for them, is no less partless; it is the absolutely simple instantaneous consciousings, of which our conscious lives are in the long run constituted. It would seem, then, that while the realists reject the possibility of consciousness's having a form of its own on the ground of its not being a composite entity, the Buddhists do not consider this as counting against their thesis that consciousness,

the simple event of conscíousing, has a form of its own. Obviously they must be using the world *ākāra* in a sense different from the realist's. What then do the Buddhists mean by saying that consciousness is *sākāra*?

In relation to perceptual consciousness, the Buddhists hold that, for example, the cognition 'This is blue' has the form 'blue'. Now of course an event of consciousing, as the Buddhists construe it, cannot itself be blue, but is a consciousing-of-blue. In other words, being-of-blue is constitutive of it. In order to appreciate the precise nature of the Buddhist position, contrast it with a view pertinently expressed by G. E. Moore.[4] Moore held that consciousness of blue and consciousness of yellow agree, i.e. are the same inasmuch as they are consciousnesses; they differ only with respect to their objects, i.e. blue and yellow. Since the objects fall outside consciousness, the two states of consciousness, *qua* consciousness, are the same. (They may, to be sure, differ in many other respects, such as their temporal location, ownership, etc.) This the Buddhists would regard as an intellectual abstraction. Being nominalists of a sort, they are unwilling to hypostatize 'consciousness as such'. Every event of consciousing is different from every other. Being idealists of a sort—and we are talking of the Yogācāras at present—they do not accept the independent existence of an external object, so a consciousing's being of blue is really, phenomenologically that is to say, being-of-blue. This being-of-blue as a constitutive feature of that event is its *ākāra* or form. It is a distinct concrete event with its inner distinctive feature that is not borrowed from an alleged external object, namely, the patch of blue over there I think I see.[5]

The Buddhist writers often use their idealism as a premiss for proving that knowledge is *sākāra*, but they also use the latter thesis to establish idealism. One and the same author can do both only at the risk of circularity. Of course, if idealism is already established and it is admitted that there are no external objects, then it would follow that the blue which appears as the object of an event of consciousing cannot but be a constituent *in some sense* of that event. But it seems to me that while a denial of external objects entails that knowledge is *sākāra*, the latter thesis by itself does not entail the former. For it is arguable that while the consciousing-of-blue has its own 'blue'-form, there is also something out there in the world which 'corresponds' to it: this in fact

would be the view of the Buddhist Sautrantikas, who were representationists of a sort. For the present, we cannot assume the validity of any ontological thesis. Realism is as much possible as is idealism. To determine the nature of consciousness, we need to interrogate consciousness itself as the primal source of all evidence. If consciousness cannot testify to its nature, how can it testify to the nature of anything else?

The Buddhist Yogācāra view is open to two serious objections. One is the extreme difficulty of making it clear in what mode blue could belong to an event of conscіousing. The other problem is its seeming inability to account for how that which appears as the object of one event of consciousing could also appear as the object of another, numerically distinct event—as the object of a prior experience appears as the object of a later memory—if the former object were a constitutive moment of the event in which it was given as an object. I think these are almost insuperable difficulties, and there is no way of answering them without either denying the legitimacy of the transcendental question raised (for example, by saying we never do have the same object in two different acts; memory never has the same object as a prior perception) or pointing out, in some other way, that the objection begs the issue.

But there is, in fact, an undeniable core of truth in that position: to recover that truth we need to contrast it with its opposite, the Nyāya–Mīmāmsā view, and also to look briefly at the sorts of arguments that have been advanced on both sides. The Nyāya–Mīmāmsā view is that consciousness itself—not consciousness in general, but every particular state of consciousness—is *nirākāra*, formless, very much in the manner in which G. E. Moore took consciousness to be 'diaphanous'. Whatever form (*ākāra*) it appears to have is derived from its object. Since the object is blue, the consciousness *seems* to be a consciousness-of-blue. To put it in another way, consciousness, of course, is of an object, but supposing that its object is a patch of blue, one is not entitled to say that being-of-blue is internally constitutive of that state of consciousness.

The following are some of the main arguments the Buddhists put forward in favour of their position and against the Nyāya–Mīmāmsā view:

1. The relation of knowledge to its object must be in some sense an identity between the two, from which it follows that the

knowledge of blue ('This is blue') should itself be (in some sense) 'blue'.

2. Truth is *sārūpya*, or having-the-same-form (*rūpa*), of knowledge with its object. This requires that knowledge has the form of its object. As Dignāga writes, validity of a cognition consists in its having the form of object (*viṣayākāra eva asya pramāṇam*).

3. Consciousness is always experienced as having form; the alleged formless consciousness is the product of conceptual abstraction.

4. If consciousness were formless, there would be no difference between consciousness of blue and consciousness of yellow, and in that case the former could manifest yellow and the latter could manifest blue, which is just absurd.

5. To say that the seeming form of a state of consciousness is due to its contiguity with its object (just as a white crystal looks red owing to its contiguity with a red flower) will not do, for the object may not exist at all, as in the case of past or future objects or when the state of consciousness is hallucinatory or a dream.

6. With regard to one and the same object we often have different cognitions. Some of these cognitions are mutually incompatible (e.g. 'This is long' and 'This is short'). In such cases, these incompatible forms could not belong to the same object, so that they must really be forms of the cognitions concerned. Even when the cognitions are not incompatible, as when the same jar is simultaneously apprehended as a jar, as a substance, or as a knowable entity (*prameya*), which of these predicates 'appears' in a cognition could not be accounted for by the object, which possesses them all and even more.

Now, in these arguments there are some very strong points, but others are weak. The first argument's premiss that there must be some sort of identity between knowledge and its object is weak, for the precise sense of this identity-requirement is not satisfactorily explicated, and any unrestricted sense of identity simply won't do. There is an important sense in which knowledge and its object have also to be different. The second argument, however, is on stronger ground: given some form of correspondence theory of truth, you need, on the cognitive side, a structure which is to correspond, in some sense or other, to the structure of the object. And if one is not willing, quite understandably, to stop with the structure of the sentence which expresses the cognition, but wants

to relate it to the structure of the cognition itself, then the Buddhist's position would make perfectly good sense. I find the third argument unhelpful, for even if it were true, as I think it is, that we do not experience consciousness in general but always a particular state of consciousness of an object, this can be construed either way and so does not necessarily entail the thesis that being-of-an-object is internally constitutive of a state of consciousness.

The last three arguments are indeed the most significant. Argument (4) expresses the felt need that if a state of consciousness is to be of one object rather than of another, there must be something constitutive of that state that makes it possible for that state to be of that object and of no other. I think this is a genuine need, and I will return to the question how best to take it into account. The next two arguments point to three groups of phenomena which any theory of intentionality has to consider: (*a*) those in which the object of a state of consciousness is simply non-existent; (*b*) those in which the state of consciousness misrepresents its object; and (*c*) those in which one and the same object is presented as *F*, as *G*, as *H*, etc., where some of these predicates are, but some are not, mutually incompatible. Naïve realism of G. E. Moore's sort fails to take these into account. The Buddhist Yogācāras resorted, in order to be able to account for these, to an equally naïve representationism, making the form into a real property of the state of consciousness. Such a naïve representationism, by itself, is hardly satisfactory; it confuses the *real* and the *intentional*. It is as little capable of accounting for phenomena (*a*) to (*c*) as naïve realism is.

Let us now turn to the arguments of the Nyāya–Mīmāmsā realists. Again, overlooking many minor controversial issues, their chief arguments are the following:

1. Consciousness is not the sort of thing that could have the form of an object, that could, for example, be 'blue', 'triangular', etc.

2. Consciousness is not experienced as something like a mirror in which an object is reflected. It is rather experienced as what is in itself formless and yet apprehends objects with form.

3. If consciousness assumed the form of its object, then it would be inexplicable why objects would seem to be 'near' or 'distant', for—on the representationist view—what would be directly presented is the form belonging to consciousness itself.

4. If consciousness had the form of its objects, it would be like its object; the two, however, are experienced as radically different. The object, for one thing, is experienced as being out there, knowledge as being within. To require total sameness of form (*sārūpya*) is absurd, it would reduce consciousness to its object.

5. How is the alleged form of knowledge itself known? Wouldn't knowledge of the form of knowledge be required to have a form of its own, which would be the form of that form?

6. To the Buddhist argument that contradictory or contrary forms could not possibly belong to the same thing and must therefore belong to consciousness, one may reply that there is no hard and fast rule that one object must have one, and only one, form. We must accept everything just as it is perceived. There can be no other criterion except cognition for whether a thing has one or many, this or the other, form or forms.

Of these arguments, the second begs the issue, and even otherwise is helpful as little as the third argument of the Buddhists. Argument (3) can be answered by the Buddhists only if they make spatiality ('being far' and 'being near', in this case) itself a form of consciousness, somewhat on Kantian lines. Arguments (1) and (4) present serious difficulties for Buddhists, and force them to provide some account of what it is for a state of consciousness to have form (*ākāra*) without courting the absurd consequences of saying that, for example, a state of consciousness is blue or is triangular. This also requires that they either give up the idea of truth as sameness of form (*sārūpya*) or construe it in a sense that is very different from the naïve idea of similarity. Argument (5) is controversial, and the Buddhist way out is to say that on their theory a cognition is self-intimating and so does not need a second knowledge in order to be known. We shall return to this issue later in this chapter.

It is really argument (6) which, even if it does not decisively prove the Nyāya–Mīmāmsā position, certainly holds out the promise of a fruitful philosophical outcome. For what the argument insists upon is that what a thing is in itself has to be ascertained only in terms of how it is perceived or presented to be or known to be. If one perceptual appearance proves illusory, that is because it is corrected by another. What the argument points out is that a thing is presented to consciousness as *F*, *G*, *H*, etc.—not all of which are mutually compatible, and some of which may not

in fact belong to the thing. What the realist is saying is that what the thing is has to be construed in terms of how it is presented, and the predicates *F*, *G*, *H*, etc. through which the thing is presented must somehow belong to the thing itself.

If now we regard these descriptions under which the thing is presented to consciousness (seeing the thing as a jar, as a work of art, as a Greek vase, as blue, as a substance, as a knowable entity, and so on—quite irrespective of which of these descriptions are indeed true of the thing, or whether all of them are) as, in a certain sense, forms or contents of particular cognitions, then we need next to make sure that the sense of 'form' or of 'content' is rightly construed. For this purpose, I will introduce a distinction between real content and intentional content. Of a blue jar, its blue is a real content, it is in fact a real part of the jar. The jar *is* blue. But of the cognition 'This jar is blue', it is odd to say either that it is blue or that it is not, for cognitions are just not the sort of thing of which colour predicates can be meaningfully affirmed or denied. Even if the cognition were blue, that fact, odd in itself, would not make the cognition *of* a blue patch. This captures the truth in the thesis that cognition is formless (*nirākāra*). But we need also to save the truth in the Buddhist thesis that a cognition that was unstructured in any sense would have no 'partiality' towards its own object, and so could just as well 'present' any other object. In order to do that, we need to say something like the following: a cognition has an intentional structure, form, or content, but no real structure. By this we are able to preserve the truths in both the realist's and the idealist's positions, without having to decide between their metaphysical positions, i.e. realism and idealism. Instead of the word *ākāra*, which was rightly suspected by the realist as meaning a real form, we shall use the word *prakāra* ('qualifier'), picking up suggestions from the later Nyāya writings. We shall say, consciousness is *saprakāraka*, that is, it always has a qualifier, i.e. an intentional and logical structure, in spite of being formless (*nirākāra*) in the standard sense.

This would explain why the Nyāya, while insisting on the content or formless character of a state of consciousness, nevertheless proceeds to give elaborate logical analysis of it (and not merely of the sentence which expresses it).

IS CONSCIOUSNESS A SUBSTANCE, A QUALITY, OR AN ACT?

In this section, I will insert only a brief discussion of the second of the four questions listed earlier. The question is essentially metaphysical, but has far-reaching implications for what is being attempted here. I leave out of consideration, for the present, the view that consciousness or knowledge is a substance (*dravya*). This is indeed a strange view, and later in this chapter I will try to interpret it in a manner such that it may at least look plausible, and indeed helpful. For that purpose, we need to switch from the empirical to the transcendental point of view. Now, however, at the empirical level of discourse where we belong at the present while beginning to philosophize, the two options before us are: is knowledge, or rather knowing, an action (*kriyā*) or a quality (*guṇa*)?

The view that knowledge or knowing is an action had its supporters among Indian realists. In fact, it has been argued that only such a theory may save realism,[6] by accounting for the difference between the thing itself and the thing as known, i.e. as *viṣaya*—a difference which is intrinsic to realism. The best-known form of this view is to be found in the Mīmāmsā of the Bhāṭṭa school, for whom that difference—namely, the difference between the mere thing and the same thing as known—is a basic premiss and is precisely what needs to be accounted for in epistemology. An act alone can make a difference and in fact brings about that difference in what is acted upon. An act which makes no difference is an absurdity. The act of knowing is precisely that which transforms the mere thing to a known thing. On the Bhāṭṭa theory, the act of knowing is not itself known at the same time as its object is. It is rather inferred from the experience of that difference, which is but the new property knownness (*jñātatā*) now accruing to the thing that is known.

The act theory is hopelessly unsatisfactory, however. Leaving aside the many technical objections raised against it, it may suffice for us to note that the purpose of knowledge is to manifest or reveal the thing (that is known) precisely as it is, to make it bodily self-present, as it were, but not to alter it by producing in it a new property such as the alleged knownness. That supposed 'epistemo-

logical difference' is not an implication of knowing, for any difference would be inconsistent with what knowing is by its intention. What, however, is an implication of knowing is that what is known does not come into being by virtue of being known, that the object of knowledge had a prior unknown existence (*ajñātasattā*) so that the function of knowing extends only as far as removing this unknown status and bringing the object into its self-givenness.

What we need in order to preserve the truth in the act theory is to recognize the conception of knowledge as intentional. Not all intentional states are activities, although all actions may be regarded as intentional. Knowledge is intentional, i.e. it is *of* an object that falls outside it; over and above this it need not be an activity that alters its object. When the Nyāya insisted that it is a quality (*guṇa*) of the self, it also recognized that as a quality it is radically different from the other qualities of the self inasmuch as it alone has the irreducible property of being-of-an-object.[7] Desire and aversion, for example, are also of, or for, something or other, they are intentional, but their intentionality is derived from that of the consciousness or knowledge which 'presents' the object in the first place. In the Nyāya ontology, there is no other category for a particular to fall under if it is neither a substance nor an action. Knowledge is not a substance, for although partless it is nevertheless non-eternal—the rule being that a substance that is not composite must be eternal. It cannot be an action for it is devoid of motion, an action being defined in terms of displacement of spatial position in time. Knowledge is accordingly classified as a quality, but of such a type as is characterized by being-of-an-object (*svābhāvikaviṣayapravaṇatva*).

IS CONSCIOUSNESS INTENTIONAL?

In effect, the preceding section concluded with the assertion that consciousness and knowledge are intentional (*saviṣayaka*). What, then, of the large question, whether there is any consciousness that is non-intentional, that is not of an object? Let us call such consciousness, irrespective of whether it exists or not, 'pure' (*śuddha*) consciousness. (In the usage I am recommending 'pure consciousness' and 'transcendental consciousness' are not the

same concepts. I will introduce the concept of transcendental consciousness later in this chapter.)

There is no doubt that the concept of pure consciousness figures prominently in Indian thought, religious as well as philosophical. Amongst the philosophies, it occupies a central place in some schools of Vedānta, notably Śaṃkara's Advaita, in Sāṃkhya, and in Yoga. I think one may even want to distinguish between two concepts of pure consciousness, one weaker and the other stronger. According to the weaker concept, pure consciousness, non-intentional though it is by definition, is still individuated. It has no *viṣaya*, i.e. object, but is has an *āśraya* or locus, i.e. it belongs to someone. The stronger concept is that it has neither *viṣaya* nor *āśraya*, it is both non-intentional and non-egological. Even this last would admit of a great deal of variation, depending upon how one wants to construe the non-egological character: one may, as the Buddhists more often do, regard pure consciousness as a succession of events of consciousings without a locus or owner, or one may regard it as a cosmic spirit, not limited by space or time or body. In either case, the sense of 'I' does not belong to the essential structure of consciousness: it is either constituted within the stream of consciousness, or superimposed upon the universal spirit by contingent circumstances (*upādhi*).

Without attending to these differences for the present, we can insist that pure consciousness, in its minimal signification of being non-intentional, is not a phenomenological datum of non-mystical experience. It is at most either a deliverance of mystic experience of some sort, or an implicate of ordinary, non-mystical experience, or a conclusion towards which logical and metaphysical reasonings lead us, or it has to be accepted on faith resulting from acceptance of the validity of scriptural texts. I do not enjoy mystical experience, so cannot use its concept to support a philosophical position. Faith is no path for philosophizing. For philosophy, only two possibilities remain open. Starting with ordinary intentional consciousness, one may want to show that intentional consciousness presupposes the non-intentional, or one may argue that consciousness, by its nature, cannot be—on logical grounds—intentional. Or, there is still the path open to try to show that even within the limits of ordinary experience one has access, however fleeting, to a mode of consciousness that is non-intentional. All these three paths have been followed by those Indian philosophers

who believe that consciousness, at a certain level, is, in fact, non-intentional. Philosophers belonging to Śaṃkara's school of Advaita Vedānta have tried all three: they have argued that a non-intentional consciousness is what makes ordinary experience possible; that consciousness cannot admit of any difference (*bheda*) within it (for all such differences must be its object), so that the subject–object difference must be extrinsic to it, i.e. must belong to the world and not to consciousness; and finally that an undifferentiated awareness does in fact always accompany all waking life and even persists through dreamless sleep. The first, if valid, would be a transcendental thesis ('transcendental' in the Kantian sense), the second, a metaphysical thesis, and the third, a phenomenological thesis. The logical reasoning which is used by the second sort of move may be intended to show either that all difference is metaphysically unreal (somewhat in the manner of F. H. Bradley's attack on relations) or that all difference must characterize, or belong to, things in the world but not to consciousness. The former proves too much, and, even in proving what it is meant to, presupposes a criterion of reality; the latter falls short of proving that consciousness is not consciousness of an object, for it does show that relations and differences are objects of consciousness. The transcendental and the phenomenological thesis will be of great interest to us.

What is the transcendental argument in this context? It must show that ordinary, intentional consciousness presupposes pure consciousness. But how would the argument run? It is one thing to say that all experience presupposes consciousness, but this does not entail that the consciousness that is so presupposed must be pure. To argue that experience is intentional and what it presupposes must be non-intentional is begging the issue. One may want to argue that the essence of consciousness is to be self-illuminating (*svayamprakāśa*) and that it is only an accident that it also 'manifests' an object other than itself. But how does one fix the essence of consciousness save by way of ascertaining what is in fact, or can be in principle? To rule out a feature by definition would be an arbitrary decision; one could as well decide to define consciousness by intentionality and rule out 'purity' and 'self-illumination'. Why can consciousness not be, by its essence, both self-illuminating and intentional? I am not saying that it is, for I do not want to bring in the notion of essence or to rule out a

possibility by definition. Only, I do not recognize any inconsistency in its being both. I have been left unconvinced by Śaṃkara's point in the opening sentence of his commentary on the *Brahmasūtras*, that consciousness and object, *asmadpratyaya* and *yuṣmadpratyaya*, self and not-self, are opposed to each other like light and darkness.[8] What is this alleged opposition like? Consciousness is self-illuminating, object is not. But why should this contrast, fundamental though it may be, render the fact of intentionality (*saviṣayakatva*) unintelligible? As one commentator on Śaṃkara recognizes, the opposition is not to be understood as that between the destroyer and the destroyed (*badhya-bādhaka-bhāva*): consciousness does not annul objects, but rather manifests them. Nor is the opposition to be understood in the sense that the two cannot coexist (*sahāvasthānasāmarthyābhāva*). In fact, light and darkness do coexist in a dimly lit place, consciousness and object do coexist in the web of ordinary experience. The opposition, then, amounts only to this: they have such radically different properties that they cannot be confused with one another.[9] This much opposition is consistent with the fact of intentional reference. Śaṃkara's conclusion that intentionality must therefore be metaphysically false[10] is hardly warranted by the mere fact that consciousness and object have very different features. In the simple fact of consciousness's being of an object, one need not apprehend the possibility of ascribing to one the properties of the other. It is true that you may have a naturalistic interpretation of intentionality which tends to misconstrue consciousness as an object; and likewise with an idealistic misconstrual.

Rāmānuja impresses me by his clear perception that consciousness is both self-illuminating and intentional. I think, however, that he ties these two features too closely: only when consciousness is intentional, he seems to be saying, does it reveal itself.[11] This, to my mind, is unnecessarily strict, and would rule out the very possibility of pure consciousness, which I do not want to rule out by definition.

The phenomenological approach to show the possibility of pure consciousness can start only with ordinary experience, the sort of experience to which you and I have access. There is one specially attractive way of doing this. One may distinguish, within any particular state of consciousness, between the aspect of awareness (which must be like a universal feature, present in all states of

consciousness) and the aspect of intentionality (which varies from state to state, depending upon the object, the knowing persons, time, and the mode of intention). The latter, by itself, is not a state of consciousness; in order to be so it needs to be accompanied by awareness. Once this distinction is conceptually made, two possible theses seem to follow. On the one hand, it is now plausible to say that a mental state can be, without being accompanied by awareness: this, indeed, is in consonance with the dominant interpretation of modern psychoanalysis. By the same token, one may want to assert that simple awareness can equally well be dissociated from any particular mental state it may happen, contingently, to accompany. This argument, which at a stroke seems to be able to reconcile the psychoanalytic theory of the unconscious and the Yoga belief in cultivating the attitude of mere awareness (of which, to be sure several different possible variations are conceptually conceivable) is impressive, but its very simplicity makes it suspect. Granting the distinction between the two aspects, the universal awareness and the particular mental state, the possibility of a separation does not immediately follow, nor does it follow that the two aspects cannot be separated. Awareness, on this account, is like any universal feature shared in common by members of a class, but from this fact the thesis of universals *ante re* does not logically follow (nor does the Freudian thesis of unconscious mental states). But both options are open and that is the best we can expect under the circumstances.

Pure awareness, then, in the sense of a universal detachable from the particular mental states with which it is associated, is at best a goal whose possibility philosophy can keep open. From a practical standpoint, one has to show that attainment of such separation is a demand that is implicit within the range of ordinary experience and also an axiological demand, i.e. it ought to be realized. I will return to this theme at another place. For the present, we have no means of, or need for, getting beyond the intentional consciousness.

IS CONSCIOUSNESS SELF-MANIFESTING?

Some of my remarks in the preceding section may appear to indicate my commitment to the thesis that consciousness is

self-illuminating. But this is only one of the alternatives in an issue which greatly concerned the Indian philosophers. The issue is: is a state of consciousness known to its owner at the very moment of its coming into existence, i.e. by virtue of its merely being a state of consciousness; or, is it the case that being intentional it is other-directed and cannot be also 'of', or 'about', itself? In the latter case, a state of consciousness, while manifesting its object, remains itself unmanifested; in other words, the knower knows the object but not his own knowledge. There would then be a parity between knowledge and its object; both are capable of being manifested by being 'objectified' by knowledge. If an object is manifested by *its* knowledge, that knowledge, on its part, can be manifested only by another knowledge, of which the former becomes the object.

Opposed to this extreme position, held by the Nyāya, is the view held in common, in spite of enormous differences between them on other matters, by the Buddhists, the Advaita Vedānta, and the Prābhākara Mīmāmsā: they all hold the view that a state of consciousness or knowledge does both things at once, it reveals its object and it reveals itself. To be conscious of an object is *eo ipso* to be aware that one is so conscious. To know is to know that one knows.

On the Nyāya theory, the judgement '*S* is *P*' (expressing a primary, pre-reflective knowledge) is different from the judgement 'I know that "*S* is *P*" '. On the latter, the 'self-intimating' theory, the 'I know that' adds nothing to the original cognition and only elaborates what was there all along. Slightly modifying the famed Kantian statement,[12] one can say that knowledge is self-intimating in the sense that the 'I know' necessarily accompanies all our cognitions.

A time-worn objection against the Nyāya theory is that it entails a vicious infinite regress. For it seems as though we are unavoidably led to postulate an endless series of cognitions, each member of which has its preceding member for its object. But it is not at all clear why there should be such an endless series. For an object to be known, you need no more than *its* knowledge, you do not need that knowledge itself to be known. In that case, no vicious infinite regress is involved in so far as the possibility of first-level knowledge is concerned. You can, if you so desire, reflect on any level of knowledge and, thereby, have a knowledge of the

next-higher level, but you need not, and ordinarily one does not go beyond the first reflective knowledge of the form 'I know . . .'.

The Nyāya theory, however, is at pains to steer clear between two possible views, both of which it rejects: that all first-order knowledge is necessarily succeeded by reflective knowledge about it; and that first-order knowledge is succeeded by reflective knowledge just in case one has a desire so to reflect. The first of these two is rejected on two grounds: in the first place, if it were necessary that first-order knowledge be succeeded by reflective knowledge about it, it would be impossible to have a continuing perception of one and the same thing over a stretch of time. This kind of knowledge, known as *dhārāvāhika-buddhi* really consists of a series of cognitions having precisely the same object. Such a series would be impossible, if it were the case that the first cognition would necessarily be succeeded by reflective knowledge. Secondly, there may, quite naturally, be hindrances which would stop reflective knowledge from coming into being. Thus, for example, immediately after a person has a first-level cognition, he may become unconscious, or may even die. Nor is the second view acceptable to the Nyāya. If reflective knowledge were made possible by a desire to reflect, that desire to reflect upon the first-level cognition would not itself be possible unless there were already an acquaintance with the latter, which is what the Nyāya theory denies. If a cognition itself is not known, how can there be a desire to know it at all?

The fact seems to be, however, that one may have the intent to reflect on a mental state that has just occurred. There must, then, be something seriously wrong with the Nyāya account. At the same time, the objections raised against the view that a first-level cognition is necessarily succeeded by reflective cognition about it are not all convincing. The first objection making use of the idea of a series of homogeneous cognitions rests upon a theory of the individuation of cognitions that is highly questionable. The theory rests upon the ontological thesis that a mental state lasts for a 'moment' (*kṣaṇa*) (excluding the moment of its origination and the moment of its termination), so that even if it is highly problematical whether one can phenomenologically identify how long (or, how small) a (Nyāya) moment is, there would be no problem in the assertion that a fairly long stretch of time (say, a minute) would consist of several moments. In that case, if I am looking steadily at

a thing for a minute, that would consist of a series of homogeneous cognitions, although phenomenologically I would consider it one cognition just in case the thing that is perceived continues to be perceived exactly under the same description. The second objection makes a valid point, but it can be taken care of by adding, as the Nyāya logicians frequently do, *ad hoc* conditions to the rule, which would, then, look somewhat like this: a first-order cognition K_1 will necessarily be followed by a reflective cognition K_2 (which has K_1 for its object), provided there are no 'preventing conditions' (*pratibandhaka*). The problem with such a rule is not that it would make the alleged serial cognition impossible. Even without making ontological commitments on how to individuate cognitive occurrences, one would be confronted with the seemingly absurd consequence that any two consecutive first-order mental states must be separated by a reflective cognition. If a perception is followed by a desire, and the desire by a sentiment, in fact one has to juxtapose between the first pair a reflective cognition of the perception, and between the second pair a reflective cognition of the desire. Now this is rather an odd picture of our mental life, where reflections do occur but not with that obstinate regularity. We do reflect, objectifying a prior mental state; it is also obvious that such reflection, to be possible, requires a desire for it. But desire to reflect on K_1 (a first-order cognition) would not be possible unless there were an acquaintance with K_1. Here the strength of the Vedānta–Prābhākara Mīmāmsā theory becomes evident.

However, I would distinguish between two varieties of the 'self-illumination' theory, a strong and a weak version. According to the strong version, every state of consciousness has the form 'I know . . .': it is a Cartesian cogito. According to the weaker version, every state of consciousness has the necessary *possibility* of becoming a Cartesian cogito; its actually becoming one requires an act of reflection, but even prior to reflection it has a transparency of its own. I find the stronger version too intellectualistic and not borne out by the testimony of experience. When I see a thing I am not saying to myself 'I see that thing over there'. I am more likely to say 'That is an automobile'. Every state of consciousness, then, is not self-conscious and reflective in the sense of the Cartesian cogito.[13] It is, however, for that reason, not an opaque thing to be manifested by another supervening

objectifying act, as the Nyāya takes it to be. When an act of reflection for the first time objectifies it, one does not have the same sense of a new discovery as one has when one comes to know a hitherto unknown object; on the contrary, one has the experience that it was known all along. In order to be able to account for all the facets of the phenomena, I will distinguish between pre-reflective transparency and reflective objectification. A state of consciousness is self-intimating only in the sense that its owner has a pre-reflective acquaintance with it, or, what amounts to the same, the state of consciousness has a pre-reflective transparency. It is this pre-reflective familiarity which makes subsequent reflection possible. Reflection analyses what was originally given.

CONSCIOUSNESS AS TRANSCENDENTAL: RÉSUMÉ

In the strictly Kantian sense, something is 'transcendental' only if it is the non-empirical condition of the possibility of knowledge and objective experience. I have earlier defined 'pure consciousness' as consciousness that is not of an object, and have left the question open for practical philosophy whether such a pure consciousness can be realized, and then ought to be realized or not. With the failure of the transcendental argument for the validity of the concept of pure consciousness, we *cannot* any longer say that the supposed pure consciousness is also transcendental consciousness. But one can still look for intentional consciousness to play a transcendental role. Obviously, the transcendental role cannot be played by any specific intentional state with its specific object. But that to which a transcendental role could be assigned has to be, for one thing, *not* your or my consciousness regarded as yours or mine, but something in general, consciousness in general, if knowledge and objectivity are to be possible. This is the sense of subjectivitity used earlier, when it was said that the subject is the who of knowing, the one who knows, while the person is the who of acting. Of course, my consciousness is mine and yours is yours. But what I can know, you can also. Knowledge can be shared, if feelings and emotions cannot be. One needs at some stage a universal feature of consciousness in general shared by all cognitive beings. Similarly, since to be able to play a transcendental

role, this consciousness must be intentional, and yet not of this or that particular object, one needs to have the concept of an intentionality that refers to object-in-general. We then get a transcendental structure: consciousness-in-general → object-in-general. The only place, but for that reason not less important, in Indian thought to look for this concept is Kashmir Śaivism, which, after distinguishing between various grades of consciousness, speaks of consciousness's inherent tendency to posit an object.[14]

The theory of consciousness to which this discussion had led may be stated in the following propositions:

1. Although consciousness is formless (*nirākāra*) in the sense of lacking real content, it has an intentional content or logical 'qualifier' (*prakāra*), permitting a logical analysis of its structure.
2. Knowledge is neither a substance nor an act, but a state which is distinguished from other states of the self by being intrinsically intentional.
3. Consciousness, within the limits of ordinary experience, is of objects (*saviṣayaka*). (Although pure awareness may be a distinguishable aspect within each state of consciousness, we do not know that it is separable. The possibility of 'pure', i.e. non-intentional, consciousness is left open, especially in the context of practical philosophy.)
4. Consciousness is self-illuminating in the (weak) sense of possessing a pre-reflective transparency. Reflection can always objectify it, but such objectification is no new discovery. It is rather a clarification of what one was already familiar with.
5. The true transcendental is not the alleged pure consciousness but the generalized consciousness-in-general → object-in-general structure.

To this summary, I shall add a remark. A study of consciousness is needed as the first step in understanding the concept of rationality in Indian thought, because all arguments for a position, all evidence for an epistemic claim and justification for ontological commitment ('such and such an entity exists') must eventually be presented to one's consciousness.

But there is a problem here, which I will put in the form of a dilemma: Rational evidence must be evidence *for* one position and *against* another. Consciousness, regarded as an impartial spectator, cannot fulfil this function: it will be as much awareness of truth

as of error. It is not surprising that the Hindu philosophers, e.g. the Sāṃkhya authors, characterized it as neutral (*madhyastha*) and uninvolved. To certify truth as truth and to reject error as error you need more than the 'manifesting' function of consciousness, you need a critical, engaged, and committed role. And yet a neutral consciousness would be too tolerant. Rational consciousness needs to be both involved and impartial. Its neutrality is not tantamount to refusal to take the side of truth. And its taking the side of truth is not a partiality, but a giving itself over to the norms of critical thinking and to how the things themselves present themselves to be. The Hindus thought at both levels. The universal consciousness is a necessary but not a sufficient condition of the possibility of knowledge and truth. For that the critical norms are needed. These norms are provided by the theory of *pramāṇa*.

NOTES AND REFERENCES

1. For critical examination of the view that the self is the body, see *Nyāyasūtras* III. i. 27–30, III. ii. 37, 42–47, along with the *Bhāṣya* on them.
2. For the view that the self is identical with one or more of the sense-organs, see *Nyāyasūtras* III. i. 2–6, 11–14, III. ii. 19, along with the *Bhāṣya* on them.
3. Thus Śaṃkara: 'Upalabdhari tu sandeho'pi na kadācidbhavati, —sa evāhaṃ syāṃ, tatsadṛśo veti' (*Bhāṣya* on Brahmasūtra II. ii. 25).
4. G. E. Moore, 'The Refutation of Idealism', repr. in his *Philosophical Studies* (London: Routledge & Kegan Paul, 1922).
5. See M. Hattori, *Dignāga on Perception* (Cambridge, Mass.: Harvard University Press, 1968).
6. See P. K. Mukhopadhyaya, 'Cognitive Act', *Journal of Indian Philosophy*, 2 (1973), 115–37.
7. See Vallabhācārya: 'jñānatve cechādivyāvṛttasvabhāvasya viṣayapravaṇatvamapekṣitamiti' (*Nyāyalīlāvati*, Chowkhamba Edition (Varanasi; 1933), 814).
8. 'Yuṣmadasmat pratyayagocarayorviṣayaviṣayiṇostamaprakāśavadviruddhasvabhāvayo' (Śaṃkara, *Adhyāsabhāṣyaṃ*). For my criticism of Śaṃkara's thesis, see my 'Consciousness in Vedānta', in S. S. Rama Rao Pappu (ed.), *Perspectives on Vedānta*, Essays in Honor of Professor P. T. Raju (Leiden: E. J. Brill, 1988), 8–17.

9. '. . . parasparātmatāsāmarthyābhāvalakṣaṇasya virodhasya iha vivakṣitatvāt' (*Vivaraṇaprameyasaṅgrahaḥ*, Vasumati Edition (Calcutta, 1941), i. 71–2).
10. '. . . mithyeti bhavituṃ yuktaṃ' (Śaṃkara, *Adhyāsabhāṣyaṃ*).
11. 'yattvanubhūteḥ svayaṃprakāśatvamuktaṃ, tadviṣayaprakāśana—velāyāṃ jñāturātmanastathaiva, na tu sarveṣāṃ sarvadā tathaiva iti niyamo'sti' (Rāmānuja, *Śrībhāṣyaṃ*, Catusūtrī Edition, ed. T. Srinivasa Sarma (Bombay: Nirnayasagara Press, 1916), 83–4).
12. 'It must be possible for the 'I think' to accompany all my representations' (Kant, *Critique of Pure Reason*, B 131).
13. Cp. J. P. Sartre, *The Transcendence of the Ego: An Existentialist Theory of Consciousness*, ed. and trans. Forrest Williams and R. Kirkpatrick (New York: Noonday, 1957). Also, J. N. Mohanty, *The Concept of Intentionality* (St. Louis: Warren H. Green, 1972), 132–7, 154–60.
14. See K. Sivaraman, *Śaivism in Philosophical Perspective* (Delhi: Matilal Banarasidass, 1973).

3

Language and Meaning

INTRODUCTION

To help us find our way through the large and variegated discussions of the Indian philosophers on the issues arising in theory of meaning, I will begin by isolating some of the crucial issues and then a set of important distinctions.

The three issues on which I will, in this chapter, make some remarks, expository and critical, occupied considerable attention of the Indian philosophers. They are:

1. Is word-meaning the primary unit, out of which sentence-meaning is composed? Or, is sentence-meaning the primary unit from which word-meaning is abstracted? An affirmative answer to the former question will yield us the so-called 'composition principle'. An affirmative answer to the second question will yield the so-called 'context principle'. Modern semantics since Frege has been concerned with these two possibilities, so also were Pāṇini, Patanjali, Bhartṛhari, and the Mīmāmsā and Nyāya philosophers.

2. In sentential meaning, are nominal expression or verbs primary? This issue as such has not been addressed by modern semantics, but has been of interest to linguists.

3. Is the meaning of a word (*a*) the particular entities it denotes, (*b*) the universal which those particulars exemplify, (*c*) the particulars, not as such (i.e. not the bare particulars), but as characterized by the universal, or (*d*) the mere exclusion of those particulars from all others (*anyāpoha*)? These alternatives have loomed large in discussions in classical Western philosophy.

The distinctions I wish to introduce at this stage, and which need to be borne in mind for discussions in this chapter, are derived from modern Western semantical theories which could be used as a foil to bring out the significance and nature of the Indian theories. The resulting strategy should not be construed as simple

comparative philosophy; it is, rather, an inevitable attempt to think from the intellectual position in which I find myself.

Taking the clue from Husserl's *Logische Untersuchungen* and Frege's 'Sinn und Bedeutung', I will distinguish between three aspects of the meaningful use of language. These three, which by no means exhaust all that is involved, are: the intention of the speaker; the sense that the word or sentence expresses; and the reference, i.e. the entity it denotes. Since most modern semantics is either an elaboration of the Fregean sense–reference distinction or reaction against it, it provides a useful starting-point. As the original distinction stands, the sense that an expression has is neither a mental entity (image, or whatever else) evoked by it nor the entity denoted by it. It is not a mental entity, for the sense must be intersubjectively identifiable, shareable, and communicable, while the mental is subjective, private, and particular. It is also not to be identified with an entity denoted or named by the expression, for then a term such as 'unicorn' which has no denotation would be rendered senseless, which it is not.

In relation to the three aspects of meaningful use of language, four possibilities may be sketched. First, omit intention but retain the other two distinctions, and you have Fregean semantics. Secondly, omit sense but keep intention and reference, and the theory would become a psychological theory of reference: reference would depend upon intention alone. Thirdly, omit intention and sense, keeping reference alone, and the resulting semantics would be a causal theory such as that of Kripke. Finally, keep all three, knit together, if you can, and you will have a phenomenological theory such as Husserl's.

One of the leading questions I will ask in this chapter is how these three—intention, sense, and reference—appear in the Indian semantical theories. But before we do that, there are still issues (1)–(3) that need to be reviewed.

WORD-MEANING (*PADĀRTHA*)

What is a word (*padaṃ*)? A word is the smallest meaningful unit of language. The Indian philosophers, it must be borne in mind, were thinking of language primarily as speech, and not as written text. Speech consists in utterance of meaningful sounds. If a discourse

can be decomposed into sentences (*vākyāni*), a sentence can be decomposed into words (*padāni*), and a word into phonemes (*varnāni*). A phoneme, however, is not by itself meaningful; a word is. A word (*padaṃ*), then, is not mere sound (*dhvani*), but a meaningful sound. It is *śakta*, i.e. possesses the power (*śakti*) to denote or refer to whatever is its object (*artha*).

If the spoken word is an aggregate, or rather succession, of phonemes, how may the unity of the word, as well as our perception of *one* word as one, be accounted for? We have here both an ontological and an epistemological question. What is a word as one entity, if it consists in a succession of phonemes? How is the word as one entity perceived? The Indian thinkers had several different answers to these questions. If the word consists of a succession of perishing phonemes, the unity of the word as one entity can consist only in the unity of meaning, and a word as one word can be perceived only by a synthetic act of the mind which joins the accumulated impressions of the preceding phonemes to the perception of the last phoneme (*pūrvapūrvavarnajanita samskārasahito'-ntyavarnapratyāyaka*). Or, one may separate the ontology from the epistemology, and hold that while ontologically each phoneme, and so also each word, has a timeless existence, epistemologically the unity of a word is perceived only as a result of the sort of synthetic act admitted in the first answer. Or, one may want to free the account of the synthetic act from the psychological atomism underlying it, and hold, as *Vyāsabhāṣya* on *Yogasūtra* iii. 17 does, that the mind grasps the word as an indivisible (*abhāgaṃ*), non-sequential (*akramaṃ*) unit in one intellectual act (*ekabuddhiviṣayaṃ*). Or, following Patañjali, one may distinguish between the perishing sound (*dhvani*) and the essential phonetic structure (*sphoṭa*), the former varying from speaker to speaker and the latter constant and unaffected by the vagaries of speaker's intonations and inflexions. The former would then be the 'modified' sound (*vaikṛta dhvani*), modified by the peculiarities of the speaker, the latter would be the primary, phonetic word-form (*prākṛta dhvani*). The sequential account of apprehension applies to the former; the latter, however, being a non-sequential structure, can only be grasped in one act. The Nyāya–Mīmāmsā account captures the first, the Yoga and the grammarian accounts capture the second.

But these two aspects do not exhaust the structure of a word. If

the perishing sound events 'manifest' the timeless phonetic word-form, the latter expresses a meaning. We are now encountering the important question what theory of meaning the Indian thinkers had. However, we still have to present many preliminary considerations before we are able to enter that central area of problems. A helpful way to begin is to enumerate the following functions of a word, combining an insight of Pāṇini with one from *Yogasūtra* iii, 17.[1] A word, first of all, as Pāṇini emphasized, denotes its own form. This is the grammarian's point of view. When he *qua* grammarian uses a word, he is using it to refer to the word itself. In other words, the grammarian's use is one of mentioning. As used by us, i.e. by non-grammarians, a word means its object (*artha*) and expresses a cognitive state (*pratyaya*). The idea of a word expressing a cognitive state, though to be found in the *Yoga sūtras*, receded into oblivion in the main philosophical tradition. One understands why this should happen if one asks what cognitive state a word could express when it is after all a sentence, not an isolated word, that expresses a cognition. The later theories of understanding of a sentence (*śābdabodha*) which we shall discuss would be continuations of this idea of a cognitive state expressed by a word.

What is it that means, denotes, or refers to an object? According to the Nyāya, Mīmāmsā, and the great majority of Indian thinkers, it is the word-sound, the sound made in uttering a word, that refers. This in a sense is true, but the perishing sound, with all the idiosyncrasies of the speaker, is meaningful only because it is the *same* as word-sounds uttered by other speakers, and they are the same only in the sense that they express the same word, i.e. are tokens of the same word-type. A word-token refers in the way it does, because it is a token of a word-type. It is this word-type, not the perishing particular, that is denoted by the word *sphoṭa* in one of its many uses. In the primary sense, then, it is the *sphoṭa* that is the bearer of meaning.

What is the meaning of the word *artha*? It clearly means, in the Indian philosophical discussions, the object denoted or referred to rather than the Fregean sense. The issue is, what sort of entity is denoted or referred by a name? Taking a typical common name 'cow', the Indian philosophers discussed four possibilities. The name 'cow' can be regarded as meaning any of the following: the individual cows, the cow shape, the universal 'cowness', or the

individual cow as possessing the cow shape and the universal cowness. Let us consider these four alternatives.

The view that the name 'cow' means individual cows is the standard reference or denotative theory of meaning. It has a certain appeal to the pre-philosophical mind, and is supported by a superficial reading of linguistic usages such as 'Bring the cow'; you could only bring an individual cow. However, the view is hardly tenable, and that for at least two reasons. In the first place, there are an infinite number of individuals, past, present, and future, which were, are, and will be called cows. If the name 'cow' designates all of them, we have to postulate an infinite number of powers (*śakti*) of the word to signify these infinite numbers of individuals. One may want to counter this objection by arguing that the so-called power (*śakti*) should not be construed as a real link between a word and its meaning, for it is only on such a construal that it makes sense to say that one would need an infinite number of powers for an infinite number of individuals. However, this rejoinder won't do, for even if power is not to be understood as a real link, it must be understood in some manner, ontologically the least committed being the Nyāya understanding of it as a conventional decision of the form 'Let this word mean this thing', and even on this last-mentioned construction one needs to postulate an infinite number of such conventional decisions or 'baptisms' of the form 'Let this individual be called a cow'. Secondly, understanding the meaning of the word 'cow' is not knowing all individual cows, but does include the ability to recognize any given individual as being or not being one.

If the meaning is not the individual or individuals, is it then the shape, form, or structure (*ākṛti*)? To understand the meaning of 'cow', then, would be to know the shape, form, or structure that any given individual must exemplify in order to be called a cow. This, however, will not do, for the same shape, form, or structure may be exemplified in a cow image, a statue, figure, or painting, which for that reason would not be called a cow.

A more plausible answer is that the word 'cow' means the generic property of cowness. That takes care of the problem arising out of the infinite number of individual cows. They all are unified by possessing cowness. One does not need to possess an infinite number of signifying powers, although one still needs some explanation of how, from understanding the meaning of 'cow',

which is the same as grasping the generic property cowness, one could be led to think of the individual that is intended in a given context. The Mīmāmsakas who hold this theory of word-meaning insist that the generic property first comes to the mind of the hearer (*prathamaṃ upasthitatvāt*),[2] for otherwise he cannot identify an individual cow as a cow. This theory of meaning has certain evident advantages over the other two. It has greater explanatory power and involves postulation of fewer entities: one signifying power for a word would suffice to explain why the word applies to any number of individuals. However, all is not well with it. When one hears the command 'Bring the cow and feed her', the hearer proceeds towards a definite individual. The verbs 'bring' and 'feed' cannot meaningfully relate to the generic property cowness; a unified sense of the sentence requires that the accusative 'cow' signifies a particular individual. Furthermore, there is a word that signifies the generic property: that word is 'cowness'. If the word 'cow' has the same meaning, the two would be synonymous, which, in fact, they are not.

If none of the three by itself—neither the individual nor the form, shape, or structure, nor the generic property—is the meaning of the word, it may very well be the three together. This in fact is the Nyāya theory, according to which a word signifies an individual as qualified by both a form, shape, or structure and a generic property (*jātyākṛtiviśiṣṭavyakti*). It is noted that even this qualified (*viśiṣṭa*) entity is none the less an individual, only it is an individual as possessing or exemplifying a certain structure and a certain generic property. The almost nagging problem still remains: which such individual is meant by the word 'cow'? If *X* and *Y* are two cows, *X* as possessing cow-structure and cowness is not yet the same as *Y* as possessing the same. Of course in one context the word 'cow' refers to *X* and in another to *Y*. Shall we then say that the meaning changes from context to context, though retaining an invariant core, namely the component 'as possessing . . .'? This problem is almost insoluble in terms of the Nyāya as long as a Fregean distinction between sense and reference is not introduced. But if such a distinction is introduced, the correlative distinction between 'understanding' and 'knowing' will destroy, or at least considerably weaken, the claim of *śabda* to be an autonomous mode of knowing. This is an issue to which I will return later in this book.

If none of the four alternatives hitherto considered provides for such a distinction between sense and reference, inasmuch as each of them identifies the meaning with an entity belonging to the world, four other theories appear to be grappling with that Fregean distinction in one way or another: first, the *sphoṭa* theory of Bhartṛhari, the *Yogasūtra* idea of *pratyaya* (cognitive state), the Buddhist theory of *apoha* (exclusion), and the Nyāya concept of *śakyatāvacchedakadharma* (the property which limits the designated entity as such).

Mark Siderits has argued for the thesis that although, generally speaking, the Indian philosophers subscribed to a referential theory of meaning, it is in some rather unexpected quarters that a theory of sense may be discerned.[3] One such place is the Buddhist theory of *apoha*. The reason why the *apoha* theory may be construed as a theory of sense is not far below the surface. The Buddhists are led to it by their metaphysical thesis that reality is an instantaneous, unique particular which, not further characterizable by any property, is what it is by virtue of its difference from other such particulars. In such an ontology there is no place for any shared property, and so for any universal. The Buddhists, therefore, reject the primacy of the name-bearer relation. Words do not function by naming objects, nor do they function by characterizing them (with properties). They seek to refer to reality—which is a unique particular—by excluding all others. (I say they seek to refer, for, strictly speaking, no linguistic entity can succeed in achieving unique reference; its success lies only in its practical applicability). The word 'cow', then, means 'not non-cow'. For my present purpose, I need not go into the various logical,[4] psychological,[5] and semantic[6] variations on this general theory. What is of central interest is the nature of the theory that the meaning of 'cow' is given by 'not non-cow'. It surely is an attempt to avoid the familiar (Indian) referential theory and to dispense with the name–bearer paradigm. But Buddhist nominalism is equally up against any sort of Platonic theory of meaning as an abstract entity. If you want to avoid both these paradigms, the idea of 'difference' as what confers meaningfulness on signs is an attractive way out. One finds it in Saussure, in much of structuralist theory, and of course, in Derrida. But the Buddhist theory is different from these inasmuch as they make use of the

idea of difference amongst the elements of a system of signs, whereas the Buddhists speak of the difference of each unique particular from all others. In the long run, however, the Buddhists cannot, in this semantic theory, make use of the (ontological) differences amongst the unique particulars, for even if these differences obtain, language would have no direct access to them. Language would be using its own internal resources—i.e. its internal differences—to talk about those (ontological) differences. In 'not non-cow', the 'non-cow' would be a pseudo-predicate, itself language-bound. The Buddhists—if they are Sạutrantikas—want to overcome this purely linguistic character of differences by making use of mental representations which one associates with the word 'cow', and ascribe a certain capacity to that representation to exclude other representations. It is in this psychological machinery that one may detect something like the sense, but—as Siderits rightly notes—this machinery is "semantically invisible", it tells me nothing about the meaning of the word 'cow'.

There is nevertheless something else about the *apoha* which looks like a theory of sense. Two different terms may refer to one and the same particular, but each may effect the exclusion in a different manner, in which case one may not know that they are co-referential even when one separately knows their meanings. Thus, even when one knows the meaning of 'impermanent' and 'product', and knows that this is a product, one may not know that this is impermanent. The way this example works, in the context of the Buddhist theory, depends uon the thesis that one may understand the meaning of 'is a product' in 'This is a product', without understanding the general term 'impermanent' in 'This is impermanent'. However, it seems to me that the semblance of referential opacity in this case is due to the fact that while one is wedded to the *apoha* theory of the meanings of 'product' and 'impermanent', one is still making use of their non-*apoha* meanings. Given a grasp of their non-*apoha* meanings, it is reasonable to say that one may understand their meanings and yet not know that both refer to this. But that both in fact refer to the unique this, follows only from the *apoha* account of their meanings, and it is not clear why one who grasps their *apoha* meanings should not *eo ipso* know that they are co-referential. I conclude therefore that the *apoha* theory is not a theory of sense, it is a strategy to

make sense of our talk about what is posited as intrinsically ineffable and unspeakable.

The theory of the linguistic universal (*sphoṭa*), in many respects the very opposite of the *apoha* theory, promises to be a close kin of the Fregean sense theory. But before we jump to conclusions, we should take note of the fact that the *sphoṭa* theory itself has many different versions. There is, first, a purely linguistic theory of *sphoṭa*, and then, a semantic theory. The linguistic theory is best stated by Nagesa in his commentry on Patañjali's *Mahābhāṣya* thus: "the existence and the oneness of *sphoṭa* is evidenced by the cognition 'This is one word, this is one sentence' "[7] The actual sound produced in uttering a word may vary from speaker to speaker, but the word itself is the same amidst such changing manifestations: hence Patañjali's statement that *sphoṭa* is the word, sound is a property of the word (*sphoṭa śabdo, dhvaniḥśabdaguṇaḥ*).[8] *Sphoṭa* is of such and such size, but it is sound which causes increase in length. It is, then, the abstract sound-pattern which is auditorily perceived. But, soon, *sphoṭa* also becomes a timeless, indivisible entity, over and above the constituent phonemes, in itself partless—but manifested by any actual utterance of the word (or of the sentence, if one is talking about the sentence-*sphoṭa*). From this purely linguistic theory of *sphoṭa*, which is a theory about the identity of a linguistic expression type (cf. Husserl's theory of the ideality of the *Sprachlichen*[9] as distinct from the ideality of meanings), we should distinguish the later semantic theory which regards the *sphoṭa* as the integral meaning-bearing sign, the word (or sentence)-in-itself *together with* its meaning, much like Saussure's sign wih its twofold aspects of the signifier and the signified. But what precisely is the signified, the *artha*, the meaning? In Saussure's theory, it is the concept or the image, the mental representation. We need not consider, for our present purpose, whether *sphoṭa* is of a phoneme, or of a word, or of a sentence (there were advocates of all three positions), and whether, accordingly, the word or the sentence is an indivisible entity. One thing seems obvious: as a theory about the identity of the linguistic entity, or about the meaning-bearing entity, it is not to be construed as a theory of meaning itself.[10] The meaning (*artha*) is still the referent. Not unlike Saussure, several amongst the *sphoṭa*- philosophers regarded the *artha* to be subjective.

Yogasūtra iii. 17 suggests that a word means its object (*artha*) and expresses a cognitive state (*pratyaya*). The commentary *Bhāsvati* on *Yogasūtrabhāṣya* explains:

> Owing to mutual superimposition, word, object and cognition get mixed up, so that the word which designates appears to be the same as its meaning, and that again appears to be the same as cognition; thus their seeming identity. By distinguishing between them, and by controlling each separately one comes to know the truth of all things, i.e. one knows what is the object designated by all the words that are uttered.[11]

After saying that the three—word, object, and cognition—are different, the commentary goes on:

> Sign is of the nature of that remembrance which consists in mutual superimposition of word and its object. In other words, what is sound (or the denoting word) is the same as the object, what is object is the same as word. One who knows their distinction, i.e. is capable of separating them and fixing his mind on each separately, is all-knowing, i.e. can know all those objects which are signified by all uttered words.

The identification to which *Bhāsvati* draws our attention is the same phenomenon as is described by Husserl thus:

> The sounded word is first made one with the meaning-intention, and this in its turn is made one . . . with its corresponding meaning-fulfilment. . . They rather form an intimately fused unity of peculiar character. . . .
>
> The relation between name and the thing named, has, in this state of union, a certain *descriptive character*, that we previously noticed: the name 'my inkpot' seems to *overlay* the perceived object, to belong *sensibly* to it.[12]

What, however, is needed is to go back behind this seeming identification and to isolate the different components—the act of uttering, the act of meaning, and the experience of the object out there—that have entered into this peculiar synthesis of unification, so that the object, a table, for example, seems to be clothed with the word 'table' and the experience seems to be linguistic.

But the cognitive state (*pratyaya*) which *Yogasūtrabhāṣya* talks about is a mental representation, a *cittavṛtti*, an internal modification in accordance with the form of the object. I have already argued, in Chapter 1, for the thesis that consciousness cannot assume the form of the object, that it cannot undergo a real modification. The Sāṃkhya-Yoga theory of cognitive states

(*pratyaya*) is therefore of no use to us. Furthermore, we are in need of a cognitive state whose 'form' would be independent of the real existence or non-existence of the object which is being designated. A cognitive state corresponding to a perceptual experience, for example, cannot be the same as the cognitive state that is expressed by language. A perceptual statement 'This is a cow' expresses perceptual cognition, but the sentence 'This is a cow' expresses a sense, no matter if it is or is not uttered with a perceptual backing.

The Yoga philosophy has another concept which may be of use: this is the concept of 'conceptual construction' (*vikalpa*). The commentary *Bhāsvati* on *Yogasūtrabhasya* on sūtra i. 9 explains *vikalpa* thus:

> It is [the mental representation] which follows linguistic (*śabda*) cognition, which arises along with the linguistic expression designating an object that lacks existence, which comes into being in conjunction with cognition of that linguistic expression and which lacks (real) object. It is not included in [the means of] true cognition (*pramāṇa*) nor is it included within 'error'. It is not a [means of] true cognition (*pramāṇa*), because it does not have a real object; owing to its 'use', which is due to the influence of linguistic cognition, it is not error. Error has no 'use' in the sense that once one knows it to be erroneous one no longer uses it. But the objects of *vikalpa* have 'use'. Even if one knows that time etc. are imaginary constructions and so unreal, one still continues to speak about them.[13]

A *vikalpa*, then, is a cognitive state that accompanies a purely linguistic use, and to which, as well as to the animated linguistic expression, there corresponds no real object. Thus the expression 'man in general' or 'redness'—if you happen to be a nominalist in your ontology—does not designate any real object, but is understood. The cognitive state its understanding gives rise to must then be a *vikalpa*.

If now we further generalize this notion, and look for a cognitive state which arises with linguistic understanding, irrespective of whether the linguistic expression concerned does or does not designate a real object out there, then we would be looking for a (Fregean) *Sinn*. The *vikalpa* shows the way, but we cannot take it to be the *Sinn* inasmuch as *vikalpa* requires that it not have a real object.

This brings us to the Nyāya concepts of 'the property which limits the referent as such' (*śakyatāvacchedakadharma*), 'qualifier-

hood' (*prakāratā*), and 'the reason of behaviour' (*pravṛttinimitta*). If the word 'cow' refers to cow-individuals, the individual cow is the referent (*śakya*) only as qualified by the property cowness. In the Nyāya vocabulary, in this case, the property of being the referent (or *śakyatā*) is limited (*avacchinna*) by the property cowness. In other words, cowness is the limiter of being the referent (or *śakyatāvacchedakadharma*) of 'cow'. This concept captures one ingredient of Frege's notion of *Sinn*:[14] it is, like *Sinn*, the mode of reference. It answers the question precisely how, in what manner, as what, the individual is the referent of 'cow'. *Prakāratā* generalizes that notion to all cognitive states. Instead of restricting itself to linguistic cognition, it captures the idea of mode of presentation in so far as 'presentation' means the cognition's reference to its own object. Every cognition not only has its object, but cognizes its object in a certain manner, *qua* such and such, or again, in Nyāya vocabulary, as limited by some property or other. There is still another allied concept: the reason for the application of a word to an object (*pravṛttinimitta*). Why is this individual called a cow? Because, it possesses cowness. All these concepts, in one way or another, capture an important ingredient of the Fregean *Sinn*: the idea of mode of presentation or of the precise manner of reference.

So far it all seems very hopeful. Let us, however, look closer at the Fregean *Sinn*. It is itself a multi-faceted notion. In Dummett's language, it has many ingredients, some of which are in tension with some others. These ingredients are: (1) the mode of presentation or reference; (2) that which to recall Kripke's well-known terms, fixes reference; (3) that which determines reference (i.e. of which reference is a function); (4) that which is grasped in thought; and, finally, (5) that which is the object of oblique discourse. Keeping these in mind, let us now look at the Nyāya concepts at our disposal. We have just seen that (1) is captured by the Nyāya concepts of qualifierhood (*prakāratā*) and reason for behaviour (*pravṛttinimitta*). The idea of the limiter of the property of being the referent of a word (*śakyatāvaccheda-kadharma*), on one reading, is the idea of the common and essential properties by virtue of which individuals belonging to a class are designate by the same term. An individual is designated 'cow' in so far as it possesses cowness. The limiter of an individual's being designated by a proper name such as Caitra would, then, be

the essence of that individual, *Caitratva*. On a certain reading, *pravṛttinimitta* or the reason for behaviour (i.e. the application of a word to an object) has similar ontological emphasis. Vardhamāna's definition includes the clause *vācyavṛttitve sati*, which means that the property (which is to count as the reason for application) must belong to the referent. In fact, if the referent of the cow is not the bare individual, but the individual as possessing the universal, then cowness is only another component of the referent. The problem we are encountering is the problem of identifying the sense as the mode of presentation with a property of the referent, be it its essence or simply a contingent property (*upalakṣaṇa*), as Raghunātha Śiromaṇi wants. For, one must have to keep the possibility open that a thing *x* is presented as *y*, even if the property of being *y* does not belong to *x*.

Do we find (4) and (5)? The object of reference in oblique discourse was construed as the word itself. Nor was a separate sort of abstract entity postulated as that which is grasped in thought (or, correlatively, in understanding). Two things need to be recalled in this context. In the first place, for Indian philosophers there is no simple translation for 'thought'. There is no thinking which is not either perceptual judgement or inference, or any of the other *pramāṇas*, so that in every case the object is the thing that is being known, the referent, and not a 'third' layer of abstract entities. Likewise, the attitude of 'understanding' the meaning of a linguistic expression was not, by itself, thematized, except as it functioned within the context of *śabda* as a *pramāṇa*, i.e. as a means of knowing. There is, however, a concern in the literature that appears to be close to a phenomenology of understanding. This is the theory of linguistic grasping (*śābdabodha*). What precisely is grasped through language? To understand this question, with which all the various schools of Indian philosophy were concerned, we need to keep in mind that nothing is grasped through a mere word, that it is only a sentence that, under appropriate conditions, generates *śābdabodha*. What the question is about, then, is the object, or content, of sentential grasping. If an auditor knows something on the basis of a speaker's utterance of a sentence (we assume that all conditions necessary for knowing are satisfied), what precisely is the object that he grasps? Obviously, it cannot be a simple, unqualified particular. Since the sentence is a complex entity in which various components are

syntactically connected together, the resulting knowledge also must reflect, in some appropriate manner, that complexity in the structure of what is known. But how and in what order? What is the primary element—the nominal element or the verbal element? Thus the theory of *śābdabodha* reflects the attempt to have a relational objectivity, still out in the world, as corresponding to the sentence. I will return to this theme later in this chapter when dealing with sentence-meaning.

The above discussion leads to the conclusion that the only ingredient of the Fregean *Sinn* that clearly emerges in Indian philosophy is the idea of mode of presentation. *By itself*, this notion is compatible with an overwhelmingly referential theory of meaning—as Evans and McDowell's interpretation of Frege shows.[15] Alternatively, there is the theory of structure of a cognition—analysed in terms of qualifiers (*prakāratā*) and qualificands (*viśeṣyatā*), but each component of this structure is a mode of presentation of an object, or component of an object that is being known, and so is inseparable from the latter. So we find either a 'thin' notion of mode of presentation, which escapes reification, or a theory of cognitive structure, to whose analysis the Nyāya logicians devoted a great deal of ingenuity.[16]

SENTENCE MEANING *(VĀKYĀRTHA)*

So far we have been talking about the meanings of words. But not all Indian philosophers of language thought that isolated words had their own meanings. Many of them, in fact, held the view that a sentence is the unit of meaningful expression, and that a sentence is a further (semantically) indivisible unit. In between the two extreme views—that isolated words have their own independent meanings, and that sentences are the smallest, indivisible units of meaningful expression—represented by the Naiyāyikas (and the Bhāṭṭas) and the grammarian Bhartṛhari respectively, there is the third possibility, namely, that words have meanings of their own but only in the context of the sentences in which they occur.

The indivisible sentence theory (*akhanda-vākya-vāda*) is succinctly stated by Bhartṛhari in the well-known verse: "Pade varnā na vidyante/varneṣvavayavā iva/vākyātpadānāmatyantaṃ/

praviveko na kaścana', which may be rendered as 'The phonemes do not exist in a word, just as the phonemes themselves have no parts. The words do not have complete distinction from the sentence [in which they occur].' A sentence is neither a unified collection nor an ordered series of words, nor is it sufficient to add the standard requirements (on many Indian theories) of contiguity, expectancy, and appropriateness. A word is an artificial construction, an isolated word a fiction. A sentence alone is the unit of utterance, a single indivisible entity with a single undivided meaning that is grasped as a unity in a flash of insight (*pratibhā*). This theory is based on some fundamental consideration of how language functions: it takes the point of view of discourse and communication, for which sentence, and not word, is primary. It is also cognizant of the role which language plays in expressing knowledge. Sentences, and not words, express knowledge. Sentences, and not words, are either true or false. The theory also appears to be in consonance with how language is learnt: the familiar Indian account is in terms of a young learner's observing how instructions embodied in sentences are carried out. Another merit of the theory, I think, is that it shows recognition of the fact that only sentences express complete thoughts in a sense in which words do not, and that understanding the meaning of a sentence does involve—whatever else—a grasping of the thought it expresses. However, the theory, despite these merits, is unacceptable. It is a metaphysical reification both of the sentence and of its meaning. None of these is indivisible—not merely in the real sense, but also semantically. And it misconstrues the account of language—learning that it, like most other theories, accepts.

While it is true that language is learnt by learning sentences (i.e. by correlating instructions such as 'Bring the cow' with the actions which they stimulate in the competent auditor), there is another process which takes place alongside it. The learner does not merely accumulate a list of such sentences, but, by a process of insertion and deletion—*āvāpa* and *udvāpa*—is able to separate the meanings of the component words from just those sentential contexts which have been presented to him. Thus by learning the meanings of 'Bring the cow' and 'Tie the cow' and 'Milk the cow', he is able to identify the meaning of 'cow'; likewise from 'Bring the cow' and 'Bring the horse', he learns the meaning of 'bring'. Unless language-learning took this step, the learner would add

more and more sentences to his inventory but would never show the power to construct, or understand, new sentences consisting of words which have figured in the sentences he has already learnt. Thus the indivisible sentence theory cannot give a good account of language-learning. It is this which underlies the standard objection against this theory in terms of 'heaviness' (*gaurava*), i.e. greater assumption.

I will therefore set this theory aside, and turn to the other two, both of which recognize the semantic divisibility of sentences into component meaningful parts. In order to contrast these two theories, and review the issues and arguments that were at stake, I will—as a foil—introduce a pair of concepts from modern semantic theories.

A word has a meaning only in the context of a sentence, said Frege.[17] This is called the context principle. Once the concept of meaning is further differentiated into those of sense and reference, the context principle becomes twofold: as applied to sense and as applied to reference. A word has sense, we can then say, only in the context of a sentence. As applied to reference, the principle is thus stated by Dummett: 'it is only as occurring in the context of a sentence that a name can so much as be said to stand for an object'.[18] Both the forms of the principle are indeed difficult to understand, and to formulate precisely. For the present, I am following Dummett's interpretations of them. As applied to sense, the principle does not say that a word does not have an invariant sense; it does not say that the sense of a word varies from one (sentential) context to another; it only states the condition under which a word can have a sense. In that case, the sense of a word is its contribution to the senses of sentences in which it does or may occur as a constituent. Likewise, as applied to reference, the principle would be: to say that a singular term or a predicate has a reference is to say that sentences in which it occurs have a truth-value. A singular term or a predicate does not name, or otherwise refer to, objects, independently of its role in sentences in which it functions appropriately. (To say that there are numbers is to say that some sentences containing number words in their subject place are true.).

The context principle is prima facie in conflict with the so-called composition principle. If the former makes the sense (and reference) of a word dependent upon the word's role in sentential

context, the latter regards the sentential sense (and reference) as built out of the senses (and references) of the component words and expressions. Frege seems to have held both the views. If we can assume that he never indeed gave up either, the question is how he, or anyone, can hold both without contradicting himself, and yet it may reasonably be supposed that a satisfactory semantic theory should take cognizance of both. With this problem in mind, let us turn to the Indian discussions of what appear to be the same, or at least very similar, issues.[19]

What I have in mind is the dispute between, and the arguments and counter-arguments that were advanced by, the defenders of the related designation (*anvitābhidhāna*) and the relation of designata (*abhihitānvaya*) theories. Since the Indian philosophers carried on these discussions over several centuries, and refined and strengthened their arguments seemingly endlessly, we may as well drop all historical references, and take a look at the issues, concepts, and arguments that turned on this controversy and hope that the Fregean insights may both supplement and be supplemented by the Indian. I am not taking this as merely an exercise in comparative philosophy, but also in systematic, analytic thinking intent upon reaping the benefits of a long and rich tradition to throw light upon a young but vigorous one, and vice versa.

The theory of related designation (*anvitābhidhāna*), which is the Indian counterpart of the context principle, is the view that isolated words do not have any meanings of their own, and that it is only a sentence that expresses an independent meaning. A word has meaning only in so far as it functions in a sentence in co-operation with the other words that belong to the sentence so that a word signifies its meaning only as related to the meanings of those other words.

The theory of relation of the designata (*abhihitānvaya*) which is the Indian counterpart of the composition principle, is the view that words convey their own meanings, and that the sentential meaning is composed of word-meanings as related in a certain manner.

While these are very general formulations of the two theories, each of these was given many different specific formulations. There were also several intermediate theories which sought to retain some part of each. Instead of pausing to mention some of

these, let me proceed to state what are indeed the more pertinent objections raised against the context principle by the defenders of the composition principle. There are six of these objections, if we overlook many minor, ancillary problems:

1. If a word always expressed its meaning only as related to the meanings of the other words belonging to a sentence, all the words of the sentence save possibly the first one that is uttered would be redundant. Since, on this theory, the word 'bring' in the sentence 'Bring me the cow' already expresses a meaning that is related to the meaning of 'the cow', the word 'bring' alone would suffice for the purpose of expressing the complete sentential meaning; the rest of the sentence would indeed be superfluous.

2. (*a*) If a word expresses its meaning only as related to other specific word-meanings (just as 'bring' may be taken to express its meaning only as related to the meaning of 'the cow'), then one has to face the following problem: there are a large number of such words ('the cow', the horse', 'an apple', etc.), and the verb 'bring' would express its meaning as related to *all* of these, which is indeed absurd. One word cannot signify, at the same time, an infinite number of entities. It would also be odd to bring in meanings not expressed by any word in the sentence under consideration. The verb 'bring', as occurring in the sentence 'Bring the cow', cannot express its meaning as related to the meaning of the expression 'the horse'.

(*b*) If the verb 'bring' expresses its meaning as related to the meaning of the expression 'the cow', and the expression 'the cow' expresses its meaning as related to the meaning of 'bring', then there will be the fallacy of mutual dependence or *parasparāśrayatā*.

(*c*) In order to avoid the difficulties raised in (*a*) and (*b*), one may want to say that a word expresses its meaning as related to some type of word-meaning in general, but not to any specific meaning. Thus, one may say, the verb 'bring' expresses its meaning as related to the meaning of some appropriate name, definite description, or indefinite description. One may want to insist on the necessary reference of meaning of a certain categorial type to the meanings of another appropriate categorial type (adjectival meanings to substantival meanings, nominal meanings to verbal meanings, and so on). However, such a move, although

it succeeds in avoiding the difficulties (*a*) and (*b*), makes it impossible for the theory to give an account of how a sentence then comes to have a specific meaning of its own. The word 'bring' will always express a meaning as related to some appropriate nominal meaning or other, just as 'the cow' will express its meaning as related to some appropriate verbal meaning. How will the two be related to each other specifically so as to constitute the specific meaning of the sentence 'Bring the cow'?

3. On the theory that a word is understood only as related to other words in a sentence, it would be inexplicable how one could understand a new sentence. A new sentence signifies a new relational structure of meanings, which, *ex hypothesi*, the hearer has not learnt. Even if the new sentence contains an already familiar word, that word would, in this new context, convey a new relational meaning. Since the auditor is not acquainted with this new relational meaning, he will be able to apprehend neither the meaning of even that familiar word nor the complete sentential meaning.

4. If words did not have, i.e. were unable to express, their own independent meanings, the classification of words into nouns, adjectives, verbs, etc. would be without justification, for any such classification is based on the nature of the word-meanings, as well as the possibility of apprehending them by themselves.

5. The context principle is also incompatible with the undeniable fact that no one can understand the meaning of a sentence if he does not already understand the component words. This cannot be the case if the meanings of the words themselves were dependent upon the context of the sentence in which they function.

6. A logical consequence of the context principle is that every sentence is an indivisible, partless entity. The putative parts, i.e. the words, are only abstractions from this entity which in reality is indivisible and which alone has its own meaning. The words, not having their own meanings, are not semantic components of the sentence. The situation is not unlike the relation between a word and its component phonemes. A phoneme (*varna*) by itself has no sense: a word is the simplest meaningful unit. As such it is further indivisible. The context principle should lead to a radical extension of the same point of view: if words by themselves have no meanings of their own, they are therefore not semantic parts of a

sentence, if by 'part' is to be meant an independently meaningful unity that has entered into the composition of a larger meaningful whole.

The defenders of the context principle have replied to these objections, and a close look at their replies will give us a better understanding of what they mean by their thesis than what the initial formulation yields. Let me therefore summarily state their replies. The reply to each of the above objections bears the same number as the objection, but with an asterisk added to it.

1*. Although each word expresses its meaning in so far as that meaning contributes to the total sentential meaning, the sentential meaning requires the contributions of all the component words. The first word, or, for that matter, any one of the component words, cannot, then, by itself express the completed sentential meaning; it can express only what it contributes to that meaning. What is more, it can make its contribution only in co-operation with the other words, but not alone. Therefore, the other words are also essential to the constitution of the sentential meaning.

2*. (*a*) The argument that there are innumerable word-meanings to which the meaning of a given word can be related is right in its starting-point, but wrong in the conclusion it draws. The fact that there are many such word-meanings does not entail that a word, as functioning in a sentence, expresses at once a correspondingly large number of relational meanings. For a word to express its meaning as related to some other word-meanings, such conditions as mutual expectancy (*ākānkṣā*), semantical appropriateness (*yogyatā*), and nearness or contiguity (*āsatti*), of course, need to be satisfied. These rule out all but the meanings of the other words figuring in the same sentence.

(*b*) The point about mutual dependence may also be set aside on the ground that in fact the meaning of the sentence 'Bring the cow' consists of two different relational structures: cowness-as-qualified-by-the-act-of-bringing, and the-act-of-bringing-as-qualified-by-cowness.

(*c*) Faced with the alternatives—either a word expresses its meaning as related to some other word-meaning of an appropriate type but to none specifically, or it expresses its meaning as related to another appropriate and specific word-meaning—the proponent of the context principle responds by emphasizing that one need not make an exclusive choice. As a matter of fact, while a bare word

expresses its meaning as qualified in general ('bring' means the act of bringing some appropriate object but none specifically), a sentence alone succeeds in specifying that generic implication ('Bring a cow, not a horse', for example).

3*. Can the context principle leave room for a plausible explanation of an auditor's understanding of an entirely new sentence? It should be noted that the question concerns not how meanings of new words are learnt, nor, for that matter, how sentences containing entirely new words are understood. With regard to these latter cases, the two theories are equally better off or equally worse off. The related designation theory is especially ill at ease with sentences in which the individual words are familiar to the auditor, but are nevertheless such that the auditor had never before apprehended the relational structure of which they are components in the present case. Suppose that our auditor is familiar with 'Bring the cow', 'Bring a pitcher of water', and their like, but has never before heard 'Bring a car' although he understands the word 'car', i.e. knows the meanings of other sentences containing that word. This presents a problem inasmuch as his understanding of the verb 'bring' is such that for him, if the theory is correct, its meaning is always related to either a cow or a pitcher of water; he has not yet apprehended the relation of the act of bringing to a car. How then can he understand this new sentence (even if it contains old, familiar words)? Note that the same problem arises with regard to his first encounter with the (now familiar, but then unfamiliar) sentence 'Bring a cow'. The proponent of the context principle contends, in reply, that the objection is based on too strong an interpretation of the idea of sentential context. It is not the case that the meaning of *this* word is always related to the meaning of *that* word. The idea of a sentential context requires only the idea of appropriate relata in general (*sāmānyena yogya-itara-anvitābhidhāna*). Once this general relatedness is apprehended—and this is all that is constitutive of the meaning of a word—the specific relations can be apprehended depending upon what specific terms occur at the appropriate places.

4*. To the objection that if words did not have, i.e. were unable to express, their own independent meanings, the classification of words into nouns, adjectives, verbs, etc. would be without justification, the proponents of the context principle reply that the

type of a word depends upon the sort of contribution it makes to the total sentence-meaning.

5*. But how to preserve the truth of the fact that one can understand a sentence only if one has prior knowledge of the meanings of the component words? What would such a prior knowledge of word-meanings amount to, on the theory of related designation? One answer is already implicit in the preceding remarks. The putative prior knowledge of word-meanings is nothing but, in the first place, understanding of some other sentences in which the words under consideration occur, and in the long run knowledge of the generic contexts in which they may possibly occur. One is pushed back to the question, how does one learn the meanings of new words? But the theory of related designation does have some room for the pure word-meaning *per se*, only it does not want to assign a place to it within its semantic theory. This accommodation is done in the following way: as a word is heard, it *reminds* the auditor of its pure meaning, but it does not *signify* that pure meaning. Since semantic theory can take into consideration only what expressions mean, signify, or denote, the pure word-meaning *per se* is of no relevance for it. I will turn to this important distinction later on.

6*. The reply to (6) may now be formulated. It is not the case that words do not have their independent meanings *per se*, only that the meanings *per se* are not signified by words which always occur in sentences. Since a word's meaning *per se* enters into the relational structure which that word signifies, the word can still be regarded as a meaningful unit, and so as a component of a sentence. The sentential meaning may then be the simplest independent unit of meaning, but neither it nor the sentence signifying it needs to be, for that reason, an indivisible, partless entity. The task is to avoid the extremes of atomism and holism in theory of meaning.

Consider now, again briefly, the standard objections which were raised against the composition principle laid down by the relation of designata (*abhihitānvaya*) theory.

7. The process of language-learning shows that the child learns simple sentences as wholes, and then, by the processes of insertion (*āvāpa*) and deletion (*udvāpa*), separates word-meanings from the specific contexts in which they were learnt. When the sentences

'Bring the cow' and 'Bring the horse' are learnt, the meaning of 'Bring . . .' is isolated as the invariant in those two or similar sentences. Likewise, the meaning of '. . . the cow' separates itself out when the sentences 'Bring the cow', 'Tie the cow', and 'Milk the cow' are learnt. If one learns language in the context of practice, it is the related meanings rather than pure unrelated meanings *per se* that are learnt.

8. If words signified their own independent meanings *per se*, the sentential meaning as a relational structure could not emerge. What we would have is a string of unrelated meanings (and a sentence would be a string of words).

9. No entity is experienced merely as such; it is experienced, at least, as existing ('padārthāstāvat nāvyatiśaktaḥ kvacit upalabhyante/antato' styarthena'—*Bṛhati*). Thus *Vyāsabhāṣya* on *Yogasūtra* iii. 17 says: 'Every word contains sentential power. When the mere word 'tree' is uttered, it is understood that it [the tree] exists' ('Sarvapadeṣu cāsti vākyaśaktiḥ/vṛkṣa-ityukte astīti gamyate'). "Where there is no other verb, there the verbs 'exists', 'becomes', etc. have to be imported" ('Yatra anyat kriyāpadaṃ nāsti tatra astir bhavanti—paraḥ prayoktavyaḥ').

The proponents of the composition principle have responded to these objections in various ways, some of which are worth noting.

7*. Even if we grant, as most Indian philosophers do, that language is learnt in the context of practice, it does not follow that once word-meanings are learnt words cannot signify their own meanings *per se*. What else could be the significance of the processes of insertion (*āvāpa*) and deletion (*udvāpa*), but to free the word from its home in the sentence, so that after it is learnt it can signify its own meaning? Moreover, it is not entirely uncontroversial that word-meanings are learnt only and always by learning sentences. As Jayanta recognizes, one can learn the meanings of words by indexical ostension: "Elderly persons are often seen instructing children by pointing fingers to things in front of them" ("angulyagreṇa nirdiśya kancidarthaṃ purasthitaṃ, vyutpādayanto dṛśyante vālān asanvidhā api").

8*. Various accounts, all closely related, are given of how a relational sentential meaning is rendered possible even on the theory that each word signifies its own meaning. Some of these are:

(*a*) Each word directly signifies its own meaning, i.e. the appropriate entity. The word-meanings, however, together secondarily signify (i.e. by indirect signification, *lakṣaṇā*) the related sentential meaning (*vākyārtha*). This is the standard view of the Bhāṭṭas, which amounts to saying that the sentential meaning is conveyed by the word-*meanings* and not by the words.

(*b*) Word-meanings (which are really referents, for the theory of word-meaning at our disposal is really a theory of reference), be they universals (such as cowness) or particulars (this cow), are not the sorts of thing which could, even indirectly, signify anything. Both direct signification (*abhidhā*) and indirect signification (*lakṣaṇā*) are functions of words. The sentential meaning is built out of word-meanings, when the words are related by *ākānkṣā* (hearing a word arouses the expectation of a word of an appropriate sort to follow), *yogyatā* (what is to follow should belong to an appropriate semantic type), and *āsatti* (close contiguity, spatial or temporal, between the words).

(*c*) The words directly signify their own meanings *per se*. But together they exercise a special significative function by which the syntactical relation between word-meanings comes to be conveyed. This special function is sometimes called *tātparyaśakti*, or the power of conveying the speaker's intention or general purport of the utterances.

Although these three accounts differ on (i) whether it is the words or the word-meanings that are instrumental in conveying the sentential meaning, and (ii) whether the sentential meaning is conveyed by secondary signification (*lakṣaṇā*) or by the speaker's intention (*tātparyya*) (both being secondary signifying functions, as distinguished from the primary function of denoting), they all agree that when words are related by expectancy, appropriateness, and contiguity, they *together* succeed in expressing the relational sentential meaning. There is, however, a common core of the theory: words do express their own meanings *per se*, and then—provided the conditions of expectancy, appropriateness, and contiguity are satisfied—cumulatively convey the relational structure, that is, the sentential meaning.

9*. Although a single word may express a sentence, as when 'jar' expresses 'The jar exists', it need not always do so. When it does, there are two meanings that are expressed, one by the uttered 'jar' and the other by the unuttered 'exists', and the usual

account or accounts, as in (8*), will be given of how the sentential meaning is conveyed. When it does not, what we have is a simple word-meaning *per se*.

This brief exposition of a rather large and widely ramified discussion in the literature should enable us to isolate the main issues and to reflect on them constructively.

Both the theories have a concept of word-meaning (*padārtha*), even of unrelated word-meaning (*ananvita padārtha*). They differ, however, on what role such a concept could be allowed to play in semantic theory. Each word has its own meaning, hearing a word even reminds the auditor of its meaning *per se*—even according to the proponent of the context principle. But this reminding is not signifying or denoting, and belongs not to semantic theory but, let us say, to psychology. The same word, in so far as it exercises its denoting or signifying function, refers to other appropriate meanings, generic or specific. I think whether hearing a word calls up memory of its referent or not is almost irrelevant at present. There is (taking this 'is' in the broadest sense) a referent, an entity, which the word denotes—so far there is an agreement. But does the word denote simply that entity *per se* or not? Our answer to this question depends upon whether we would want to say that the true *home* of a word is in a sentence (and not in the lexicon, for example,), so that it never denotes its referent except in a sentential context, i.e. as related to other word-meanings.

It is important, in order to be able to reflect fruitfully on this discussion in Indian philosophical literature, to keep in mind what the philosophers who took part in the controversy understood by 'word-meaning' (*padārtha*), or for that matter, by 'sentential meaning' (*vākyārtha*). I believe that neither the Nyāya nor the Mīmāmsā philosophers had anything like the Fregean concept of sense as contradistinguished from reference. What they called *padārtha*, to my mind, is nothing other than what a word denotes or refers to. (In quite another context, *padārtha* means the most general classes to which all entities that words refer to may be assigned.) The concept of *padārtha* does not include anything like the Fregean mode of presentation or that which determines reference. It is the referent itself. This, I think, is valid in spite of the different views which were held on what precisely is the meaning (*artha*) of a word. As has been pointed out, the word 'cow' was taken to mean either the particular cow being talked

about on any specific occasion, or the universal cowness, or the particular as qualified by cowness. Each one of these is an entity in the world, not a mode of presentation, not a sense but a referent. When we talk, then, in the present context, of the context principle or of the composition principle, we interpret both principles only as applied to reference but not as applied to sense. How then are we to understand the two theories under consideration?

Just as a word refers to an entity, a sentence also refers to a complex relational entity. To understand a word is to know what entity it denotes, and it is the same in the case of a sentence. In both cases, according to both the theories, understanding amounts to a peculiar presentation (*anubhava*), but not recollection, of the entity denoted. In the Fregean language, one grasps the referent, but not a sense.

But how does this theory work? The word 'cow' means, denotes, refers to, either the universal cowness or a particular cow as possessing that universal. The sentence 'The cow (is) white', expresses, means, or refers to a relational structure whose components are the referents of '(the) cow' and 'white'. If the cow over there is in fact white, there is an ontological structure: that individual over there which possesses cowness is characterized by an instance of colour white, i.e. a colour-particular which possesses the universal whiteness. Is it this structure that is grasped by the auditor who understands the sentence 'The cow is white'? In a sense, we should say 'yes'.

Neither the Mīmāmsā nor the Nyāya is concerned, in the strict sense, with what one can call 'understanding the meaning of an expression'. One is rather concerned with how hearing a sentence, under appropriate conditions (e.g. when the speaker is honest and reliable and known to be so), serves as a means of acquiring valid knowledge, i.e. as a *pramāṇa*. When those appropriate conditions are fulfilled, understanding amounts to knowing, i.e. grasping, not the sense, but rather the ontological structure that obtains, e.g. the individual over there as possessing cowness, and as characterized by a colour-particular which possesses the universal whiteness.

One may still wonder in what sense such verbal knowing is a grasping of the (relational) ontological structure? Since one may also perceive (visually) the same relational structure (namely, a white cow over there), how is the purely linguistic grasping of that

structure (upon hearing the sentence uttered by a reliable speaker) different, *qua* grasping, from a perceptual grasping of it, especially from the sort of perceptual grasping that, according to both Nyāya and Mīmāmsā, is shot through (*anuviddha*) with linguisticality? It could not be said that that which is grasped is different in each case, for on the theory of 'overlapping of the means of the cognition' (*pramāṇasamplava*), which both Nyāya and Mīmāmsā accept, one and the same objectivity may be the object of perception, inference, and language (*śabda*). Of course, one may want to explain the cognitive difference by means of the different way each is caused, but what we are at present interested in is how the one cognition, as a grasping, is different from the other, when both are graspings of the same objectivity.

Perhaps it may help to emphasize a fundamental distinction between two sorts of grasping: direct (*aparokṣa*) and indirect (*parokṣa*). Perception is direct grasping, inference and *śabda* are both indirect. In both direct and indirect cases, one knows a relational structure. Perhaps the locution of 'grasping' is misleading. Not all cases of knowing are cases of grasping. Only perceptual knowing is grasping. The others are knowing, but not grasping. What one knows in each case may not be quite the same.

Thus though the Fregean thesis that in understanding one grasps a sense is of no avail, we are not very far from the other Fregean thesis that in judging one is recognizing its truth-value, for truth-values are referents of sentential senses. Judging that *p* and knowing that *p* by hearing a speaker utter the sentence '*p*' in the affirming manner are closely related mental acts.

So we can at best be said to have on hand an issue concerning reference. We have seen that, according to Dummett, the context principle, as applied to reference, may be formulated thus: words name or refer to objects only in the context of their roles in sentences in which they occur. This is capable of a weaker and a stronger interpretation. On a weaker version, 'what justifies us in regarding an expression as standing for an object is, first, that it behaves like a proper name'.[20] The stronger version is the holistic thesis that a word can be said to denote an object only in the holistic context of the language, discourse, or theory to whose vocabulary the word under consideration belongs. Clearly this sort of holism is not maintained, explicitly or implicitly, by any of the Indian philosophers under consideration.[21]

The weaker thesis is too weak. The related designation theory (*anvitābhidhāna*) says more than merely maintaining this: what it says is that a word, even one that behaves like a proper name, does not denote an entity *per se*, but always as related to other entities denoted by some other words. These other entities themselves, in so far as they are denoted by their names, are likewise related to each other. Note that we do not have here an ontological thesis to the effect that there are *no* unrelated entities: even if there *are* unrelated entities, words do not denote them as such—this is the core of the theory. The theory pertains to the denoting function of words; this function is defined in terms of sentential context, so that words can be said to denote only in that context. What they denote then is a relational state of affairs, not the entity *per se* which is its referent. We have, then, neither an ontological theory nor a theory of sense, but a theory of denotation or reference.

What then is the point of the concern about the unity of sentential meaning? If each word, we are told, denoted its own meaning *per se*, what we would have is a string of such entities and not a unified sentential meaning. Now, as far as the sentence itself is concerned, there is no difference of opinion: it is in fact a string of words (a succession, if we are talking about spoken words), unified into a sentence by virtue of the features of expectancy, appropriateness, and contiguity. As far as the ontological fact is concerned, there is indeed a relational structure out there, independently of what theory of meaning we adopt: a particular cow, for example, possessing cowness, and characterized by a colour that is an instance of whiteness. The issue, then, can only be, how can a string of words each denoting its own meaning *per se* together denote that relational structure? If this is the issue, the Nyāya theory of 'relation amongst designata' has a quite plausible account. By accounting for the unity of a sentence (by virtue of mutual expectancy, appropriateness, and contiguity), it also accounts for how the component expressions together could denote that ontological structure. What is it, then, that this theory cannot satisfactorily explain and which the Prābhākara version of 'related designation' theory can explain better? What is it, then, for the explanation of which the proponents of the Nyāya theory appealed to modes of secondary signification—be they *lakṣaṇā* or *tātparya*, of the words or of their denotations?

There is something for which, it may be argued, a crude

composition principle cannot provide a smooth account: this is the unity of sentential sense or, what is the same, the unity of the proposition expressed by a sentence. Some sort of context principle, it would seem, has a better account of it at its disposal. Such an account would have two component theses, both reputedly Fregean: first, that a sentential sense itself is a complete unit and needs no further completion; secondly, that it must be made possible by a peculiar linking of a saturated element and an unsaturated element. Taking the latter thesis into consideration, one may say as against the Nyāya theory that a sentential sense cannot consist of a juxtaposition of several complete subsentential senses. Since, the Indian theory, as we have said, has no Fregean 'sense' at its disposal, what we can say instead is that the reference of a sentence cannot consist in a juxtaposition of complete referents of the subsentential expressions. What we need is the recognition that the referents of subsentential expressions are, as such, unsaturated and need completion by other entities of appropriate types. Whereas the Fregean name denotes a saturated entity, only the predicate expression denoting something unsaturated, the Indian counter part, i.e. the Mīmāmsā theory, entails that no word means or denotes an entity *per se*, but only as related to some other entity of an appropriate sort. No meaning of a subsentential expression can be a complete, independent entity. This is true of both (Fregean) names and predicates.

We are then led to the following conclusion: the Nyāya theory is correct in holding that each word has its own reference *per se*, and that the sentential meaning is built out of these. But it goes wrong if it supposes that the subsentential meanings are self-complete, or, in Fregean language, saturated entities. This is precisely where the strength of the Mīmāmsā theory lies. It sees rightly that the sentential meaning is not a mere juxtaposition of component meanings, and that any closer unity than a mere juxtaposition requires that in some sense the meanings of the component expressions need each other and so must be, taken *per se*, unsaturated. To the idea of an unsaturated entity belongs the idea of a mode of completion. Hence the Mīmāmsā thesis that a subsentential expression denotes its meaning as related to some other meaning of an appropriate sort. The theory would go astray if it held that a subsentential expression has no denotation of its own *per se*. It has its own meaning, but its meaning is unsaturated.

This is to radicalize the Fregean thesis so as to apply (à la Ramsey) to names as well. It is in this sense that we have to understand the claim that meanings of words are related in general (*sāmānyena anvita*), but unrelated specifically (*viśeṣeṇa ananvita*).

How to construe this claim in its ontological bearing, such that it would be both a plausible ontological theory and consistent with the Prabhākāra pluralistic ontology, is a question we can neither avoid nor attend to in the present context. But this much can be said for the present. The theory is a theory of *śābdabodha*, i.e. of understanding of language. Ontologically, each sentential unit has its reference *per se*, some of which can be by themselves, some need other entities for being what they are. But, as has been said, none of these is denoted, signified, by itself, but only as related to some others. The unsaturatedness that one is thereby imputing is being ascribed not to the things—individuals or universals—that one admits into one's ontology, not to the referents. And yet the theory has no fully fledged theory of Fregean sense. I want to suggest that the theory needs a weaker, less ontologically committed theory of sense; it needs a theory of mode of presentation, not of another ontological stratum of abstract entities. Let us call it quasi-*Sinn*. The Indian logicians had such a theory in their general notion of *viṣayatā* (objectness)—a theme to which I will revert later in these pages.

LINGUISTIC UNDERSTANDING (*ŚĀBDABODHA*)

I maintained earlier that the theory of *śābdabodha* was a theory of what relational structure was known when one knew something on the basis of hearing a sentence being uttered. (We assume that all requisite conditions for such knowing are satisfied.) Let me, however, construe *śābdabodha* as linguistic understanding, the theory as a theory of what it is that is grasped when one understands a sentence. Construing it in this way takes us beyond the constraints of classical Indian modes of thinking, but there is nothing as such about the theories of *śābdabodha* which makes such construal impossible. It is only under such construal, but not on the standard construction of the Indian semanticist, that Matilal's statement would be justified: 'To describe the content of *śābdabodha* can be said to be equivalent to describing the

'meaning' of the utterance.'[22] The standard construal would be that the account of *śābdabodha* is an account of what relational structure is *known* by means of hearing the sentence concerned. The construal I propose (and which lends support to Matilal's statement quoted above) interprets the structure as being not of the object being known (for, in fact, the sentence may be false and yet may generate a *śābdabodha*), but as being of the cognitive state produced in the auditor. Thus, the theory purports to give a cognitive structure. If the sentence is true, and there is a knowledge, the objective structure corresponds to the cognitive structure. Let us recall that, according to the Indian epistemologists, all cognitive states have the qualificand–qualifier structure and that although in a complex cognitive state what functions as qualificand may itself be a qualifier in relation to some other qualificand, there must be a qualificand which is not a qualifier. In the cognition '(the) rose (is) red', 'rose' is the qualificand and 'red' is the qualifier. But 'red' is also a qualificand whose qualifier 'redness' is not 'mentioned'. 'Rose', in this case, is no longer a qualifier of any cognitive component, and therefore is the chief qualificand (*mukhyaviśeṣya*). Every sentence must have a chief qualificand which is the component around which all others cluster.

Consider a simple Sanskrit sentence:

(1) Caitro grāmam gacchati.
(Caitra is going to the village.)

The grammarians, who were impressed by the centrality of the verb in sentential structure, thought that one who understood it would be grasping a structure whose core element must be the meaning of the verb. In the technical jargon just introduced, the grammarians theorized that the cognitive state produced by understanding a sentence has a relational structure in which the chief qualificand, the linchpin, as it were, holding all other components together, is the verbal meaning.

Śābdabodha, on this theory, then, has the verbal meaning as the chief qualificand (*dhātvarthamukhyaviśeṣyaka*). How then does the structure corresponding to our sentence look? What the auditor apprehends, when he understands it, is, on the grammarian's theory, the relational entity: 'the act of going which has the village as its accusative and Caitra as its locus.'

The Naiyāyikas accorded this centrality, the status of the chief qualificand, to the meaning of the word with the nominative case-ending whose meaning is a substantive (*prathamāntārtha-mukhyaviśeṣyakaḥ*). The relational structure grasped in understanding our sentence (1) then has to be something like: 'Caitra as possessing the activity of going which has, as its accusative, the village'.

The Mīmāmsaka's theory is closer to that of the grammarian's, excepting that this theory has a different account of the meaning of the verbal expression. The verbal expression means, primarily—according to the Mīmāmsaka—not the actual act, but rather the effort (*bhāvanā*), the idea of bringing something into being, the thought that causes you to act. Accordingly, on his theory of sentence-understanding, the verb still—as on the grammarian's theory—plays the role of the chief qualificand, but since the verb *means* the idea of bringing something into being, the provoking thought, the effort, the structure grasped in understanding becomes: 'the thought—residing in Caitra—conducive to such activity as would lead to reaching the village'.

A detailed examination of these theories especially with regard to action sentences will not be undertaken in this volume. For the present, it may be useful to look at the way the rival theories were assessed by each party—the arguments and counter-arguments often give us a better idea of the issues involved than the preliminary formulations of theses. The grammarian's theory requires that every sentence must have a finite verb, just as the Nyāya theory requires that every sentence must have a nominative. But consider, on the one hand, a sentence such as

(2) Caitraḥ brāhmaṇaḥ.
(Caitra [is a] brahmin.)

and, on the other hand, a sentence such as

(3) Caitreṇa supyate.
([It is being] slept by Caitra.
= Caitra is sleeping.)

The former lacks a verb (a copula is not needed for a Sanskrit sentence), the latter has no word with a nominative case-ending. Even if there is a finite verb, it may not indicate effort or *bhāvanā*—thus causing embarrassment for the Mīmāmsaka, as in

(4) Ratho gacchati.
(The chariot is moving.)

In all three cases, the strategy of the theorist is to import what is not ostensively there, to import the copula in (2) and to import the sense of activity favourable to going by indirect signification (*lakṣaṇā*) in (4). In (3), the Naiyāyika will admit that the chief qualificand is the word designating sleeping, and so, again, a noun. It would seem, from this rather quick consideration, that the Mīmāmsā theory suffers from a serious weakness, which derives from its taking human voluntary actions as paradigmatic, which requires construing all verbs as designating, directly or indirectly, an effort or *bhāvanā*. The Nyāya and the grammarian's theories would appear to have equal strength—both can take care of all cases either by importing what is lacking, or by introducing a nominative that is a verbal noun. Is there then any consideration which may help us to choose between these two? It is interesting that in the case of impersonal sentences such as 'It rains' or 'Caitreṇa supyate', all theories agree that what is grasped in understanding is a structure in which the name for action ('raining', 'sleeping') is primary. As the author of the *Nyāyakośa* recognizes, that understanding in such cases has an action as its chief qualificandum (*kriyāmukhyaviśeṣyakaḥ*) is admitted by all theories (*sarvatantrasiddhaḥ*). You have then a noun which designates an action. The two possibilities of transformation are always there. Both theories have something to say in their favour: the same nominal word takes on different case-endings, depending on the meaning of the verb, so that the verb would seem to be more 'powerful', but likewise, tenses and moods and number of the verb would be determined by the nominative, in which case the nominative would seem to be the determining factor.

Is the difference one of ontology? In one case, it would seem, one is making use of an ontological primacy of substance, in the other of the primacy of actions. We know that in the Nyāya ontology, individual substances have a central position: members of other categories, qualities, actions, universals, and even absences reside in some substance or other, either proximately or remotely. But we cannot say that in the grammarian's ontology actions, processes, and events occupy a similarly central position. Besides, even if it might seem as though nominatives mean

substances, that is indeed misleading. For the nominative case-ending may very well attach to words designating actions, processes, and events.

The difference, then, if not traceable to ontology, may be due to the very different linguistic theories the grammarians and the Naiyāyikas support. The linguistic theories are reflected in the definitions of sentences that the theorists give. A sentence, according to Kātyāyana's *Vārttika*, is an expression 'possessing one finite verb' (*ekatin*). Patañjali, in his *Mahābhāṣya*, insists: "there is no sentence which is devoid of a verb" ('*na hi kriyā-vinirmuktaṃ vākyaṃ asti*'). The Naiyāyikas reject this, and go back to the other ancient linguistic tradition: a sentence is one which arouses no expectation to complete its meaning, as *Kātyāyanaśrautasūtra* I. iii. 2 states ("teṣāṃ vākyam nirākānkṣaṃ"). For Nyāya, then, there are sentences without verbs, as, for example, 'nīlo ghataḥ' ('the blue jar'), 'trayāḥ kālāh' ('the three times'). Even a single word may suffice as in 'ghataḥ' ('the jar'). The grammarian is naturally expected to reply that in all such cases the verb is understood and should be 'imported'.

In fact, the difference in linguistic theory goes deeper than the account of sentence: it concerns also the nature of words. Already Yaska's *Nirukta* mentions two such accounts: most grammarians, notably Sakatāyana, we are told, held the view that names are derived from verbs, while Gārgya, along with some grammarians, reportedly held that not all names have verbal origin. For the Naiyāyika, even conjugational affixes and case-endings, the *bibhaktis*, are words. If we take this last point into consideration, then the Naiyāyikas' one-word sentence such as '*pacati*' ('cooks') really has two words, *pac* and *tin* (or, 'ghataḥ' ('the jar') consists of two, *ghata* ('jar') and *sup* ('one in number')).

The most reasonable account, then, of the source of the differences in theories of *śābdabodha* is linguistic theory rather than a description of the content of consciousness at the moment of understanding. In other words, it would *not* be a phenomenological account of the structure of the act of linguistic understanding. It is, rather, an attempt to set up a theory that would be able to take care of all empirical data about sentence-understanding. It is interesting that whatever it is that is grasped in an act of sentence-understanding, that entity—the thought (shall we say?) expressed—can be described in either of the two ways: one way

which makes the verbal element the linchpin, the other way which makes the nominative the linchpin. We could, then, say that *something* is grasped when a sentence is understood, but this entity can be analysed in two different ways. The thought expressed by (1) can be analysed either in terms of 'Caitra' as the chief qualificand and the other components as its qualifier or in terms of 'is going' as the linchpin.

A RÉSUMÉ

Looking back, I have maintained that some theory of sense, or rather of a quasi-*Sinn*, is needed to support many of the theories discussed: the Prābhākara theory of related designation, the Nyāya theory of objecthood (*viṣayatā*), especially of qualifierhood (*prakāratā*), and the theory of linguistic understanding (*śābdabodha*). One may not need to go so far as to admit an entirely different realm of entities like the Fregean *Sinne*. But one needs more than the mere reference. One needs the idea of mode of presentation, to say the least. But the mere mode of presentation—to which Evans and McDowell want to reduce the Fregean *Sinn*—won't do. We want something that is grasped in *śābdabodha* or linguistic understanding. My present claim is that the Nyāya idea of objecthood (*viṣayatā*) is able to take care of both: the mode of presentation and that which is grasped in understanding (and it also helps to talk about the context of a cognitive state in which something is known).

When an entity *A* is known, thought of, presented, it becomes the *viṣaya* or object of the appropriate cognitive state. In that case, one would say that there is in the cognitive state a *viṣayatā*, an objectness, attaching to *A* (*A-niṣtha*). If the entity *A* is a complex structure (e.g. a white horse), then in fact the objecthood (*viṣayatā*) attaching to it divides into several specific modes: a qualificandness (*viśeṣyatā*) attaching to the horse and a qualifierness (*prakāratā*) attaching to white. This is to give the simplest analysis.

Such an entity as the qualificandness-attaching-to-horse is a very peculiar entity. It is not a real property of the horse as the colour of the horse is. It is not also a real property of the cognitive state as, for example, temporal and egological locations are.

The Nyāya logicians never quite succeeded in properly categorizing this group of entities. But they did perceive their ambiguous character in so far as the dichotomy between that which really belongs to a cognition and that which is really out there in the object is concerned. I would prefer to call them intentional contents which are *of* the cognition in one sense of 'of' and *of* the object in another sense of 'of'. The cognition refers to its object. This reference (along with its specific modality) is precisely the objecthood (*viṣayatā*) (or its specific form) attaching both to the cognition and to its object. One then begins to see how by using this concept of objecthood (along with its specific modalities), the Indian epistemologists succeed in talking about a cognitive state and yet in terms of the objects that are being known. We have then a sort of quasi-*Sinn*, a minimal entity which yet is the mode of presentation.

In purely linguistic understanding—which does not amount to knowing—what is grasped would be such a structure—a structure which would be a concatenation of such intentional meaning-contents. I am not thereby attributing to the Indian theorists this purified theory of linguistic understanding (*śābdabodha*). There is no doubt, in general, that the Indian theorists, in talking about *śābdabodha*, are talking about a mode of knowing what is the case. I am attempting to suggest that the distinction between *śābdabodha* as linguistic understanding and *śābdabodha*, if one insists on using the same term, as linguistic knowing is important and should be brought to explicit recognition. That something like this was on the horizon is suggested by the recognition that even if there is doubt about semantical competency, *śābdabodha* may occur. This recognition is glossed over by a commentator thus: *Śābdabodha* arises from the cognition of competency, it does not matter if such cognition is assertive or is a case of doubt.[23] There is a serious equivocation here. If there is doubt about competency, there cannot be *śābdabodha* as a mode of knowing, but there can be *śābdabodha* as a mode of linguistic understanding.

MEANING INTENTION?

Besides the concepts of sense and reference, the concept of intention (to mean) has played an important role in theories of

meaning. Let us now look at the role this concept plays in the Indian theories of meaning.

There is an extreme subjectivist view ascribed by Vācaspati (in his *Tātparyaṭīkā* on *Nyāyasūtra* I. i. 7) to Dignāga, according to which there is nothing in the connection between a word and its referent save the individual speaker's arbitrary desire. A word is neither identical (*tadātmā*) with the referent, nor is it caused by the latter. Even without there being any referent, a word can be used owing to the mere desire to speak on the part of a person. Likewise, Manorathanandi, in his *Vṛtti* on Dharmakīrti's *Pramāṇavārttika*, writes that words do not invariably designate an existent object.[24] What words do indicate, then, is rather the intention of the speaker. And this intention does not always come out true.

This Buddhist view has been severely criticized by the Naiyāyikas as well as Jains. The following summary of their criticisms follows the text of Prabhācandra's *Prameyakamalamārtaṇḍa*.[25] First of all, the auditor, to whom the speaker is addressing himself, cannot possibly determine the speaker's intention, as it is not perceivable by him; as far as the speaker himself is concerned, his uttering the words to convey his intention to himself is pointless. Why then should he utter the words that he does?

Secondly, if all that words do is to convey the intentions of the speaker, then every word—all sentences particularly—would be true to their intention. The Buddhist's utterance then would be no more valid than an utterance of the Jain's, for each would express its utterer's intention.

Just as there may be utterances in the absence of their referent, as the Buddhists insist rightly, so also there is no invariable relationship between an utterance and the intention behind it. One may intend to mean something and utter the wrong word, as is especially seen in the case of mistakes in referring to a person by the wrong name.

What is this desire or intention (*vivakṣā*)? Is it the simple desire to utter a word? Or is it the intention to mean such and such thing by such and such word? In the former case, listening to an utterance or studying the scriptures would be pointless—if all that one can gather at most is the intention of the utterer or writer. Furthermore, all sentences would be alike inasmuch as each would

express its utterer's intention. If what is meant by *vivakṣā* is an intention to mean such and such thing by such and such word, then clearly such an intention is absent in the case of utterances by a parrot or by a person who is out of his senses.

Finally, does a sentence indicate the intention of its speaker by itself or does it do so only by depending on a language? In the former case, everyone would understand every language, which is absurd. In the latter case, why not say that a word conveys its meaning, as belonging to a language?

If these arguments are sound, as they seem to be, to reduce the function of a linguistic utterance to indicating merely the intention of the speaker won't do. It is true that there is no relation of invariable co-presence between a word and its referent. It is also true that an utterance is not caused by the presence of its referent. It would be wrong to say that the way we know on the basis of hearing an utterance (or reading a text) is but a case of inference. There is an important element of truth in the claim of most Indian philosophers that *śabda* is an irreducibly unique sort of true cognition—although I have questioned this thesis as it is generally put forward. I will say more about this later in this book.

If the sole function of speech is not to indicate the intention of the speaker, that should not be construed to suggest that in my view the speaker's intention has no place at all in a theory of meaning. Since I have pleaded for a (mildly ontological) theory of sense, I would suggest that an utterance indicates to the hearer the intention of the speaker, while at the same time performing the other two functions: namely, expressing a sense (or thought) and referring to a (real or putative) thing out in the world. As long as the subjective intention of the speaker does not affect the last two functions, there seems to be no great harm. But does it leave them totally untouched by subjectivity? At two points, the spectre of subjectivity raises its head.

First, even on the Nyāya view, so opposed to the Buddhist's, the connection between a word and its meaning is conventional, and 'convention' is explicated by 'the desire "let this word mean such and such thing" '. To say that the desire which assigns meanings to words in a language is but God's—as the Naiyāyikas often said—is to escape from subjective relativism, but at what cost? There is not only the problem whether one act of desire on God's part can

objectify all things by assigning names to them, there is also the problem about languages in the plural: which vocabulary did God sanction, which names did he choose? No, appealing to God's desire won't do, but at the same time we may admit that there must have been some original 'baptism' (to borrow Kripke's term) or some *Urstiftung* (in Husserl's sense). However, once such a baptism has been performed, the *Urstiftung* established, the connection becomes objective; subjective intention plays little role subsequently. We assume, unless otherwise indicated, that the speaker intends to use the words he utters in the sense in which the community uses them. If he intends to use them otherwise, he should say so, or give indications thereof. So subjectivism is no threat at this point.

Secondly, for a string of words to constitute a sentence and so to have the capacity to generate a proper linguistic understanding, the words must not only be in close contiguity, but the succeeding words must fulfil the expectations aroused by the preceding ones. This last feature is what is called *ākānkṣā*. The imperative 'Open', when uttered, arouses the expectation 'the door' or some such appropriate (*yogya*) object name, in the accusative case, to follow. However, to characterize the syntactic point as a case of *ākānkṣā* would seem to be letting a subjective concept intrude into our semantic (or syntactic) theory. Whose *ākānkṣā*, we may ask? That of the preceding word? Or, of its meaning? Or of the speaker, or of the hearer? Since both the word and the meaning are not conscious, we cannot literally ascribe to them anything like *ākānkṣā*. It is really the speaker (or the auditor) who, upon uttering (or hearing) 'open', intends to utter an accusative noun immediately after (or expects to hear such an expression soon after). In fact I believe that when the Indian semanticists characterize the syntactical relation as one of *ākānkṣā*, they are taking the point of view of the hearer.

But, as Jayanta adds, a person's expectation is not, by itself, a *pramāṇa*. Expectation cannot by itself establish the nature of things. But, as depending upon *śabda*, the expectation can be a factor in bringing about connectedness of meanings. The attribution of the word *ākānkṣā* to the words themselves, then, is a case of 'transferred epithet'.

LANGUAGE AND THE INEFFABLE

In their metaphysical thinking, many Indian philosophers, from very ancient times, insisted that reality is unspeakable. Thus, the Upaniṣads said that the *Ātman*, the Self, cannot be described by language ("Yato vācā nivartante aprāpaya manasā saha"). The Buddhists regarded the real as the *sva-lakṣaṇa*, being-of-its-own-nature, which shares nothing with any other, the unique particular which therefore cannot be referred to or described by language. However, at the same time, the very same philosophers sought to talk about the ineffable, and, being self-conscious and self-critical to a high degree, had to work out a theory of how language works in such cases.

Referring to an individual need not be by way of giving a set of predicates which are uniquely true of it. The philosophers who held that reality is ineffable used many different strategies to talk meaningfully about it. Some of these are as follows:

One may say what the thing is not, if it is not permissible to say what it is. This is the root of the Buddhist theory of *apoha*, or meaning as exclusion. It is also at the root of the Advaita Vedānta thesis that when the Upaniṣads speak of *brahman* as *satyaṃ, jñānaṃ*, and *anantam* (truth, knowledge, and infinite), what the three constituent words mean, in such a context, is to exclude all that is *a-satya* (false), *ajñānaṃ* (non-knowledge), and *sānta* (finite). Since *brahman*, on the Advaita view, is without any attributes (for all determination is negation), the three words are not to be taken as ascribing properties but only as saying what *brahman* is not—while referring to one and the same entity in itself (and not as characterized by three different properties).

Or, one may be using words as indexicals, thereby pointing to, drawing the attention of the auditor towards, enabling him to identify the entity. The logic of such pointing accompanied by discourse as an aid has been called by many Sanskrit authors *Arundhati-nyāya*, the logic of Arundhati. *Arundhati* is the name of the smallest star in the polar configuration. Simply saying 'That is Arundhati' would not help a novice in astronomy. You have to say something like this: 'You see that big star. See the star next to it. That is not Arundhati. See the one to its north. That *is* Arundhati.' Ostension and the discourse jointly lead the auditor to successful identification. The role of language is to aid this process.

Or, consider the Vedānta theory of immediate knowledge which is yet brought about by linguistic discourse. To recall the well-known fable: ten supposed fools swam across a river in spate. Once reassembled on the other bank, they wanted to make sure that all ten had arrived, that none had been drowned in the river. Everyone who did the counting did not count himself, and so came up with the number nine, so arousing the anxiety that one of them had not made it. A wise brahmin was passing by and, seeing their plight, said to the last man who had just finished counting nine and was looking for the tenth person, "You are the tenth person" ("Daśamastvamasi"). This verbal instruction makes him aware of his own being, not indeed conceptualizable but, in that context, capable of being identified non-conceptually as a result of an appropriate verbal discourse.

Finally, to the grammarian philosopher Bhartṛhari we owe the paradox:

What is sayable (*vācya*) by the word 'unsayable' (*a-vācya*) is made sayable by that word. But to say that it is sayable of the word 'unsayable' is to contradict oneself.[26]

His solution proceeds as follows:

Just as doubt, giving up its own nature, renders its object doubtful, so the word 'unsayable' (*a-vācya*), giving up its own self, expresses the object by objectifying it. But the word 'unsayable' does not express unsayability (*a-vācyatva*) of itself. The operation of the word 'unsayable' in referring to its object is *not* accompanied by another operation directed towards itself, i.e. to the word 'unsayable', so that in addition to denying that the object cannot be described by any word, it does not, by the (supposed) second operation, deny its own expressibility. Hence no contradiction.[27]

The example of doubt is to be understood thus: in doubting if an object is such and such or not, the object is rendered doubtful and, by implication, the doubtfulness of the object's being such and such is made free from doubt. In this sense, doubt 'gives up its own nature'. Likewise, in saying of a thing that it is unsayable, *its* unsayability is being spoken of, not the unsayability of unsayability itself. Due to this 'giving up of its own nature', or dropping its self-referentiality, even the ineffable can be linguistically referred to as the ineffable.

IDENTITY SENTENCES (*SĀMĀNĀDHIKARAṆYA VĀKYĀNI*)

In view of the concern of this chapter with a theory of sense, as distinguished from reference, it would be appropriate to conclude it with a brief discussion of how identity sentences were dealt with by some Indian philosophers. If anywhere it is here that a theory of sense is approached. The typical identity statement is one in which all the words are *samānādhikaraṇa*, i.e. have the same (nominative) case-ending. We choose as example a sentence already briefly quoted: 'Brahman [is] truth (*satyaṃ*), knowledge (*jñānaṃ*), infinite (*anantaṃ*)' (*Taittirīya Upaniṣad* II. i. 1). The grammarian Patañjali defines *sāmānadhikaraṇya* or 'having the same case-ending' as "the application [or belonging] of [many] words, having different reasons for application, to one and the same entity" ("bhinnapravṛttinimittānāṃ śabdānāṃ ekasminnarthe vṛttiḥ"). The identity statement 'Brahman [is] truth, knowledge, infinite', then, expresses either Brahman's identity with itself, or the linguistic thesis that the different words apply to one and the same entity but for different reasons so that the statement is not trivial (which it would be on the first interpretation).

Given this explication of identity statements, the Indian philosophers proceeded from here in at least two directions. One is represented by the theory of the followers of Śaṃkara, the other, with slight variations, by all the rest. On Śaṃkara's metaphysical theory, reality is pure identity, and so he was looking for how discourse, even identity statements, although containing internal differences (such as differences amongst meanings of component words), could yet refer to that purely self-identical, undifferentiated reality. The other philosophers reject this idea of abstract self-identity, and have an easier task of showing that what discourse can refer to must be an identity-in-differences.

Consider again the sentence 'Brahman [is] truth, knowledge, [and] infinite'. If the last three words are synonymous, then the sentence would be trivial, repetitious, and, in the end, a string of names for one and the same thing. One must then recognize that they are not synonymous, that they have different meanings. How then can they all refer to a self-identical and purely undifferentiated entity? The explanation consists in distinguishing three different modes of meaning: the primary or literal meaning

(*abhidhā*), a secondary meaning (*lakṣaṇā*) and the intended meaning (*tātparya*). We leave out of consideration the question whether the intended meaning is nothing but what the speaker intends, or whether it is a function of the words themselves. The sentence 'Brahman [is] truth, knowledge [and] infinite' intends to refer to a pure identity. But in doing so each component word gives up part of its meaning, and retains part of its meaning. What it retains is the negative exclusion, conveying that exclusion as its secondary meaning (*lakṣaṇā*). How the secondary meanings of the words are to be construed depends upon what the intended meaning of the sentence is. If the intended meaning is to refer to a pure identity, the component words cannot be taken as ascribing predicates of it, but have to be taken, in the secondary signification, as referring to the appropriate exclusions. What the intended meaning is can be ascertained without determining the actual intention in the mind of the speaker: all that we need is to take contextual factors into account—factors such as introduction, conclusion, repetition, etc. in the text. Hence the sequence of interpretation is:

Context → Intended Meaning → Secondary Meaning.

We can apply the same interpretation to more mundane identity statements such as 'This is the same Devadatta as that', the context of the utterance being somewhat like this: two persons *A* and *B* had seen a man called Devadatta in the same place and at the same time. The same two persons now see him again in a different place and at a different time. *A* recognizes him to be the same person, *B* takes this Devadatta to be different from the one seen in the past. *A* tries to persuade *B* to believe that this is the same Devadatta as that. The statement is asserting that: this Devadatta = that Devadatta. Once this intention is determined, it becomes clear that the expressions 'this Devadatta' and 'that Devadatta' are not here to be taken as expressing their complete meanings. For 'this Devadatta' refers to Devadatta as qualified by the properties of occupying the present time and the space in front of the utterer, while 'that Devadatta' refers to Devadatta as qualified by the properties of occupying past time and space away from here. This is to leave out of consideration other differences such as: then Devadatta was younger, now he has grown older. In the identity statement, then, on the Vedāntin's theory, the two expressions

give up part of their meanings, the reference to differing spatiotemporal locations (or to age, for example), and retain only a part, i.e. reference to Devadatta himself: hence the reference to the pure identity of Devadatta with himself.

Such is the theory of the followers of Śaṃkara. On the opposed theory, defended amongst others by Rāmānuja in his commentary on *Brahmasūtra* I. i. 1, the notion of an indivisible object (*akhandaekarasavastu*) which is referred to through a series of exclusions is rejected. A *sāmānādhikaraṇya* or identity statement, on this theory, is nothing but 'the reference of all words of the sentence to one object, where each word ascribes a different property to that object'.[28]

The commentary *Śrutaprakāśikā* on Rāmānuja's commentary on I. i. 1 distinguishes between three kinds of words:

1. Some are co-referential, both denotatively and connotatively ("viśeṣaṇato viśeṣyatascaikārtha"). Such are the synonyms such as *ghataḥ* and *kalaśaḥ*, both meaning 'jar'.
2. Some are of different denotation and different connotation ("ubhayataśca bhinnārthaḥ"). Such are the two words *gauḥ and aśvaḥ*—the former meaning 'cow', the latter 'horse'.
3. Some connote different properties, but denote the same entity ("viśeṣaṇato bhinnārthaḥ viśeṣyataḥ ca ekārthaḥ"). Such are the words 'Devadatta [is] dark, young, and of red eyes', or, to take the other example given by the author, 'the blue lotus.' It is in this last case that *sāmānādhikaraṇya* or identity statements are possible.

To add one remark, on a superficial reading (3) suggests a sense–reference distinction—if we take the property connoted to be the sense. There is no doubt that Frege sometimes spoke of senses as properties. However, if we examine closely the examples given, we find them to be logically very different from Frege's 'the Morning Star = the Evening Star'.

NOTES AND REFERENCES

1. Pāṇini: "svaṃ rūpaṃ śabdasya aśabdasaṃjñā", I. i. 68; *Yogasūtra* iii. 17: "śabdārthapratyāyanaṃ itaretarādhyāsāt śaṃkaraḥ".

2. "gavādiśabdānāṃ jātāveva śaktiḥ viśeṣaṇatayā jāteḥ prathamanupasthitatvāt" (*Tarkasaṃgrahadīpikā* on Annaṃbhaṭṭa's *Tarkasaṃgraha* on *śabda*).
3. M. Siderits, 'The Sense–Reference Distinction in Indian Philosophy of Language' (preprint).
4. The two kinds of negation involved had to be sharply distinguished in order to make sense of 'not non-cow'. For the problems involved see J. F. Staal, 'Negation and the Law of Contradiction in Indian Thought: A Comparative Study', *Bulletin of the School of Oriental and African Studies*, 25 (1962), 52–71; Hans Herzberger, 'Double Negation in Buddhist Logic', *Journal of Indian Philosophy*, 3 (1975) 3–16; J. L. Shaw, 'Negation and the Buddhist Theory of Meaning', *Journal of Indian Philosophy*, 6 (1978), 59–77, and M. Siderits, 'Was Śāntarakṣita a "Positivist"?' (preprint).
5. The psychological aspect of the theory concerns the role which mental representations—themselves also particulars—play in the linguistic reference to external particulars.
6. Semantic complexities arose in connection with the question whether the meaning of 'cow' is entirely negative, or whether it consists of a positive element as well, and if so, what the relative weights of those components are.
7. "Idaṃ ekaṃ padaṃ, ekaṃ vākyaṃ iti pratyayaḥ sphoṭasattve tadekatve ca pramāṇaṃ" (Nāgeśa, in *Mahābhāṣyapradīpoddyota*, i. 11).
8. Patañjali on Pāṇini I. i. 70.
9. E. Husserl, *Formale und transzendentale Logik* (Halle: Max Niemeyer, 1929), §2.
10. Thus Raja: "*sphoṭa* is not the idea or the meaning, but it is that indivisible symbol which brings to light the idea of the thing meant" (K. Kunjunni Raja, *Indian Theories of Meaning* (Madras: Adyar, 1963), 154).
11. "śabdārthapratyayānāṃ itaretarādhyāsāt saṃkaraḥ—yo vācakaḥ śabdaḥ sa evārthaḥ tad eva ca jñānaṃ iti saṃkīrṇatā, tatpravibhāgasamyamāt—pratyekaṃ vibhajya samyamāt sarvabhūtānāṃ ṛtajñānaṃuccaritaśabdārthajñānaṃ bhavediti sūtrārthaḥ" (Hariharānanda Āraṇyaka, *Bhāsvati* on *Vyāsabhāṣya* on *Yogasūtra* (Calcutta, 1930, 127).
12. The text from *Bhāsvati* is at p. 129. The Husserl texts are from the *Logical Investigations*, ed. and trans. J. N. Findlay (New York: Humanities Press, 1970), i. 281–2, ii. 688.
13. "śabdajñanānupātī—avastuvācakaśabdajñānasyānujātaḥ tajjñānānibandhano vastuśūnyo vikalpaḥ sa na pramāṇo—pārohi—pramāṇāntarbhūtaḥ, na ca viparyayopārohī. vastuśūnyatvāt na pramāṇaṃ tathā śabdajñānamāhātmya—nibandhanād vyavaharānna viparyayaḥ. pramāṇasya viṣayo vāstavaḥ. viparyayasya nāsti vyavahāraḥ

. . . vikalpasya viṣayānāṃ cāsti vyavahārah, yathā vaikalpikaṃ, kālādi avastu iti jñātvāpi tad vyavahṛiyate" (*Bhāsvati*, p. 13).

14. For the various ingredients of Frege's notion of *Sinn*, see M. Dummett, *The Interpretation of Frege's Philosophy* (London: Duckworth, 1981), 101–4.
15. See G. Evans, *The Varieties of Reference*, ed. J. McDowell (Oxford: Clarendon Press, 1982), ch. 1. For criticism of this interpretation, see Dummett, *The Interpretation of Frege's Philosophy*, 105 ff.
16. For more on this theory of cognitive structure, see my *Gaṅgeśa's Theory of Truth* (Santiniketan: Centre of Advanced Study in Philosophy, 1966), 25–37.
17. G. Frege, *Die Grundlagen der Arithmetick* (Darmstadt and Hildesheim: Georg Olms, 1961), Introduction, and §60, §62, §106.
18. Dummett, *The Interpretation of Frege's Philosophy*, 366.
19. An earlier version of the next few pages on the theme of sentential meaning was first read at an international conference on Theory of Meaning at the Jadavpur University, Calcutta, 1983. Since then the paper has been read and discussed in various places. After these pages were written, B. K. Matilal and P. K. Sen published an important paper on this theme ('The Context Principle and some Indian Controversies', *Mind*, 97 (1988), 73–97).
20. Dummett *The Interpretation of Frege's Philosophy*, 382.
21. Possibly, Bhartṛhari was the most radical holist in the Indian tradition—at least, Professor Matilal reads him so. See B. K. Matilal, *Perception: An Essay of Classical Indian Theories of Knowledge* (Oxford: Clarendon Press, 1986), esp. 386–98.
22. B. K. Matilal, *Logic, Language and Reality* (Delhi: Motilal Banarasidass, 1985), esp. 408 and 41b.
23. "Tattatpadārthasmaraṇe sati kvacitsaṃśayarūpasya kvacit niścayarūpasyāpi yogyatāyā jñānasya sambhavāt" (*Siddhāntamuktāvali* on *Bhāṣāpariccheda*, *kārikā* 83).
24. "nāntarīyakatāyā avinābhāvasyābhāvāt vastubhiḥ saha śabdānāṃ, tataḥ śabdebhyo nārthasya siddhirniścayaḥ. kiṃ tarhi tebhyo gamyate? ityāha—vakturabhiprāyasya vivakṣāyāste śabdāḥ sūcakāḥ, tadanvayavyatirekānuvidhāyitvāt" (Manorathanandi's *Vṛtti* on Dharmakīrti, *Pramāṇavārttikaṃ* (Varanasi: Bauddha Bharati, 1968), 323).
25. Prabhācandra, *Prameyakamalamārtaṅda*, ed. Pt. Mahendra Kumar Shastri (Bombay: Nirnaya Sagara Press, 1941), 449–51.
26. *Vākyapadīya*, iii. 20–21.
27. Ibid. iii. 23–8.
28. "anekaviśeṣaṇābhidhāyināṃ śabdānāmekasminviṣaye paryavasānaṃ sāmānādhikaraṇyaṃ" (*Śrutaprakāśikā* on Rāmānuja's *Śribhāṣyaṃ* on I. i. 1).

4

The Nature of Indian Logic

ANUMĀNA

The word 'logic' is not easily translatable into Sanskrit philosophical language. *Pramāṇaśāstra* readily translates into 'epistemology'. *Ānvīkṣikī*—one of the four branches of inquiry, the other three being *adhyatmika* (spiritual, leading to *mokṣa* or liberation), *trayī* (the three Vedas), and *vārtā* (agriculture)—is discursive, analytical philosophy, including logic and all the rest. *Nyāya*, apart from naming an entire philosophical school (with an emphasis on reasoning and logic), stands for reasoning itself. *Tarka*, in strict parlance, stands for a definite sort of argument—using a counterfactual. But, in informal language, *nyāyaśāstra* and *tarkaśāstra* have been used to render 'logic'. In this discussion of Indian logic, I will be primarily concerned with theory of inference (*anumāna*) or, rather, certain aspects of it.

In a work devoted to the concept of reason, a theory of inference must occupy a central place. In a pre-eminent sense, reason is exercised in reasoning, which is what a theory of inference theorizes about. A theory of consciousness (*cit*) and a theory of (linguistic) meaning (*śabda*) are, of course, presupposed in any reasoning. The two preceding chapters therefore, have set the stage for a discussion on inference. We exclude perception (*pratyakṣa*) from consideration: reasoning in the strict sense begins where perception ends. The idea of an unconscious (e.g. associative) reasoning that is embedded in perception is alien to most Indian philosophies. The Buddhists alone have a semblance of it, but they, in effect, reduce perception to inference.

There are two general features of theory of inference in Indian philosophy which we may start by noting at this stage. First of all, in *anumāna* (or inference), the prefix *anu* signifies 'after'; a standard etymology shows the word as meaning knowledge which comes *after*—i.e. after some other knowledge, notably perception and *śabda*. The premisses of inference are derived from either

source, proximately or in the long run. However, the sort of cognition inference yields is *sui generis*. Where this irreducible distinctness lies we have yet to ascertain. The second feature of the theory of inference we are to take a look at is that it is embedded in a larger epistemology. Inferential knowledge is a variety of knowledge; inference, as a *pramāṇa*, i.e. as the unique cause of such knowledge, is one amongst other *pramāṇas*. Theory of inference, then, is part of theory of knowledge. But knowledge itself is an entity. It has causal conditions; it belongs to someone (i.e. the knower). It has properties. Theory of knowledge, then, is embedded in an ontology. Thus the theory of inference is enventually inseparable from ontology. It makes use of ontological concepts such as 'cause'.

With these two general remarks let us take a look at how the inferential process and the structure of a completed inference are portrayed.

THE INFERENTIAL PROCESS

A very cursory account of the inferential process—making use of the rather hackneyed example of the Sanskrit textbooks—would be as follows:

A person *sees* a column of smoke on a mountain top. Assuming that he has already, in the past, acquired the knowledge—by generalization on particular instances such as the stove in the kitchen—that wherever there is smoke, there is fire, he now—upon seeing the column of smoke—*remembers* that universal correlation between smoke and fire as exemplified in the case, familiar to him, of the kitchen stove. This memory makes him *see* the smoke *as* that with which fire is, without exception, co-present. This last cognitive phase inevitably (unless certain powerful impediments occur at this stage) and immediately leads to a cognition of the form 'This mountain possesses fire', which is an inferential cognition (*anumiti*). Whatever happens to be the distinguishing (*asādhāraṇa*) cause of the cognition is inference as a *pramāṇa* or source of knowledge.

Sanskrit philosophical literature abounds in such accounts, with slight variations, of this example or its likes. There are several striking features of this account. It describes what is purportedly a

process occurring within the mental life of a person. Seeing, remembering, inferring are mental acts, and are always acts performed by someone or other. To this extent, and in a further sense to be determined, the account is of a psychological process. It is also an account of a process in time. These acts, in the order described, succeed each other. There is a causal account that forms part of the description. One act causes another, under appropriate, specifiable conditions. Besides being an account of a psychological, temporal, and causal process, the description is also of a process that is embedded in the everyday, perceptual context. These features raise serious questions about the suitability of the account to form the basis of a logical theory of inference. And it is, in part, this and related questions that I will pursue in this chapter.

While such is the mental process involved in inferring, there are also specifiable psychological conditions which must be satisfied in order that an inferential process may take place. These conditions have been discussed by the Nyāya logicians under the title *pakṣatā*. In the example given above, the mountain which is inferred to be fire-possessing is the *pakṣa* (roughly corresponding to, but not quite the same as, the 'minor term' of the Aristotelian syllogistic). '*Pakṣatā*', then, means the property of being the *pakṣa*. When is the mountain a *pakṣa*? When one infers something of it. But when does one do so? In reply, the Nyāya logicians want to exclude all those circumstances under which one would not infer.

The two variables that are relevant for this purpose are: the presence or absence of desire to infer (*siṣādhayiṣā*) and the presence or absence of a prior certainty (about what is to be the conclusion of the inference). Of the four possible combinations of these factors, three permit the possibility of inference, and only one rules it out. If a person has the desire to infer, no matter whether there is or is not prior certainty, inference may take place. For, even in the presence of prior certainty that there is fire on the mountain top (the certainty may have been arrived at by a reliable informer's report), one may, on seeing the column of smoke, establish it by inference. If a person has neither desire to infer nor prior certainty he may still infer: on hearing thunder one may spontaneously, without any desire to do so, infer the presence of a rain cloud. So only one combination excludes the possibility of inference. This is the combination of: (1) absence of desire to infer and (2) prior certainty. If a person is already certain and has no

desire to substantiate that certainty by an inference, he will not infer. The psychological condition, then, of inference—or *pakṣatā*—is: the absence of a conjunction of absence of desire and prior certainty (*siṣādhayiṣā-viraha–viśiṣta-siddhyabhāva*).[1]

The Indian logicians loved to lay down, on the basis of intuitive–inductive generalizations, laws about the relative strengths of different sorts of cognitive acts.[2] Three such laws relevant to our present discussion are:

(1) With regard to the same object, if the conditions of both perception and inference are present, those of perception will prevail, they are the stronger ones ('samānaviṣaye pratyakṣasāmagrī balavatī').

(2) If there are two different objects, with regard to one of which the conditions of perception are present and with regard to the other the conditions of inference are present, the latter will prevail, being the stronger of the two ('bhinnaviṣaye anumānasāmagrī balavatī'). One argument in support of this rule is that if it were not valid, inference would never take place, for with regard to some object or other, at every moment of waking life, the conditions for perception are present.

(3) In all cases, the conditions of desire (*icchā*) are stronger and so will prevail over any other cognitive possibility.

THE STRUCTURE OF INFERENTIAL COGNITION

When this inferential process, as described above, is given a linguistic form, we can treat the temporal process as though it were frozen. There would still be a sequence of sentences that is ambiguous as between logical order and temporal order.

If the cognizer is simply expressing his cognitive process to himself he will utter the following enthymeme:

That hill possesses fire, because of smoke.

This is what has been called inference-for-oneself (*svārthānumāna*). If the cognizer wants to persuade another person, then he has not only to expand the enthymeme, but also to follow the most effective strategy for persuasion. He then has to state the following five-part structure:

(1) The mountian possesses fire.

(2) Because it possesses smoke.

(3) Whatever possesses smoke possesses fire, as does the kitchen stove.

(4) The mountain is like that (i.e. possesses smoke, with which fire is universally co-present).

(5) Therefore, the mountain is like that (i.e. possesses fire).

This five part discourse produces in the hearer an inferential cognition. It is also called 'inference-for-another'.

Obviously, at first sight in any case, this discourse does not conform to the rigour of modern Western logic's predicate calculus. The order of sequence is determined by the needs of the discourse, i.e. the dialogical disputational context, rather than the context of strict proof. One also wonders whether the parts, i.e. the component sentences, express propositions in the familiar sense of Western logic or not. They certainly do express cognitions--perceptions, memories, as the case may be, and they are intended to produce in the hearer who has understood parts (1)–(4) a cognition such as is expressed by (5). Let us not worry at present about the so-called psychological aspect of this theory: I intend to return to it a little later. Let us take these sentences as they stand, and let us assume that together they constitute the inference-for-another.

From the point of view of Western predicate calculus, (2) and (3) alone could, by *modus ponens*, yield the conclusion (5). (1) is the same sentence as the conclusion, only it is not asserted, while (5) is asserted as true. In other words, (1) is not asserted as true, but is stated only as that which is to be proved. It therefore does not function as a premiss, if premisses are those truths from which the conclusion is drawn. However, it does serve as a step in the *anumāna* regarded as a dialogical–disputational discourse. The first cognizer who has already inferred it for himself knows that (1) is true. The other, for whom he is now discoursing, does not know that (1) is true. So, for the purposes of the latter, (1) is yet to be proved. It is the natural beginning of the discourse; it lends it its *telos*. When the discourse reaches its goal in (5), (1) is proved to be true, i.e. asserted on the basis of (2)–(4).

Also remarkable is the sentence (3). (3) states the universal

rule, previously learnt by the original cognizer. For the other, it is not enough to state the rule 'Whatever possesses smoke, possesses fire'. The other would like to know, since he has not himself acquired this knowledge, the cases in which the person stating it had found it exemplified—these cases must be such as to be acceptable to him as well. In other words, the example must be an agreed, uncontroversial case of co-presence of smoke and fire. This one example (in the present case, the kitchen stove) or possibly another, negative one (the lake in which there is neither fire nor smoke), will not prove the truth of the rule for the other. But the example will make it plausible for him; the argument can get off the ground. Without this, part (3) can still play its role in validating, in the sense of Western logic, the inference, but it will not serve the purpose of inference-for-another.

Sentence (4) appears to repeat (2), but there is an important difference. Now that (3) has been stated, the smoke that is now (seemingly repetitively) predicated of the mountain is no more the smoke *per se*, but smoke *qua* that with which fire is universally co-present. In other words, the rule is applied to the particular case in hand. It might seem strange that the application of the rule to the case on hand should itself be stated as a premiss, even if it is uncontroversial that the universal rule has to be applied to the particular case coming under it. But why make the application or the sentence describing it a premiss? Would not the logical form of the argument show that this is being done? Again, from the point of view of Western logic, this indeed is so. But for Nyāya *anumāna*, even inference-for-another is a cognitive structure, each component intended to facilitate taking a cognitive step on the part of the hearer. Hence (4), which is an indispensable, for some the most important, step. Once this step is taken, i.e. the cognition expressed by it is aroused in the hearer, the final cognition expressed by (5), the drawing of the conclusion, is almost unavoidable. The drawing of the conclusion, the cognitive step, is indicated by 'therefore' (*tasmāt*).

One thing stands out clearly: we have here a discourse whose internal order, coherence, and economy are guided, not only by the norms that are operative in Western logic, but by a striking combination of cognitive psychology together with the needs of a dialogical-disputational context and the strictly logical demand of validating a belief. To the question 'Is the structure of *anumāna*

logical?' one must not give a hasty answer. Of course, the word 'logic' is of Western origin, and has gathered a connotation of its own. The *anumāna* theory is a system by its own right. If it is not the same as either Aristotelian syllogistic or modern predicate calculus, it is not for that reason illogical. Using 'logical' in a transcultural sense, our task is to perceive its internal logicality, if there is any such: let us call it '$logical_2$', reserving '$logical_1$' for the standard use in the Western context (with appropriate subscripts for 'logic'). How is $logical_2$ related to $logical_1$?

ATTEMPT AT AN INTERPRETATION

I will attempt an interpretation of the nature of $logical_2$ by dealing with a number of issues—and oppositions—in terms of which the concept of $logical_1$ has traditionally been determined, if not defined. These oppositions are between (1) the logical and the psychological, (2) the formal and the material, (3) the necessary and the contingent, (4) the logical and the real.

The Logical and the Psychological

One way of determining the $logical_1$ has been to distinguish it from the psychological. This is done by saying that while both are concerned with thoughts, they are concerned with thoughts in rather different ways. Logic, we are told, is concerned with how men ought to think; psychology is concerned with how men do in fact think. Another way of drawing that distinction is to say that psychology is concerned with the process of thinking, whereas $logic_1$ deals with the product of thinking, with thought as an atemporal structure, no matter who arrived at it or by what process. $Logic_1$, then, although concerned with thoughts, has nothing to do with human minds, with what goes on in them. If this is how the distinction is drawn, then the theory of *anumāna*, and so $logic_2$, contains a heavy and disturbing intrusion of psychology. Can there be a logic, if $logic_2$ claims to be one, which thus contains large measures of psychological considerations?

During the second half of the nineteenth century there was a fashionable theory of logic known as psychologism. Psychologism is the view that the theoretical foundations of logic lie in

psychology, that ideal logical thinking, being but a species of thinking in general, must be governed by the same laws that hold good for all thinking. Now, some of the most powerful logicians of the West—Frege, Husserl, and Russell—fought psychologism, and laid it to rest. Psychologism, they argued, reduced, in effect, the necessary truths of logic to the inductive, probabilistic laws of psychology. It also conflates the laws of being-true (which are the laws of logic) and the laws that determine taking-something-to-be true (which are laws of the psychology of thinking); and it confuses the objective entities, such as concepts, propositions, theorems, and theories, and subjective, private events in people's minds, such as beliefs, convictions, doubts, desires to know, etc.[3]

Thus while psychologism is clearly at fault in seeking to derive the laws of logic from the way the human mind works (note that the idea of 'deriving' itself involves logical principles), the extreme anti-psychologistic position leaves us with an unmitigated Platonism in the strong sense, a domain of abstract entities such as meanings, propositions, and theories, divorced, on the one hand, from the mental acts of thinking and understanding which grasp them, and, on the other, from the linguistic signs which 'express' them. Is there any way to avoid these two alternatives?

The anti-psychologistic philosopher such as Frege is right in his argument that the entities with which logic deals could not be privately owned, temporally individuated particulars, and that logical truths are not inductive generalizations. But, it may be pointed out, he has an impoverished conception of mental life. This is certainly true of Frege, for whom the mental is the private particular and the laws about the mental are necessarily inductive generalizations. The question then for us is: why need we restrict ourselves to this impoverished concept of the mental? Is it not possible, given a suitably enriched philosophy of mind, to give psychologism its due, while preserving the intuitions on which the anti-psychologistic positions are based?[4]

I think that is possible. Indeed, there are several such systems already available. One is the Brentano–Husserl conception of an eidetic psychology. Another is to be found in the Indian logical theories, especially the Nyāya. In any case, what one needs is a conception of the mental according to which a mental event (or act) exemplifies or embodies a universal structure such that two or

more numerically distinct mental events may exemplify or embody identically the same structure. In that case, within a mental event, one may distinguish between its particularity (which it shares with no other) and its universal features. Amongst universal features are to be counted not only such generic features as the property of being a belief or the property of being a desire, but also such specific features as 'being a belief that *p*' or 'being a desire for a cup of tea'. In brief, what one needs is the conception of a structure of mental acts. Once you have such structures, then you can talk about essential truths about different sorts of mental act. In that case, a logic of propositions and an eidetic psychology of mental acts in which those propositions are entertained would have a closer relation than the radical anti-psychologism of Frege would like to admit, and yet both that relation and the nature of the relata would preclude one from falling into the obvious errors of psychologism.

In the light of these general remarks, let me now give a brief sketch of the Nyāya concept of (mental) acts. If *m* is a mental act, it has an owner, i.e. a self, it occurs at a time, it has what Husserl calls an act-quality (i.e. it is either a perceptual act or an act of remembering, an inference, a desire, or a hope, and so on) and finally it has a structured content (about which I have more to say below). Of course, the act has an object, but the object falls outside the act. What represents the object within the act is the structure. The act *m* then may be represented as an ordered quadruple (self, *t*, *q*, content), where *t* stands for the time of the occurrence and *q* for the act-quality. Our present concern is with the content.

The content of an act is neither the object of that act (which is, on Nyāya realism, always out there in the world) nor a real constituent of the act (which, in Nyāya ontology, has no parts, and so is formless, *nirākāra*, if 'form' signifies the structural arrangement of parts). To begin with, let us call it—using a concept handily available in phenomenology—intentional content. It is the object not as it is in itself but precisely as it is being presented in the act under consideration. The object out there in the world may remain the same, but for a different act having the same object, the structure of the content may very well change, depending upon precisely how that object is presented in the new act. Consider the two perceptual acts expressed in the sentences

(1) nīlo ghataḥ.
((This is a) blue jar.)

(2) ghatasya nīlaṃ.
(The blue (is) of the jar.)

It would appear that whatever is the object out there is not changed by the change of one's perspective. In (1), the primary object is the jar, which is being perceived as qualified by the colour blue. In (2), the primary object is the colour blue, which is being perceived as belonging to the jar. I will not expound in detail the Nyāya analysis of these structures. It suffices to note that for Nyāya such a structure is a concatenation of a whole set of (epistemic) entities, each of which serves a specific function of either qualifying, determining, or limiting, or being qualified, determined, or limited by some other. These peculiar entities are epistemic, for they do not exist in the object *per se*, they arise only when a cognitive act is directed towards the object. These entities as well as their concatenated structures are, in an important sense, universal-like: another cognitive act may embody precisely the same structure. What the logician has directly to deal with is a cognitive act in so far as it exhibits such a structure. We have then a criterion of identity for acts for the purposes of logical analysis. Two acts m_1 and m_2 are *L*-identical, if they have the same act-quality and the same structure of their contents. The fact that they occur at different times and/or in different selves is irrelevant.

At this point, one may wish to argue that the supposedly repeatable structure is nothing other than the proposition of Western logic. Two numerically distinct acts of belief are then *L*-identical in so far as they are beliefs in the same proposition. If the structure is nothing but the proposition, and since the proposition is an abstract entity towards which one may take different attitudes, or the same attitude at different times, then a logic of propositions would have to be separated from a psychology of those attitudes. Now to appreciate the nature of the Indian logical theories, it is important to see why the content of a mental act as understood in the Indian logics is not the proposition of Western logic, not at least in one of the senses of 'proposition'. In this sense, which is also the sense in which detaching the proposition from the mental acts may be most persuasively

effected, a proposition is that entity towards which many numerically as well as qualitatively different attitudes and acts, belonging to the same or to different selves, may be directed. Now on the Nyāya analysis of the content of an act, the quality of the act often makes a difference to the content. In the sense of 'proposition' just indicated, the supposition '*S* may be *p*', the question 'Is *S p*?', the denial '*S* is not *p*' and the affirmation '*S* is *p*' are all directed towards the same proposition. This is not the case in Indian logic, where analysis reveals a different structure in the case of 'Is *S p*?' from that in the case of '*S* is not *p*', and a different structure in the latter from that in '*S* is *p*'.[5] But the affirmative categorial 'This mountain has fire' does express the same content, not only when it expresses the cognitions of two different persons, or of the same persons at different times, but also when it expresses cognitions of different types: perception, inference, or cognition brought about by language (*śabda*). This justifies bringing these three under one generic group called *anubhava*. This is not to deny that there are attempts to individuate still more finely the content even across these variations, so that the structure of the content would be different in the case of language-generated knowledge from that in the case of inferential knowledge, both again different from the structure of perceptual knowledge. The proposition of Western logic is not as finely individuated across the range of varying propositional attitudes.

There is still another difference between the proposition and the content of Indian logic. The proposition is an abstract entity towards which a mental act is directed. Irrespective of how strongly one may want to ascribe to it an ontological status, it is independent of, and transcends, any act directed towards it. But the content which one, through reflective analysis, discovers in an act is that act's structure, not its object, not a transcendent entity.

Let us now see how this applies to the case of an inferential knowledge with which logic$_2$ is concerned in the first place. This would involve determining in what sense the theory of inference proposed is, or is not, psychological. Consider the account of inference given earlier:

A woman sees smoke on a distant mountain. This leads her to remember the rule 'Wherever there is smoke; there is fire' which she recollects as having been instantiated in cases such as the familiar stove in the kitchen. She now recognizes the smoke that

she saw on the mountain as a mark of fire in accordance with the rule she just remembered. At this point, if there is no unexpected hindrance, the woman would as a matter of course, be led to draw the conclusion: 'therefore, there is fire on this mountain'. This last sentence is an expression of an inferential cognition that has been produced in her.

What we have is a sequence of psychological events: a perception, a remembrance, a recognition, leading finally to an inferential cognition. These events belong to one and the same self, and are individuated by both ownership and temporal position. Now how can any such temporal sequence yield a logical rule? We can derive such a rule (*a*) by replacing the particular person concerned by a variable and making a universal quantification over it; (*b*) by retaining appropriate relations of succession, but doing away with the actual temporal positions; (*c*) by identifying the cognitions involved by their contents and temporal positions relative to the other cognitions figuring in the rule; and (*d*) by requiring that all cognitions figuring in the rule must have one and the same owner. Then, following the five-part discourse, we then get a rule such as the following:

(6) For any knower *S*, if *S* has a perceptual cognition, *Fx*, and then remembers the rule 'Wherever there is *F*, there is *G*' as instantiated in the uncontroversial case *O*, and then perceives in *x* the same *F* as before but this time as figuring in the remembered rule 'Wherever there is *F*, there is *G*,' then *S* will experience an inferential cognition of the form *Gx*, provided there is no relevant hindrance.

This indeed is as much a law of eidetic psychology as one of epistemic logic of inference. It is arrived at by an intuitive induction over particular cases; it is not a probabilisitic inductive generalization.

Another set of such laws with which Nyāya logic operates consists of rules of the form:

(7) If a cognition of type $\emptyset$ and with a structure T occurs at time t_i in a self S, then a cognition of the type ψ and with a specific structure T would not occur at time t_{i+1} in S.

A simple and intuitively clear case of such a law is: if a person perceptually ascertains that *-p*, she cannot, at the immediately

following moment, have a perceptual cognition that *p*. Or: if a person perceptually ascertains that *p*, that perceptual cognition will prevent the emergence, at the immediately succeeding moment, of an inferential cognition that -*p* (even if other conditions for the latter cognition are present).

These rules are further strengthened by bringing into consideration non-cognitive causal conditions such as desire to have a certain sort of knowledge. One cognitive type $\emptyset$ is said to be stronger than another cognitive type ψ, just in case if the causal conditions of both are present the one belonging to the type $\emptyset$ will occur and the one belonging to the type ψ will be prevented from occurring. Thus, if the causal conditions for a perceptual cognition of the fire on the yonder mountain are present, as well as conditions for an inferential cognition of the same in the same person, then the perception will occur, preventing the inference from occurring. But suppose, in addition, that there is a desire to infer: then the presence of this new factor will cause the inferential cognition to occur even if the perception has just occurred. One may infer 'There is fire on the mountain' even if one saw the fire on the mountain top, if one desired so to infer.[6]

Given such an eidetic psychology of cognition of which rules such as the above are fundamental principles, one can have a theory of inference which is indifferently a logic and a psychology of inference, but which is not psychologistic in the pejorative sense. But given this formulation of theory of inference, a serious question arises. If the rule formulated in (6) is also a psychological law, then it would seem as though all persons would necessarily make the right sorts of inference under right conditions, and it would be nearly psychologically impossible to commit a logical fallacy. For if the logical rules of inference are also rules of appropriate cognitive occurrences, then it would be impossible for men, given the psychological constitution that we have, to violate those rules. Now this indeed is the most difficult question for a psychologistic theory of logic to answer. However, let us try. The place we need to look at is the theory of invalid inference, or what has been called *hetvābhāsa* (to be construed as either defective *hetu* or the defects of *hetu*, *hetu* being the mark from which an inference is made). The standard definition of a defective *hetu* which would vitiate the inference in which it functions as *hetu* and would render it invalid is this: 'the object of such a valid

knowledge as acts to prevent inferential cognition'. What is meant, in brief, is this: an inferential cognition of the form '*S* is *p*, because of *m*' would be prevented from occurring if the person under consideration had a valid knowledge of a situation which was, in fact, a defect of *m* as a mark of *p* in *S*. Consider the obviously fallacious inferential cognition 'This lake posseses fire, because it possesses water'. Such an inferential cognition can occur in a person only if she believes in the truth of the universal rule 'Wherever there is water, there is fire'. However, if the person recognizes that wherever there is water there is the absence of fire, which amounts to recognizing that the mark (*hetu*) is characterized by the defect known as 'opposed' (*viruddha*), or that the mark is a *viruddha hetu*, then the inferential cognition would be prevented from taking place. This is rather a curious way of putting the matter. Instead of being told that the person made an inference that is fallacious, we are told, rather, that she would not have made the inference if she had known that the mark that was being employed was defective.

One way of understanding all this—the one I prefer, for it meshes well with the account I have developed earlier in this chapter—is to take the thesis to imply that as rational beings we cannot make a fallacious inference: we only appear to be doing so. Since the causal conditions of inference require, in accordance with (6), that the person concerned must believe in the appropriate rule 'Wherever there is *m*, there is *p*', she can infer only if there is such a cognitive occurrence in her mind, so the inference she makes will always be formally valid. Now that she learns that in fact 'Wherever there is *m*, there is *-p*', this cognition will prevent that other rule-cognition and so eventually the inferential cognition from occurring. The implication, of course, is clear: even when we are apparently making an invalid inference, we are making it not only because we do not detect the fallacy involved but also because we are so construing the terms and the premisses involved that the inference would turn out to be valid. Since psychologically it is impossible to make a fallacious inference, when we make an inference which by objective criteria is fallacious, what is happening is that we have given the premisses and the terms, interpretations under which the logical and the psychological requirements are in fact satisfied. If those interpretations are changed—and this is what happens when the defect

in the mark is recognized or pointed out—that inferential cognition would be prevented from occurring.

This is the price one pays for making the psychology of cognition and the logic of propositions coincide at least within the limits of elementary inferential operations. There is a concomitant commitment to rationality which rules out the possibility of making such obviously invalid inferences as 'All men are mortal, Socrates is a man, therefore Socrates is not mortal'. However, one who does make such an inference must be misconstruing the sense of the logical terms 'all' and 'not'.

The thesis is not as improbable as it may look to be at first. Mary Henle has discovered,[7] by considering empirical data about errors in syllogistic reasoning by adults, that "where error occurs, it need not involve faulty reasoning, but may be a function of the individual's understanding of the task or the materials presented to him". In another experiment, this time with children, Henle fails to find evidence that thinking transgresses the rules of syllogism. In most cases, the subjects understood the premisses in a manner that accounted for the error, while no faulty reasoning process was employed. The implications of her findings, as Henle sees them, are that "the two blind alleys of psychologism and of the radical separation of logic from the study of thinking" have to be avoided. Saying that our actual thinking process exhibits an (implicit) logical structure does not, in her view, amount to psychologism, for it does not make "logic coextensive with thinking by making it illogical. Rather than denying logical requiredness, denying the demands of necessary implication, it seeks to show that such requiredness is central in actual human thinking." Such a conception of actual human thinking, I want to emphasize, is germane to the Indian logical theories, especially the Nyāya, which finds the logical in the texture of everyday actual processes of reasoning. This is done, as we have seen, by construing the mental processes of reasoning as rule-governed patterns of successions of cognitive events (*jñānāni*), the rules being not empirical generalizations but Brentano-like intuitive inductions.

I would add, finally, that the logical structure of a cognition should not be taken to coincide with the structure of the sentence which expresses that cognition. For one reason, amongst others, there will always be constituents of the cognition—e.g. the mode of presentation (the Fregean *Sinn*)[8]—which cannot be expressed

but can only be shown in that sentence. In other words, for an expressed sentential constituent, there will necessarily be an unexpressed epistemic constituent. This should not be construed as suggesting an ineffability thesis, for what is unexpressed in that sentence can be expressed in another, which, for its part, will have its own unexpressed epistemic constituent. A given sentential-structure does not, then, provide a clue to eliciting the epistemic structure unless it is aided or rather supplemented by reflective analysis of one's own cognition. Structural analysis and reflection on the inner cognitive events are, ideally, made to supplement each other.

Here we have a possibility which neither Frege nor Husserl, in their eagerness to reject and overcome psychologism, saw; but Husserl was closer to seeing it than Frege.

Formal Validity and Material Truth

A commonplace claim about $logic_2$ has been that it did not have a concept of formal validity as distinguished from material truth. The obvious support for this claim is the need for citing an instance in which the universal rule of co-presence (between smoke and fire, in the illustration of *anumāna* at hand) is instantiated. The instance is not merely of illustrative value, but is given an unavoidable role in the structure of *anumāna*. Given such a requirement, an *anumāna* could not possibly contain a false premiss. A (Western) syllogism in which both the premisses and the conclusion are materially false, but which is nevertheless formally valid, i.e. instantiates a valid schema, is just not admissible within the Indian logician's theory of inference.

But to say that mere formal consistency and mere deductive implication were not thematized by the Indian logicians is not *eo ipso* to say that they did not know of them, or to deny that when the premisses were taken to be materially true, they were still looking for some relation between them such that a conclusion could be legitimately drawn. In other words, even if the dialogical–disputational and cognitive context limited logical imagination to those arguments in which component sentences were taken to be materially true, still the relation between those sentences must have had some feature which justified drawing the

conclusion. This feature of the inference-for-another discourse precisely is nothing other than formal validity.

Thus that commonplace claim is in a sense true, in another sense not quite so. To be able to assess this claim more accurately, I will introduce the following critical considerations:

(α) First of all, what is called *tarka*, in Indian logic, has, as a premiss, a statement of the form 'If p, then q', where p and q are both counterfactuals. The rest of it, in most cases, appears to be a case of *modus tollens*:

(1) $p \rightarrow q$
(2) $-q$
(3) $\therefore -q$

Or, in predicate calculus, after making the reasoning fully explicit, a *tarka* may look like this:

(1) Pa	assumption
(2) $Pa \rightarrow Qa$	premiss
(3) Qa	from (1) and (2) by *modus ponens*
(4) $-Qa$	premiss
(5) $\therefore -Pa$,	

which is a type of the *reductio ad absurdum* argument. Filling the schema out in a concrete argument:

(1) God created the world.
(2) If God were the creator, then he would possess a body, suffer pain, etc.
(3) God has a body, suffers pain, etc.
(4) But God does not have a body, etc.
(5) Therefore, God is not the creator.

Now, clearly *tarka* is a case of logical implication—a structure which has a counterfactual as a premiss. We have, then, in the theory of *tarka* incontrovertible evidence that, within logic_2, there is a fragment that conforms to the austere norms of logic_1. This, however, is not the whole truth of the matter. While recognizing that *tarka* is a form of reasoning, the Indian logicians did not accord it the status of a valid mode of knowing (*pramāṇa*). It was not dignified as a *pramāṇa* for various reasons: because of its use,

as the ground (*hetu*) of terms which are empty, non-denoting, 'not-established' (*asiddha*), or indecisive (*anaikāntika*); because of the misleading subsumption of *tarka* under doubt (*saṃśaya*); and because one of the sentences in the chain of reasoning is just false (*Qa* in the above schema). None of these is a decisive reason to exclude *tarka* from valid inference (*anumāna*), or from valid cognition (*pramā*) generally. As Lawrence Davis has pointed out, instead of rendering *apramā* as falsehood, and then taking *tarka* as a species of falsehood, it would be more appropriate to take *apramā* as what is other than *pramā*, and then say that *apramā* comprises falsehood, doubt, and *tarka* (which may often lead to truth).[9]

In fact, as *Varadarāja* in *Tārkikarakṣā* recognizes, *tarka* is subsidiary for all valid modes of knowing (*pramāṇas*) and not merely of inference. It helps dispel doubts about error in the object of a valid cognition. It is an accepted doctrine of the Naiyāyikas that *tarka* aids the process of inductive generalization. Thus, one argues, if there could be smoke without there being fire, then the causal law that only fire causes smoke would be contradicted, and one would be justified in making the (vain) effort to produce smoke without making fire.

(β) Lawrence Davis has shown that, given suitable translations from the canonical language of predicate calculus into Sanskrit (and vice versa), any argument in the predicate calculus can be translated into the *anumāna* language (and vice versa), which strengthens our point that, in a certain fragment, predicate calculus and *anumāna* coincide. However, the real danger remains the example (*dṛṣṭānta*). How can a place be found for it? This takes me to my third point in the present context.

(γ) Introduction of the *dṛṣṭānta*, to my mind, served three roles, all of which should be kept in mind in order to be able to appreciate the nature of $logic_2$. First of all, as is obvious, it determined the parameters of an effective dialogue and disputation. It did not permit introduction of a premiss which, even if true, is, to say the least, implausible for the other *ab initio*. The introduction of the *dṛṣṭānta*, which must be an uncontroversial instance and which must be agreed upon by the other, guarantees that the other will go ahead, even if provisionally, with the premiss being introduced. Hence its role in the dialogical–disputational context.

Secondly, the *dṛṣṭānta*—by ruling out both false premisses and premisses which, even if true, are not known to be true—succeeded in preserving the epistemic purity of the *anumāna*. One would not then, be arguing for the sake of argument, but in order to make a point that one knows to be true, and to be able to generate in the other the same cognition.

While these two functions are useful, I am suggesting that the *dṛṣṭānta* also played a more fundamental formal-logical role. This thesis is similar to that attributed by Hintikka to Kant when he says that mathematical proof must involve construction of a figure (in geometry) or counting (in arithmetic): it is the introduction of an individual by the rule of existential instantiation.[10]

The Necessary and the Contingent

A third distinction that has determined the concept of the logical_1 is that between the necessary and the contingent. Logical truths are necessary truths; factual truths are contingent truths. Of course, to be sure, not all necessary truths are logical truths, but certainly the reverse does hold good. The concept of necessity—both in the broader sense and in the narrower sense as applied only to the logical truths—is difficult to explicate. Some ways of explicating the narrower sense of necessity are: that logical truths are analytic and tautologous; that they are true by virtue of their form; that they are true in all possible worlds. As contrasted to these, factual truths are synthetic and informative; true by virtue of what the world happens to be; and, therefore, true in some possible worlds and false in others. However, essential laws, which are grounded in the essences of the things related by those laws, are—should one accept any such—necessary but not analytic, true in all possible worlds but not true by virtue of form alone. Let us then distinguish between purely logical necessity, essential necessity, and causal necessity.

In the light of this distinction, we may now ask what concept of necessity we find in the Indian logics. In what sense is the logical_2 necessary?

I have already shown that inference-for-oneself is a causally necessitated sequence of inner episodes. Of such a succession of inner episodes, it makes no sense to say that it is logically necessitated. As Hume would have said, one event could not be

said to follow logically from another. However, inference-for-another is a discourse whose components are sentences; it is only to this structure that one may want to ascribe necessity of a non-causal sort. Two considerations complicate the issue, and make it so difficult to identify the sort of necessity that characterizes this structure. In the first place, logical necessity holds good amongst propositions, where propositions are abstract entities to be construed in any of a number of ways. Indian logic does not countenance any such abstract entity. The sentences that constitute inference-for-another express cognitions which besides being episodes in someone's mental life have each a structure that is shareable by any number of such cognitive episodes. The necessity, then, that can be ascribed to the structure of an inference-for-another has to obtain amongst the structures of the cognitive episodes which the component sentences express. It may very well be that this necessity is the same as that which obtains amongst propositions, but it is not obvious that it is. When the relata of two relations are of different sorts, one is tempted to say that the relations are also of different sorts. In the present case, one may make out a case for the thesis that propositions as abstract entities which define the domain of $logic_1$ are abstracted from the cognitive structures which define the domain of $logic_2$. This indeed is a plausible thesis, at least for a fragment of logic—a thesis whose anticipations are to be found in Husserl.

The second consideration that casts doubt on ascribing to the $logical_2$ the sort of necessity which characterizes the $logical_1$ is that the opposition between causal necessity and logical necessity is softened with regard to $logic_2$. If the sequence of episodes constituting inference-for-oneself is causal, the sequence of cognitive structures expressed by inference-for-another is logical. The two, far from being opposed, are, rather, two aspects of one and the same thing. This indeed is an attractive thesis. What concerns me at the moment is, however, this: the very fact that $logical_2$ necessity is not opposed to the causal suggests that the nature of this necessity must be different from $logical_1$ necessity, which is sharply opposed to the causal. Again, one may plausibly argue that this sharp opposition is false, that an original unity of the two is what we should have, as is exemplified in present-day computational theories of mind.

The point that I am at pains to make is that if we ascribed to

$logic_2$ a conception of necessity, that conception would have to be somewhat different from that which is true of the $logical^1$. I am also suggesting that the $logical_2$ may in fact be the original structure from which the $logical_1$ is derived by abstraction.

This position about the availability of a conception of necessity in the Indian logics is somewhat different from the position I have advocated in several earlier papers. On earlier occasions, I have asserted that Indian logic had no conception of necessity. I still regard this to be true, but only within limitations. There is no indubitable truth. Given suitable epistemic conditions, anything whatsoever can be doubted (except such transcendental truths as 'I am')—such is the view of the Indian epistemologists. It is also true, I believe, that the universal major premiss of the Nyāya syllogism—asserting a relation of invariable co-presence between the mark or the middle and the major—is not to be understood as a necessary relation (excepting on the Buddhist view as formulated by Dharmakīrti). Subject to these two constraints, one may very well contend that there is a sort of necessity that characterizes the $logical_2$, but this needs to be clearly distinguished from the necessity that belongs to the $logical^1$.

There are two other places where one may look for the concept of necessity in Indian logic. One may look for recognition of fundamental logical principles such as the principles of non-contradiction and excluded middle. One may also look for the concept of an inference-schema whose instances would be all valid inferences. The first is undertaken by Matilal in his *Logical and Ethical Issues of Religious Belief*;[11] the latter by Sibajiban in his paper 'Middle Term'.[12] Matilal quotes Udayana's *Nyāyakusumāñjali* iii. 8, and his commentary on it, to show that the principles of non-contradiction and excluded middle were in fact recognized by the Naiyāyikas. What is more, since the principles are not traced to any of the *pramānas*, they were regarded—according to Matilal—as a priori. Udayana's verse iii. 8 runs thus:

> Parasparavirodhe hi na prakārāntarasthitiḥ
> Naikatā'pi virudhānāmuktimātravirodhataḥ.

"There is no other sort, when there is mutual opposition. The opposed cannot be [in] one and the same, since the very utterance would be contradictory." Udayana proceeds to explain: "A kind other than the positive (*bhāva*) and the negative (*a-bhāva*) is not

possible, for they are of the nature of mutual affirmation and negation," and adds, "By merely denying the positive, the negative is affirmed."

There is no doubt that this text clearly enunciates the logical principles of both non-contradiction and excluded middle. However, a close attention to the context shows that the passage should not be read as formulating the principle as a principle. What Udayana is criticizing is the view that similarity (*sādṛśya*) is other than the six positive (Nyāya-Vaiśeṣika) categories as well as different from the (seventh) category of negation (which is in the generally accepted Nyāya list of categories). So here *bhāva* refers to those six, and *abhāva* refers to the seventh. Emphasizing the completeness of the list, Udayana is saying that nothing can be outside the list: if positive, it falls within the first six, if negative, of course, within the seventh. This intention is best brought out by the commentary *Haridāsī*: "if [it is] a negation, it shall be the seventh category; if positive, if it possesses a quality, it will be a substance, and so on". ("Abhāvatve saptama-padārthatvaṃ. Bhāvatve ca guṇavattve dravyatvaṃ . . .") So follows a list of *bhāva* or positive categories.

I do not want to deny that taken out of context we have here a clear formulation of the famed principles. But read in context, it is a defence of the completeness of the list. The logical principles *qua* principles are at best implied in that claim, but do not imply that claim.

Sibajiban's paper 'Middle Term' emphasizes the fact that the inference

> 'The mountain possesses fire, for it possesses smoke, and whatever is the locus of smoke is also the locus of fire'

is a substitution instance of the schema:

> 'The mountain possesses fire, for it possesses that with which fire is invariably co-present,

which again is a substitution instance of:

> Whatever possesses that with which another thing is invariably co-present, possesses that other thing.

Thus—and this is Sibajiban's point—the specificity of the *hetu* (or middle term) is not needed; what is needed is a term with which the *sādhya* (or the major term) is invariably co-present.

We have here either a rule in accordance with which inference is drawn or a schema whose substitution instance is a particular valid inference. In the latter case, we have the idea of a pure form, in the former case the idea of a rule of inference claiming to be a priori.

My intention is not to challenge such a possibility. If we initially construe the Nyāya inference-for-another as a syllogism, then extracting from it, by a process of formalization, a pure schema (or rule) is possible. But one still has to ask if the inference-for-another is a syllogism, and I turn to this next.

The Logical and the Real

The concept of the $logical_1$ is also determined by its contrast with the real. (If in some systems such as the Hegelian the two coincide, the result is a considerable modification of both the concepts.) Logic, on this construal, is concerned with such entities as concepts, propositions, and complexes of propositions. Real things, events, and processes do not enter into logical discourse, although logical discourse may be about them (in a sense of 'about' that is, however, explicated variously).

It is with this distinction in mind that we can take the syllogism of $logic_1$ to consist of propositions and the propositions to consist of concepts. The terms express concepts. The language of terms (of the minor, major, and the middle terms) is to be understood in this way. We can now ask, does the Indian *anumāna*, construed as inference-for-another, consist of terms? Are *pakṣa* (the mountain, in the illustration employed), *sādhya* (fire), and *hetu* (smoke) to be understood as the minor, major, and middle *terms*?

One extreme view is to the effect that an Aristotelian reading of the Indian *anumāna* is a total mistake. For one thing, *liṅga* (or mark, or *hetu*) and the middle term are not the same, the former being the smoke arising from the hill top, the latter being the term 'smoky'. Indian logic, on this view, deals directly with things (the real hill over there, the column of smoke visible on it, and the real fire), while Aristotelian syllogistic deals with terms. If this way of drawing the distinction is right then the *dharmi–dharma* distinction (the hill, in the example on hand, is the *dharmi* and the fire the *dharma*) is not the same as the subject–predicate distinction. *Dharmi* is that which possesses a property, *dharma* is the property

it possesses. Both are things, neither is a term. In order to evaluate this claim about Indian logic *vis-à-vis* the Aristotelian, let us look at (1) the *dharmi–dharma* and the *subject–predicate* distinctions, and (2) the claim that Indian logic deals with things rather than terms.

(α) As regards the first, the Indian logicians distinguish between three different pairs: property–location (*dharma–dharmi*), qualificand–qualifier (*viśeṣya–prakāra*), subject–predicate (*uddeśya–vidheya*). Contrary to the views of many writers on these matters, I maintain that, of these three, the first is ontological, the second cognitive, and the third logical. In so far as the major term (*sādhya*) is a property (*dharma*) occurring or located in the minor (*pakṣa*), which is the location (*dharmi*), we have an ontological situation. Although the words mean 'property' and 'that to which the property belongs', the fire and the smoke are said to be properties of the hill in a very peculiar sense. Anything is a *dharma* if it has a location. If blue colour is a property of a cup, the cup is a property of the table on which it is. *Viśeṣya* and *prakāra* are categories applicable to cognitive states. The cognition expressed by 'The cup is blue' has 'the cup' as its qualificandum (*viśeṣya*) and 'blue' as its qualifier (*prakāra*). The cup, however, is cognized as a cup, i.e. as characterized by cupness, and the blue is cognized as blue, i.e. as characterized by blueness. 'Cupness' therefore is a qualifier of 'the cup', 'blueness' of 'the blue' (so that 'blue' is a qualifier in relation to 'the cup', but a qualificandum in relation to 'blueness'. The resulting concatenation of qualificandum and qualifier as well as of the corresponding abstract entities qualificandumnesses (*viśeṣyatās*) and qualifiernesses (*prakāratās*) gives an analysis of the cognition into components that are themselves epistemic. Finally, *uddeśya* and *vidheya* capture the logical distinction between that of which something is said and what is said of it. The same grammatical sentence 'Ram is cooking', in one context, would be used to say of Ram that he is cooking; but, in another context, would be saying of the act of cooking that Ram is its agent.

These distinctions show that transposing the subject–predicate form (along with the copula) to the Indian logics would be to overlook the vast differences that exist between the two logical traditions. The subject–predicate distinction itself is ambiguous and can be made at many different levels, and nothing will be

gained in understanding the nature of Indian *anumāna* if we cast it into the strait-jacket of Aristotelian syllogistic. On the contrary, a plausible case may be made for the thesis that Indian logic is closer to modern mathematical logic than to Aristotelian logic. To do this, the *anumāna* example on hand needs to be rewritten thus:

> Whatever posssesses smoke, possesses fire, as e.g. the kitchen.
>
> The mountain possesses smoke.
>
> The mountain possesses fire.

Let the predicate '. . . possesses smoke' be *S*, and the predicate '. . . possesses fire' be *F*. Then we rewrite it as:

(1)	$(x)\ Sx \rightarrow Fx$	vyāpti, premiss
(2)	Sa . Fa	example (EI, construction)
(3)	Sm	premiss
(4)	Fm	from (1), (2), and (3) by *modus ponens*

(2) assures that the domain is non-empty, and so is not a redundant sentence. The familiar Sanskrit locution (*yatra yatra . . . . tatra tatra*' reads as 'whatever is the location of . . . is the location of . . .', in which there is clearly a universal quantification over *x* where *x* is the location of . . . This translates into (1) if '*x* is the location of smoke' is read as *Sx* and '*x* is the location of the fire' is read as *Fx*. There are clearly other features of (1) I will point out later, but what has been said at least shows that Indian logic was not a logic of noun expressions.

(*ß*) How then are we to understand the point that Indian logic is concerned with things (mountain, smoke, and fire, in our example) and not with terms? Obviously, there is a clear sense of 'is concerned with things' in which logic, no logic whatsoever, could be so concerned. (Lighting fire, putting out fire, producing a column of smoke, and climbing a mountain are examples of such concern.) There is another sense in which all cognition, inferential cognition not excluding, is of, or about, reality, and not about itself: it would not be cognitive if it were not so. Even if the Aristotelian syllogism consists of propositions and these latter consist of terms, the syllogism is about realities, about men, their being mortal, about Socrates, and so on.

The contrast, then, cannot be between being about terms and

being about things. It has to be between two different ways of being about things: the way a conceptual proposition is, and the way a cognitive state is. The Indian *anumāna*, as a discourse, consists of sentences which express cognitive states, the latter being about realities. The Aristotelian syllogism consists of sentences which express propositions consisting of terms, which, in the long run, are about realities.

In the context of Western logic, the notion of terms being-about-reality may be shown to be possible in many different ways. One may hold that terms express concepts, and concepts are abstracted from realities. Alternatively, one may say, concepts are applied to realities. In either case, a reference to reality is missing. In a logic of propositions, one may locate the real within the structure of the proposition as its subject-component: different versions of this position are to be found in Kant (a judgement must contain an intuition) and in Frege (a thought consists of an object and a function). By locating the real (or, as in Kant, what directly refers to it, i.e. an intuition) within a proposition, one succeeds in showing that even propositional thinking is about a reality. A modern variant of this view is Russell's position that in 'This is blue', the thing demonstrated by 'this' is a constituent. Eventually, a proposition can be about a reality through some component of it which is a demonstrative, or a singular term which expresses an intuition of a reality.

The Aristotelian syllogism does not permit a singular term, a proper name, or a demonstrative to be substituted for the variables *S* and *P* and *M*. In Indian logic, on the other hand, a demonstrative or a singular term occurs at every step: '*This* mountain possesses smoke. Whatever possesses smoke possesses fire, as in the kitchen (*I* or *we* have seen before). Therefore, *This* mountain possesses fire.'. Based as it is, at every point, on intuition or intuitability, the being-about-a-reality is readily on the surface.

Is Indian Logic Intensional or Extensional?[13]

The issues between the extensionalist and intensionalist camps in philosophy of logic are many and varied, and in fact the labels are not univocal and precise. There are intermediate grades between the two extremes; there are both hard and soft

extensionalists as well as hard and soft intensionalists. However, speaking broadly, the two camps are divided over admitting or not admitting into their discourse various sorts of entity or rather names of such entities. Whereas the intensionalist admits propositions, the extensionalist would have only sentences. For the intensionalist's properties or attributes, the extensionalist would substitute open sentences and classes or ordered pairs. The intensionalist admits modal concepts like 'necessity' and 'contingency', operators like 'strict implication' and 'entailment', while the extensionalist wants to rid logic of such notions.

Why does the extensionalist regard propositions and attributes to be undesirable? He is bothered by the fact that they are not individuated as adequately as classes. Classes are the same when their members are the same, but it is not always conceded that properties are the same when they are possessed by the same objects. The law of extensionality fails for attributes. For the extensionalist, therefore, predicate-expressions are not names of attributes but are open sentences. What attributes are to open sentences, propositions are to closed sentences. The notion of sameness of attributes as well as of propositions requires the notion of synonymy, and the extensionalist does not find any suitable criterion of synonymy and so suspects this notion altogether. The extensionalist is also bothered by the failure of substitutivity of identity in intensional contexts, by 'referential opacity', as also by the failure to quantify.

It is in this context that we have to try to locate Nyāya logic. For the present I will pass over the concern with cognitions (*jnānāni*), though only to return to it later on. Clearly enough logic$_2$ has no explicit conception of necessity; in its theory of truth it does not make any distinction between necessary truths and contingent truths. 'Pervasion' (*vyāpti*) is defined—to take one of the many definitions as a sample—not as the impossibility of occurrence of the middle, but as its mere non-occurrence, in the locus of constant absence of the major. To put it symbolically, the *vyāpti* '*x* is pervaded by *y*' has to be written *not* as:

$$- \Diamond (\exists z) \quad (Oxz \, . - Oyz),$$

where '$- \Diamond$' is to be read as 'it is impossible that' and O stands for the relation of occurring (*vṛttitva*), but as:

$$- (\exists z) \quad (Oxz \, . - Oyz).$$

The notion of 'If there is smoke, there is fire' is understood extensionally as 'Wherever there is smoke, there is fire', and the latter as 'Whatever is a locus of smoke is also a locus of fire', which again may be restated, à la Matilal, as:

> (x) (x is a member of the class of loci of smoke. x is a member of the class of loci of fire).

This last is equivalent to:

> – ($\exists$ x)·(x is a member of the class of loci of smoke. x is not a member of the class of loci of fire),

which restates the first of Gaṅgeśa's definitions of *vyāpti* as non-occurrence (of the middle) in all loci of the absence of the major (*sādhyābhāvavadavṛttitvaṃ*). This indeed is an extensional entity. Where then does the supposed intensionalism of Nyāya come in?

Intensionalism comes in at least at two points. First, the Nyāya does not make the class membership relation fundamental, but rather uses the relation of occurrence as the primitive relation. Matilal shows this very carefully on various occasions.[14] Instead of saying that the mountain is a member of the class of loci of smoke, the Nyāya would rather say:

> The mountain possesses an occurrence of fire.

Matilal has aptly pointed out that this proposition is a universal one if the assertion is about the predicates being limited by the limiter of subjectness, i.e. by mountainness. The limiter does the job of the quantifier. When the assertion asserts the predicate as being concurrent with the limiter, the proposition is existential; when the predicate is asserted to be limited by the limiter, the proposition is universal. The limiter is a property, an attribute. Hence the intensionalism.

The second point regarding Nyāya intensionalism may be made by referring to a bewilderment expressed by Quine regarding modal concepts. For the intensionalist, mathematicians are necessarily rational and not necessarily two-legged, while cyclists are necessarily two legged and not necessarily rational. What then of an individual, Quine asks, who happens to be both a mathematician and a cyclist? Which of the two properties is necessary and which is not? It would seem that just in so far as we are talking

referentially of the person, no attribute is contingent and none necessary. There is no doubt that the attributes which belong to an individual object do belong to it, and so far there is no hierarchy amongst them. But the intensionalist will at this point make a typical move. He will say, "Well, there is no mere reference to the object. We always talk about an object, refer to it, think of it or know it in a certain context, as possessing such and such property, as belonging to such and such class, as satisfying such and such description, etc. The person (who is both a mathematician and a cyclist) may be referred to as a mathematician, or he may be referred to as a cyclist, or he may be referred to as one who is both. These three surely do not exhaust all the various ways he may be referred to. In each case, the properties which are asserted of him and the precise manner they would be asserted of him would be different." This is again another use the Nyāya would make of its concept of limiter. If in the proposition 'This man is rational' the limiter of subjectness is the property of being a mathematician, then the predicate is being asserted as limited by that limiter. If, however, in uttering the same sentence, one intends the limiter of subjectness to be the property of being a cyclist, the predicate would be asserted only as being concurrent with that limiter. This would be the Nyāya explication of the intensionalist's use of modal concepts in such contexts. Though this explication makes no use of modal concepts, it surely makes use of the language of attributes and limiters.

What about the problems of individuation of attributes and relations, the problem of referential opacity, and the problem of substitutivity of identity? Intensional abstracts are individuated by their loci and conditioners, by their subjuncts and adjuncts, and therefore unless they are generic properties (*jāti*) they are treated by the Nyāya as non-repeatable particulars peculiar to each occurrence. Thus 'fatherhood as conditioned by Rāma and as occurring in Daśaratha' names a different intensional particular from 'fatherhood conditioned by John and occurring in Joseph'. The same principle is applied to individuate relational abstracts as well. However, while it thus holds good that attributes or relations which have different loci and different conditioners are different, it does not nevertheless follow that attributes or relations having exactly the same loci and same conditioners are therefore identical. And yet it is precisely this latter which the extensionalist

would say to be the case. To take Quine's example: the class of all marine mammals living in 1940 is the same as the class of all whales living in 1940, but the property of being a marine mammal alive in 1940 is different from the property of being a whale alive in 1940. What the extensionalist would like to do, therefore, is to eliminate properties in favour of classes, or so to qualify the notion of property as to make properties identical when their instances are identical. Matilal seeks to formulate an identity condition for relation-particulars which may be sought to be extended to all intensional entities. His identity condition requires that two intensional entities, in order to be identical, should have the same conditioners and subjuncts and/or have the same loci. Now I have grave doubts if this identity requirement would be acceptable to Navya-Nyāya. Knowability (*jñeyatva*) and nameability (*abhidheyatva*) are different attributes even if they occur precisely in the same loci. 'The property of being the author of *Waverley*' and 'the property of being the author of *Ivanhoe*' are names of distinct abstract properties even if they are present exactly in the same locus (*anyūnānatiriktavṛtti*). One may of course add another identity condition to take care of these: one may require of two intensional entities φ and ψ that, in order to be identical, they must be capable of being substituted in intensional contexts (e.g. that whoever believes that *a* possesses φ also *eo ipso* believes that *a* possesses ψ, and vice versa). But this identity condition cannot be formulated by an extensionalist. It leaves the above two properties distinct intensional entities even if they have exactly the same locus.

What I am trying to do is to take a look at the nature of the intensionalism of Nyāya—i.e. to pinpoint those places where the intensionalism makes itself felt most. I am also trying to bring out the peculiar character of its intensionalism—which surely is different from many other varieties of intensionalism. I would certainly consider it a softer variety of intensionalism which (1) retains the epistemic language and the language of propositional attitudes (*niścaya* or certainty, *saṃśaya* or doubt, etc.); (2) makes use of the language of attributes, properties, and relations instead of the language of classes; but (3) which curiously enough does not take recourse to modal concepts. This last makes us feel that it has a strong extensionalistic strain. This feeling is further strengthened by the consideration that Nyāya logic did quantify. But again the

quantification was effected with the help of the concept of the limiter—an intensionalist device—as well as by the use of such locutions as 'wherever . . . there' (*yatra yatra . . . tatra tatra*).

We have in fact, in Nyāya logic an excellent example of a logic of cognitions. There are many difficult issues involved in making clear what precisely such a logic is concerned with. Each cognition is a private particular. If it happens to be a qualificative (*saprakāraka*) cognition, it is very closely connected with some verbal form. What this close connection is I have never been able to get clear about. Surely, in analysing a cognition, even a qualificative cognition, the Nyāya does not analyse the verbal form, the sentence, which it happens to be closely connected with. Does it analyse the proposition which is the meaning of the associated verbal form? There are difficulties in extending the concept of proposition to the Nyāya analysandum. My difficulty does not arise out of the problem of synonymity, nor out of distrust for abstract entities. A proposition in one important sense is precisely that identical content which can be the object of different mental attitudes like believing, affirming, denying, doubting, etc. Now, for the Nyāya, with the change of the mental attitude, the content also changes. An instance of doubt like 'Is this a tree or not?' shows a different content structure from an assertion 'This is a tree'. What, then, is the identical invariant proposition? I have said elsewhere[15] that what the Nyāya analyses is a cognition which is propositional, it does not analyse a proposition. Or, one may distinguish between the epistemic attitude and the objective content, and hold that what the Nyāya analyses is the objective content, which is not private. It is important to bear in mind the fact that this objective content, though unaffected by changes in the knower and changes within the range of the same generic class, by the particular object that is known (e.g. 'This is fire' would always have the same objective content and the same analysis, no matter whoever asserts it and which fire particular is being known), undergoes change with change in the epistemic attitude. So any doubt having the form 'Is this a tree or a man?' has the same objective content; any *niścaya* or certainty having the form 'This is a tree' has the same content, and so on. I should think Husserl's distinction between act-quality, act-matter, and intentional essence of an act are surprisingly relevant in this context. Identity of objective content assures for

purposes of analysis identity of cognitions, however else two cognition-particulars may differ. For Husserl, what is required is identity of intentional essence.

A RÉSUMÉ

What, then, does our interpretation of $logic_2$ amount to? It is time to gather together the various strands of this interpretive effort. In $logic_2$, logic (in a generic sense) and psychology are blended together in a manner which avoids the opposed stances of psychologism and Platonism: this is achieved as much by psychologizing logic as by logicizing psychology. $Logic_2$, further, is a logic of cognitions, and not one of propositions, although the contents of cognitive events are construed propositionally. The requirement that the inference contain a case in which the universal rule $(x)Fx \rightarrow Gx$ is existentially instantiated is not to be taken as an indication that $logic_2$ does not have a concept of formal validity. It is, rather, a consequence of the cognitive–disputational context into which a logic of inference was inserted. We also found that the concept of necessity that $logic_2$ operates with is different from that which $logic_1$ has; and there are two different ways in which the two logical traditions are about reality. Regarding the extensional–intensional issue, $logic_2$ is extensionalist in the sense that it does not make use of modal concepts, but intensionalist inasmuch as its domain is primarily one of cognitions: it makes use of properties (and not of classes) and other intensional abstracts. In many respects, thus, $logic_2$ shows that many of the sharp oppositions that dominate Western thinking about logic do allow for a middle ground, so that we need not treat the logical and the psychological, the epistemic and the causal, the extensional and the intensional as though they are irreconcilable opposites.

NOTES AND REFERENCES

1. *Siddhāntamuktāvali* on *kārikā* 70.
2. For more on this, see Sibajiban Bhattacharya, *Some Principles and Concepts of Navya-Nyāya Logic and Ontology* (Calcutta, 1978).

3. For the most systematic critique of psychologism, see E. Husserl, *Logical Investigations*, ed. and trans. J. N. Findlay (New York: Humanities Press, 1970), i: *Prolegomena to Pure Logic*.
4. See my *Husserl and Frege* (Bloomington: Indiana University Press, 1982). Also my 'Psychologism', in Mark A. Notturno (ed.), *Perspectives on Psychologism* (Leiden: E. J. Brill, 1989), 1–10.
5. For more on this, see my 'Nyāya Theory of Doubt', *Visva Bharati Journal of Philosophy*, 3 (1965), 15–35; repr. in my *Phenomenology an Ontology* (The Hague: Martinus Nijhoff, 1970).
6. "Siddhou satyāmapi siṣādhayiṣāsattve'numitirbhavatyeva" (*Siddhāntamuktāvali* on *kārikā* 70).
7. M. Henle, 'On the Relation between Logic and Thinking', *Psychological Review*, 69 (1962), 366–78.
8. Sibajiban and J. L. Shaw have emphasized this.
9. See Lawrence Davis, '*Tarka* in the Nyāya Theory of Inference', *Journal of Indian Philosophy*, 9 (1981), 1105–20.
10. See J. Hintikka, 'Kant's Theory of Mathematics Revisited', in J. N. Mohanty and R. E. Shahan (eds.), *Essays on Kant's Critique of Pure Reason* (Norman: University of Oklahoma Press, 1982).
11. (Calcutta: University of Calcutta Press, 1982).
12. *Notre Dame Journal of Formal Logic*, 9 (1968), 229–32.
13. For earlier discussions of this issue, see J. F. Staal, 'The Theory of Definition in Indian Logic', *Journal of American Oriental Studies*, 81 (1961), 121–6. Karl H. Potter, '*Astitva jñeyatva Abhidheyatva*', *Wiener Zeitschrift für die Kunde Sud—und Ostasiens und Archiv für Indische Philosophie*, 12–13 (1968–9), 275–89; B. K. Matilal, 'The Intensional Character of *Lakṣaṇa* and *Śaṃkara*', *Indo-Iranian Journal*, 8 (1964), 85–95; and J. N. Mohanty, 'Review of B. K. Matilal's *The Navyanyāya Doctrine of Negation*', *Journal of Indian Philosophy*, 1 (1971), 197–201.
14. See, in particular, B. K. Matilal, *Logic, Language & Reality: An Introduction to Indian Philosophical Studies* (Delhi: Matilal Banarasidass, 1985), esp. 112–40.
15. See my *Gaṅgeśa's Theory of Truth* (Santiniketan: Centre of Advanced Study in Philosophy, 1966), esp. 31.

5

Indian Theories of Truth: Their Common Framework

In this chapter, I want to begin by reflecting not on some one or other amongst the theories of truth (*prāmāṇya*) in Indian philosophy, but rather on that common framework which encompasses them all, or perhaps the most important amongst them, or on that common horizon within which these theories and their mutual dialogues have moved. Taken separately, there are, in the large spectrum of the Indian philosophies, theories that exhibit remarkable affinities to the major Western theories of truth. Thus the Nyāya theory of truth is a sort of correspondence theory, the Mīmāmsā a sort of self-evidence theory, and the Buddhist a sort of pragmatic theory. There are theories, such as the Nyāya, which combine a correspondence theory of the nature of truth with a sort of coherence theory and a sort of pragmatic theory of the test of truth. Some others, like the Mīmāmsā, question the very distinction between the nature and the test of truth. Comparative philosophy, bent on tagging theories on to theories, promises to be a rewarding enterprise.

On the other hand, closer acquaintance with the Indian philosophical texts cannot but impress one by their distinctive flavour, by a most peculiar tenor of their discussion, and by the slant given to formulations of problems, as well as by their concerns, proximate as well as remote. In a word, the world which one enters is a different world from that within which Western philosophical thinking moves. This is as much true of the philosophies in general as of their theories of truth. How can that distinctiveness be captured and conceptualized? This chapter will make a contribution towards that end, but from the limited perspective of the concept of truth. It is not as though East is East and West is West, and never shall the twain meet. But it is only after we are able to lay bare and thematize the horizon of Indian concern with truth that any tagging of theories on to theories

would be fruitful and rewarding, without leading to deceptive affinities and easily available clichés.

COGNITIONS AS BEARERS OF TRUTH

It may be useful to begin by ascertaining what it is of which truth (and falsity) may be predicated by the Indian philosophers. In Western philosophy, there are several well-known candidates for this position: sentences, statements, propositions, beliefs, and judgements. A sentence is a physical (when regarded as a token), linguistic (if regarded as a type) entity; a statement is what may be made with a declarative sentence. A proposition is an abstract entity, the alleged meaning of a sentence in the indicative mood. Belief is a psychological state—be it an episode or a disposition—a person may be in. A judgement is the mental act of affirming or denying a proposition. Of these, the dominant view has been that even if truth may be, and in fact is, predicated of all these on different occasions, what is true in the most fundamental sense is the proposition, understood not alone as the signification of an indicative sentence but also as the identical content towards which a large variety of mental acts, both numerically (e.g. many different acts of believing) and qualitatively (e.g. an act of believing and an act of doubting) distinct and belonging to the mental lives of different persons, may be directed. At the cost of a rather risky generalization, I would like to say that the concept of 'proposition' underlies the main line of Western thinking on truth. A sentence is true if it expresses a true proposition; a belief is true if it is belief in a true proposition; a judgement is true if it is the affirmation of a true proposition or the negation of a false one; a statement is true if the sentence which is used to make it expresses a true proposition. The abstract and objective character of propositions accounts for the fact that what is true is true-in-itself, that truth is not relative to any person or mind, and that the true cannot become false or vice versa. Western formal logic is a logic of such propositions. Those who have felt reluctant to admit such abstract entities into their ontologies have nevertheless felt constrained to account for those alleged abstract entities in terms of whatever entities they have admitted. Even as an explicandum, the proposition looms large on the horizon of Western thought.

In the Indian philosophies, truth is the predicate of a *jñāna* or

cognition. And a *jñāna* is a concrete occurrence: a property (*guṇa*) or action (*kriyā*) of the self in most systems; a modification or *vṛtti* of the inner sense (*antaḥkaraṇa*), with consciousness reflected in it, according to Sāṃkhya-Yoga and Vedānta. In any case, it is something that belongs to, occurs in, or attaches to, a self, that of the person who knows. The cognition, if it is not a non-conceptual, pre-predicative (*nirvikalpa*) perception, is expressed in language; if it is a language-generated cognition, it is essentially linguistic. But it is neither the sentence which expresses it, nor the meaning of the sentence, i.e. the proposition, for there is in these philosophies no such abstract entity, no such sense as distinguished from reference, proposition as distinguished from fact.

What sort of entity, then, is this cognition? It is a real occurrence which is of an object, which, in Nyāya and Mīmāmsā systems, being an act or a quality, is formless (*nirākāra*) (for form is a function of arrangement of parts and only a substance can have parts),but in Sāṃkhya-Yoga, Vedānta, and Vijñānavāda Buddhism, has a form (*ākāra*), being either a definite modification of a substantial entity or a momentary existent arising with its own form, which appears to be an external object. But leaving Buddhism out for the present, we can say that for all Hindu systems no matter if knowledge is formed (*sākāra*) or formless (*nirākāra*), it does have a logical structure of its own, a structure that is evident only to reflective analysis but not given in the primary living through a cognition. The logical structure is different from the structure of the sentence which expresses the cognition, for one reason, amongst others—as has variously been pointed out—that there necessarily will remain logical constituents of a cognition which are unexpressed in the sentential structure. In other words, for an expressed sentential constituent, there necessarily will be an unexpressed epistemic constituent. If the cognition is expressed in the sentence 'This is a pot', that the pot is being comprehended *as* a pot, i.e. as qualified by 'potness' is not expressed but understood. Nevertheless, the sentential structure does provide the clue to eliciting the epistemic structure, but only when aided by reflective analysis into one's own cognition. A purely third-person, external analysis of the structure of a cognition is not possible. But given that a cognition has such and such structure, logic can draw conclusions about what follows or does not follow from it.

It is such an occurrence, then, that is true or false. It is not quite what, in Western epistemology, goes by the name of 'belief'. Belief is either a feeling, or a disposition to act in a certain manner, which attaches to a proposition that is external to it, for the same proposition may well be the object of disbelief of the same person at another time or of another person at the same time. Here, in the Indian epistemologies, a true cognition (*pramā*) is indeed characterized as a certainty (*niścaya*), but not as a certainty that may be tagged on to a proposition external to it, but as having a propositional structure, so that the doubt about the same would have a quite different structure. Whereas, the certainty (*niścaya*) 'This is a pot' has the structure:

> The qualifier (*prakāra*) 'pot' as limited by 'potness' determines the qualificandum 'this' as limited by 'thisness' in the relation of identity (*tādātmya*),

the doubt (*saṃśaya*) 'Is this a pot?' has the structure:

> The mutually contradictory qualifiers 'pot' (as limited by 'potness') and 'absence of pot' determine the qualificandum 'this' as limited by 'thisness'.

An identical propositional content thus does not emerge, so that neither in the sense of 'meaning' (as distinguished from reference) nor in the sense of object of propositional attitudes is something like a proposition admitted by the Indian philosopher.

The implication of all this for theory of truth is of decisive importance. For one thing, the entire distinction between analytic truth and synthetic truth, between truths that are true by virtue of meanings of the component terms, and those that are true by virtue of the circumstances obtaining in the world, does not appear in the Indian philosophies. For another, since the occurrence called 'cognition' itself has a logical structure, any law that applies to such structures applies also to the relationship between such occurrences or cognitions, as a consequence of which the distinction between logic and psychology could never be drawn. The logical laws are also the laws in accordance with which men must think. Or, more appropriately, it is psychologically impossible to violate a logical law, the seemingly logical errors being, in reality, errors in construing the relevant terms. No one who understands the sense of 'pervasion' (*vyāpti*) and the connected

concepts such as the universal quantifier, locus, etc., and, if he has the cognitions that *F* is pervaded by *G* and that *A* is the locus of *F*, would infer anything else but that *A* is the locus of *G*. The so-called fallacies (*hetvābhāsas*), in Indian logic, are not errors of inference, but factors which, if present and if recognized, would stop the inferential cognition from arising. This lack of distinction between the psychological and the logical cuts both ways: it logicizes the psychology of cognition and psychologizes logic. There is no room for the purely formal analytical concept of logical truth, subsisting apart from all relation to mental life; just as the purely empirical-associationist account of mental life is equally ruled out. The Indian logicians and epistemologists had grasped, without their knowing it and without even adequately conceptualizing it, a middle ground between psychologism and logicism. This, of course, we have already pointed out in the preceding chapter.

What happens to the concept of necessary truth? Indian logicians and metaphysicians have generally recognized several types of necessary truth, none of which coincides with the true-by-virtue-of-meaning sort of analytic truth. These are: (1) rules of inference such as whatever is a locus of *F*, in case *F* is pervaded by *G*, is also a locus of *G*; (2) rules determining the emergence or non-emergence of specific types of cognitive events, generally based on the so-called preventer–prevented (*pratibandhaka–pratibadhya*) relation (e.g. a certainty that *A* is *F* would stop the emergence of a doubt 'Is *A F*?'); (3) existentially necessary truths, i.e. truths whose denial, though not involving formal self-contradiction, cannot be asserted (e.g. 'I am');[1] and (4) truths which are claimed to be presupposed by all other truths (e.g. the self-luminousness of consciousness).

The universality and necessity of mathematical truths did not attract the attention of the Indian epistemologists as much as they fascinated their Western counterparts. There is, indeed, no truth whose opposite is inconceivable, none that is indubitable. Given suitable epistemic conditions anything and everything can become the subject-matter of doubt, and one can err about anything whatsoever. This is so not merely according to those who regard truth (*prāmāṇya*) as extrinsic (*parataḥ*) but also according to those who regard it as intrinsic (*svataḥ*). Even on the *svataḥ* theory (leaving aside the extreme Prābhākara view, according to which

there is no error at all), the claim to truth which is held to be intrinsic to every cognition is at the same time recognized to be defeasible by 'extrinsic' circumstances. On the contrary, likewise, even according to the Nyāya theory that truth is extrinsic to cognitions, there are cognitive occurrences such as inference and perception of a familiar situation (*abhyāsadaśāpanna*), where doubt is ruled out by the very nature of the factors that generate such cognitions, so that we are neither achieving indefeasible certainty nor hopelessly threatened by the possibility of skeptical doubt.[2] In fact, this middle ground is assured as much by the refusal to separate psychology of inference from its logic as by the connection of cognition to the overall contexture of practical life. As Udayana, the great logician, put it, skeptical doubt is limited by contradicting practical behaviour (*vyāghātāvadhirāśaṅkā*).[3]

TRUTH-DETERMINATION: INTRINSIC (SVATAḤ) OR EXTRINSIC (PARATAḤ)?

In the above section, we insisted on the significance of making 'truth' a predicate of a cognitive occurrence, on the lack of a theory of meaning as contradistinguished from reference, and on the consequent lack of the concept of analyticity. The domain of necessary truths was thereby greatly narrowed down to existential truths ('I exist'); transcendental truths ('consciousness is'); rules, arrived at by intuitive induction on introspective data, about the emergence or non-emergence of cognitive occurrences of various types; and finally, rules of inference (which contain no material terms, and so are not analytic in the sense of being true by virtue of meanings alone). I ended the section, however, by noting how the threat of scepticism was overcome by recognizing the role of practice in cognitive life. It is to this last point that I now turn.

For my present purpose, I shall begin by stating a problem which has been raised by Vācaspati in the context of Vātsyayana's opening statement: 'A cognition *has* an object, when the object is being apprehended by a cognitive instrument, because there is successful practice' ('pramaṇato' rthapratipattou pravṛttisāmarthyāt arthavat pramāṇam'). Determination of the nature of the object (*arthaniścaya*) requires ascertainment of truth (*prāmāṇyāvadharaṇa*); the latter requires successful practice (*samarthap-*

ravṛtti); but, the last, for its part, is dependent upon determination of the object (*arthaniścaya*). We have then a case of vicious mutual dependence. All those philosophies which make ascertainment of truth dependent upon successful practice have to face this problem and, in order to appreciate the frequently asserted affinity with modern pragmatism, we need to recall what was meant by *pravṛtti* and what place it occupied in the total cognitive context. No matter what the theory or truth they upheld, all Hindu and Buddhist philosophers asserted the schema:

> an instrument of true cognition (*pramāṇa*) → true cognition (*pramiti*) →desire (*cikirṣā*) → practical behaviour (*pravṛtti*) → success/failure.

Worldly persons, who are knowers as well as agents, are of two kinds: they are either attached to the enjoyment of things, or they are free from such attachments. Accordingly, practical behaviour (*pravṛtti*) is also of two kinds: the actions of a non-attached person are aimed only at prevention of things not desired (*aniṣta*)—such a person does not act with a view to acquiring a desired thing. But the actions of the other sort of person, i.e. the 'attached', are of two sorts: he acts either for acquiring the desired things or for preventing the undesired, the former arising out of attachment, the latter out of hatred. Either may be successful or unsuccessful. It is successful when the person, setting out to acquire a thing, indeed acquires it, or, setting out to avoid an undesired thing, indeed avoids it; it is unsuccessful when one reaches a thing one wanted to avoid or cannot get a thing one had set out to reach.

A classification of practical behaviour (*pravṛtti*) more relevant for our present purpose is the following: it is either one whose result is empirical or this-worldly (*aihikaphalā*) or one whose result is other-worldly (*āmuṣmikaphalā*). Further, the knowledge which is the cause of the former may be either knowledge of an already familiar (*abhyāsadaśāpanna*) object or knowledge of an unfamiliar object. Now in these three cases, the conditions required for the possibility of practical behaviour (*pravṛtti*) are different.

Where the object of knowledge is empirical and familiar (such as water), the knowledge, by virtue of its likeness to other cognitions tested and validated on earlier occasions, is at once taken to be, i.e. inferred to be true, and then acted upon.

Truth is inferred on the basis of 'belonging-to-that-type' (*tajjātīyatva*), and action follows upon it. However, in such cases, it may be argued, appropriate action does not wait for determination of truth. Udayana contends that ascertainment of truth takes place because the causes of such ascertainment are present, but not as a necessary prerequisite for action. Gaṅgeśa goes further than Udayana and maintains that, for such action, all that is presupposed is absence of doubt about falsity of the knowledge as well as absence of certainty about its falsity. If there is no determination of falsity and if there is no doubt about falsity either ('Is this knowledge of water a hallucination?'), perception of water would lead a thirsty person to approach the water perceived with a view to quenching his thirst. It is not needed that the thirsty person should first ascertain the truth of the perception and then act accordingly. Even where the knowledge is unfamiliar, i.e. its object is new, but empirical, appropriate practical response requires, not determination of truth, but ascertainment of the object and an inferential knowledge of the sort 'This object would serve this desired purpose'. The farmer knows that ploughing the land, sowing seeds, etc. would lead to harvesting corn, but this relationship of means and end is only probable. The farmer does not know whether possibilities such as drought or flood which may frustrate the achievement of his goal will set in. However, the farmer's actions are caused by knowledge of the possibility of harvesting corn and knowledge that his work will be a (likely) means to achieve that goal. In other words, as Vācaspati says, appropriate practical response depends on knowledge of the object (*artha-pratīti*), not on determination of the true nature of the object (*arthāvadhāraṇa*), the latter requiring determination of the truth of the former. Vācaspati adds, men sometimes do act even if they have doubt about the truth of their knowledge (*arthasaṅdehādapi prekṣāvatām pravṛttiḥ*).[4]

Thus in the case of empirical objects, appropriate action does not require determination of truth; it requires only apprehension of the object. But does not, as suspected earlier, certainty about the object (*arthaniścaya*) itself depend upon determination of truth? How can one have certainty about the object until one has also ascertained that the knowledge one has of the object is true? In fact, this is what the Mīmāmsā theory of *svataḥprāmāṇya* assumes. Gaṅgeśa has argued convincingly that the Mīmāmsā

theory assumes more than is warranted by the facts; we may indeed know an object without knowing that our knowledge is true. The function of knowledge is to reveal its object, to show what is the case, but not *eo ipso* to reveal its own truth. On Gaṅgeśa's view, then, when the object of knowledge is empirical, no matter if it is 'new' or 'familiar', action does not require determination of truth. Knowledge gives a cetainty about its object, which gives rise to appropriate practical response; if that leads to successful result (*phala*), one is led to infer that the knowledge was true. Ordinarily, if the knowledge is of a familiar sort, one immediately infers its truth, although action is caused by the knowledge, not by such inference of its truth.

In this account of the role of truth-determination and of appropriate practice in ordinary experience, a crucial question concerns the nature of the knowledge of the fruit (*phala*) or result. If the truth of a cognition (where its object is unfamiliar and empirical (*laukika*)) is determined inferentially, upon satisfaction of the action that follows from that cognition, then how is the truth of the experience or cognition of the final 'result' (in the case of perception of water, of the quenching of thirst, of the judgement 'My thirst is quenched') to be ascertained? It seems as though there are only two alternatives: either the cognition of the result is to be regarded as intrinsically (*svataḥ*) true, not in need of any further confirmation, or, if there is need of confirmation of this cognition (which is itself a confirmatory cognition), there would be a vicious, infinite regress for which there is no corresponding series given in experience. The Buddhists call this confirmatory cognition of result *arthkriyānirbhāsaṃ*. Dharmottara in his *Nyāyabindutīkā* maintains that 'even if there is immediate reaching [the object] in the case of the appearance of causal efficacy, that does not yet need to be examined' ("arthakriyānirbhāse tu yadyapi sākṣāt prāptiḥ tathāpi tanna parīkṣaṇīyaṃ"), for with this cognition the person's (i.e. the knower's) goal is attained and there is no occasion for doubt which could justify further examination of its truth.[5] The Naiyāyikas have rejected this account. Udayana has argued that although generally a confirmatory knowledge such as having one's thirst quenched is not doubted, but rather taken as valid on the basis of 'belonging-to-that-type' (*tajjātīyatva*), the possibility of doubt is not, as a matter of principle, to be ruled out. Not only is an unfamiliar sort of confirmatory experience liable to

be doubted, but even a familiar sort of confirmatory experience carries no unfailing assurance of its objectivity, for one may experience quenching of one's thirst in dream as well.

The alleged infinite regress is, then, stopped either by saying that the cognition of result (*phalajñāna*) is intrinsically (*savtaḥ*) true (which might have been the view of earlier Buddhists such as Dignāga and was refuted by Kumārila in *Ślokavarttika*) or by saying that, although not intrinsically true it is still not a subject-matter for enquiry since one never doubts its validity (which is Dharmotara's view, criticized by Vācaspati and Udayana), or by saying that although in most cases and ordinarily it is not doubted such doubt is not to be ruled out in principle.

The Nyāya fallibilism then does not amount to scepticism. Even if every epistemic claim can be doubted, as a matter of fact, however, inferential cognitions, cognitions whose objects are familiar and empirical, and familiar confirmatory cognitions are not generally doubted. They provide bases of certainty in the empirical search for truth and successful action, but none of these provides that apodictic basis which rationalist philosophy has hoped to be able to discover for knowledge and action.

However, there is another type of epistemic claim and another type of action with which, most probably, the Indian thinking about truth was concerned in the first place. This is the knowledge which is to cause such practical behaviour as is alleged to yield non-empirical consequences. The scriptures recommend the performance of certain sacrifices if one intends to enjoy certain benefits in the afterlife or wants to go to heaven. The scriptures also say that one who knows *ātman* gets rid of all fear. Now, even if one grants the Nyāya view that, for performing actions with empirical consequences, determination of the truth of the knowledge upon which such action is to follow is not required, no one, it would seem, would undertake to perform courses of action recommended by the scriptures unless she were sure of the truth of the scriptural sentences (i.e. of the knowledge produced by understandingly hearing those sentences). The latter, however, is agreed upon by all schools of Indian philosophy, including the Nyāya, which admits of such knowledge. Thus Udayana writes: 'Practical behaviour whose result is non-empirical requires prior ascertainment of truth.'[6] Jayanta states the position most clearly: "In cases of valid cognitions such as perception whose objects are

empirical, since action is possible without determination of truth, there is no necessity for asking, whether in those cases truth is intrinsic or extrinsic; rather non-determination of truth is, in those cases, conducive to ordinary practice. It is different, however, with non-empirical objects. . .".[7]

Although the Mīmāmsakas insist that, even in cases of empirical knowledge, action requires determination of truth and so defend their position that a cognition is both born as true and is apprehended *ab initio* as true, they and the Naiyāyikas agree that in cases of scriptural knowledge, truth-determination is a necessary pre-condition of practice. Both agree that it is here that the question of truth—especially the issue 'Is truth (*prāmāṇya*) intrinsic or extrinsic?'—is particularly relevant. In fact, one may even contend that that issue has its origin in this concern, although its satisfactory solution required consideration of all sorts of cognition. While agreeing in this much, the Naiyāyikas, Buddhists, and Jains, in fact all those who believe that scriptural texts are composed by persons, defend the thesis that their truth is extrinsic, and the Mīmāmsakas, who believe that scriptural texts do not have any author, defend the thesis that their truth is intrinsic. Both extend their respective theses to all cognitions, empirical and non-empirical. In order, therefore, to understand the deeper grounds that sustain this difference in theories of truth, one needs to consider the fundamental philosophical insights which underlie the differing attitudes towards scriptural texts. Since I am not at present able to see clearly and adequately into those, the following remarks are unavoidably brief and provisional.

Let us suppose, as appears to be the case, that the scriptures contain two sorts of sentence: some purporting to be statements of fact (e.g. 'sarvaṃ khalu idaṃ brahman') and others expressing prescriptions or prohibitions ('svargakāma yajeta'). If scriptural cognition is to be a sort of knowledge *sui generis*, i.e. if its objects are not, and cannot, be known in any manner except through the scriptural texts, then only the prescriptions or prohibitions are what, in the strict sense, deserve to be counted as scriptural. In other words, our knowledge of what one ought or ought not to do is alone what we acquire from the scriptures. Such ought-sentences are not simply capable of empirical verification: the prediction of a non-empirical consequence amounts to saying that no empirical consequence could possibly confirm them. To say, then, that such

moral beliefs cannot be empirically confirmed or disconfirmed, and that acting upon them can never be contingent upon prior truth-determination by such confirmation, i.e. by successful practice, amounts to saying—in so far as they are moral beliefs—that they are not entertained as hypotheses or even simply as beliefs which are not known to be false or doubted to be so (as the Nyāya regards empirical cognitions to be) to begin with. Consequently, they have to be accepted as true, i.e. as binding upon one's will, in order that one may act in accordance with them. In this sense, they are intrinsically true. The question who authored those texts is irrelevant for the moral force of those prescriptions, for the fact that someone *X* authored the injunction 'one ought to Ø' has no logical connection, as is well known, with that ought-sentence. Since the authorship is irrelevant, and since their disconfirmation is, on logical grounds, ruled out, their truth is intrinsic. One may then go on to argue that those who hold the scriptural texts to be authored by persons and so regard their truth to be extrinsic (contingent upon determining that their authors were free from any human defects, the possibility of verification in this case being ruled out) are really deducing the 'ought' from the 'is'.

What I am suggesting, in effect, is a combination of intrinsic truth theory with regard to the moral knowledge delivered by the scriptures and extrinsic truth theory with regard to factual knowledge of all kinds. I am aware that this combination is not one of the alternative positions defended in the tradition. Such a view would have been repugnant to the tradition, when that tradition did not clearly perceive the radical difference between the senses of 'truth' in the two cases. All the participants in the intrinsic–extrinsic controversy wanted *one* theory to cover both. But that requirement is what I am wanting to call in question.

SOME DEFINITIONS OF 'TRUTH'

Even with regard to factual cognitions, the participants in the intrinsic–extrinsic controversy did not all define truth in the same manner. In fact, some of the differences between the intrinsic and the extrinsic theories may be traced back to different conceptions

of truth underlying them. Without claiming exhaustiveness, I am giving below some of the decisive definitions of 'truth':

$$(1)\ \text{is true} \overset{\text{Df}}{=} \text{is not known to be false.}$$

(1) is, obviously, a psychological sense. Many Mīmāmsā arguments make use of it, so that the intrinsic thesis is rendered analytically true. Since Gaṅgeśa so clearly defends the position that a cognition can cause action only if it is not known to be false, his position is compatible with saying that a cognition (which is a certainty) is true in this sense, to begin with. But that renders the dispute pointless. There would still be the difference between the intrinsic and the extrinsic theories that on the latter theory this sense of truth will be replaced by a stronger sense (to be specified below) once the cognition is confirmed by successful practice, whereas on the former theory this sense of truth is the only sense of truth we have at our disposal, there being no further possibility of confirmation, although the possibility of disconfirmation is always left open. To be noted, then, is that this sense of truth is common to all certainties (*niścaya*) prior to disconfirmation; if the cognition is disconfirmed, ascription of truth in this sense is retracted.

To be sharply distinguished from this are the various epistemological senses:

$$(2)\ \text{is true} \overset{\text{Df}}{=} \text{has } \textit{that} \text{ as its qualifier } (\textit{tatprakāraka}).$$

On this definition, a knowledge 'This is silver' is true if it has 'thisness' and 'silver' as its qualifiers. But that would render every cognition to be true, which in fact is the view of the Prābhākaras, according to whom there is no error: the alleged false cognition is but a failure to distinguish between several component cognitions each of which is true in sense (2).

A stronger, but still epistemological, sense is:

$$(3)\ \text{is true} \overset{\text{Df}}{=} \text{has a qualificandum which is qualified by that.}$$

Gaṅgeśa refers to this as a possible Mīmāmsā definition of truth which makes truth of a cognition intuitable in the introspective inner perception (*anuvyavasāya*) of that cognition. Note that this

is a purely epistemological concept. A cognition 'This is silver' is true if in it the 'this' is known as qualified by 'thisness' and 'silverness'. This, of course, is the case in all judgemental certainties (*niścaya*). The definition refers to the qualificandum–qualifier structure of a cognition, and says nothing about what the thing that is known is like. Raghunātha Śiromaṇi in his *Dīdhiti* on Gaṅgeśa's text explains the difference thus: even if a cognition is known as having the qualifier 'silverness' with regard to the object yonder ('this'), it is not known *as* having the qualifier 'silverness' with regard to the piece of silver yonder ("tena purovartini rajatatvaprakārakamiti grahe api purovartini rajate rajatatvaprakārakamiti na grahaḥ").

Sense (3), unlike sense (2), belongs only to certainties (*niścava*), and cannot be retracted, for even a so-called false cognition would have a qualificandum which is qualified by *that*. Like sense (2), then, it is common to what is ordinarily called true and false cognitions.

(4) A restriction, on the Mīmāmsā senses (2) and (3) is imposed by adding to either of them the requirement 'and has the property of being an object which was not known before' (*anadhigatatva*). The explicit purpose of this restriction is to exclude memory from the scope of true cognitions: this eagerness to regard memory as invalid (*a-pramā*) has been justified either by appealing to its lack of independence in manifesting its object, or by sheer appeal to conventional usage of the word *pramā* (as Vācaspati does in his *Tātparyyaṭīkā*), or on the ground that it simply is not true to its object, for the remembered past is not now (as Udayana argues in his *Pariśuddhi* on Vācaspati's text).

I have on an earlier occasion[8] expressed my dissatisfaction with all these moves by saying that they are all unfair to memory. No one seems to have realized that tradition is preserved and continued through memory. I would now like to recognize this element of truth in almost all Indian theorists' refusal to count memory as a *pramā*. True knowledge is required to be an originary mode of disclosure of its object. Memory, to be sure, is not such an originary mode of disclosure: it is parasitical upon, and is a derived mode of, a past originary cognition. However, one could still want to argue that memory is the originary mode of disclosure of the

past *qua* past. This is at least true of what Husserl calls primary memory, if not of what he calls secondary memory.

There is still another sense of 'truth' which makes the *svataḥ* thesis analytically true. According to this,

(5) is true $\overset{\text{Df}}{=}$ is a knowledge (*jñāna*),

or, elaborating a metaphysical thesis about the nature of knowledge,

(5*) is true $\overset{\text{Df}}{=}$ is a modification of the inner sense (*antaḥkaraṇavṛtti*).

Later writers on Advaita Vedānta, such as Madhūsadana Saraswati and Brahmānanda, have defended such an account which, they have contended, does not extend to error, doubt, and memory—for none of these three is on their theory a modification of the inner sense (*antaḥkaraṇavṛtti*) but rather each is a modification of ignorance (*avidyā*): they are not knowledge (*jñāna*) but only seeming-knowledge (*Jñānābhāsa*). Abstracted from the theory of knowledge as an *antaḥkaraṇavṛtti* (as distinguished from *avidyāvṛtti*) and from the rejection of memory as a sort of knowing, definition (5) has a remarkable affinity with the linguistic thesis that '*S* knows that *P*' entails '*P* is true'. The late K. C. Bhattacharya appealed to the introspective evidence that knowing is never known as an 'indifferent psychical fact', but always as 'the implicate of the awareness of truth' so that truth 'cannot be taken simply as additional confirmation of what already is known indifferently'.[9]

Finally, I will mention a definition of truth which is neither psychological nor merely epistemological, but which has a component which describes an epistemological fact about the cognition under consideration and a component which describes an ontological fact. This is the Navya-Nyāya view, according to which

(6) is true $\overset{\text{Df}}{=}$ is a cognition whose qualifier is such that it belongs to its object (*tadvati tatprakārakaṃ*).

If the cognition is 'This is silver', its being true is nothing other

than having a qualifier, i.e. 'silverness', which belongs to its object, which then is silver.

It is this concept of truth which I have elsewhere characterized as making of truth a 'hybrid' entity. Gaṅgeśa's point, then, against the intrinsic theory amounts to arguing that although reflection or introspection reveals what the qualifier of a cognition is, i.e. that it has 'silverness' as its qualifier (*rajatatva-prakāraka*), it cannot reveal what in fact the object is, i.e. whether in fact silverness belongs to it. That the object in fact is so, quite apart from what the internal epistemic structure of the cognition is, can only be inferred: chiefly from successful practice, but in appropriate cases from the mark of 'belonging to a familiar type' (*tajjātīyatva*).

The crucial question, then, on which the validity of Gaṅgeśa's point rests is, is the distinction between epistemic structure and ontological structure in the long run valid? Furthermore, the problem for Gaṅgeśa becomes all the more pertinent inasmuch as he upholds a realism according to which a cognition, formless in itself (*nirākāra*), derives all its forms from its object. How can there be an epistemic content (*viṣayatā*) which does not refer to an objective content out there? On this matter, I would refer to Sibajiban Bhattacharya's interesting interpretation of Navya-Nyāya,[10] and will add, for my present purpose, only the following: some Naiyāyikas were led to the position, closely similar to that defended by Russell in his *The Problems of Philosophy*, that what is lacking in the case of an erroneous cognition but present in the case of a true cognition is a total unitary, not further analysable content (*vilakṣaṇa viṣayatā*)—in addition to the component contents—such as 'the-this-as-qualified-by-silverness'.

I had set out with the idea of bringing out some of the distinguishing features of Indian theories of truth. Now, they are: (1) a peculiar concept of a cognitive event; (2) absence of a theory of meaning as distinct from reference; (3) a consequent position that steers clear of logicism and psychologism; (4) a restricted theory of necessary truths, a fallibilism with regard to empirical truths, and an infallibilism with regard to moral truths; (5) a perception of a close connection between cognitive enterprise and practice; and, finally, (6) an epistemology which relies heavily upon reflective, introspective analysis of the cognitive situation.

NOTES AND REFERENCES

1. Vācaspati in his introduction to the commentary *Bhāmatī* (on Śaṁkara's *Bhāṣya*) writes: 'Na hi jātu kaścidatra sandigdhe—ahaṃ vā nāhaṃ veti, na ca viparyasyati nāhameveti.'
2. For this, see my *Gaṅgeśa's Theory of Truth* (Santiniketan: Centre of Advanced Study of Philosophy, 1966), 49–55.
3. Udayana, *Nyāyakusumāñjalī*, iii. 7.
4. Vācaspati: 'arthapratītyadhīnā tu pravṛttirnārthāvadhāraṇādhīnā arthasaṅdhehādapi prekṣāvatāṃ pravṛtteḥ' (*Nyāyatātparyaṭīkā* on *sūtra* I. i. 1, *Nyāyadarśana*, ed. A. Thakur, Mithila Institute Series, (Dharbanga: Mithila Institute, 1967), i. 29).
5. Dharmottara, *Nyāyabinduṭīkā (Dharmakīrti, Nyāyabindu*, ed. Āchārya Chandraśekhara Śāstri (Varanasi: Chowkamba Samkrit series, 1956), 6).
6. 'tatra āmuṣmikaphalā prāmāṇyāvadhāraṇapūrvikā eva' (*Pariśuddhi* (on *Tātparyaṭīkā*) on *Nyāyasūtra* I. i. 1).
7. 'pratyakṣādiṣu adṛṣṭārtheṣu, pramāṇeṣu prāmāṇyaniścayaṃ antareṇaiva vyāvahārasidhestatra kiṃ svataḥprāmāṇyaṃ uta iti vicāreṇa na naḥ prayojanaṃ aniścayena eva tatra śreyān, adṛṣṭe tu viṣaya . . .' (Jayanta, *Nyāyamanjari*, bk. 1, §8).
8. *Gaṅgeśa's Theory of Truth*, 40 n. 33.
9. K. C. Bhattacharya, *Studies in Philosophy* (Calcutta: Progressive Publishers, 1956), ii. 157.
10. Sibajiban Bhattacharya, *Some Principles and Concepts of Navya-Nyāya Logic and Ontology* (Calcutta, 1978).

6

The Concept of Being and the Ontologies

PRELIMINARY REMARKS

If a cognitive episode is true, i.e. *pramā*, it establishes a being, or the Being of a being. There is thus a close relation between 'Being' and 'being-true',[1] between, in Sanskrit, the three terms: existence (*sattā*), truth (*satyaṃ*), and validity (*prāmāṇyaṃ*). One may want to distinguish, following Heidegger, between two senses of 'being true': one logical, the other ontological.[2] In the logical sense, 'being-true' refers to the truth of a judgement, in the Indian context, of a structured cognitive episode: this is *prāmāṇyaṃ*, discussed in the foregoing chapter. In the ontological sense, 'being-true' refers to the unconcealment, *aletheia*, of a being as what it is, the manifestation of an entity in its own nature: this is *satyaṃ*. For an ontology that wants to say what the world is like, what things are, the merely logical concept of *prāmāṇya* is not enough. One needs the possibility that things can be presented as they are. Hence, both the Indian realists (the Nyāya-Vaiśeṣika and Mīmāmsā schools) and the Indian idealists (the Advaita Vedānta school) needed a theory of preconceptual, pre-predicative (*nirvikalpa*) perception in which things are presented as they are—which provides the ontological underpinning for their logical–epistemological theories.[3]

But, one may ask, did the Indian philosophies after all raise the question of Being? And, furthermore, can we ascribe to them ontological theories?[4] With regard to such questions, one needs to avoid two extremes: there is on the one hand an Eurocentric point of view which regards philosophy (as also its various subdisciplines, especially metaphysics and ontology) as a Western discipline emerging in Greece for the first time, and, on the other hand, a universalist point of view which is insensitive to the cultural variations that permeate seemingly similar questions. I

will not pursue these general concerns here. As a matter of fact, this work is intended to provide concrete case-studies to illustrate the thesis that both the above extremes are mistaken points of view. Returning to the question of Being and the idea of ontology (or even of metaphysics), one may want to ask if the idea of questioning with the spirit of open-ended enquiry that ancient Greek thought allegedly brought into being and itself so brilliantly exemplified is to be found in the Indian philosophies, each of which, founded on already specified commitments that are embodied in the aphorisms (*sūtras*), had only a limited logical space available for genuine questioning and engaged only in exegetical and hermeneutical work. There is no doubt that this contrast does point to an important difference in the nature of philosophizing in the two traditions. Philosophizing, in the Indian tradition, was fundamentally hermeneutical when you consider each system of philosophy separately. Each such system thought and questioned from within a conceptually defined tradition, and not in an open logical space. (How open this space can be, and whether Greek questioning took place within an open space, not delimited by any conceptual framework, are questions I will not ask for my present purpose.)

However, there are two other aspects to that situation which should set the anxiety about this questioning's philosophical nature at rest. In the first place, exegetical hermeneutics is compatible with creative thinking—as the history of Indian philosophy amply shows. Each system developed far beyond what its original founders could have intended: such was the plasticity of meaning of the founding texts. In the second place, when trying to assess the nature of Indian questioning, one needs to go beyond the distributive point of view which focuses on a system, each one separately, but must rise to that point of view from which one can survey these systems in endless dialogue amongst themselves—a dialogue and a conversation that abandons the exegetic–hermeneutic concern and adopts the stance of relentless critical examination of oneself and of the other. This total phenomenon, as it grows in history, is an impressive reconciliation between intrasystemic demands and intersystemic challenges, between the need for defending one's topos through self-development and appropriating into one's thinking the truth in the other's point of view. If this is not genuine questioning—especially when each

system's best self-defence consisted in rendering itself problematic in the eyes of the other and then rescuing itself from collapse through building up the edifice anew—that can only be so when judged against an illusory standard of questioning in allegedly unlimited open horizon.

But can there be metaphysics and ontology outside the Western tradition? A negative answer to this question has acquired a certain self-evident character as a result of the Heideggerian historiography of thought. To render this self-evidence problematic, one needs to ask: what is it about the question concerning 'Being *qua* Being' that makes it so Greek to begin with? A science of 'Being *qua* Being' may mean either a science of the most general predicates of being, i.e. of categories, or a science of the highest being, i.e. theology, or an enquiry into the meaning of Being, i.e. (Heideggerian) fundamental ontology, or a science of the regions of being with their modalities (Nicolai Hartmann). To hold that, since the specific question about the meaning of Being (raised by Heidegger) was not asked in the Indian tradition that tradition's concern with Being cannot yield ontology,[5] would be misleading, for not all those who thought about metaphysics and ontology in the Western tradition asked the Heideggerian question about the meaning of Being. If by 'categories' are meant the most general predicates of beings regarded as beings, the Vaiśeṣika doctrine of meanings of words (*padārtha*) did amount to a doctrine of category: anything whatsoever is either a substance (*dravya*) or a quality (*guṇa*) or an action (*karma*) or a universal (*sāmānya*) or the relation of inherence (*samavāya*) or an absence (*abhāva*). Whether it is a good theory is another question. This is not to say that the Vaiśeṣika is Aristotelian. It is to say that both exhibit the same sort of enquiry, the same concern—though in different culture-relative contexts. Metaphysical or ontological thinking is not Greek in origin: a certain variety of it is. The words 'metaphysics' and 'ontology' are Western; the type of thinking, in its generic features, is not. That this is so should not be surprising if language is a major determinant of our mode of thinking and if Sanskrit and Greek share large linguistic structures. It is rather the Heideggerian historiography which would appear to be arbitrary.

TERMINOLOGY

The three Sanskrit words crucial for any thinking about Being are: the verb *asti*, having for its root *as*, the abstract noun *sattā*, and *bhāva*, derived from the root *bhu*.

The root *as* has, among its meanings, to live, to exist, to be present, to take place, to happen, to abide, dwell, or stay, and also to become. Grassman's *Wörterbuch zur Rig Veda* singles out as its primary meaning *sich regen* and *leben*—out of which the concept of being is said to have developed. The root denotes, as just said, both to be present and to happen as well as to become. *Astitā*, or existence, is then that which is common to them all, existence in a sense which applies both to that which is present, to a happening or occurrence, and to becoming. They all are.

The word *sat* is more commonly used in philosophical literature. While it retains the ontologically and valuationally neutral meaning of *astitā*, it goes beyond that in its connotation so that besides meaning being, existing, occurring, happening present, living, and enduring, it also came to mean the true, the good, and the right. Both these aspects together lead to the idea of true being—the veridical sense, as Kahn puts it.[6] The word *sat*, as well as its abstract derivative *sattā*, are closely related to the word *satya*, which, besides meaning truth, reality, also has valuational meanings such as genuineness, sincerity, honesty, truthfulness, purity, virtue, goodness. Attempts to give *satya* a metaphysical meaning are already found in *Bṛhadāraṇyaka Upaniṣad* V. v.1, where the three syllables constituting the word (*sa*+ *ti* + *yam*) are interpreted as standing, respectively, for the real, the unreal and the real, so that the word is made to refer to the fact that the unreal is enclosed on both sides by the real. *Taittirîya Upaniṣad* (II. 6) does the same with the concepts of the formed and the formless so that *satya* is interpreted as meaning the unity of both.

The word *bhāva*, along with the root *bhu*, is more unambiguously a becoming word: it means to become, to arise, to come into being, but also to live, to stay, to abide, to exist, and also to happen, to occur. By implication, it comes to mean the place of coming into being, i. e. space, the world, the place, piece of ground, the earth. The root has two derivative abstract nouns:

bhava, which predominantly expresses the sense of becoming and especially continuity of becoming, in Buddhist writings: and *bhāva*, where the sense of what has been comes to the fore—*bhāva*, as the state of being of anything, also means the essence of a thing but essence in the sense in which, according to Hegel, the German *Wesen* points to what has been (*gewesen*).[7] There is a narrower sense of *bhāva* to be distinguished from this, where, as in classical philosophical literature, it came to qualify *padārtha* (*bhāvapadārtha*) to mean positive entity as distinguished from *abhāvapadārtha* or negative entity. It meant neither that an *abhāvapadārtha* or negative entity has no nature of its own nor that negative entity does not possess being in some sense or other. Thus when Yāska, the author of *Nirukta*, refers to the view of Vārsyāyaṇi that there are six modes of *bhāva*—is born, is, undergoes change, grows, decays, and perishes—he is evidently referring to positive and non-eternal entities.[8]

The philosophical usages of the three words *astitā, bhāva*, and *sattā* may be specified as follows: *astitā* belongs to all entities, positive and negative, particular and universal, permanent and changing; *bhāva* belongs to all entities which, contrasted with negative entities, have a positive nature of their own, *sattā* belongs to all positive entities excepting universals and certain other entities in which a universal cannot be said to inhere.

It was this scheme which determined the Nyāya-Vaiśeṣika attitude towards the question of being, and which was opposed by both the Buddhists and the Vedāntins.

IS BEINGNESS A UNIVERSAL?

The Nyāya-Vaiśeṣika position is based on a clear distinction between *sattā* and *astitā*. *Sattā* is a real universal (*jāti*, in the technical vocabulary), *astitā* is not. The reason lies deep in the categorial structure of the system. A real universal (*jāti*), according to this system, has to be in any of its instances in the relation of inherence (*samavāya*), and so cannot belong to that relation itself. Nor can it inhere in another real universal (*jāti*), for otherwise there would be an infinite series of them nested in succession. As contrasted with *astitā, sattā* belongs only to positive entities, and not to absences and other varieties of negative

entities the system admits. Consequently, of the seven types of entity the system recognizes, *sattā*, as a real universal, inheres only in substances, qualities, and actions. The other type of positive entity the system recognizes in order to preserve its pluralism is 'ultimate particularity' (*viśeṣa*). These particularities, characterizing the ultimate, further indivisible, reals—atoms, souls, etc.—cannot be taken as exemplifying a real universal called 'particularitiness', for that would be incoherent. Now substances, qualities, and actions are, in the system, particulars—not bare particulars to be sure, for they exemplify various kinds, but particulars, nevertheless—and so only particulars have *sattā*, they alone *are* in the strict sense, they *are* by being related, in the relation of inherence, to the real universal *sattā*. Although the categorial framework of the system admits other entities such as real universals, the relation of inherence, particularities, and a host of negative entities, all these do not exist in that strict sense, nor do they exemplify real kinds. They exist, not as possessing the real universal *sattā*, but 'by themselves' (i.e. they possess *svatvasattva* or *svarūpasattā*), which is a theoretical construct intended to convey how entities could be without exemplifying beingness. *Astitā,* as characterizing all entities that are (both those which are in the strict sense, i. e. the substances, qualities, and actions, and those that are in the other, weaker sense), is not a real universal at all; it does not delimit any real class, and so is rather a construct (*upādhi*).[9] Hence the justification for ascribing to Kaṇāda the view that not everything exists in the same sense: no univocity of 'Being'.[10]

That the concept of being is thus radically split from within is recognized by philosophers outside the Indian tradition,[11] so this by itself should not be regarded as a sign of the weakness of the Vaiśeṣika view. I think, the problem with that view, rather, is that it tends to understand *sattā* as a real universal. Even though it is recognized as the highest (*parā*) universal, it is still a universal as much as 'substancehood' (*dravyatva*) and 'cowness' (*gotva*) are. It is the highest universal only extensionally—all the particulars belonging to the class of substance, all the particulars belonging to the class of quality, as well as all particulars belonging to the class action—all these particulars come under the extension of *sattā*. But, of course, there is no entity that belongs to the class *sattā* which does not belong to any of the other three classes.[12]

Furthermore, if the other entities such as real universals have *sattā*—as noted earlier—but not in the relation of inherence (*samavāya*), one can say that *sattā* does in fact belong to everything, only in different relations, or, better still, that *sattā* is related to different things in different relations.[13]

These considerations suggest that it may be better to deny that *sattā* is a real universal (perhaps even that substancehood, qualityhood, actionhood are real universals). It may be necessary to recognize that beingness is not like cowness, that the difference between them is not simply one of scope. To bring home the point I am trying to make, let me consider the following judgements:

(1) This jar is blue.

(2) This jar exists.

Judgement (1) is roughly analysed as a certainty (niścaya) whose content is the fact that blue, as determined by blueness, serves as a qualifier (*prakāra*) of the jar which, on its part, is determined by jarness and thisness. This provisional analysis needs expansion in the light of further details of the Navya-Nyāya theory.[14] What is important for our present purpose is that nowhere in this analysis does 'existence' enter as a component of the fully analysed expression—so that one may say that the existence of the jar, as also the existence of blueness in the blue colour, are presupposed rather than asserted. The Sanskrit linguistic form *ghato nīlaḥ* correctly reflects the situation by letting the copula 'is' remain unsaid, and even when it is explicitly said, it stands not for assertion of existence, but either for the relation obtaining between the epistemic contents, or for the subjective certainty about it. It is also worth noticing that, in the Nyāya epistemic analysis, the term that is directly designated by the word actually used is to be taken as qualified by the class-property designated by the corresponding unsaid (*anullikhita*) abstract noun: the word 'blue' in (1) does the job of invoking blueness as the unsaid qualifier of the blue that is predicated. The same holds good of 'jar' and 'this'.

Judgement (2), however, is an existential judgement in which, instead of blue, existence is predicated of this jar; and, as before, the particular existence of this jar is to be taken as determined by the universal generic property of existenceness or beingness. Here, it seems to me, the Nyāya analysis of (2), if construed in

terms parallel with that of (1), runs into difficulties, for one then has to distinguish between the particular existence of this jar and existence in general, which the Nyāya does not want to do in accordance with its principle that qualified being (*viśiṣṭasattā*) and pure being (*śuddhasattā*) are identical.[15] But then one has to say that the predicate *sattā* directly attributes the universal *sattā* to this jar: directly, i.e. without the mediation of an unsaid qualifier.

The Nyāya took care to see that there is no infinite regress in speaking of existence as a universal, for if universals are ontologically real, they too may be said to exist—so that existence may be predicated of the universal *sattā*. To avoid this regress and self-predication, the Nyāya restricted the domain of ascription of *sattā* only to substances, qualities, and actions—but, as we have noted, this has been a source of major philosophical embarrassment for the system in view of its realism with regard to universals. The one plausible answer, in terms of the system, is to say that *sattā* belongs to particulars alone in the relation of inherence; to all others that are, it belongs in the *svarūpa* relation, which is but another way of saying they *are*, but not by virtue of exemplifying the universal *sattā* but of themselves (*svarūpa*). Śriharṣa subjects this conception to devastating criticism, the main thrust of which is the following: if an entity is made existent by being related to the universal *sattā*, the entity *per se* must be a non-existent (*asat*) and it is not intelligible how a non-existent entity could enter into a relationship. If the entity must in some sense already *be* in order to be related to *sattā*, then we must distinguish between that sense of being from the fully fledged existence deriving from relationship to *sattā*. Since particulars alone exist in the strict sense—in the Nyāya-Vaiśeṣika system—one may also ask how the particularity of a particular is different from and related to its existence.[16]

If something can be, without exemplifying the universal *sattā*, why after all consider *sattā* as a universal? Two proposals were around, should we reject this view: the first, from within the Nyāya system, is made by Raghunātha Śiromaṇi, who defined *sattā* as 'relatedness to time in the mode of presence' (*ghatādau sadvyavahāraśca vartamānatvanibandhanaḥ*) or as 'relatedness to time' (*kāla-sambandhitvaṃ*); the second is made by the Prābhākara Mīmāmsā, which defines *sattā* either as relatedness to a true cognition (*pramāṇasambandhaḥ*) or as 'fitness to be related to a true cognition' (*pramāṇasambandhayogyatā*),[17] or, following

the Buddhist, one may define *sattā* as causal efficiency (*arthakriyākāritva*).

Raghunātha Śiromaṇi's innovation would virtually amount to retracting the Nyāya position on this matter, and one consequence—a revolutionary consequence in any case—is the need to take time out of the list of entities and to accord to it an altogether different status. The Prābhākara Mīmāmsā view identifies being with being an object of cognition, or in its other version, with the capacity to be such an object: by definition it rules out any entity that is, but is unknown and unknowable. Let me now turn to the Buddhist view.

EXISTENCE: NEITHER A UNIVERSAL NOR A REAL PREDICATE

For the Buddhist thesis that existence is not a real predicate, I will quote the following statement from Vasubandhu: "We say matter 'is produced', 'it exists', but there is no difference between existence and the element which exists."[18] The point of the argument is thus developed by Vācaspati Miśra in *Nyāyavārttikatātparyaṭīkā*: consider the existential affirmative judgement 'The cow exists' and the existential negative judgement 'The cow does not exist'. In both cases, the predicate is 'existence'. But of what is 'existence' predicated? If the word 'cow' designated a real existent, then affirmation of existence would be tautologous (*punarukti*), and denial of existence self-contradictory (*virodha*).[19] Therefore 'existence' is not a predicate of the real; it is affirmed or denied of a conceptual construction. Of what is real, 'existence' need not be affirmed and cannot be denied. In fact, the existent and its existence are one and inseparable. As Vasubandhu said, "there is no difference between existence and the element which exists".

This argument, though not the Buddhist's use of it, is precisely that which Russell advanced to prove that 'existence' is not a predicate. As he put it, in 'Lions exist', 'existence' is predicated not of things designated by 'lion', but of the concept 'lion' or the propositional function 'x is a lion'—so that to say that lions exist is to say that this propositional function is true for some values of x.[20] Russell also held, like the Buddhist, that if 'Socrates' were a

proper name and not a concept or a description, then 'Socrates exists' would be tautologous and 'Socrates does not exist' would be self-contradictory. For the Buddhist as well, when 'existence' is being predicated—affirmed or denied—it is being predicated of what does not exist, namely of a concept, a *vikalpa*. Of what does exist, 'existence' is not a possible predicate. But the Buddhist thesis is stronger than Russell's: nothing in fact is a predicate of the real—the real is ineffable.

Vācaspati asks: what then is the similarity between that which is pure existence and the universal 'cow' which can be affirmed and denied?[21] He then goes on to formulate the Buddhist's answer thus: It is the fact that both are not non-cows. If the constructed object (*vikalpaviṣaya*) 'cow' is nothing but its contrast with non-cows, the similarity (with the point-moment of reality expressed by 'this') becomes possible and explains the possibility of the existential judgement 'This is a cow'. Both the concept and the real underlying it have only this much in common that both exclude non-cows, even though the real is purely positive, *bhāvasvarūpa* or *vidhisvarūpa*. What is excluded from it is all that we can affirm *and* deny.[22] The concept, however, is constituted by such exclusion (*anyāpoha*). The real underlies the concept, renders the exclusion possible, but is not itself conceptualizable: it is *vikalpajñānapratibhāsa-yogya*. It is its own nature (*sva-lakṣaṇa*); it cannot even be named. Names are as much constructions as concepts are. There are no Russellian proper names which merely denote but do not describe. Even 'this' ascribes 'thisness' and so excludes.

If the Buddhist had completely separated the two realms, the existent and the construct, his position would have been simpler but only at the cost of overlooking the complexity of the situation. However, he did realize that mental constructions cannot hang in the air, and that there is a sense in which some judgements are true and some false. Even if the criterion of truth within empirical discourse be pragmatic success (pravṛtti-sāmarthya) one would expect that success to be rooted at some point in the contact with the real. With a view to taking care of these considerations, the Buddhist made the ineffable, unutterable, unconceptualizable real the underlying support of conceptual construction, and also made pure, pre-predicative perception in which the real is encountered the basis of perceptual judgements. To that extent, and only to

that extent, is the real, though transempirical, also immanent in ordinary experience: hence also the possibility of the otherwise misleading ascription of 'existence' to what are mere constructs.

It is now understandable why the Buddhist should admit the possibility of making significant statements about what are empty subject terms. The context in which the issue has generally been introduced is the Buddhist statement 'Whatever is non-momentary is non-existent' (or 'The self, *ātman*, does not exist'), to which the Nyāya objection, based on the theory that the subject term of any significant assertion must be referring, is obvious: 'How can you talk about the non-momentary (or the self, *ātman*) when no such thing exists according to you?' I do not intend to discuss how the Buddhist defends such talk, or how the Naiyāyika would paraphrase such sentences to dispense with the non-referring expression. What I wish to point out is simply this: given the philosophical intuition that the existent is unspeakable, unconceptualizable, indescribable, it follows that what we in fact talk about are constructions (though in a rather attenuated sense of 'about' our talk is about existents). Though within the realm of constructs, one should distinguish between those that have empirical reality (such as cows) and those that do not have it (such as dragons), yet the fundamental situation is the same, and it is only natural that the Buddhist will defend the possibility of talk about fictions—for, after all, what else is any talk about?

My purpose here is not to enter the details of Buddhist metaphysics or even to survey, in barest outlines, the major Buddhist theories. What I have tried to do is to highlight one dominant Buddhist concept of being. According to this view, then, 'being' or 'existence' or *sattā*, taken as a universal term, designates constructions (like all general terms); logical predicates of the forms 'exists' and 'does not exist' are predicated only of other constructs ('cow' and 'dragons'). What is real is the existent which is non-different from its existence. The picture of the existent as a substance possessing properties, or even as an aggregate of properties of which 'existence' is one, is misleading. Each is a unique entity. Such a series of unique entities underlies and supports (mental) constructions, and lends whatever plausibility there is in talking of truth and validity (as well as of falsity and invalidity) with regard to these constructions.

SATTĀ AS THE UNIVERSAL SUBSTANCE

If, for the Nyāya, *sattā* is the most general predicate, the extensionally widest real universal (*parājāti*), and if, according to the Buddhist, there is no existence as such but only the unique occurrence, the Advaita Vedānta, as contrasted with these schools, regards 'existence' as the ultimate subject of all predication, the enduring substratum of all qualification. The Advaita Vedānta agrees with the Nyāya that 'existence' is the highest generality, but it differs in regarding it not as a universal but as a substance (*dravya*); it agrees with the Buddhist that it is not a predicate, but differs in regarding it not as an instantaneous occurrence but as a timeless, simple substance underlying all things and permitting them to borrow their existence—claims from their 'association' with it. Again, another of its affinities to the Buddhist thesis is apparent: just as, according to the Buddhist, any empirical judgement derives its validity from the uniquely existing occurrence that underlies and supports the mental constructions constituting the judgement, so also for Advaita Vedānta, any existential judgement, in fact any judgement, presupposes the self—manifesting being as the ground of its possibility.

Thus runs a well-known Advaita couplet:

> Asti bhāti priyaṃ rūpaṃ nāma ca iti aṁśapañcakaṃ
> ādyatrayaṃ brahmarūpaṃ jagadrūpamatodvayaṃ.

"Of the five 'parts'—'exists', 'appears', 'pleases', 'form', and 'name'—the first three are of the nature of *brahman* (ultimate Reality), and the remaining two of the nature of the world." In other words, according to the Advaita thesis, whenever we assert of anything that it exists, its existence is of the nature of *brahman*, but only as limited by the content of 'it'. Likewise, whenever we say of anything that it appears, the bare element of manifestation as abstracted from the content that is manifested is the *brahman*. It is also the same in the case of value-judgements. This shows, according to Advaita Vedānta, that being is as much immanent as transcendent with regard to ordinary experience: it is immanent as the indwelling condition of its possibility; it is transcendent inasmuch as in its purity it is beyond the limitations of contents encountered in experience.

In saying that Advaita construes being in the manner of a substance, I am aware that my contention is liable to serious objections and disclaimers. I will therefore adduce two evidences in support of my contention, and then proceed to subject it to an important qualification. First, let us recall the famous statement of the *Chāndogya Upaniṣad*, of which Śaṃkara makes much use: "Just as, good sir, when the one lump of clay is known, all things made of clay are known, so all formations are merely differences of name; the clay alone is the truth."[23] The priority of substance in Śaṃkara's ontology is most clearly stated in his commentary on *Brahmasūtra* II. ii. 17:

> We ascertain the difference between smoke and fire from the fact of their being apperceived in separation. Substance and quality, on the other hand, are not so apperceived; for when we are conscious of a white blanket, or a red cow, or a blue lotus, the substance is in each case cognized by means of the quality; the latter therefore has its Self in the substance. The same reasoning applies to action, generality, particularity, and inherence.[24]

It would then seem that, according to Śaṃkara, the one being is the one universal substance; it is different from the finite substances *qua* substance in that the finite substances have qualities, whereas the one being has no distinguishable quality; furthermore, of a finite substance, existence appears to be a predicate, whereas this one being is the existence of which all finite substantial contents are, in reality, predicates. The qualification, then, to my contention that Śaṃkara regards being as a substance is this: of all finite ontological categories, the category of substance, being the most fundamental of them, comes closest to a true understanding of the nature of being; where this category fails, none other can do the job any better.

Unlike the Nyāya-Vaiśeṣika, for whom everything whatsoever *is* (whether by relatedness to the universal *sattā*, or intrinsically), the Advaita Vedānta operates with a criterion of being, and in this it shares a common mode of thinking with the Buddhist, who also has his criterion of causal efficiency to begin with. The criterion with which Advaita Vedānta operates—the criterion both of being and of reality, for the two are identical in it, as in Buddhism—is non-contradiction. Now there would seem to be two ways of formulating the criterion of non-contradiction, one logical, the

other experiential. The former is employed by Nāgārjuna and F. H. Bradley: that is real which is free from logical self-contradiction. It seems to me that the philosophers who apply the logical criterion are primarily metaphysicians; even if they seek to demolish metaphysics, they do so through metaphysical thinking. Their concern is reality. Śaṃkara's criterion is experiential: being must be that which admits of no experiential contradiction—it must be that whose negation is not possible—for it must be the all-pervasive, ever-present support of all that appears to be. If the illusory snake is, upon correction of the illusion, negated as non-existent, the being of the snake-phenomenon is not. Of no empirical content as such can we say that it cannot possibly be negated by subsequent empirical evidence. There is only one thing which, with absolute certainty, precludes the possibility of experiential contradiction, and that is consciousness. For the absence of consciousness, to be a possibility, must be established and testified by consciousness. To say that an entity is, but cannot be proved, perceived, or otherwise known, talked about, etc., is to be inconsistent. If there were absence of consciousness, such absence would have to be an object of consciousness, which would be a manifest absurdity. Consciousness alone can posit its own absence; hence, although absence of this or that modality of consciousness, this or that content of consciousness, is clearly conceivable, absence of consciousness as such is inconceivable. Being is consciousness. Any content whatsoever appears to be, because consciousness is. As the *Vedāntaparibhāṣā* puts it: "*Brahmasattayā eva sarveṣām sattāvyavahāraḥ.*"

Consciousness alone does not appear to be; it is. For, in the case of consciousness, appearance and reality coincide; it is fully transparent, its being is manifestation (*prakāśaekarasa*). Whatever is an object of consciousness may be negated; consciousness, not being an object of consciousness, cannot be negated, for any such negation would be a negating consciousness. From this thesis that consciousness is not a possible counter-positive (*pratiyogi*) of negation, the Advaita philosophers proceed to deduce various propositions about consciousness. Negation is either difference or absence. Difference is either homogenous (*sajātīya*) as of one cow from another, or heterogeneous (*vijātīya*) as of a cow from a horse, or internal (*svagata*) as of parts of a whole. Absence is either absence antecedent to origination, or absence consequent upon

destruction, or absence of a thing at one place or time while it is present at another place or another time. Now if none of these modes of difference, as well as none of these modes of absence, are applicable to consciousness, consciousness becomes one being, undifferentiated, eternal, changeless. All differences and absences are its objects; none belongs to its nature.

In this conclusion, phenomenology and metaphysics get blended together. Here, as in Buddhism, the link between the two is provided by a most elusive concept, the concept of ignorance or *avidyā*. If being is consciousness, and if, as being, consciousness provides the foundation and the support for all beings and makes possible ascription of existence to any object whatsoever; if, that is to say, any ascription of existence as a predicate is, in fact, an ascription of a predicate to existence or being, then why is it that this inversion takes place? Why is it that what is, in itself, appears as attaching predicatively to what is in reality not a substantive? Why is it that consciousness seems to be my state when in fact it is my being, and 'I' am its modification? Why is it that consciousness—self-illuminating and autonomous in its self-concern—should come to exhibit that intentionality, or being-towards-the-world, which characterizes ordinary experience? The answer is: due to ignorance (*avidyā*); but even the being of ignorance is the same self-illuminating consciousness. Ignorance both rests on it and seeks to conceal it, i.e. to conceal that which lends it its own being; in this consists the paradoxical nature of ignorance.[25] Ignorance conceals being but in so far as it itself is experienced, as in the judgement 'I am ignorant', being is not totally concealed. For were it in total concealment, ignorance itself would not be manifested; in fact, there would be, as some Vedānta authors put it, utter darkness (*jagadāndhyaprasaṅga*). Experience is the chiaroscuro of light and darkness—neither complete, unhindered illumination, nor all-enveloping darkness, but darkness resting on, concealing, and yet revealed by, light.[26]

But darkness is not sheer non-being. Ignorance is a positive being, a beginningless power which is conceived of as having the two functions of concealment of being and projection of empirical forms on the formless being. In order not to appear to be identifying the world of entities with sheer non-being, some Vedānta authors distinguish between three orders of being: *pāramārthika* or metaphysical being; *vyavahārika* or empirical

being; and *prātibhāsika* or apparent being. These three are ordered in such a manner that the third form of being derives its being from the second, while its content is its own; and the second, likewise, derives its being from the first, while its content is its own. The first is contentless being, the mere 'that' without any 'what'. In fact, all 'that,' the 'that' of an empirical object or even of a hallucinatory object, derives from it. When an apparent being is negated by cancellation of an illusion, what is cancelled is the content, not the fact of its appearing. The same holds good, when—as in spiritual knowledge—the reality of the empirical being is cancelled. The unnegatable, uncancelled abstraction of mere 'appearing', 'manifestation', 'awareness', abstracted from all contents that appear, is being. It is time now to tie together some of the loose ends in the exposition given above, and to use this to throw light on some fresh aspects of the problems concerned.

RÉSUMÉ AND FURTHER ISSUES

We began by asking whether 'being' is a real predicate. To this the Nyāya offered an affirmative answer, but its answer ran into difficulties owing to its exclusion of all entities other than substances, qualities, and actions from existing in the primary sense. It had to search for a common and generic sense in which all entities recognized in the system might be said to exist, and that led Raghunātha Śiromaṇi to the conception of 'relatedness to time in the mode of presence'. We pointed out some likely consequences of such a theory. The Buddhist rejected the theory that existence is a real predicate of existing particulars, for such existents are unique and ineffable; he admitted, however, that it is a logical predicate of concepts, which are but logical constructions. To exist, in the primary sense, then—for the Buddhist view expounded—is to be a member of a series of instantaneous occurrences; to exist, in this sense, is for a mental construct to be related to such a primary construct by the relation of co-ordination or *sārūpya*. The Advaita Vedānta understands being as that which is in principle unnegatable, that which is the principle of manifestation, the self-manifesting and other-manifesting awareness abstracted from all contents, to be understood on the analogy of the most universal substance, but again, as Hegel said,

substance understood as subject. To be, in the primary sense, is to be self-manifest*ing*; to be, in the derived sense, is to be manifest*ed* by consciousness.

How are these three concepts of being reflected in the respective ontologies and also in their epistemologies? The following points are worth recalling. In the Nyāya ontology, since all entities possess being in some sense or other, each has a being of its own, so that there is a resulting pluralism of entities. But at the same time, substances, qualities, and actions have being in a pre-eminent sense, requiring thereby that all other entities must inhere in, be residing in, some entity belonging to one or other of these three types. A particularity (*viśeṣa*) must inhere in, by its very conception, an ultimate, indivisible substance; and absence must 'reside in' an entity of some such kind. Consequently, the Nyāya needs a relation which is both adequate to tie such diverse types of entity together and compatible with their type-differences. Of the three basic types, substance, quality, and action, again, qualities and actions must belong to substances by the same sort of relation which would 'tolerate' their type-differences, and yet bind them inalienably. Such a relation is *samavāya*, by which the Nyāya succeeds in reconciling a pluralistic ontology required by its concept of being with a systematically structured conception of the world in which the category of substance and the relation of *samavāya* occupy an especially basic status.

Advaita Vedānta denies the legitimacy of a relation that would inseparably bind entities and yet tolerate their type-differences. Either deny inseparability or deny difference. Śaṃkara chooses the latter. He writes in his commentary on *Brahmasūtra* II. ii. 17:

> Or else let the qualities, etc., depend on substance; then it follows that, as they are present where substance is present, and absent where it is absent, substance only exists, and, according to its various forms, becomes the object of different forms and conceptions (such as quality, action, etc.); just as Devadatta, for instance, according to the conditions in which he finds himself, is the object of various conceptions and names.

The relation, then, between the blue of the blue lotus and the lotus is not inherence of a quality in a substance but *tādātmya*, which is not mere identity, but 'the relation of having that (*tat*) as one's own self (*ātman*)'.[27] The self is the being. Substance is the being of qualities, etc., and of empirical substances. Being is the unnegat-

able principle of manifestation. Thus it follows from the Advaita Vedānta conception of being that such a relation should be fundamental to its ontology. But note that this relation is not one of undifferentiated identity, for that would not be a relation at all. Tādātmya is that identity which tolerates differences (bhedasahiṣṇu), but here it is not the difference between two types of reals, but between the real and its appearances.

For the Buddhist, the real is the instantaneous event; the only relation that such a concept allows is one of succession. But, with only the instant being real, there is no real relation that could relate the successor to the predecessor; moreover, the relation itself would tend to be a recurrent relation and so could not be real. It is a mental construction. But that which connects a mental construct, like a concept, to its founding instant is not causation, not correspondence, but co-ordination (*sārūpya*). Most nominalistic ontologies, of course, recognize resemblance as a basic relation, but for the Buddhist *sārūpya*, though literally meaning 'resemblance', is to be understood as 'similarity between two things absolutely dissimilar' (*atyantavilakṣaṇānāṃ sālakṣaṇyam*), a 'similarity' produced either by non-apprehension of difference (*bhedāgraha*) or by a common exclusion (*apoha*).[28]

How is being known? It seems to me that, in general, consistent with the thesis of the priority of perception common to most systems, to every concept of being there is a correlative mode of perception in which it is given. Even in their theory of perception all three theories distinguish between a primary, 'non-qualificative' (*nirvikalpaka*) pre-predicative, non-judgemental perception, and a subsequent, qualificative, predicative, judgemental perception. This distinction, as is well known, is made in different ways. It seems, however, that in each system being is apprehended in non-judgemental perception. This contention should be immediately accepted in the case of the Buddhist and the Advaita Vedānta systems. For the Buddhist, perception, in the strict sense, is but the pure sensation in which a unique, ineffable particular is apprehended; even for the Advaita Vedānta, the primary, pre-predicative encounter with any object presents us with the mere 'that' (*sanmātraṃ*) which subsequent predicative perception characterizes with a 'what'. But I would even ascribe a type of the same thesis to the Nyāya. What I mean is this: if the Nyāya had only the theory of judgemental perception

which it has, knowledge would always apprehend, e.g. the jar as qualified by jarness and as possessing the blue which itself is qualified by blueness. But, in that theory, there is no way to validate, even in principle, its basic pluralism, i.e. the separate being of each term of this predicative complex. This latter is validated by the putative primary, non-qualificative perception, in which there is no relational complex, no epistemic entities or relations (*viṣayatā, prakāratā*, or *samsargatā*, etc.) and which apprehends, as Matilal puts it, 'the Thing'.[29] But the domain of the object of such a pre-predicative perception ranges over all types of entity—substances, qualities, actions, etc.—which is in accord with the thesis that they all have being.

It is indeed difficult to decide whether in each of these cases the conception of being determines or is determined by the epistemological thesis. It seems to me plausible that in all these cases the epistemological thesis is a consequence of, a necessary concession to, the ontological thesis. Neither the Buddhist's pure sensation in which an instantaneous event flashes forth, nor the Advaita Vedānta's pre-predicative perception of the mere that, seems to me to be phenomenologically self-evidencing; the Nyāya non-qualificative perception, on the Nyāya admission, is not self-evidencing, but is rather inferred. Another way of looking at the three theories is to note that, for the Nyāya, the concept of being, in the widest sense, is the concept of an indifference. To be is extrinsic to the intrinsic nature of the entity. There is a sense, as was pointed out, in which all entities are. Let us call it 'being as indifference'. Being in this sense is not exhausted by being an object of an act of consciousness, for a being may as well not be such an object. And even in the case of an entity that is also an object, being-an-object is not the same as mere being. Further, in the later systems of Navya-Nyāya, such epistemic entities as objectness (*viṣayatā*) are also entities and have being; just as an act of consciousness also is. An act of consciousness is, of course, directed to an object, but its being is not other than that of any other entity. In this widest sense there are types of entity, but there are no types of being. Again, just as all entities may be objects of knowledge, but the being is in no case exhausted by being-an-object, so also every entity may be named (*vācya*) but the property of being nameable (*vācyatva*) does not define being.

To be contrasted with this conception of being as indifference are the more restricted concepts of being, which allow distinctions between entities *qua* entities, not all of which have being in any commonly ascribable sense. Such are the Buddhist and the Advaita Vedānta theories. As pointed out earlier, Advaita Vedānta distinguishes between three orders of being, so that illusory objects and empirically real objects have being in different senses from that in which *brahman*, or pure consciousness, has being. The same holds good of the Buddhist view expounded. Particularly in Advaita Vedānta, then, we have the overarching contrast between consciousness and the world: the former self-revealing, the latter not self-revealing but manifested only by being an object of consciousness; the former independent and self-supporting, the latter dependent upon it in the sense of being an object of the former. To be sure, the being of the world does not consist in its being perceived; the world certainly—unlike the hallucinatory object—possesses unknown existence (*ajñātasattā*). But even as unknown, it is an object of consciousness. As the author of the *Vivaraṇaprameyasamgraha* expresses it: "all things whatsoever are objects of pure consciousness, either as known or as unknown".[30] Thus we can say the following:

(1) The being of hallucinatory objects consists in their being perceived.

(2) The being of the empirical world consists in its being an object of consciousness—either in the mode of knowledge or in the mode of ignorance (*jñātatayā ajñātatayā vā*).

(3) The being of consciousness is precisely its self-manifesting nature.

However, there is no Husserlian doctrine of the constitution of the world in consciousness, for, first, consciousness is understood here as pure transparence, but not as intentionality; second, being simply the principle of manifestation, consciousness has no content of its own. Thus, empty of all contents, consciousness more resembles the Sartrean 'nothingness'; the world is given to it as an inexplicable absurdity, *anirvacanīya*, whose sense cannot, in principle, be entirely explicated.

PLURALISM VERSUS MONISM: A STUDY IN CONTRASTS

No two philosophical schools, in Indian philosophy, are so unlike each other as Nyāya-Vaiśeṣika and Advaita Vedānta. Nyāya is realistic, while Vedānta is idealistic. The former is pluralistic, the latter monistic. If, then, we can gain some philosophical understanding of this difference—some insight into differences in basic presuppositions as well as methodological commitments—we may be on our way to a better understanding of Indian philosophical thinking as a whole. In this section I wish to take up that task.

An Indian philosophical system, a *darśana*, is a surprisingly close-knit system, whose boundaries have been sharply defined and loose ends tied together fairly well during centuries of its historical development. In such a system, it is often a frustrating experience to look for an absolute beginning. Should the point of beginning be the scriptural texts which are then explicated and rationally justified? Should it be a primary cosmological and/or spiritual intuition which is then conceptually elaborated and defended against other rival intuitions? Should the beginning be in the epistemological theory of *pramāṇas* or means of knowledge (with which the classical expositions began) from which the ontology or theory of *prameya* (or objects of such knowledge) then follows? Or, is the theory of *pramāṇas* itself a consequence of the implicitly presupposed metaphysics? Or, as may appear not unlikely to readers of Sanskrit philosophical texts, do the philosophers begin with ordinary experience and ordinary language (*lokānubhava* and *lokavyavahāra*) and then unravel their implications by a peculiar combination of description, analysis, and transcendental argument? If only we could settle these issues, our understanding of the methods of philosophizing in ancient India could be substantially enhanced; but the difficulties facing any such move are enormous. In fact, it does seem that metaphysics and epistemology, theory of *prameya* and theory of *pramāṇa*, depend upon each other; and the use that is made of a scriptural text is determined by, rather than determining, these commitments.

In the *Nyāyasūtras* I. ii. 18–19, just before considering separately the various means of knowing, Gotama considers an

objection that is apparently raised by the Mādhyamika Buddhist. The objection is developed in several stages, but its main point seems to be that the epistemological thesis about 'means of knowledge' and the ontological thesis about what there is to be known so determine and presuppose each other that the Nyāya cannot even account for its own beginning. Gotama's and his commentator Vātsyāyana's response to this rather radical questioning is worth recalling: partly, it amounts to arguing that denial of the validity of all means of knowledge cannot be coherently stated, for this denial itself needs to be validated; partly, it consists in pointing out that the Buddhist had wrongly formulated his alternatives as mutually exclusive possibilities when he asked: does the *pramāṇa* precede or succeed the *prameya* or is it contemporaneous with it, and then went on to deny all three—the first on the ground that if the *pramāṇa* preceded its object, then the perceptual object could not be a cause of perceptual knowledge; if the object preceded *pramāṇa*, then *pramāṇa* could not be the source of 'establishing' the object; if the two were contemporaneous, then we would come to know many things at once, which would violate an accepted principle that cognitions are successive rather than simultaneous. These apparent difficulties are avoided by the Naiyāyika by pointing out that all these three possibilities are instantiated in different cases, the first when the causes of knowledge precede the object of that knowledge; the second when the object is first there, later to be known and established; the third when the two are contemporaneous (as when smoke is a cause of the inference of fire). These three possibilities correspond to three tenses of the verb 'to know': 'he knew', 'he will know', 'he is knowing', respectively. These usages will be unaccounted for unless we admit all three possibilities. To look for one pattern of dependence is false; the scepticism arising from not finding such a pattern is unjustified, apart from being incoherent.

This shows that the Nyāya philosophy makes constant appeal, particularly when encountering scepticism, to ordinary usage and ordinary experience. It also appeals, on other occasions, to the universal practice (*pravṛtti*) of mankind. A rather well-known illustration is its reply to the sceptic who questions if the universal major of a syllogism is at all valid, who questions, for example, on what grounds he is to assume that all occurrences of smoke are also occurrences of fire. The Nyāya answer is, if the evidence of

uncontradicted experience (all positive instances and no negative instance) does not satisfy the sceptic, it should be pointed out to him that the contrary assumption that there may be smoke without fire (when the fuel is not wet) would upset the practice of mankind with regard to the production of smoke and fire. Udayana, in his *Nyāyakusumānjali*, formulates this principle most clearly: 'That may be doubted (*tad eva hi āśaṃkyate*), by doubting which (*yasmin āsaṃkyamāne*) the fallacy of contradicting one's own actions does not arise (*svakriyāvyāghātādaya doṣā na avatarantīti*); this is the prestige of ordinary experience (*loka-maryādā*).' One's own action, writes Vardhamana in his commentary on this text, is the ultimate limit of doubt (*svakriyayā eva śaṃkāpratibandhakatvāt*).[31]

I will give one other illustration of the same procedure. There was a theory, held originally by the so-called grammarians but later assimilated into various theological–metaphysical schools, that a name and what is named by it are inseparable. Against this theory, Udayana—in his *Pariśuddhi*—argues that it contradicts the distinction between merely recalling the word 'fire' and directly experiencing the warmth of fire.[32]

If these examples serve to make any point, it is that philosophical theory should not contradict ordinary experience, ordinary usage, and ordinary practice. The Nyāya accordingly sought to exhibit its ontological theses as, at least, implicates of ordinary experience and usage, and also as compatible with ordinary practice. This is not to say that the ontological framework was derived from ordinary experience, but the system tried to validate the framework—perhaps developed a priori—by reference to ordinary experience and usage. I will illustrate this with reference to two key elements of Nyāya ontology: its realism and its pluralism.

Consider the sentence 'This is a jar'. It is distinct from the sentence 'I see that this is a jar'. This difference is essential for the purposes of Nyāya. The two sentences give expression to two different cognitions, the former to the perceptual cognition whose object is the jar before me, the latter to the reflective cognition whose object is the first cognition. Any analysis of the content of the first sentence, 'This is a jar', for Nyāya, should not contain reference to the cognition whose expression the sentence is; on the other hand, an analysis of the second sentence, namely 'I see that

this is a jar', must contain reference to that original, perceptual cognition. In other words, although the sentence 'This is a jar' expresses the perceptual cognition of the jar lying before me, it describes the object of that cognition, not that cognition itself. The expression 'the knowledge that this is a jar' names that cognition, but does not express it; for this expression is possible only when the original cognition itself is cognized in a reflective inner perception.

From this it follows that, for Nyāya, a cognition is not self-referential, it is wholly and fully referring to its own object. The form of the cognition ('This is a jar) is fully and wholly determined by the form of the object; other than the form of the object, the cognition itself has no form of its own. The two theses jointly lead to Nyāya realism, but these two rest upon Nyāya analysis of knowledge. I will briefly comment upon the two assertions I just made.

First, as I have already discussed in Chapter 1, the two theses—(1) that knowledge is not self-referential and (2) that its form is in fact the form of its object so that in reality knowledge is formless—jointly entail a realistic ontology. One has only to bear in mind that since knowledge is not self-referential, it does not 'show' itself; what does appear in knowledge is not itself but its object. Further, all the forms, 'this', 'jar', for example, are originally forms of the object, and not of the knowledge. The idealist, e.g. the Buddhist Vijñānavādin, holds, to the contrary, that knowledge is self-manifesting and also that it has its forms—both conjointly lead him to the thesis that what 'shows' itself in a cognitive situation is the knowledge itself with its own immanent forms. The Nyāya rejects both these premisses and so also the consequent idealism.[33]

The realism that is thus entailed by (1) and (2) further needs to be strengthened by the following considerations:

In so far as the sentence 'This is a jar' expresses a cognition, its analysis must contain elements which are essentially cognitive, and not ontological—or, even if ontological, certainly of a 'hybrid' character.[34] For example, in this knowledge the substantive 'this' is determined by the qualifier 'jar'. Without going into further details of the analysis, we have already introduced concepts that are epistemic: 'substantive', 'qualifier', 'being determined by'. It may be that they correspond to the ontological structure, but the

correspondence is not simple. In 'This jar is blue', the term 'This jar' functions as substantive, and 'blue' as the qualifier. In principle, the question is this: if cognition does involve elements that are epistemic, what grounds do we have for separating these out from those that are ontological? Further, do not these epistemic concepts characterize the structure of cognition itself, and if so how could one say that a cognition is formless, or that all its forms derive from the object? The Nyāya attitude, in consonance with, and in support of its realism, has been twofold: first, to admit that any epistemic object has also an ontological status is an admission which makes especially the Navya—Nyāya an *aniyatapadārthavādin,* i.e. one whose list of entities is 'irregular'. But, perhaps, philosophically the more decisive move is that the propositional form of cognition which we are considering is preceded by a non-propositional, pre-predicative perception in which things are given as such, each by itself, without their having to enter into a predicative complex. I believe this admission is vital to Nyāya realism, for only such an awareness opens an access to things as they are, and such an awareness itself has no form of its own, not even the epistemic characteristics whose ontological status was under question. This pre-predicative awareness in which individual substances, their qualities, universals, and relations are presented, each separately by itself, is perhaps a necessary condition for a pluralistic ontology of the sort maintained by the Nyāya.

Now, contrast the situation with the Advaita Vedānta. In Advaita Vedānta, 'This is a jar' and 'I know this is a jar' are equivalent, the latter expressing no new cognition, for every cognition is self-referential, i.e., self-manifesting. Every cognition, therefore, manifests both itself and its other, the object. But it can manifest its object—it is argued—only by assuming the form of its object. Form originally belongs to the objects—the Advaita Vedānta agrees with the realist as against the Buddhist; but it also agrees with the Buddhist in holding that a cognition, being essentially self-manifesting, can manifest only that with which it identifies itself by assuming its form. Empirical consciousness, then, with all its diverse forms and modalities is distinct from the original nature of consciousness, which, in its purity, is formless. The cognition 'I know this is a jar', therefore, has to be analysed somewhat as follows:

(1) My consciousness has assumed the form 'This is a jar'.

More accurately, (1) has to be expanded into:

(2) A mental state of the form 'This is a jar' is reflecting my consciousness (just as a mirror may reflect the sun's rays).

Better still:

(3) Consciousness (which is in itself one and differenceless) as limited by the predicate 'belonging to me' and consciousness as reflected in the mental state of the form 'This is a jar' are identified.

Consciousness, as described in (3), is still consciousness knowing itself; all knowledge is self-knowledge, but subject to limiting conditions, both on the subjective and on the objective sides—on the subjective side by the 'ego', on the objective side by the 'objective form'.

The basic issue, then, on which the vast difference between Nyāya and Advaita Vedānta rests is: is all knowledge self-knowledge? If knowledge is not *eo ipso* self-knowledge, then what it apprehends is the other. If knowledge is *eo ipso* self-knowledge, what it apprehends is really itself, though always under a different modality. For the realist, everything whatsoever is a possible object of knowledge, *sarvaṃ prameyaṃ*. For Advaita Vedānta, in the long run, there is no object of valid knowledge except consciousness itself, for the rest are apparent modifications of it; but since consciousness is also the subject under the limitation of 'I', it is in truth subject and object in one—the ever self-revealing differenceless unity to begin with.

Further differences follow. 'I know this is a jar' is analysed as:

(4) A cognition having the form 'This is a jar' belongs to me, where the 'me' refers to the knower of whom consciousness is a state.

But, again, consider

(5) When I was expecting my guests, and was busy arranging the table, I heard the doorbell ring and felt happy.

It becomes clear that the same I who is the subject of hearing is also the subject of expecting, the agent of the act of arranging, and

the enjoyer of the feeling of happiness. Thus the 'I' stands for the same entity who is the subject of knowledge, the agent of actions, and the enjoyer or sufferer of emotions. This indeed is the Nyāya self (*ātmā*). Just as it is true of this I that it knows, acts, and enjoys or suffers, the following is also true of it:

(6) I soon fell asleep, and was not aware of anything.

(6) implies, on a very straightforward analysis, that the self denoted by 'I' sometimes does not possess any consciousness—so that consciousness is a contingent state of the self rather than a necessary property.

The Advaita Vedānta analysis of sentences (5) and (6) is far from being straightforward, as was the analysis of the sentence 'This is a jar'. In (5), as in 'This is a jar', the I, the expectant state with its intentionality towards guests, and the actional state as also the affective state, are all equally well modifications of consciousness; so that, in each case, a differenceless consciousness is being appropriately modified as belonging to an I, as an expectant state, as an actional or an affective state. For an analysis of (6), the Advaita Vedānta wants to consider it together with:

(7) I slept well,

which, on a surface analysis, bears out—provided it is taken as a recollective judgement and not as an inference—that there was a consciousness of well-being accompanied by an awareness of ignorance in general ('I was not aware of anything') during dreamless sleep, which of course fits very well with the Advaita Vēdanta metaphysics.

Trying to understand the ontological difference between Nyāya pluralism and Advaita Vedānta monism, we have seen, in the first place, how the two theories may be seen as implicates of ordinary language sentences. We have also seen how the two theories require different basic relations, inherence (*samavāya*) in one case and a sort of identity (*tādātmya*) in the other. This latter choice is necessitated by the requirements of the system, rather than determining the system itself. (The Nyāya-Vaiśeṣika need for a fundamental relation which should be able to preserve category differences and yet weld entities from different categories into the unity of a thing makes sense only when one already presupposes that categorical system. Likewise, the Advaita preference for a

sort of identity is clearly motivated, as well as necessitated by an ontology in which all categorical differences are obliterated in the identity of substance.) Can we say the same of the former and contend that how the ordinary-language sentences under consideration are analysed is no less dependent on the ontological framework adopted? This appears in fact to be so, as will be argued below.

There are four decisive issues to which attention was drawn in the foregoing. The first of these is the Nyāya commitment to a methodology that would be consistent with the implications of ordinary language and ordinary cognitive as well as practical experience. The other three are substantive issues: Is knowledge or consciousness self-referential or not? Is knowledge or consciousness formless (*nirākāra*) or formed (*sākāra*)? What precisely is given in pre-predicative, non-linguistic perception, which precedes and is the presupposition of all predicative and linguistic perception and thought? Regarding the methodological issue, the Nyāya requirement may be opposed in either of two ways. One may reply that what precisely is implied by ordinary language and ordinary experience depends upon how one interprets the latter, and this interpretation itself cannot be tested by the same requirements of consistency with the implicates of ordinary language and experience. In other words, it is not with ordinary language and ordinary experience as such, but rather with a certain analysis of it that a philosophical theory may come into conflict. When the Nyāya insists upon this criterion, and in most cases when the school applies it, it makes use of an implicit, and often an explicit, interpretive analysis of ordinary language and ordinary experience, and in most such cases such analysis is system-dependent. Secondly, and this would be a more radical reply and likely to be advanced by the Buddhist, there is no reason to accept ordinary language and experience as authoritative. To argue against a philosophy that purports to be a radical critique of all accepted modes of thinking that such a philosophy would conflict with the way we habitually talk about the world is to beg the very question at issue. Both these responses place themselves on the level of hermeneutic thinking and wish to deny any phenomenological access to the given *qua* given. But of these, the latter, the more radical, alone is consistent. The former leaves room for some such counter-reply: granted that many interpretations of ordinary

language and experience are system-dependent, it is nevertheless possible to show that a given ontology or a given epistemology is at odds with ordinary experience itself, and not merely with an interpretation of it. This is particularly so when a theory contradicts not a proposition, but the possibility of a certain mode of acting, as the Nyāya argues in the case of universal sceptical doubt, or against the thesis of identity of the name and the named.

Nevertheless, it has to be conceded that neither the Nyāya nor the Advaita Vedānta ontology is a bare, phenomenological description of what is given. While the Nyāya-Vaiśeṣika ontology does have the semblance of a certain closeness to common sense, yet the system proceeds by providing ordinary language with a semantic interpretation[35] in terms of its own categorial system, which at all points does not capture the given, but rather, if necessary, reconstructs it—as becomes more and more evident as the old Nyāya makes room for the new. Description and interpretive reconstruction go hand in hand. In fact, a good description becomes none other than a satisfactory semantic interpretation. Given this understanding of the Nyāya project, one can still compare how successfully rival schools do this. Here possibly the Nyāya fares better. But the same methodological criterion, even in its revised form, cannot be applied to the Buddhist Mādhyamika critique, which, by its radicalness, questions all criteria whatsoever and so disavows all ontology (and correlative epistemology). Provisionally one can then say, if you want to do ontology, the revised criterion is as good as any other. But it surely does not provide a test or point of departure outside a system.

But is it not that all Indian systems recognize a certain primacy of perception as a means of valid knowledge? In Nyāya, this is almost a methodological absolute. Inference follows perception, and has no right to contradict it. The truths that verbal testimony of the scriptures delivers are perceivable by the yogis, if not by ordinary men. The same in Advaita Vedānta: if ordinary perception is metaphysically impotent, and even if it is true that the scriptures alone testify to the oneness of Being, it is at the same time a thesis of the system that pure undifferentiated being (*sanmātra*) is given, even if fleetingly, in every pre-predicative perception, and in its full metaphysical significance, in a perceptual immediacy resulting from meditative reflection on the

scriptural texts (*śabda-janya-aparokṣānubhūti*). What one suspects is that the primacy of perception provides no extra-systemic test of validity, for not merely the analysis of perceptual statements, but even the content of pre-predicative, pre-linguistic perception itself is understood in terms of the system. What is ontologically real in the system—the unrelated entities, universals as well as particulars, substances as well as their qualities and actions, in the one case, and pure, undifferentiated Being in the other—is exactly what is said to be given in pre-predicative perception.

The Nyāya is, in this regard, on relatively stronger ground than the Advaita Vedānta; for believing as it does that no knowledge is self-illuminating, the Nyāya can, without inconsistency, rule out direct perceptual evidence for its thesis regarding the alleged pre-predicative perception, and may, as in fact it does, depend only upon a sort of transcendental argument in its support: an argument to the effect that a predicative perceptual judgement of the form *S* is *P* is possible if and only if it is immediately preceded by the direct, i.e. non-qualificative, acquaintance with each of the terms involved in that predicative structure. The Advaita Vedānta, in contrast, cannot appeal merely to such or any other inferential argument in support of its thesis. Since it believes that every knowledge is self-illuminating, the fact that predicative perception in each case is preceded by a direct apprehension of undifferentiated Being, the mere 'that' which is only subsequently determined by a 'what' should be borne out by the testimony of one's own self-illuminating cognition, and yet it is precisely here that testimonies are likely to differ. On the other hand, even if the Nyāya is entitled to an inferential argument in support of its thesis, the argument establishes the thesis only when the perceptual judgement (whose possibility the transcendental argument is to account for) is interpreted, to begin with, after the Nyāya manner, i.e. in terms of precisely that categorial framework for which the non-qualificative perception was to provide supporting evidence. Thus an extra-systemic evidence eludes our grasp.

What shall we say about the two remaining substantive issues, namely those concerning the self-illuminating nature of consciousness and its formlessness? It seems to me as though here we are on stabler ground. If consciousness is self-illuminating or not, the question whether or not to know is *eo ipso* to know that one knows, it seems, can be decided without making use of the

analytical tools of the Nyāya or the metaphysics of the Vedānta. In fact, the only way—one may claim—that the question can be decided is by interrogating, without theoretical preconceptions, one's own cognitive experience. Here, I believe, the self-illumination thesis is on a stronger ground. The Nyāya arguments against it stem from the inability of the system to accommodate the testimony of one's experience, and so much the worse for the system. But the variety of self-illumination thesis which, on my view, is phenomenologically certified is not the stronger version according to which every cognition is already and *eo ipso* an 'I know', but the weaker version to the effect that every cognition can be elaborated into an 'I know', the latter not adding any new content to the original cognition but explicating what it was implicitly all along. It was shown earlier that the thesis that knowledge does not illuminate itself when combined with the thesis that knowledge is formless provides the strongest plea for a realist ontology. If knowledge is self-illuminating, that is compatible with realism, provided we still have the thesis that knowledge is formless (a thesis basically agreed upon by the Nyāya and the Advaita Vedānta). Only, we have now a weaker case for realism, a position ascribable to the Prābhākara school of Mīmāmsā. But to be able to decide whether likewise the issue about form can be settled on extra-systemic grounds or if one inevitably appeals to considerations arising from within the system, one has to consider the nature of supporting and opposing evidences and argumentations offered by the Nyāya and the Buddhist philosophers, which I do not intend to take up here.

The result of these critical considerations has been rather mixed: both unsettling and illuminating. It is unsettling, for we find that choice from amongst the systems was not entirely on the basis of the so-called means of true cognition or *pramāṇas*. *Pramāṇas* were used to certify the ontology, but the doctrine of the *pramāṇas* itself was incorporated into the latter. The Mādhyamika Buddhist critique, then, has a point, but the point was radically to transcend philosophy, for while doing philosophy one had to be within the epistemology–ontology structure of a system—a structure whose basic categorial framework remained an a priori, relative to the system. What is illuminated by this otherwise unsettling conclusion is the reason behind the Indian tradition's attitude towards doing philosophy: to do philosophy was not to examine philosophical

propositions as such, but always to examine other systems from within one's own and to defend and/or develop one's own from within. This alone was, for that tradition, responsible philosophizing as distinguished from irresponsible, intellectual sophistry. While this was a major component of the tradition's self-understanding, it happily was not the sole component. The really pertinent question is, what range of development and self-criticism of a system was to count as taking place from within? Where do we place some one like Raghunātha Śiromaṇi, or the transition from the old to the new Nyāya? Furthermore, should not the need for more radical philosophical criticism break open the bounds of the systems, and move along either the more radical path of the Mādhyamika critique of that systematic discourse, or be in search for extra-systemic grounds of phenomenological evidence?

NOTES AND REFERENCES

1. On this relation, in Greek thought, see C. Kahn, *The Verb 'To Be' in Ancient Greek* (Dordrecht: Reidel, 1973). Also Aristotle, *Metaphysics*, Theta 10.
2. See J. J. Kockelmans, 'Being-True as the Basic Determination of Being', in J. J. Kockelmans (ed.), *A Companion to Martin Heidegger's 'Being and Time'* (Washington, DC: University Press of America, 1986).
3. In other words, every system's ontology is reflected in its conception of *nivikalpa* perception.
4. See W. Halbfass, 'On Being and What There Is: Indian Perspective on the Question of Being', in M. Sprung (ed.), *The Question of Being: East-West Perspectives* (University Park: Pennsylvania State University Press, 1978).
5. See ibid.
6. Kahn, *The Verb 'To Be' in Ancient Greek.*
7. Hegel, *Wissenschaft der Logik*, ed. G. Lasson, pt. 2 (Leipzig: Felix Meiner, 1970), 3.
8. *Nirukta*, i. 2.
9. B. K. Matilal, *Perception: An Essay on Classical Indian Theories of Knowledge* (Oxford: Clarendon Press, 1986), 381; P. K. Mukhopadhyaya, *Indian Realism: A Rigorous Descriptive Metaphysics* (Calcutta: K. P. Bagchi, 1985), 196.

10. Mukhopadhyaya, *Indian Realism*, 196–7.
11. See E. Husserl: 'We do not deny, but in fact emphasize that there is a fundamental categorial split in our unified conception of being' (*Logical Investigations*, ed. and trans. J. N. Findlay (New York: Humanities Press, 1970), i. 353).
12. For more on this issue see Mukhopadhyaya, *Indian Realism*, 94–8.
13. Ibid. 99.
14. For Nyāya analysis of cognition see B. K. Matilal, *The Navyanyāya Doctrine of Negation* (Cambridge, Mass.: Harvard University Press, 1968), Introduction, and J. N. Mohanty, *Gaṅgeśa's Theory of Truth* (Santiniketan: Centre of Advanced Study of Philosophy, 1966), Introduction.
15. D. H. Ingalls, *Materials for the Study of Navya Nyāya Logic* (Cambridge, Mass.: Harvard University Press, 1951), 69.
16. Śriharṣa, *Khandanakhandakhādyaṃ*. Also see S. Mookerjee, 'The Absolutist Standpoint in Logic', in *The Nava-Nālandā-Mahāvihāra Research Publication*, i, ed. S. Mookerjee (Nalanda, 1957). For further criticisms see, *Prameyakamalamārtanda*, 618–19.
17. Śālikanātha, *Prakaraṇapañcikā*, ed. A. S. Sastri (Varanasi: Banaras Hindu University, 1961), 97–100; Rāmānujācārya, *Tantrarahasya*, ed. R. S. Sastry (Baroda: Oriental Institute, 1956), 19.
18. T. Stcherbatsky, *Buddhist Logic* (New York: Dover, 1956), ii. 347.
19. 'Yadi punarsādhāraṇo bhāvo bhaved astiśabdo na prayujyeta, punaruktatvāt. Nāstīti api na vaktavyaṃ virodhāt' (on *Nyāyasūtra* I. i. 1).
20. B. Russell, *Introduction to Mathematical Philosophy*, 2nd edn. (London: Allen & Unwin, 1920).
21. Vācaspati, *Tātparyaṭīkā* on *Nyāyasūtra* I. i. 4, ed. and trans. from Stcherbatsky, *Buddhist Logic*, ii. 417.
22. Ibid. See Stcherbatsky, *Buddhist Logic*, ii. 416.
23. *Chāndogya Upaniṣad* VI. i. 4.
24. The Vedānta *Sūtras* of Bādarāyaṇa with the commentary of Śaṁkara, trans. G. Thibaut (New York: Dover, n.d.), pt. 1, p. 395. Śaṃkara's text runs thus: "bhedapratītestu tatrāgnidhūmayoranyatvaṃ niściyate, ihatu śuklaḥ kambalaḥ rohiṇī dhenuḥ, nīlamutpalamiti dravyasyaiva tasyatasya tena tena viśeṣeṇa pratīyamānatvāt naiva dravyaguṇayo-ragnidhūmayoriva bheda-pratītirasti. Tasmād dravyātmakatā guṇasya. Etena karmasāmānya viśeṣa-samavāyānāṃ dravyātmakatāvyākhātā."
25. This follows the interpretation of 'avidyā', by the Vivaraṇa school.
26. 'Sarvaṃ vastu jñātatayā ajñātatayā vā sākṣicaitanyasya viṣaya eveti' (*Vivaraṇaprameyasaṅgrahaḥ*, ii. 148).
27. See R. V. De Smet, 'Patterns and Theories of Causality', in C. T. K. Chari *et al.* (eds.), *Essays in Philosophy*, presented to T. M. P. Mahadevan (Madras: Ganesh, 1962), 347–67, esp. 366.

28. See Stcherbatsky, *Buddhist Logic*, i. 213.
29. B. K. Matilal, *Epistemology, Logic and Grammar in Indian Philosophical Analysis* (The Hague: Mouton, 1971), esp. 90.
30. 'Sarvaṃ vastu jñātatayā ajñātatayā vā sākṣicaitanasya viṣaya eva.'
31. Commentary on *Nyāyakusumānjali*, iii. 7.
32. *Nyāyatātparyatīkāpariśuddhi* on *Nyāyasūtra* I. i. 4.
33. For a more detailed discussion of this, see my 'Consciousness and Knowledge in Indian Philosophy', *Philosophy East and West*, 19, (1979), 3–10.
34. See my *Gaṅgeśa's Theory of Truth*, Introduction.
35. The possibility of such an understanding was first pointed out to me by Lawrence Davis.

7

Time, History, Man, and Nature

AN EXCURSUS INTO THE CONCEPT OF TIME

How is thought of being related to thought on time? It seems undeniable that, generally speaking, no Indian philosopher accorded to time that central place in ontology which modern Western philosophy has. But there were certain tendencies which could have led in that direction. What I have in mind are the following:

The *Maitri Upaniṣad* (vi. 15) says that there are two forms of *brahman:* time and not-time (*kālaścākālaḥ*), and then goes on to add: 'Time cooks all things' (*kālah pacati bhūtāni*). 'He who knows in what time is cooked, he is the knower of the Vedas.' But this primacy of time was never fully developed.

The Nyāya, as noted in the preceding chapter, came to hold the view that being (*sattā*) is relatedness to time in the mode of presence. But this, as was also pointed out, would have required taking time out of the list of entities that are and giving it a primacy in speculations about being. That this turn of thought, namely, founding the concept of being on that of time, did not take place is partly due to a strong tendency in the opposite direction that is anticipated very early in Vātsyāyana's commentary on the *Nyāyasūtras II.* i. 41–3.[1] Vātsyāyana argues that the present time is apprehended in two ways: first, as dissociated from the past and the future, and, secondly, as associated with them. The first kind of apprehension is made possible by the being of an object, the second by a series of actions such as cooking and cutting. This suggests that instead of the concept of being being rooted in the temporal mode of presence, the present is apprehended through the being of an object. The priority of time is replaced by the priority of being.

This is the occasion to make a few remarks on the place of time in Indian thought. First of all, there are two widely held clichés which need to be set aside. One of these is the view that for Indian

thought time was unreal, at most a mere appearance. The other is the view, accepted unquestioningly by modern Indian as well as Western writers, that the Indians held a cyclic conception of time as contradistinguished from the Judaeo-Christian conception of linear time. Both these views, as stated, are false. As regards the first, it may suffice to point out that time is held to be unreal (in a deep metaphysical sense) only by the Advaita Vedānta system, but that too must be understood in the larger context that for Advaita Vedānta the empirical order with all its categories (space, time, causality, amongst others) are metaphysically unreal. Seen in this context, the unreality of time is not a special position; space, too, is unreal. Although in many of the other systems, especially in Sāṃkhya-Yoga, the status of time is anomalous, there are indeed powerful systems of philosophy which regarded time as metaphysically real. This is especially true of the Nyāya-Vaiśeṣika. The Sāṃkhya did not admit the existence of any real time only in the sense that time had, according to this school, no existence separate from the movement of the atoms so that time as a separate entity is a creation of *buddhi*.[2] The questions on which the Indian philosophies differed were: Is time atomic or discrete, or is the continuity of time real? Is time inseparable from the changing events that fill time, or is it a separate entity in which finite entities have their places? Is time, however conceived, perceived or can it be known only by inference? It is these issues rather than the large question whether time is metaphysically real that occupied the bulk of the attention of the philosophers.[3]

A brief mention of the Nyāya-Vaiśeṣika theory of time may help to bring to clear consciousness a definitely realistic conception of time. The existence of time is proved by a reasoning which assigns a noninherent cause to the quality of determinate (*niyata*) farness (*paratva*). If *A* is later than *B*, this 'being later than' (which is a 'farness', *paratva*) is determinate (*niyata*) in the sense that *A* is later than *B* for all persons. (But what is to my east may be to your west, so that spatial farness is non-determinate, *aniyata*.) Now, farness of the former sort is then proved to be due to the conjunction of the entities concerned with time. In the (technical) language of the system, time is the non-inherent cause of the determinate farness (for such farness, as a quality, does not inhere in time).[4] Time, in Nyāya-Vaiśeṣika, is an all-pervading, partless substance (*dravya*) which appears as many only in association with

changes in it. 'Past', 'present', and 'future' are owing to an extrinsic adjunct (*upādhi*). But time is also the cause of the origin, continuation, and destruction of all effects;[5] it is a general cause for all effects.

Annaṃbhaṭṭa defines time as the cause of usages of 'past etc.', i.e. of 'past', 'present', and 'future' (atītādivyavahārahetu).[6] Under 'etc.' are to be included also usages of 'older' and 'younger' and 'simultaneity' and 'non-simultaneity' (*yougapadya-ayougapadya*).[7] Since all effects are, on this theory, related to time as its general cause, one may also define time as what is the efficient cause (*nimitta*) by being the locus (*adhikaraṇavidhayā*), where this causality is determined (*nirūpita*) by an effectness (*kāryatā*) that is limited (*avacchinna*) by temporal relation (*kālikasambandha*). Temporal relation is a relation in which all effects are in time (though they may be in other things in other relations).[8]

Even if Vedānta does not regard time as real, a Vedānta writer defines time as what is manifested by the uses of 'past', 'present'. 'future', etc. owing to the limiting adjunct (*upādhi*) of the sun's movement.[9] A different account is given by Patañjali in his commentary Mahābhāṣya: time is that because of which (*yena*) growth (*upacaya*) and decay (*apachaya*) of things are to be noticed.[10]

These should suffice bring home the point that it is very far from the truth to say that the Indian thinkers regarded time to be unreal.

Did they, however, regard time as cyclic? To the larger issue, whether the metaphors of 'arrow' and 'circle' are mutually exclusive, and if the metaphor of 'circle' does not appear within the Western, even the Christian, and also the scientific view of time, I cannot attend in this work.[11] First of all, it should be borne in mind that these are convenient 'geometrical' metaphors. Secondly, the theory of cyclic changes (the cycle of creation and dissolution, the cycle of happiness and suffering, the cycles of birth and death, and so on, pictures of which abound in Hindu and Buddhist religious and mythological writings) should not be confused with a theory of cyclic time. If these cycles succeed each other, such succession requires a non-cyclic time. Thirdly, to represent time as beginningless and endless (*anādi* and *ananta*) is, as should be obvious, not representing it as cyclic. The idea of *yugas* or epochs (or their larger multiples) is not *eo ipso* the idea of

time cycles: it is at one level determining units of cosmic time-calculation, at another amounts to an idea of recurring valuational types—but not in any case one of 'eternal recurrence'. Let me conclude this excursus by suggesting an analogy. In economic theory, one talks of economic cycles, of cycles of inflation and recession. These cycles do not imply a theory of cyclic time. The Indian philosophers did *not* hold such a theory.

Underlying the ascription of a conception of cyclic time to the Indians, there is also a confusion between the sacred time (of religious mythologies) and the profane time (of natural and historical order). It is wellknown in modern phenomenology of religion that sacred time is cyclic—no matter in what religion. Thus writes Mercia Eliade:

> [The] religious man lives in two kinds of time, of which the more important, sacred time, appears under the paradoxical aspect of a circular time, reversible and recoverable, a sort of eternal mythical present that is periodically reintegrated by means of rites.[12]

Not only does the religious point of view look upon, or rather experience, sacred time as 'perpetually returning', but it regards this mythical time as providing the foundation for the profane time of nature and history. From this perspective, the profane time, despite its linear character, experiences the eruption of the cyclic, ever-returning sacred time (as, for example, when the religious events return and are re-enacted in the sacred calendar). But this is a feature of all religious experience, and not of the Hindu or the Buddhist alone. When the latter are singled out as eschewing a cyclic view of time, the readers of the appropriate texts obliterate the distinction between the two levels of discourse, and, as a consequence, end up regarding the time of nature and of history—the profane time—to be cyclic as well.

HISTORY

One cannot at this point avoid the question: what then accounts for the insensitivity of the Indian mind to history, that is to say, for its well-known ahistorical stance? If we restrict ourselves to the philosophical schools (*darśanas*), it is undeniable that a philosophical concern with history is indeed missing in them. None of

the *darśanas* recognized, for example, historical knowledge as an irreducible variety of true cognition (*pramā*) or as caused by a distinct sort of means of true cognition (*pramāṇa*). We know that some, called the Paurāṇikas, did regard tradition (*aitihya*) as an independent source of knowledge. This came, I suppose, nearest to a recognition of historical knowledge as being *sui generis*. But the Paurāṇikas never gained importance amongst the classical schools, and even the most traditionalist amongst them, such as the Pūrvamīmāmsā did not accord to tradition that epistemic status. While the question of why the Indian thinkers were indifferent to history remains, one must, while doing comparative philosophy, also keep in mind that Western thought came to take history seriously only in modern times (despite the nascent historicity of Judaeo-Christian self-understanding).

Writing history and taking history as philosophically significant are two different things. The Greeks did produce a Thucydides, but classical Greek thought was at least as ahistorical as Indian thought was. The classical Indians did not produce great history nor did they show philosophical concern with history. Before dealing with the latter, i.e. with their ahistorical philosophical stance, let me briefly mention what we know about the classical Indian understanding of history itself.

The dictionary *Vācaspatyam* gives the following definition of *itihāsa* (the closest, but not exact, equivalent of 'history'): *itihāsa* means 'arranged in the form of stories and past happenings, conveying instruction in *dharma, artha, kāma*, and *mokṣa*, i.e. in [the goals of] righteousness, wealth, sensuous love, and spiritual freedom'.[13] Kautilya writes that *itihāsa* includes the *purāṇas* (tales of past ages),[14] *itivṛtta* (dynastic chronicles; also accounts of men and times that are past), *ākhyāyikā* (short tales), *udāharaṇa* (exemplary stories), *dharmaśāstra* (laws), and arthaśāstra (political economy).[15] *Itihāsa* and *purāṇa* seem to be identified or at least closely juxtaposed as early as *Bṛhadāraṇyaka Upaniṣad*.[16] An old etymology of the word *itihāsa* is given by Durga's commentary on *Nirukta* ii. 10: it lets us know 'thus it was'.[17] The *aitihāsikas* or historians were the traditional story-tellers. According to Pusalkar, history (*itihāsa*), for the ancient Indians, comprised political, social, economic, and religious histories, but also polity, philosophy, cosmography, and genealogy of sages and of gods[18]—both profane history and sacred history. C. H. Philips notes that the

Purāṇas, around the first millennium A.D., exhibit the fundamental assumption that the universe changes through 'enormous cycles of time' (which, in view of my earlier remarks, really are enormous cycles of change) and inculcate the supreme lesson of history for man as cultivation of a sentiment of calm resignation (*śāṅtarasa*). (A far more reliable sense of chronology is exhibited, according to Philips, by the Jain[19] and the Buddhist authors.) Even this Puranic sense for history is absorbed into the poetic literature, and history tends to become legend.[20]

The historian R. C. Majumdar notes that the practice of keeping chronicles of kings continued in Nepal, Kashmir, Gujarat, and a few other places, and quotes from Hiuen Tsang to the effect that each province had its own official for recording events, good and bad. However, the extant historical biographies (such as *Harṣa-carita*) and historical narratives (such as *Prabandha-cintāmaṇi*) do not 'reach the standard which entitles them to be ranked as 'historical' in the proper sense of the term'. 'They are limited in their objects, eulogistic in character, rhetorical or poetic in style, and aiming more at edification and entertainment than a statement of positive facts.'[21] Nevertheless, Majumdar also recognizes that a true conception of history and a conception of its correct method was not altogether lacking. In fact, in his view, Kalhaṇa, whose *Rājataraṅgiṇi* is admittedly the best history book written in Sanskrit, required that the historian cultivate a detached mind free from prejudices, and he himself consult ordinances, inscriptions, written records, coins, and old monuments.[22] Kalhaṇa criticizes earlier accounts such as that of Kṣemendra. But he does not satisfy his own standards: he appeals to supernatural explanations and refers to himself as a *kavi*, i.e. a poet. He writes that his purpose is to ascertain true places and times, to please his readers, and to make them realize the impermanence of things, thereby enabling them to foster the sentiment of calmness (*śāntarasa*).[23] He makes use of the idea of fate—of fate which leads kings even against their will,[24] which brings it about that the strong are deceived by the weak,[25] but which can still be overcome by a powerful king.[26] I will conclude with Majumdar's apt remark: 'this one work is sufficient to prove that the ancient Hindus did not lack true historical sense'.[27]

It is not, then, the case that the ancient Indians did not have a historical sense. The connection between history and story was

clearly there, and much of early history, even some of contemporary historical writing, is edifying. Direct history by a participant did not exist, critical history of the past is to be found in its rudiments, and 'exemplary' history was emphasized. What was lacking, I would suggest, was a sense of the *importance* of history.

It would not do, as noted earlier, to trace this lack of a sense of importance of history to a metaphysical (or religious) belief in the unreality of time, for not all, not even most, Indian philosophers regarded time as unreal. We also cannot hold the conception of cyclic time—the endless and beginningless recurrence of events—responsible, for it is highly doubtful if this conception of time was held by anyone. Even if it were found in the *Purāṇas* (it can be read into them only by misinterpreting cycles of change as cycles of time), none of the philosophical schools made any substantial use of such a conception in their ontologies. What the doctrine of cycles asserts is not the recurrence of events, but rather of broad patterns of values. It is not that every single event or individual belonging to one epoch or cycle had been prefigured in an infinite number of other such cycles preceding it. No cycle is identical with another in content. Only the moral and spiritual ideals, the human virtues and failings, the patterns of social and individual behaviour—the form, in brief—is what is supposed to repeat itself. Character-types, symbolized in mythical figures, are repeated, not particulars or individuals.

History as the series of events or as the record of events in their particularities is assured. But history as a significant process of achieving new values that were not achieved before is denied. It may still have a didactic and exemplary use. If philosophy is concerned with ultimate values and ageless, eternal truths, it need have no concern with history of events.

A recognition of the reality of time, though a necessary condition of a philosophical concern with time, is not yet sufficient for it. History is not just a temporal process. Recognition that the world is a process in which nothing abides is not an index of one's sense of history. There are Indian Heracliteans, but no Indian Hegelians (though Rāmānuja has been wrongly taken to be one). History is basically the history of man. The history of man is the history of human consciousness. What is needed for a sense of history is a recognition of the historicity of consciousness. Now, in

general, for Hindu thought, consciousness is above change. Where, as in Buddhism, the concept of process is extended to consciousness, this process is conceived as a series of instantaneous moments; with *Nirvāṇa* this flow is arrested and transcended. *Nirvāṇa* is beyond history as much as *mokṣa* is, and cannot be conceived as an achievement *of* history within history. The cycle of birth and rebirth is transhistorical. The law of *karma* made room for both determination by the past and initiative at present, but it is not the sort of determination that the idea of history requires. In the strict sense, history is not the sojourn of an individual soul through a series of its transmigrations, but a gradual advance of an institution, a race, a nation, a social group, or of mankind in general towards a far-off goal through an ordered succession of events and experiences, actions and decisions, thoughts and sufferings. *Karma* is individualistic in its conception, rebirth and transmigration are transhistorical. Collective *karma* and collective *mokṣa* could have provided a basis for concern with history. These ideas were on the horizon,[28] but were never fully exploited till modern times.[29]

The time whose reality is relevant for our present attempt to unravel the deeper motivations of Indian thinking on these matters is not just the physical time or even the cosmic time in which natural events, human experiences (as well as mythical enactments), take place. What is needed is the conception of historical time as distinguished from the cosmic time, and, whatever else may go into the notion of historical time, surely the notion of the temporality of consciousness is an essential ingredient in it. The temporality of consciousness is not just consciousness's being in time in the same way as any natural event is in it. It is rather the fact that consciousness is time itself, that every event of consciousness carries with it the original, further unanalysable and irreducible temporal significations of past, present, and future in one.[30] But such a theory of consciousness would also entail a rejection of that conception of self or *ātman* which is almost a pervasive feature of Hindu thought. For temporality is, in that case, required to characterize not empirical consciousness alone but also transcendental consciousness. In fact, empirical consciousness, as the consciousness belonging to me—this man here and now—may be located, via my body with which it is seemingly

inalienably connected, in the cosmic, physical time. But even if I bracket the empirical adjuncts of my consciousness, even if I overlook the fact that it is *my* consciousness tied to this psychophysical organism which is *in* time, the phenomenological residuum, i.e. consciousness as such, though not any longer locatable in physical time, is yet characterized by original temporality in the sense elaborated by Husserl. An essential temporality of *ātman* is a necessary presupposition of a serious philosophical concern for history.

MAN, SUBJECT AND PERSON

One remarkable feature of contemporary ontological thinking is a concern with the meaning of Being in the context of the problem of time, and since original temporality is sought to be located in the structure of consciousness (Husserl) or of human existence or *Dasein* (Heidegger), ontology has been sought to be grounded either in a phenomenology of transcendental subjectivity or in an analysis of the structure of *Dasein*. In the former case, the idea of objectivity occupies the central place, in the latter case, the idea of *Dasein* or of human existence.

While it is true, I think, that the concept of man is not directly thematized by the classical Hindu philosophies, [31] already in the Upaniṣads, the concept of *ātman* is used to understand the earlier question, what is *brahman*? A typical passage where cosmological speculations on the nature of *brahman* are abandoned in favour of a quasianthropological one is found in *Bṛhadāraṇyaka Upaniṣad* ii. 1. In this well-known text, we find Bālāki Gārgya approaching the King, Ajātaśatru, with the intention of explaining *brahman*, and he attempts to define it, in succession, as the soul in the sun, the moon, lightning, ether, wind, fire, water, etc. The king in each case points out that the entity under consideration is really subordinate and not autonomous (as *brahman* should be). Finally, he takes the brahmin to a person in deep sleep, and says that that from which he will wake up and wherein he enters during deep sleep is *ātman*, and that is *brahman*. The point of this remarkable dialogue appears to be to use the *ātman* of a person as a clue to the understanding of the nature of *brahman*.

What, however, is *ātman*? *Bṛhadāraṇyaka Upaniṣad* iv. 1 gives

six definitions by Janaka: *ātman* is the speech, the breath, the eye, the ear, the mind, and the heart, each one ascribed to a well-known teacher. Yājñyavalkya rejects these definitions: these sense organs or faculties are mere 'supports' (*āyatana*) for the manifestation of *ātman*, which is their foundation (*pratiṣthā*).

Perhaps one more text, *Chāndogya Upaniṣad* VIII. vii.1–VIII. xii. 6, may be worth quoting: The god (*deva*) Indra and the demon (*asura*) Virocana go to Prajāpati with a view to receiving instruction about the nature of *ātman*. The lessons given by Prajāpati are, in that order: the *ātman* is that which is seen looking into the eye of another, or into a bowl of water, or into a mirror, it is that which is reflected in these media, complete even to the hairs and nails. Clearly *ātman* is here said to be the body, so at least both Indra and Virocana appear to interpret the lesson when they complain, after reflecting on it, that this putative *ātman* is subject to miseries and sufferings and so could not be the real *ātman*. The context, however, leaves open the possibility that both misunderstand the lesson, that what was intended is that the *ātman* is the subject of all seeing. The second lesson insists that the *ātman* is that which 'wanders around freely in dream'. Again there is the ambiguity as between the dream-body and the dreaming subject. The objection of Indra is that, in dream, there is no doubt some freedom but the person enjoys and weeps *as if* the experiences are his own. A body (or a person) I see in dream may be enjoying or weeping, i.e. subject to the same affections as the real person in the real world. But it is also the case that the dreaming subject enjoys his dream or is afflicted by it, i.e. weeps and suffers. The assumption in both these lessons, as well as underlying the responses of Indra and Virocana, is that the *ātman*, whatever it may be, must be free from all afflictions and sufferings, from both pleasure and pain. This obviously is not the criterion one applies when one tests if a conception of self is to be accepted or not, if, for example, my body is my self: one applies such criteria as identity, possibility of memory and recognition, and self-ascription of both physical and mental predicates. Although later philosophers—such as Śaṃkara in his examination of Buddhism and the Nyāya-Vaiśeṣika writers in rejecting the theory that 'I' designates my body—do employ such criteria, the Upanisadic texts do not. This makes almost unavoidable the question whether the Upanisadic *ātman* should be translated as 'self'. There is no

doubt, however, that the *ātman*, even as it is the theme of these early discourses, has something to do with the human person—that, in other words, our access to the *ātman* is provided by the human person.

The final lesson by Prajāpati in the dialogue we are discussing is: when a man is completely immersed in deep, dreamless sleep, that is the *ātman*. But what? Not the person who is in deep sleep, for the person would be a familiar human being—J.N.M., for example, but J.N.M. is not the *ātman*. Is it the sleeping person's internal state of being in deep sleep? Indra objects that if this were *ātman, ātman* would amount to utter annihilation, for nothing is there. He does not even know himself to be *ātman*, nor does he know anything whatsoever.

The dialogue ends here, with Prajāpati adding, 'Oh Indra, this body is mortal, it is subject to death. It is the seat (*adhiṣthāna*) of the immortal and incorporeal self. One who is bodily is subject to pleasure and pain; there is no end to his pleasure and pain. He who is incorporeal is not touched by pleasure and pain.' However, the tradition looks upon his intention to be to suggest: either that the *ātman*, is the fourth, transcendent state (*turīya*) as distinguished from the first three (waking, dreaming, dreamless sleep); or that the *ātman* comprehends all four possibilities, it being that which persists through all four; or both. We do not learn what this fourth state is. Is it one alongside the other three? But these three are familiar empirical states a person goes through. The fourth may be regarded as a supernormal state of mystic experience in which one's separate individuality is transcended, and yet the *ātman*, comprehends all four. One becomes hopelessly confused.

Just when philosophical interest in 'man' was about to emerge, we find Indian thought displacing it by another powerful concept, the *ātman*, which was then construed by the tradition as being *my* (or *your*) *ātman*, and by the Anglophile as being my, or your, Self—as though capitalization of the 'S' was sufficient to prevent one from looking here for what the English usage, or Western philosophical concern, understands by 'self'. One continues to do that even when the *ātman*, is construed, as in Advaita Vedānta, as pure, undifferentiated, all-pervading Spirit or Consciousness (*cit*). It is still held to be my (or your) Self, if not my (or your) self—the conceptual confusion is only beginning to tighten its grip.

This ambiguity is reflected in the very etymology of that word *ātman*. Vinoba Bhave quotes the following etymologizing verse:

> Yadāpnoti yadādatte yaccātti viṣayāniha
> Yaccasya santato bhavas tasmādatmeti kīrtyate.[32]

The four verbal roots, according to this verse, are *ap* (*vyāptou* = to pervade), *a + da* (*ādāne* = to give), *ad* (*bhakṣaṇe* = to eat) and *at* (*satatyagamane* = to constantly accompany). Vinoba himself prefers to derive *ātman* from a pre-Vedic root *at*, which is close to both *as* and *bhū*, the former meaning mere being and the latter meaning 'to have different forms, to become', so that *ātman*, would mean the pure formless Being which, however, has become in many forms—clearly suggesting the Vedántic metaphysical Absolute Reality. Note that if we insisted on the roots meaning 'to give' and 'to eat', *ātman*, would have a clearly personal meaning, a meaning which, banished from the *darśanas*, found refuge in ordinary language. Not too far round the corner is a connection with the German verb *ātmen* (to breathe). Emphasize the root meaning 'to accompany constantly', and you are close to a sense of 'self'.

In the light of this deep ambiguity, my interpretive strategy will be to make use of a distinction between 'subject' and 'person', which I will explicate as follows:

The subject is spirit understood as consciousness, for which the world is object. If there is knowledge of the world, or of an object, that knowledge is for a subject. Subjectivity or consciousness is the source of that revelation which makes knowledge of an object possible. An object as such does not reveal itself. It needs to be made an object for a subject. The word 'subjective', in its ordinary English usage, often signifies what is relative to a subject, and so lacks universality. But that precisely is being denied, by implication: as the concept of subject is being formulated here, what is for a subject is not relative to it, but may be the content of a universally valid cognition. To be the subject of knowledge requires transcending one's personal interests and prejudices, and to attain universality, such that knowledge is, in principle, valid for everyone. Thus the epistemological subject is disinterested and also universal, for otherwise knowledge could not be objective and could not be valid for everyone. It is not being denied that there is a perfectly legitimate sense in which it is a person who knows. But,

if a person's claim to know is to be sustained, then his being the person that he is should be irrelevant to his knowing what he knows. For what he knows should be an objective truth, which could be known by any other person as well. His knowing it requires that *qua* knower he be disinterested, even if he might have been led to his knowledge by interests and his knowledge may give rise to further interests. If a person cannot raise himself above his life of interest, if he cannot go beyond, or rather escape, the point of view relative to the sort of person he is, then he cannot know. In other words, in order to be able to know, he must be a subject, over and above being a person. Furthermore, being that for which the world is an object the subject *qua* subject is also not a mundane thing, but a transcendental principle.

The person, on the other hand, is a concrete, corporeal entity which calls itself 'I', a bodily psychic unity that is appropriated into the structure of a unitary self-consciousness. It is in the world, and with others. Its mode of being in the world is not an epistemological subject's having a world stand over against it, but a concernful, caring willing and acting—temporally structured by systems of recalling, anticipating, and lack of fulfilment. In the language of the Indian philosophers, the person is characterized by agency (*kartṛtva*) and being an enjoyer (*bhoktṛtva*); he is an agent and an enjoyer; his being an enjoyer and being an agent together form one total structure of mundaneity. For the person, objects are primarily not objects (*viṣayāṇi*) of knowledge, but objects of affective–volitional concern (*arthyate anena*). They are either attractive or repulsive, either to be acquired or reached, or to be shunned or avoided. In so far as it is also the person who knows, his knowledge enters into this structure and determines the life of interest and is determined by it. As a mundane occurrence, knowledge of an object gives rise to desire (*icchā*) to acquire or shun it; such desire leads to appropriate action (*pravṛtti*), which ends either in success or in failure, giving rise to pleasure or pain as the case may be.

The Indian philosophers recognized this possibility of looking at knowledge in two radically different manners. From the point of view of the subject, knowledge is manifestation of the object; its entire purpose, its total *telos*, is fulfilled in that manifestation. From the point of view of the person, knowledge is an event which impinges into the affective–volitional structure, giving rise to

desire, appropriate action, success and failure, pleasure and pain.

It is, therefore, not true that Indian philosophy does not have a concept of person. However, the concept of subject was the dominating concept, and, under its dominance, the concept of person remained philosophically underdeveloped.

This primacy of the concept of subject is exemplified, in different ways, in several features of Indian thought:

1. First, almost all Indian theories of knowledge conceive of knowing as manifesting, revealing, illuminating, and unconcealing the object of knowledge. Even where knowledge is propositional or inferential, what is known, precisely as it is known, is out there in the world independently of the knowledge. Buddhism alone had the concept of knowledge as construction, but even there the constructing, synthesizing agent is not a subjective unity, an ego or a person; in fact, there is no agent other than the series of instantaneous cognitions with their inherited, but beginningless, tendency to conceptualize and objectify. Although most Indian epistemologies recognized the role of the body in the acquisition of knowledge, that role, as well as the role of the mental and intellectual faculties, lies only in causing knowledge to occur; however, when knowledge does occur, its sole function, *qua* knowledge, is to manifest its object. It is not surprising, therefore, that all Indian philosophies, except some forms of Buddhism, were realistic. This contrasts with the predominant tradition of modern Western thought, at least since Kant, that knowledge is synthesis, construction, interpretation of data in the light of conceptual frameworks, etc.

2. Where the concept of person is most likely to be autonomous and irreducible, namely in theory of action we also find shadows of the dominance of the concept of subject. In the mundane structure of desire, action, success or failure, pleasure or pain which centres around the concept of person, an action is done out of a desire or want and is intended to bring about a consequence which, in the long run, is satisfying the desire or removing the want. But such an action 'binds' the person to that structure. Yet the same action which binds, when performed within the mundane structure, may be a road to freedom if performed with 'non-attachment'. But how can the person who, by definition, leads a life of interest act without attachment? Is not a 'disinterested person' an inconsistent

concept, unless disinterestedness is a sort of interest? This seems to be so, when the *Bhagavadgītā* recommends that actions be performed not out of selfish interests but out of altruistic motive of 'gathering people together' (*lokasaṃgraha*). But the *Gītā* also speaks of complete non-attachment, of 'inaction in action', of renouncing the sense of being the doer, of seeing action as though it belonged to the mechanism of *māyā* (the realm of appearance). We have here an ethics of action in which the agent ceases to be the person that he is, but reduces himself to a pure subject. Universality (of moral action) is sought by progressively emptying the person of all contents and of all interests and by reducing himself to zero, to a mere witness-consciousness. What else but the primacy of the concept of subject can lead to such a concept of moral action? We should remember however, that this is not the concept of action in the tradition of Hindu liturgy, social ethics, and law, where a complex nexus of duties and obligations are taken to bind the individual person to other persons, to gods, and to nature, and where a person's actions were supposed to carry the weight of tradition.

3. The concept of person, where it does appear to emerge in the philosophies, is a 'weak' concept. A concept of person is strong if it formulates an irreducible and unanalysable unity. Examples are: the Kantian concept of end-in-itself, Scheler's concept of act-centre, and Strawson's concept of the subject of *p*-predicates. A concept of person is weak if it formulates a unity that is analysable into components none of which, on its part, yields a concept of person: such is the analysis of empirical self into the pure consciousness (*puruṣa*) and nature (*prakṛti*) which remains paradigmatic for Hindu thought. The former by itself, even if individualized, as in Sāṃkhya, or universalized as in some systems of Vedānta, is still a witness self, an uninvolved observer, disinterested, neutral (*madhyastha*), the pure subject of knowledge but not an agent or enjoyer. Nor is the psychophysical body–inner-sense–ego–intellect complex by itself a person, for it is not self-conscious; it can, for example, act without knowing that it does so. The person is a derivative unity of two heterogeneous elements: a pure witness self, i.e. pure subject, and a psychophysical complex. The latter provides the causal conditions of knowing, the former the final epistemic condition of manifestation.

Western philosophy, especially since Descartes's founding of philosophy on the *ego cogito*, has been—as insisted upon by Heidegger—a metaphysics of subjectivity. How can we, in the face of such an authoritative characterization, hope to be able to say that it is not so much the concept of subject as that of person which determines Western thought's understanding of man and his relation to the world and to others? It should be emphasized that I have said 'not so much. . .as'. In other words, while the role of subjectivity is not being denied, the hypothesis, rather, is that Western attempts to understand the subject have been, more often than not, modelled after the concept of person. For the Greeks, the subject of knowledge is the rational faculty of an individual soul recollecting what is already implicit in it. The Cartesian *ego cogito* is the pure inner reflective life of the ego of the meditating philosopher. The residue that is left, in the world of corporeal things, including the body of the philosopher himself, has been subjected to methodical doubt. It is not the subject that is the ultimate condition of the possibility of knowledge and experience, but rather the apodictic basis on which philosophy as a rational reconstruction of experience was sought to be founded. It is the person, stripped of his corporeality, in the interior of his reflective thinking, secure against possible doubt and error. But it is still the interior of a person, of a monad, but not the principle of subjectivity which is universal rather than individual. The Kantian transcendental unity of self-consciousness is, to be sure, what I have said the Cartesian *ego cogito* is not: it is the condition of the possibility of all knowledge and experience, and not the apodictic basis for philosophy as a science. It is not the interior of a person, for both the interior and the exterior belong equally well to the phenomenal world, to the domain of possible objects of experience. It is also not the ego in its reflective thinking act, but rather the unity which underlies, without necessarily surfacing to be explicitly recognized, even the most unreflective of our perceptual judgements. Thus far, it is indeed subjectivity in the true sense, subjectivity that is also the condition of the possibility of objectivity in the sense of intersubjectivity. What it constitutes are not subjective-relative, but just the opposite: objective-universal and objective-necessary. But, at the same time, it should be noted that this Kantian unity constitutes objectivity; it is the unity of synthesis. Kant appears to have wavered between saying that the

transcendental unity of apperception is the source of all constituting, synthesizing functions and saying that, whereas all synthesis is the achievement of the faculty of imagination, understanding (which is the transcendental unity of apperception in relation to the synthesis of imagination)[33] only raises the already achieved synthesis to the level of self-consciousness. The constituting, synthesizing ego is but a transcendental rational ego, caught, not in the interiority of its reflective thinking about itself, but in its activity of prescribing laws to nature. It is not unreasonable, therefore, to find, even in the First Critique, anticipations of the Second, to understand constitutive functions of subjectivity in the light of the legislative autonomy of the rational person as a moral being. The constituting ego is a transcendental, rational person. The Kantian Critique is a philosophy of the French Revolution.

The same is no less true of Husserl's constituting transcendental ego. Without entering into the complexities of this Husserlian concept, I would like to draw attention to only a couple of aspects in order to bring home my point. In the first place, the Husserlian transcendental ego is constituting, and to that extent partakes of my characterization of the Kantian transcendental unity of apperception. But its closeness to the concept of person becomes clearer still, more than in the case of the Kantian doctrine, when one recalls that, for Husserl, there is a 'wonderful parallelism' between the transcendental and the empirical, and also that the transcendental ego has a genesis, even if its genesis, as autogenesis, is radically different from the 'origin' of objects in the intentional structure of acts. The parallelism thesis is to the effect that every 'empirical' experience may be, once it is subject to purification by the epoché, i.e. divested of its naïvety, rehabilitated within the life of the transcendental ego, so that the transcendental ego and the empirical ego are both the same and yet not the same. The transcendental ego has all the richness and diversity of contents of the empirical ego, only minus the latter's naïve self-understanding as a man in the world, as a part of nature, i.e. as a mundane entity. The thesis of autogenesis is to the effect that the transcendental ego is constituted through a genetic process of development, as intentional experiences, while they, as act-intentionalities constituting the sense-structure of the objective world, are also unified, through associative synthesis and habitualities, into the unity of life of one ego.[34] Corresponding to the

'genesis' of the transcendental ego, we have—by virtue of the parallelism thesis—a possible thesis of the psychogenesis of the empirical ego, confirmed by developmental psychology of the Piagetian sort. Also instructive, in our present context, is the concept of the transcendental ego's 'sphere of ownness', as outlined in §44 of the *Cartesian Meditations.* Amongst the structures of this sphere of ownness, we have: the lived body as the field of sensations over which the ego 'rules'. It is also not surprising that the transcendental egos should belong to a transcendental community, or even that one would want to speak of a 'transcendental ancestor'.

As the transcendental ego, in its concreteness, moves closer to the concept of a transcendental person, the Husserlian 'transcendental subjectivity' comes more and more to oscillate between the 'transcendental observer' and the concrete historical life of subjective experiences, whose two poles are the constituted world of objects and the transcendental ego. It is the former, namely the 'transcendental observer', which comes closer to the Hindu concept of a witness self (*sākṣi*).

While characterizing a large segment of Western metaphysics as being both a metaphysics of presence and a philosophy of consciousness, modern critics have subjected both to a radical criticism. For this criticism, a philosophy of consciousness is committed to a metaphysics of presence inasmuch as consciousness is characterized as 'presence to itself' and also inasmuch as the world is presented to consciousness as a representation. It is to these two aspects of this criticism that we turn in order to test their validity in the context of a non-Western, namely Indian, metaphysics of subjectivity—leaving the question untouched but open whether they are true of all Western thinking on consciousness. In other words, we are asking two questions: can we say of all Indian philosophies of subjectivity: (1) that they understand its being as self-presence, and (2) that they regard consciousness as representational and the being of the world as being-represented to consciousness? The answers to both the questions should be in the negative, if the questions pertain to the entire range of Indian thought. For just as there were philosophers who denied the self-presence or *svayaṃprakāśatva* of consciousness but continued to use the discourse of consciousness, there were also those who denied its representative function. In fact, the Indian philosophies

include (1) those who regarded consciousness as self-presence and representational (*sākāra*); (2) those who regard it as self-presence but not representational (*nirākāra*); and (3) those who regard it as lacking in self-presence as well as in representational character. The Buddhists held the first view, Advaita Vedānta the second, and the Nyāya the third. It was never regarded as prima facie to be the case that consciousness was to represent reality within it. In fact, the distinction between consciousness and mind (or the mental) helped most philosophers to transcend the concept of a representing consciousness. The mind (*manas*) was regarded either as an instrumental cause (as in Nyāya) of the production of knowledge while the cognitive event was as little mental as the act of cutting was located in the knife one cuts with; or as a substance, subtle matter in fact, which undergoes modifications (*vṛtti*) to fit the shape and form of the object apprehended, but which still is not awareness. Consciousness illuminates, without representing within it, all objects—outer and inner, objects as known and objects as unknown. The illuminating consciousness is not a representing consciousness. The intentional consciousness need not have to be representing.

There are two respects in which the Indian thinking on subjectivity needs to be supplemented. In the first place, the concept of intentionality, the directedness of consciousness towards the world, has, more often than not, been neglected. The Nyāya recognizes the intrinsic object-directedness of all states of consciousness, but this recognition loses its effectiveness owing to the overall causal explanation of consciousness in the system, so that the intentional consciousness is reduced to one sort of objective property amongst others. The systems which recognize the subjectivity of consciousness, its transmundane character, tend to deny intentionality to it as in the two most influential systems: Sāṃkhya and Advaita Vedānta. Śaivism possibly, and Rāmānuja to be sure, want to have both: consciousness as an irreducible phenomenon and its intentionality. But for Rāmānuja, the subject becomes a person. The inseparability of soul and body, *cit* and *acit*, becomes the decisive ontological category. It is perhaps in Śaivism that we have the most exciting possibilities of a developed phenomenology of subjectivity.

But once intentionality is ascribed to the non-mundane consciousness, such a consciousness, as the pure subjectivity, cannot

simply manifest the world which stands over against it. For that mere illumination, the non-intentional self-presence of consciousness is enough. The intentional consciousness, if it does not simply represent the world within it as in a mirror, if it does not simply let the world emerge into light from darkness, i.e. be an object for it, will also confer on it meaning and significance. It will then constitute the world. But constitution is not an act of creation out of nothing, completed at one instant, but a historical process in which the new significations are constituted on the basis of sedimented layers of meanings. But as the intentional, temporal, historically constituting subjectivity assumes responsibility for the worlds it constitutes, the reflective consciousness which lays bare this process of world-constitution becomes the 'transcendental observer'. Realism is preserved but recedes: what is merely made to emerge into manifestedness is not the world (for that is being historically constituted), but that world-constituting function and process of subjectivity.

One of the reasons why this constitutive dimension of subjectivity was not generally appreciated in Indian thought is that the idea of grades of subjectivity, so much on the surface in the Upaniṣads and the literature on Yoga, never took root in the major systems, where subjectivity, understood as awareness, was a homogeneous source of illumination. It is here that contemporary Indian thought has valuable insights to offer and succeeded in making use of some neglected strands of the tradition. The idea of grades of consciousness has been elaborately worked out by Sri Aurobindo, and since, for him, each grade of consciousness has its own mode of intuition, there are grades of intuition too.[35] Each level of reality, material, vital, and the mental, embodies a corresponding level of consciousness. More directly pertinent for my present purpose is K. C. Bhattacharya's concept of grades of subjectivity: the bodily, the psychic, and the spiritual.[36] But at each level, subjectivity is not what constitutes the corresponding object, but what enjoys itself as freedom from it. I should add, however, combining the insights of Husserlian phenomenology and K. C. Bhattacharya, that transcendental subjectivity is both constitutive of, and enjoys its freedom from, the objectivity meant or intended. The world is constituted by transcendental subjectivity; and the latter being 'transcendental' is also transworldly.

Merleau-Ponty has often insisted that the objectification of the

world and, correlatively, the interiorization of subjectivity into a purely inner life with no exteriority, have their genesis in the 'original sin' of objectification of the body. Again, Indian thought's attitude towards the body exhibits the familiar discrepancy between a large mass of original insights embedded in the culture and practices and the systematized thoughts of the major systems. The major systems, leaving aside the Sāṃkhya-Yoga, have a fully objective conception of body. Not only is this so in the Nyāya-Vaiśeṣika, but also in Vedānta. Body is *acit*, *jada*. The distinction between self and body is the most decisive metaphysical truth to be known and experienced. Parallel to this objective conception of body, there was also, in Indian thought, a conception of body that removes body from the world of things and assigns to it a decisive and positive role in the cultivation of the subjective attitude. The understanding of the body in the language of the three *guṇas* (*sattva*, *rajas*, and *tamas*) which form the basis of the Sāṃkhya understanding of the universe in the same language, and the Yoga emphasis on the role of the body in spiritual life, are suggestive of this positive role. For K. C. Bhattacharya, the bodily subjectivity (or the felt, as contradistinguished from the observed, body) provides the first awareness of freedom from objects, and arouses a demand whose complete fulfilment requires the cultivation of the spiritual attitude.[37]

The respects, then, in which the concept of subjectivity in Indian thought needs to be improved upon are: (1) a recognition of intentionality as constitutive and (2) a thematic use of the idea of grades of subjectivity whose foundation is the bodily subjectivity. To both, Indian thought can add, from within its own resources, the idea of freedom. The constitutive intentionality, if it is to be transcendental, has to be 'free' from what it constitutes. Each grade of subjectivity, then, would represent a freedom from whatever is its constitutive accomplishment.

I began by suggesting that whereas Indian thought accorded primacy to the 'pure subject' for which the world is object, Western thought accords primacy to the person who lives in his world and the world of his community. Western attempts to comprehend subjectivity have resulted in a sort of transcendental person in a community of transcendental persons. Indian attempts to comprehend person have resulted in a 'weak' concept of person, according to which a person is a compound of two heterogeneous

principles, *cit* and *acit*, consciousness and body. Western thought has the notion of constituting and therefore historical subjectivity, but needs that of 'transcendental observer' if relativism has to be overcome; Indian thought has the concept of *sākṣicaitanya*, the witness-consciousness, but what it is a witness to is a finished, objective world, not the world being constituted, through history, by a community of intentional egos.

As a consequence of this *rapprochement*, two contrasted concepts, subject and person, exhibit themselves as two unstable poles between which man's understanding of himself necessarily moves. It is not so much in reducing the one to the other as in recognizing this unstable oscillation that the more promising future for philosophical anthropology appears to lie.

THE CONCEPT OF NATURE

Again, from the mass of Hindu and Buddhist speculations about the nature of the empirical world,[38] I will single out only a few, indeed three typical accounts—not also, even in these three cases, in their details but only in their general structures so that we can bring to clear relief the general framework within which they thought.

The problems of continuity versus discontinuity and change versus permanence concerned the Indian thinkers as much as they did the European thinkers. Hindu thinking took two forms: the atomism of the Vaiśeṣikas and the theory of original, *Ur*-Nature (*prakṛti*) of Sāṃkhya. The former found discontinuity at the root of things, the latter continuity. The former saw in the last analysis unchanging atoms, the latter understood the *Ur*-Nature as an incessant becoming—homogeneous at first, of like into like (*sadṛśapariṇāma*), and only subsequently heterogeneous, i.e. of like into unlike (*visadṛśapariṇāma*). Combined with this difference, there are two other sets of contrasting features: first, between mechanistic and teleological models, and secondly, between emergentism and causal emanationism. Let us look at these *three* sets of contrasts.

Atomism versus the Prakṛti Theory

(α) Atomism is sought to be proved by the Nyāya-Vaiśeṣika by the following arguments:

Since by definition an atom is imperceptible, its existence cannot be established by perception. The only cognitive means that can be employed in this case is inference. The inference runs like this:

(1) The smallest visually perceptible thing is composed of parts, since it is visible, as is, for example, a piece of cloth.

(The example (*dṛṣṭānta*), the piece of cloth, is both a visible thing and is made up of parts, and so exemplifies the relation of universal co-presence between the middle term and the major term, i.e. between 'visibility' and 'being composed of parts'). By (1) the parts of the smallest visible thing must be imperceptible, but if those parts themselves are composite, then they can be further divided into their parts. If this process is not to proceed *ad infinitum*, i.e. if one has to avoid the defect of infinite regress (*anavasthā*), there must be further indivisible parts (which are themselves partless) which are, by definition, atoms.

However why not allow that the process of dividing into parts shall proceed endlessly? The Nyāya-Vaiśeṣika philosophers insist, in reply, that should that be the case, i.e. if there is to be endless divisibility, certain familiar empirical phenomena cannot be accounted for. It is universally agreed that a mountain is larger in size than a mustard seed. If both consist of an infinite number of parts, if both are infinitely divisible, one could not say that the mountain consists of more of the same ultimate parts than the mustard seed—which is the only way of accounting for the difference in size between them.[39]

The *Nyāyasūtras* IV ii. 18–25 discuss various Buddhist arguments why the atom must be composite and so further divisible. Leaving aside the analytic thesis that what is composite and divisible would not be, by definition, an atom, let me mention one argument implied in *sūtra* IV ii. 18: the atom cannot be partless, because it permits differentiation with regard to space (*ākāśa*) ('ākāśavyatibhedāt tadanupapattiḥ').[40] If space is all-pervasive (*sarvagatam*), it must pervade the atom as well, must be inside it

(so that there must be a hollow inside where there are no parts—the parts surrounding the hollow).[41] If the atom has an inside and an outside, that must be due to relation to space, and then it must be divisible into parts.[42] To this argument, the Naiyāyika replies that 'inner' and 'outer' designate the parts of a substance that are caused,[43] and so do not apply to an atom, which is uncaused. To say that space is everywhere does not mean that it is inside an atom, that it is related to what does not exist. Since an atom does not have an inner empty core, not being related to that putative core does not prevent space from being all-pervasive.[44]

An argument against atomism made by Śaṃkara in his *Bhāṣya* on *Brahmasūtra* II. ii. 12 asks how atoms can have contact (*saṃyoga*) with each other, and insists that such contact can only be with respect to one part rather than another, for contact inheres in a substance only in one part, i.e. it is not *vyāpyavṛtti*. The point is that substances that can have contact with each other must have parts. Furthermore, if an atom has a shape (e.g. circular), such shape must be due to arrangement of parts. This argument is anticipated in Nyāyasūtras IV. ii. 23–4. To this argument, two replies are suggested in *sūtra* IV. ii. 25: one is the familiar point about infinite regress (*anavasthākāritvāt*); the other is brought out by Viśvanātha's *Vṛtti* thus: what determines the relation of contact (*saṃyoga*), in the case of atoms, is not a part but rather a direction (*dik*).[45]

This theory of atoms has three peculiar features, which need to be emphasized. In the first place, each atom belonging to a certain class (e.g. each earth-atom) has exactly the same properties that belong to every other of that class, and yet each one is a unique particular. In order to assign unique particularity to each such atom (as also to each soul), the system had to postulate a property known as *viśeṣa*—not a quality (*guṇa*) in the technical sense nor a universal (particularity)—which each unique but incomposite particular possesses. Each *viśeṣa* is both unique and self-distinguished (*svato vyāvṛttaḥ*). T. R. V. Murti correctly remarks: 'The boldness and enormity of this conception is astounding. Is this not tantamount to saying that each atom has a self-identical and self-distinguishing egoity of its own, by virtue of which it keeps its individuality, identity and uniqueness amongst others? Only, the egoity is *objective* and lacks experiential basis.'[46] Secondly, when the atoms combine and produce the next larger whole up

until the production of the smallest visible thing, the theory insists, the cause of the 'extension' (*parimāṇa*) of the composite product is not the extensions of the atoms (contrary to the general rule that the quality (e.g. colour) of an effect is caused by the qualities (e.g. colours) of the component parts) but the number of the component atoms. This thesis that the number can be a cause was necessitated because of the realization that since the quality of a part produces in the whole the same quality in greater degree, the atomic extension of an atom, if that causes the extension of the composite whole, can only produce the same atomicity in greater degree, i.e. an extension that is still smaller (which, in the first place, is absurd, and, in the second place, would make it inexplicable how gross, perceptible things of larger extension could arise at all). A third feature of the theory—a feature shared by other parts of Nyāya-Vaiśeṣika metaphysics—is that combination of parts (whether atoms or larger wholes) always brings into being a new entity (which is more than the mere sum of the parts), a genuine whole (*avayavin*), that is to say, which *inheres* in its own parts. I will return to this last feature and the controversy surrounding it later in this chapter. In the mean time, let me contrast this atomism with the theory of *Ur-Nature.*

(*β*) The above arguments in support of atomism have been regarded by many—the Vedāntins and the Sāṃkhya philosophers—as not compelling, and as, in the long run, begging the issue. The point has been most forcefully stated by T. R. V. Murti: why should not the process of divisibility continue *ad infinitum*? To reply, as noted already, that without stopping at indivisible parts we cannot explain why a mountain and a mustard seed have different sizes is really begging the issue. 'This objection would appeal to one who has already accepted that things of perceptible size are made up of smaller parts put together. But this is the very thesis—*ārambhavāda*—at issue . . '.[47] In other words, only on the Nyāya-Vaiśeṣika general theory of material cause (the theory that things are made up of parts) is it obligatory to stop at a last part. But it is precisely this general theory which may be called in question. The Sāṃkhya proposes a radically different alternative according to which all finite things, all empirical phenomena, are but manifestations of a primary *Ur*-Nature or *prakṛti*. This process of manifestation is not a result of new combinations of parts, but rather of internal change

in this *Ur*-Nature. It is as though a primitive, purely homogeneous stuff gets divided into determinate empirical things because of a new sort of change that takes place within it, a change that results in distinguishable things and properties making their appearance from the bosom of that original homogeneity within which they were all contained.

It is possible to construe this original *Ur*-Nature on the lines of a familiar scientific cosmology prevalent at the end of the nineteenth century and clearly formulated by Herbert Spencer. But that construal would miss something essential about the Indian theory. On the Indian theory, the root Nature, the unmanifested *prakṛti*, does not consist of atoms, only not yet forming heterogeneous combinations. It rather consists of what are called *guṇas* (provisionally to be rendered qualities). These *guṇas* are said to be three: *sattva*, *rajas*, and *tamas*. These constituents, we are told, are of the nature of pleasure, pain, and indifference respectively. Each of these latter is a title for a whole group of experiential qualities. '*Sattva*', for example, signifies peace, contentment, lightness, happiness, and much else: all these are manifestations, in human experience, of the *guṇa* called *sattva*. Likewise, saying that *rajas* is of the nature of pain is an abridged way of saying that it stands for activity, motion, striving, exciting; saying that *tamas* is of the nature of indifference is to say that it stands for heaviness, inertia, sleepiness, and such qualities. The Sāṃkhya is saying not merely that these are three basic types of human affectivity in response to things of nature, but much more: namely, that nature itself, even in its original, transempirical, unmanifested, state, is constituted of these three sorts of element.

Let us try to be clear about the exact nature of this thesis. First of all, we should note that even though the Vaiśeṣika atomism is rejected, a sort of atomism persists: the *guṇas* strictly speaking are not qualities but elements. They are called *guṇa,* because they serve the other, are meant for the other, i.e. the affective (enjoying, suffering, indifferent), self.[48] However, each of the names *sattva*, *rajas*, and *tamas* stands for an infinite number of elements, not for one element.[49] In fact, in a sense, each element is a *dravya*, i.e. a substance, not a quality-substance, because each *sattva*-element has such qualities as pleasure etc. (and only substances have qualities).[50] How then is this atomism different from the Vaiśeṣika? One commentator at least raises this

question,[51] and suggests the answer that the constituent elements here—unlike in the Vaiśeṣika—do not possess qualities such as sound, touch, colour, etc. (as Vaiśeṣika atoms do). Another answer, implied in Sāṃkhya *kārikā* 12–13, is that the qualities such as pleasure, pain, and indifference arise in the *guṇas* through mutual interaction, through preponderance of one over the others, or through accompanying each other. While this does distinguish the Sāṃkhya elements from the Vaiśeṣika atoms, the important difference between them should be emphasized: the Vaiśeṣika atoms do not belong to the world, they form the world, while the Sāṃkhya elements constitute a totality, i.e. *Prakṛti*, to begin with. Their varying combinations produce different empirical things, but they themselves do not *produce* the *Ur*-Nature but belong to it as its unmanifested elements. Furthermore, unlike the atoms they are intrinsically dynamic, even as in the *Ur*-Nature, even prior to empirical manifestation, they are in a continuous process of 'homogeneous transformation' (*sadṛśa pariṇāma*). Thus Sāṃkhya seeks to preserve the Vaiśeṣika pluralism of elements without having to bear the burden of a radical pluralism—for which Vaiśeṣika had to pay a heavy price.

Next, how are we to understand this strange thesis, seemingly psychological and subjectivistic, that the elements *qua* elements are of the nature of pleasure, pain, and indifference? There are two contrasting ways of interpreting the thesis: one naturalistic, the other psychologistic. By the former, I refer to the interpretation suggested by B. N. Seal.[52] Seal understands *rajas* and *tamas* as the energy and the mass that are needed for any moving body, and construes *sattva* as the 'intelligible essence', the (Platonic) form, which alone is in the proper sense knowable and which provides motion with its immanent goal or *telos*. Thus nature as a dynamic system of becoming must have the three aspects of energy, mass, and form. In this account, the affective language employed by the Sāṃkhya would be merely metaphorical, for the connection between these three aspects and 'pleasure', 'pain', and 'indifference' cannot but be tenuous. The contrasting psychological interpretation, having some basis in the Sāṃkhya texts, proceeds as follows: everything in nature produces in a conscious being either of the three psychological responses: pleasure, pain, and indifference; what produces pleasure in one produces pain in another and indifference in still others. From this fact, one may

argue, making use of the Sāṃkhya principle that the effect must be already, i.e. prior to its origin, contained in the cause, that everything in nature must contain elements that produce pleasure, elements that produce pain, and elements that produce indifference.[53] The difficulty with this way of understanding is that it does not fully take into account the Sāṃkhya statements that the *guṇas* are of the nature of—and do not merely produce—the appropriate feelings. How can we understand this claim without falling into an implausible psychologism?

For this purpose I turn to the interpretation of K C. Bhattacharya.[54] According to Bhattacharya, the Sāṃkhya regards things of nature primarily as contents of affective experience, and the experience and the experienced, *bhoga* and *bhogya*, as one and inseparable. 'The external world is both experience and the experienced, feeling and the felt, but the dualism does not appear here at all.'[55] The dualism appears as the dualism between the body (as the support of experience, *bhogāyatana*) and the object (*bhogya*). The *guṇas* are defined as potentialities of feelings and felt contents, 'as the feel*ables* that may not be actually felt', and as prior to the subject–object distinction they are 'the absolute(s) of feeling and felt content'. 'Objective reality,' Bhattacharya writes, 'is essentially feeling or felt content. Object as known is but such felt content to detached reflection. The *guṇas* as affective absolutes constitute the object.'[56] The *guṇas* are the substantial, but dynamic, being of the elementary feelings that constitute, in their interconnections, all experience (and so all contents of experience).[57]

At the end of this brief discussion of Sāṃkhya, I would like to reiterate the importance of the idea of dynamic interconnection and interdependence of these *guṇas*.[58] Thus the activating, energizing function of *rajas* requires the obstructing role of *tamas*, otherwise everything would be equally active.[59] The three also overpower or dominate over each other, and thereby produce different varieties of experiences. Their complete separation is brought about only by subsequent reflective abstraction. In this interconnected structure, Bhattacharya assigns the central role to *rajas*, i.e. to pain-experience. The reason, as he formulates it, is profoundly philosophical. What is other than and independent of the self must be shown by experience to be so: pain eminently qualifies for this in as much as pain is, by its very nature, rejected

by the self as extrinsic to it. In Bhattacharya's words, pain is the only entity 'that is immediately intelligible as utterly distinct from the self'.[60] It is given as other than consciousness, it, is 'the exemplar of objective reality'. The other *guṇas* derive their significance from their relatedness to pain. Since pain implies the active wish to be free from pain, pain is a freeing activity: it is restless willing to be free. Pleasure is 'restful freedom' from pain; indifference is 'not only want of freedom but is also not actively willing freedom'. Again, in Bhattacharya's words, it is the 'feeling of being stupefied before the object or being fascinated by the object'. The three *guṇas* are not only thus interdependent, they are capable of forming a complex unity—which is the unity of *prakṛti*, of the experience and its content.

At the beginning of this discussion of the concept of nature, I said that besides the controversy about atomism and the *prakṛti* theory, there are two other sets of features, the contrasts between them defining the parameters of Indian thinking on these matters. It is now time to turn to them.

Mechanism versus Teleology

Does the empirical world serve some ultimate purpose, or is it the result of a mechanical combination of atoms? The Sāṃkhya represents the first alternative, the Vaiśeṣika at least appears to opt for the second. It is generally recognized by modern writers that the Sāṃkhya is the only clearly teleological theory amongst the Indian philosophies. But is Vaiśeṣika its opposite, i.e. a purely mechanical theory? Two atoms combine, on the Vaiśeṣika theory, to form a binary atom (*dyaṇuka*), and three of the latter sort combine to form a tertiary atom (really consisting of six atoms) or *tryaṇuka*, the smallest perceptible entity (identified with the dust particles one sees streaming along the ray of light through an opening). Out of different combinations of these arise the sundry empirical objects such as sticks and stones. Is it fair to characterize this process of formation as mechanical? According to Frauwallner, 'we here in the Vaiśeṣika and for that matter, no doubt, in the whole sphere of Indian philosophy find a thorough preoccupation with the problems of a mechanistic view'.[61]

M. Hiriyanna, that incomparably astute scholar of Indian philosophy, notices several original tendencies in Indian cosmolo-

gical thinking.[62] These are: accidentalism (*yadṛcchāvāda* or *animitta-vāda*), naturalism (*svabhāva-vāda*), supernaturalism (*adṛṣṭa-vāda*) and the theory that the world is a transformation of *brahman* (*brahmapariṇāma-vāda*). Accidentalism considers the world as due to mere chance, there being no law of causation at all. Naturalism insists on law, but the law belongs to the nature of the original cause, to each one's unique nature (if one believes in many original elements), and rejects any external intervention in the causal chain. Supernaturalism brings in such external 'unseen' (*adṛṣṭa*) determinants—either by way of God's agency (*kartṛtva*) and/or by way of the role that the law of *karma* plays in determining the shape of things. The fourth, which Hiriyanna regards as a modification of absolutism under the influence of *svabhāvavāda* or naturalism, takes the world as a real modification of *brahman* and adds to the concept of nature also the concept of many distinct and eternal souls—thus in a peculiar way blending heterodoxy with orthodoxy.

Now, if a mechanistic world-view implies accidentalism (sometimes, in Western philosophical literature, one finds accounts which make it appear as though according to mechanism the world is a product of chance collocation of circumstances), then Vaiśeṣika is not mechanistic. There are two further beliefs, besides its strict commitment to the law of causation, which give it a hybrid character: the world-process is also due to an intelligent creator, Iśwara, who creates in conformity with the principle of *karma* of the souls. The law of *karma*, especially the invisible forces generated by good or bad deeds of embodied souls, influences the course of world formation, not by abrogating natural causality, but by 'influencing it in a definite way' and directing it to 'such paths as are demanded by the works or deeds of the beings concerned'.[63] However it is still not an explicitly teleological doctrine: the law of *karma* is still a law of causation, and works 'from the past' as it were, and does not provide a *telos* for the world process.

The Sāṃkhya's teleological thinking is explicit. The *Ur*-Nature, with its constituent *guṇas*, is, even if ontologically independent of the selves, yet is *for* them. Its very being, not to speak of the subsequent process of manifestation into the empirical world, is for the purpose of the souls. One of the familiar proofs given for the existence of selves is embodied in the premiss '*parārthasamghātatvāt*',[64] meaning 'all collocations of things [that

are themselves non-conscious, *acetana*] must in the long run be meant for the purposes of a conscious 'other' (*para*)'. These purposes all reduce to two: enjoyment (*bhoga*) and liberation (*mokṣa*). The idea of 'enjoyment', with its threefold primitive forms discussed earlier and their combinations, coincides with that of 'experience'. The world is intended for the experience of selves, and eventually for their liberation from mundanity. We should note two features of this idea of purposiveness.

In the first place, since nature on this theory is not conscious, the purposiveness is only to be understood in the sense of an unconscious technology. Two well-known Sāṃkhya metaphors suggest this: the rain cloud yields rain in order to sustain life on earth, the cow gives milk for the sake of her calf. What is implied in these cases is not the entertainment of a goal as a conscious representation, but rather the directedness of a structure, of a pattern of behaviour, of a process, towards satisfaction of another's need. Śaṃkara's criticism that even in the case of a cow's milk or rainfall there must be a conscious agency therefore misses the point.[65]

However, there is a certain circularity in the overall theory (but not in the mere teleological conception of nature). The needs of the selves that are being served are, as mentioned, two: enjoyment and liberation. Enjoyment, i.e. experience in the broadest sense, involves mundanity centring around the aspect of pain; liberation is freedom from this mundanity, and so presupposes a prior mundanity. Why, we ask, should nature serve to ensnare the pure self into enjoyment and so bondage (along with all that the latter entails), and then lead it, through cultivation of discriminatory knowledge (*viveka-jñāna*), to liberation from that bondage? What kind of game is it which first ensnares, captivates, and binds, and then frees? Why not leave the self untouched in its pristine purity, so that the two coeternal realities, the self and *prakṛti*, remain independent and untouched by each other—the self in its unsullied freedom, *prakṛti* in its unmanifested homogeneity? If the circularity is to be avoided, the concept of liberation must be sufficiently enriched, so that it would not be a mere return to the original innocence but spirit would be all the richer having had to pass through the test and vicissitudes of enjoyment (and suffering) in order to recover itself. But, then, time and history would gain a significance, which Sāṃkhya would not allow—and spirit would

not be the mere *madhyastha*, uninvolved spectator, but would rather be closer to the Hegelian *Geist*, dying in order to live, suffering in order to be free.

A literally suffering spirit is alien to Indian thought: all suffering (as also enjoyment) is mock-suffering, the spirit being eternally free and uninvolved. What then is the sense of that teleology or *parārthatva*?

Is a New Entity Produced?

One expects a mechanistic theory of nature to rule out emergence of new products and a teleological theory to allow it. But Indian thought belies this expectation. The Nyāya-Vaiśeṣika with its theory of atom-combinations vehemently argues for the thesis that when parts combine to produce a whole, the whole is more than the sum of those parts. The Sāṃkhya, which, as noted earlier in this chapter, argues for nature's subservience to the purposes of spirits, yet construes that process of unfolding of nature as becoming-explicit of what is already implicitly there, so that there is no new production. From this contrast one may jump to the conclusion that, in the Indian mind, atomic combination was taken to yield a novel product: some forms of Buddhism show, however, that an atomism (of a sort) need not entail emergence of novelty. It would be instructive to look at these three possibilities as laying down the parameters of Indian thought about nature.

The Nyāya-Vaiśeṣika, Buddhism, and Sāṃkhya may be regarded as pushing to the centre of their thinking three quite different metaphors. The Nyāya-Vaiśeṣika metaphor is that of a potter putting together two parts (of a would-be jar)—that being the way the potter worked—to produce a jar. The Buddhist metaphor is that of a heap of sand (consisting, obviously, of innumerable tiny grains of sand). The Sāṃkhya root metaphor is that of oil-seed being pressed to yield oil that is already in it.

The issue between the Nyāya-Vaiśeṣika and Buddhism may be stated thus: is a whole a *mere* aggregate of parts or is it more than the sum of parts, i.e. a new entity over and above its parts? If the putative whole is nothing but the aggregate of its parts, that would be tantamount to saying that there is, strictly speaking, no genuine whole. The issue then may also be stated thus: are there, besides the elements, also wholes (*avayavin*)?

The main Buddhist argument against the theory of a genuine whole consists in pressing the point that no satisfactory account is available of how this putative whole is related to its parts. The possible answers seem to be: either the whole is partially (*ekdeśena*) in each part, or entirely (*kārtsyena*) in each. The first alternative implies that there are further parts besides those in which the whole is supposed to reside partially; the latter alternative implies that the whole is really many and not one. There are also other standard objections against the theory of the whole: that you can pull a part (e.g. an arm) and not the alleged whole (the body), that you may see a part, or not see another without seeing or not seeing the alleged whole, that the alleged whole is never seen without a part being seen, that the alleged whole may be both covered and not covered and both in contact and not in contact with another given thing (thus possessing contradictory properties), and—to mention one more—the whole weighs no more than what the detached parts together weigh.[66]

These and other objections as well as the replies given by the Naiyāyikas bring out clearly what needs to be salvaged from the theory, and where valuable philosophical insights are covered up by considerations deriving from the system.

The questions about the mode of being of the whole in its parts are answered by saying that both the alternatives—either 'in part' or 'in entirety'—are inapplicable in this case. Both apply only when there are many things, some of which constitute partialness and all of which constitute entirety. They do not apply to something which is one. The alleged whole being one, one cannot ask if it is present (in its parts) partially or entirely.[67]

The other objections are used by the Naiyāyika precisely to his own advantage, i.e. to press the point that the whole is a different entity so that to cover a part is not to cover the whole, to pull a part is not to pull the whole, and so on. I think the main point is epistemological[68]—even if it is made to support an ontological thesis: if the tree yonder is a mere aggregate of atoms, each atom being imperceptible the tree would not be perceived. If the tree is not perceived, its colour, shape, size, position, and generic property would also not be perceived.[69] We not only perceive the tree but perceive it as one thing, which could be the proper referent of such a statement as 'This is one thing, that is another'. If there are mere parts, how can a mere aggregate, a plurality, be

referred to as one thing? The sense of unity ('This is one') and the sense of plurality ('These are many') cannot refer to the same thing. Even if we may *sometimes* mistake a plurality for a unity, such mistaken sense of unity is possible only if there are cases where our ascription of unity is veridical. If all sense of unity is erroneous, then even those cases where all are agreed that a plurality is being mistaken for unity would remain unexplained.[70] The needed veridical ascription of unity cannot be said to be when one says 'This is a sound', for on the phenomenalist position it is impossible to identify a sound as one sound and not as an aggregate or succession of sounds. It is more plausible to take 'This is one tree' to be the paradigmatic case of ascription of unity, and then to advance the claim that a heard sound is one sound.

The Naiyāyika's position rests on two theses: one epistemological, the other ontological. The epistemological thesis is that it is not necessary for perceiving a whole that one should perceive all its parts. In most cases of physical objects, we do not perceive all the parts of a thing, and yet do indeed perceive the thing itself. As I look at the tree yonder, I see only some of its parts; others are hidden from me. I do not see the other side, to be sure. From this uncontroversial premiss one may want to conclude that therefore I do not see this tree, I infer it, imagine it, or whatever. The Buddhist tends towards such a position. The Naiyāyika rejects such a conclusion. Even if the tree is nothing but an aggregate of parts, what is seen is one part of this assemblage, but what then is inferred? The (Buddhist) theory can only hold that from seeing this part, say the front part, we infer the unseen parts. But neither the front part nor the hind part taken by itself is the tree. What is in that case inferred is not the tree but only the unseen part of the tree. My knowledge of the tree has not thereby been shown to be inferential. The inferential theory has no better chance of success on the assumption that the tree is more than the assemblage of parts. In order to be able to infer *B* from *A* it is necessary either that *B* must be analytically contained within *A* or that *B* must always have been observed together with *A*. In the present case, only the second alternative is plausible, and yet since on the (Buddhist) theory the whole is never perceived, it could not have been perceived together with its parts and so cannot possibly be inferred. Thus the epistemological thesis of the Naiyāyika amounts to a defence of direct perception of material things—although the

idea of direct perception needs to be suitably construed so as to make room for the complicated nexus of relationships through which the percipient comes into contact with a material object.

The ontological thesis of the Naiyāyika is that a whole is a new emergent reality which inheres (technically, is in the relation of *samavāya*) in the parts whose conjunction brings it about. Both those theses together—the ontological and the epistemological—give rise to one important question which the Indian realists did not raise. This question is how to determine which assemblages of parts give rise to wholes and which do not. Not all conjunctions of (alleged) parts would give rise to a whole. The table on which I am writing, the books and papers on it, the pencils, pens, my spectacles, and the paperweights—all these do not constitute, on the Nyāya theory, an emergent whole that is being perceived by me as one thing. The Nyāya whole is also not —it should be noted—what is often called, in Western philosophies, an organic unity,[1] for its parts can be separated without detriment to their natures and identities. The Naiyāyikas often spoke of a special sort of conjunction (*saṃyoga*) called *samślesa* (where the parts come closer than merely coming in contact). But we do not learn anything more definite about it. But perhaps this much can be said: genuine wholes are produced in a manner or in a sense in which pseudo-wholes are not. The precise sense of 'production' in the above is, however, not clear. Perhaps the maker alone knows how a whole is produced. One may ask, if on the Nyāya theory the world is created by God why is not the world one genuine whole? Nyāya avoids this consequence by construing God's authorship of the world to mean not that God creates the world as one entity, but only that his authorship pertains to each thing taken separately: the world is a mere aggregate and not an emergent whole.

The Nyāya position is opposed not only by the Buddhist but also by the Sāṃkhya. The Buddhist opposes it on the ground that there is no genuine whole but mere assemblage of parts. This, however, would make ordinary perception into an inference but cannot explain how that inference is possible. The Sāṃkhya opposes the Nyāya view on the ground that causality is not production of a new entity, that in other words the effect is not a new production but was already contained, though not manifested prior to effectuation, within the (material) cause. Empirical nature is a becoming-

explicit of what is contained in the *Ur*-Nature, the original *prakṛti*.

The thesis rests upon a more basic attitude towards causality: the causal efficacy does not bring into existence anything that was non-existent (*asat*). It does not do so, for it just cannot do so: it cannot make something arise out of nothing. Oil can be pressed out of oil-seed (and not out of chips of stone) just because oil-seed contains oil. But does milk change into yoghurt because milk contains yoghurt implicitly? What about threads that are woven together to produce a sari? Should one say, the resulting piece of clothing was really in the threads implicitly? If it was, was it present (implicitly) in each thread severally or taken together? That something cannot come out of nothing is not to be disputed: it is a presupposition of all Hindu thought. But on the theory of the emergent whole, the whole does not appear out of nothing, it emerges with the putting together of the parts. The idea of the effect being implicitly contained in the cause makes use of certain paradigms, and clearly does not fit some others. But even with regard to those paradigms to whom it owes its plausibility, the idea of implicit existence is left vague. If the stuff oil is liquid, it is odd to say that the oil-seed contains this liquid (as coconut contains its water); if it did, then oil would be in oil-seed, not implicitly but in a rather straightforward sense. In the latter case, to say that it is in an unmanifest state means no more than that we cannot perceive it owing to the hard shell that covers it—not in any metaphysically interesting sense. But this is not what the Sāṃkhya means.

We have already noted that the Sāṃkhya, while rejecting Vaiśeṣika atomism, makes use of a sort of atomism of *guṇas*, and conceives of the difference amongst entities in empirical nature as being due to combinations of these *guṇas* in different proportions. Out of such a mixture, one can say, something new emerges—i.e. each distinct natural entity, although the Sāṃkhya would not formally say this in order not to violate the canonical doctrine that the effect was already contained in the cause (*satkāryavāda*).

Concluding Remarks and a Historical Excursus

Both in India and in the West, as the original mythopoeic thought was replaced by rational thinking, we find a search for the unity underlying the diversities of nature and for an impersonal law. In

the Vedic hymns this is best exemplified in the well-known conception of *ṛta* and in Greek thought in the search for a 'sustaining principle' or 'first cause' of things. The conception of *ṛta* signifies the discovery of an impersonal law amidst the welter of conflicting natural forces. The host of lesser deities are now seen to be conforming to a larger cosmic order, their individual caprices subordinated to a general interest. Gods obey the *ṛta*, which none can transgress. It was an easy step from this to the notion of a universal moral order: the idea of cosmic order was comprehended within it but transcended by extending the idea to account for moral experience as well.

The pre-Socratic search for the ultimate element of nature was not lacking in ancient Indian thought.[72] Prajāpati Parameṣthin, for example, held water to be the most fundamental principle, while for Anila, as for Anaximenes, this principle was air. While thus the search for the one ultimate element went on both in India and in Greece, four distinct trends of thought tended to emerge.

First, there emerged the conception of natural law, which itself, in ancient thought, seems to have had two forms (to borrow the distinction from A. N. Whitehead): the idea of law as immanent and the idea of law as imposed. In Indian thought, the law as imposed came to be the law of the unseen (*adṛṣṭa*): the law that combines cosmic law with moral law, the unseen law apportioning merit and demerit to appropriate actions. The idea of law as immanent, as the real source of unity underlying the plurality of appearances, led to the idea of *brahman*, the *ekam sat*, the one existent (another transformation of the Vedic *ṛta*), as also happened in ancient Greece with Parmenides.

Secondly, the atomic theory was represented by Leucippus and Democritus in Greece and the Vaiśeṣikas in India. There were no doubt differences between them, and here as elsewhere the Greeks succeeded in making greater abstraction. The atoms of the Greek theory had neither colour nor taste nor temperature—all such sensible qualities being derived from combinations of atoms. The Indian atomists, however, stopped with qualitative atoms (the earth-atom, the air-atom, the fire-atom, and the water-atom), each with its distinctive simple quality. Every atomic theory has to face the problems of original motion and the beginning of atomic combination which the Greeks sought to explain without assuming an external efficient cause. The Indian philosophers, like Aristotle,

were puzzled by the possibility of a chance origin of atomic combinations, and fell back on the hypothesis of a prime mover, a god, Iśvara, who, however, is no capricious artificer but acts in accordance with the above-mentioned law of the unseen (*adṛṣṭa*).

Thirdly, there was the idea that nature was mathematical and that natural laws can be mathematically represented. Originating possibly with Pythagoras, this idea was appropriated by Plato[73] in so far as the latter regarded the smallest particles as geometrical forms which could be reduced to and built up from other geometrical forms. This became the basis of the mathematization of nature by Galileo.[74] It is noteworthy that in spite of the Hindu love of mathematics, this mathematical conception of nature never took hold of the Hindu mind (in spite of Hindu astronomy and its mathematical basis).

To Plato we owe still another element of the Western philosophy of nature: this is what is today called essentialism, the belief that things have their ideal essences. This conception of essences strengthened the belief in laws which were construed as essential relationships amongst essences (and not contingent relations amongst passing particulars). This essentialism had the tendency to make of nature a static structure, but it was transformed by Aristotle into a dynamic one, which, together with elements derived from Christianity, laid the basis for the later historicism. Nature was construed as a process of growth through which what was potential becomes actual. The forms came then to be regarded as the final causes, implicit in nature, leading it towards their gradual actualization. A new attitude towards nature developed along with the mathematical: this is the teleological account of natural processes.

It has been said that the mathematical conception of nature was not in the forefront of Indian thought. Some form of essentialism was there in the Nyāya-Vaiśeṣika theory of real universals (*jāti*). The teleological conception, as has been noted, shows up in the Sāṃkhya and possibly there alone.

Platonism is essentialist and mathematical; modern science is mathematical and anti-essentialist; Vaiśeṣika was atomistic, essentialistic, and also not mathematical; the Sāṃkhya was essentialistic and teleological.

SCIENCE AND METAPHYSICS

Ever since Aristotle, science of nature and metaphysics have been separated in Western thought, and it is only in more recent times that philosophy has tended towards continuity with science. As the traditional distinction goes, science is concerned with things, with entities of nature, metaphysics with being *qua* being. We need not for the present purpose, recall all the various ways 'being *qua* being' has been understood in that tradition. What is important is that there was a clear line of demarcation between the various natural sciences and metaphysics.

We can say, without taking much risk, that for most Indian thinkers science and metaphysics were continuous. Both seek to understand the structure of the world; they differ only in the order of generality. (The Advaita Vedānta is the only exception in this regard: the world, being unreal on this theory, is left to the empirical sciences, and metaphysics—if that is what *parāvidyā* is—is the knowledge of the one Being underlying the many beings). Both Sāṃkhya and Nyāya-Vaiśeṣika are science and philosophy in one. For ancient Hindus, Sāṃkhya formed the theoretical-scientific basis of medicine and psychology, Vaiśeṣika formed the basis of physics and chemistry. The Sāṃkhya, as science, mirrors its cosmology in an analysis of the psychophysical entity that is the human person; the Vaiśęsika seeks to combine an atomism with emergence of new entities. Both supplement their scientific theory with a theory of self as its integral part. The self, however, is not *in* nature: it underlies its possibility. If it is the actions of the self and the moral forces (*adṛṣṭa*) generated by actions that account for empirical nature's manifestation or creation, then ultimately nature is both natural and moral: the two orders coincide. Science then becomes subordinated to the moral and spiritual goals of the self.

NOTES AND REFERENCES

1. See M. Hiriyanna, *Indian Philosophical Studies* (Mysore: Kavyalaya, 1957), esp. 121–6.

2. S. N. Dasgupta, *A History of Indian Philosophy* (Cambridge: Cambridge University Press, 1922), i. 311.
3. For the conception of time in Indian philosophy, see A. N. Balslev, *A Study of Time in Indian Philosophy* (Wiesbaden: Otto Harrassowitz, 1983). Balslev was the first to question the view that time, in Indian thought, was cyclic.
4. See M. Tachikwa, *The Structure of the World in Udayana's Realism: A Study of the Lakṣaṇāvalī and the Kiraṇāvalī* (Dordrecht: Reidel, 1981), 95–6.
5. *Vaiśeṣikasūtra* VII. i. 25.
6. *Tarkasaṃgrahaḥ* 15.
7. *Bhāsāpariccheda.* See *Nyāyadarśana* ii. 1.
8. This yields the definition of time given by the commentary *Dinakarī* (on *Siddhāntamuktāvali* on *kārikā* 45): 'Kālalakṣaṇaṃ tu kālikasambandhāvacchinnakāryatvāvacchinnakāryatānirūpitamadhikaraṇavidhayā nimittatvaṃ.'
9. 'Sūryakriyopādhivaśādatītānāgatavartamānādivyavahārabhāk kālaḥ' (*Pramāṇādipadārthaprakāśikā* by Jayatīrtha).
10. 'Yena mūrtināmupacayāścāpacayāśca lakṣyante taṃ kālamāhuḥ' (on *sūtra* ii. 25).
11. For this, See Stephen J. Gould's recent book *Time's Arrow, Time's Cycle* (Cambridge, Mass.: Harvard University Press, 1987).
12. M. Eliade, *The Sacred and the Profane: The Nature of Religion*, ed. and trans. Willard R. Trask (New York: Harcourt, Brace and World, 1959), 70.
13. Bhim C. Jhalkikar, *Nyāyakośa* (Poona: Bhandarkar Oriental Research Institute, 1928), 140.
14. *Purāṇa* means 'Old Narrative'.
15. Kautilya, *Arthaśāstra*, bk. I, ch. 5.
16. *Bṛhadāraṇyaka Upaniśad* II iv. 10.
17. " '*iti ha evamāsit' iti ya niyate sa itihāsaḥ.*"
18. A. D. Pusalkar, 'Conception of History in Ancient Indian Literature', *Our Heritage*, Bulletin of the Department of P. G. Training and Research, Sanskrit College, Calcutta, vol. 12, pt. 2, (July–Dec. 1964), 35–52.
19. C. H. Philips (ed.), *Historians of India, Pakistan and Ceylon* (London: Oxford University Press, 1961), Editor's Introduction, esp. 4.
20. R. C. Majumdar cites this Jain text: '*Itihāsa* is a very desirable subject. According to tradition, it relates to what actually happened' (Jinasena, *Ādipurāṇa* of the 8th cent. AD) in 'Ideas of History in Sanskrit Literature', in Philips (ed.), *Historians in India*, 13–28.
21. Ibid. 20, *Rājataraṅgiṇi*, i. 9–10, 14–15.
22. Ibid. 20–1. Kalhaṇa: '*Slāghyaḥ sa eva guṇavānrāgadveṣabahiṣkṛta.* bhûtārthakathane yasya stheya—syeva sarasvati' (*Rājataraṅgiṇi*,

i. 7). ('That worthy person deserves praise, whose word, like that of a judge, is free from love or hatred in narrating the story of the past.')

23. i. 23.
24. vii. 7. See A. L. Basham, 'The Kashmir Chronicle', in Philips (ed.), *Historians in India.*
25. vii. 959: '*vancyante balino'pi yat laghubalaiḥ'.*
26. i. 324: iv. 413.
27. 'Ideas of History', 25.
28. Cp. the idea of *sarvanmukti.*
29. Cp. Sri Aurobindo's ideas in this regard.
30. For an account of temporality in this sense, reference may be made to Husserl's Lectures on *The Phenomenology of Internal Time Consciousness*, and also to Heidegger's *Being and Time.*
31. See W. Halbfass, 'Anthropological Problems in Classical Indian Philosophy', in *Beiträge zur indische Forschung: Ernst Waldschmidt zum 80 Geburtstag gewidmet* (Berlin: Museum für indische Kunst, 1977), 225–236.
32. Vinoba Bhave, *Iśāvāsyavṛtti.*
33. Kant, *Critique of Pure Reason*, A 119.
34. See G. Funke, *Zur transcendentalen Phänomenologie* (Bonn: Bouvivier, 1957).
35. Sri Aurobindo, *The Life Divine* (New York: Sri Aurobindo Library, 1949).
36. K. C. Bhattacharya, *The Subject as Freedom* (Amalner: Indian Institute of Philosophy, 1930; repr. in K. C. Bhattacharya, *Studies in Philosophy*, ii. (Calcutta: Progressive Publishers, 1958).
37. *The Subject as Freedom*, 103–5.
38. For these, see amongst others, B. N. Seal, *The Positive Sciences of the Ancient Hindus* (Delhi: Matilal Banarasidass, 1958) and P. C. Ray, *History of Hindu Chemistry* (Calcutta: Indian Chemical Society, 1956). For Vaiśeṣika, see Eric Frauwallner, *History of Indian Philosophy*, ii, ed. and Trans. V. M. Bedekar (New York: Humanities Press, 1974).
39. 'Sarveṣāmanavasthitāvayavatve merusarsapayostulyaparimāṇatvāpatteḥ' (Visvanātha's *Vṛtti* on *Nyāyasūtra* IV ii. 25).
40. Vācaspati in his *Tātparyaṭīkā* on this *sūtra* explains *ākāśavyatibheda* as 'ākāśahetukam vyatibhedaṃ vibhāgaṃ'. I follow this explanation. Uddyotakara gives several possible meanings of the text, none inconsistent with Vācaspati's interpretation.
41. This structure is what Uddyotakara calls *suṣiram.* Of course, on the Nyāya-Vaiśeṣika view, this is not the structure of an atom, for then an atom would have parts.
42. Visvanātha in his *Vṛtti* explains: 'antarbahiścākāśa-samāveśāt, tathā ca sāvayava.'

43. Visvanātha formulates the reply: 'antaḥśabdo bahiḥśabdasca kāryadravyasyāvayavaviśeṣavāci na ca akārye'vayavasambhava ityarthaḥ.'
44. Uddyotakara: 'nāyam sarvagatārtho yannāsti, tena sambandha iti . . .na ca paramāṇormadhyamamasti, tasmānna tenassambandhāt ākāśamasarva-gataṃ prasajyeta iti' (*Vārttika* on *Nyāyasūtra* IV. ii. 25).
45. 'tatsaṃyogāvacchedaka digvibhāgaḥ.'
46. *Studies in Indian Thought*, Collected Papers of Professor T. R. V. Murti, ed. Harold G. Coward (Columbia, Mo.: South Asia Books, 1983), 145–6.
47. Ibid. 144.
48. 'guṇa iti parārthaḥ' (Mahādeva's *Vṛtti* on the *Śāmkhyasūtra*, 128).
49. Thus Nageśa: 'sattvāditrayamapi pratyekaṃ vyaktibhedādanantyaṃ' (*Vṛtti* on 127). That each is really many is supported by the argument that otherwise the great variety of things in the world would be unaccounted for (*kāryyānāmantavaicitryaṃ na syāt).*
50. Nageśa, again, in his *Vṛtti* on *kārikā* 127, writes: 'Atra prītyādināṃ guṇadharmāt.'
51. Mahādeva writes: 'Na ca mūlakāraṇasyānantavyaktikatve vaiśeṣikamatāt ko viśeṣa iti cet, kāraṇadravyasya śabdasparśādirāhityameva' (*Vṛtti* on *sūtra* 127).
52. *The Positive Sciences of the Ancient Hindus.*
53. It is interesting that one of Śaṃkara's criticisms of Sāṃkhya makes use of precisely this difference in response by different persons to one and the same thing. Thus writes Śaṃkara: 'śabdādyaviśeṣepi ca bhāvanāviśeṣāt sukhādiviśeṣopalabdheḥ' (*Bhāṣya* on *Brahmasūtra* II. ii. 1).
54. K. C. Bhattacharya, *Studies in Philosophy*, (Calcutta: Progressive Publishers, 1956), i, esp. 'Studies in Sāṃkhya Philosophy', chs. 9 and 10.
55. Ibid. 205.
56. Ibid. 206.
57. S. N. Dasgupta characterizes the *guṇas* as 'feelings, the ultimate substances', in *A History of Indian Philosophy* (Cambridge: Cambridge University Press, 1992), i. 242.
58. Sāṃkhyakārikā, 12: 'anyonyābhibhavāśrayajanana—mithunavṛttayaśca guṇāḥ.'
59. See Mahadeva's *Vṛtti* on sūtra 128: 'rajaḥ pravartakatayā sattvaṃ laghu sarvatra pravartayet yadi tamasā guruṇā na niyamyeta.'
60. *Studies in Philosophy*, i. 205–6.
61. Eric Frauwallner, *History of Indian Philosophy*, ii, ed. and trans. V. M. Bedekar (New York: Humanities Press, 1974), 57.
62. M. Hiriyanna, *Outlines of Indian Philosophy* (7th Impression; London: Allen & Unwin, 1968), 103–5.

63. Frauwallner, *History of Indian Philosophy*, 63. Frauwallner gives an interesting account of the many ways this 'invisible' causation doctrine influenced the (possibly) original natural-scientific conception of Vaiśeṣika.
64. *Sāmkhyakārikā*, 17.
65. Śaṃkara, *Bhāṣya* on *Brahmasūtra* II. ii. 1.
66. For a list of such objections, see Karl H. Potter, *Indian Metaphysics and Epistemology: The Tradition of Nyāya-Vaiśeṣika up to Gaṅgeśa* (Princeton, N.J.: Princeton University Press, 1977), 75–9. (For references to Sanskrit texts also see Potter.)
67. Vātsyāyana on *Nyāyasūtra* IV. ii. 11: 'Tāvimou kṛtsnaikadeśaśabdou bhedaviṣayou naikasminnavayavinyupapadyete bhedābhāvāditi.' Uddyotakara explains this thus: 'anekasyaśeṣatā kṛtsnaśabdasyārthaḥ aśeṣasya kasyacidabhidhānamekadeśaśabdasya, na caitadihopapadyate iti tasmānnāvayavini kṛtsnaśabdo nāpyekadeśaśabda iti' (*Vārttika*).
68. For more on this, see my 'Reflections on the Nyāya Theory of Avayavipratyakṣa', *Journal of the Indian Academy of Philosophy*, 1 (1), 30–41; repr. in my *Phenomenology and Ontology* (The Hague: Martinus Nijhoff, 1970).
69. *Nyāyasūtra* II. i. 34–5. Also See Vātsyāyana's *Bhāṣya* and Uddyotakara's *Vārttika* on them.
70. *Nyāyasūtra* II. i. 36. Uddyotakara: 'Mithyāpratyaya apyete na bhavanti pradhānābhāvāt' (*Vārttika* on II. i. 36).
71. On organic unity, See R. Shusterman, 'Organic Unity: Analysis and Deconstruction', in R. W. Dasenbrock (ed.), *Redrawing the Lines: Analytic Philosophy, Deconstruction and Literary Theory* (Minneapolis: University of Minnesota Press, 1989), 92–115.
72. See B. M. Barua, *A History of Pre-Buddhistic Indian Philosophy* (Calcutta: University of Calcutta, 1921).
73. See Werner Heisenberg, *Across the Frontiers*, ed. and trans. Peter Heath (New York: Harper & Row, 1974), esp. ch. 9.
74. See E. Husserl, *The Crisis of European Sciences and Transcendental Phenomenology*, ed. and trans. David Carr (Evanston, Ill.: Northwestern University Press, 1970).

8

Remarks on the *Pramāṇa* Theory

GENERAL OBSERVATIONS ON THE *PRAMĀṆA–PRAMEYA* THEORY

Pramāṇa

A philosophical theory or *darśana* not only elaborates a view about the nature of things, but also backs up this account with a theory of evidence, rational justification, and critical appraisal. It not only uses such evidence, rational justifications, and critical appraisals, but also has a theory of these theoretical practices—that is to say, a theory of rationality. We may want to look in it for generalized answers to such questions as: When is a cognitive claim valid? What sorts of justification of beliefs are acceptable? In critically appraising rival claims, what criteria are admissible? Where there are conflicting criteria, what are their relative strengths and weaknesses? These are the tasks to which the *pramāṇa* theory addresses itself. It is a singular sign of the high level of intellectual sophistication of the *darśanas* that they all, at some time or other in course of their development, came up with their theories of *pramāṇas*.

My purpose in this chapter is to draw attention to some striking features that emerge in these discussions—both with regard to the definition of *pramāṇa* and with regard to the number of *pramāṇas* and their specific natures—and thereby to be able to throw some light, however dim, on the Indian concept of rationality.

To begin with, let me note an important matter about locution that is not merely a matter about locution but also points to deep substantive issues. In the Western philosophical tradition, it was usual up until recent times, to ask: does knowledge arise from reason or from experience? The rationalists and the empiricists gave different answers. These answers, in their various formulations, determined the course of Western philosophy. In Sanskrit philosophical vocabulary, the words 'reason' and 'experience'

have no exact synonyms, and the epistemological issue was never formulated in such general terms. On the other hand, a question which was asked (and which is likely to be mistaken for the above question raised in the Western tradition) is: is perception (*pratyakṣa*) the only means of knowing or is inference also such a means? Neither is 'perception' synonymous with 'experience', nor 'inference' with 'reason'. Those who recognized perception as a means of knowing (in fact, every philosophical school did so) often did not restrict perception to sensory perception, and did not restrict sensory perception to the domain of sensible qualities such as colour and material objects such as sticks and stones. Amongst things that were taken to be sensuously perceived are: the self and its qualities such as pleasure, pain, desire, and cognition; universals such as redness; natural-kind essences such as cowness; and relations such as contact and inherence (of a quality in a substance; of a universal in its instances). That inference is different from reason (of the rationalists) is clear from the very etymology of the word *anumāna*; it follows upon perception. If we leave the Buddhists out, no school of Indian philosophy ascribed to inference a constructive role. It knows what can be known otherwise. There is always a priority of perception. There are no Indian rationalists. Neither perception nor inference pointed to any specific faculty of the mind—as 'experience' and 'reason' did in classical Western philosophies. The same faculties or cognitive instruments—operating in different manners—resulted in one case in perception, in another in inference.

I have belaboured this point in order to caution against any temptation to see in the *pramāṇa* theories near-kin of the Western epistemologies. The above remarks lead to another feature of the *pramāṇa* theories. A *pramāṇa* is the specific cause of, or the specific means of acquiring, an irreducible type of *pramā* or true cognition. There are two different reasons why a particular *pramāṇa* is not recognized by a certain school. One is that the sort of cognition which it causes is just not true cognition: this is the reason why some Buddhists would not regard inference as a *pramāṇa*, for an inferential cognition apprehends its object as an instance of a universal rule, and not in its uniqueness, and so is not true to its object's own nature. But one may give a quite different sort of reason why a putative *pramāṇa* is not really one. When the Vaiśeṣikas deny that *śabda* or words can serve as a *pramāṇa*, they

do not deny that the putative linguistically generated cognition is true; what they insist upon is that it is not of an irreducible variety, that as a matter of fact it is reducible to inference. There are thus three claims made by a *pramāṇa* theory:

(1) Some cognitions are true, i.e. *pramā*.
(2) Some of these true cognitions belong to a type that is irreducible to some other type.
(3) True cognitions belonging to such an irreducible type are caused by a unique aggregate of causal conditions.

Thus, a sort of causal theory of knowledge is built into the *pramāṇa* theory:[1] a true cognition must not only be true to its object (*arthaavyabhicāri*), but must also be generated in the right manner, i.e. by the appropriate causes. Expressed in a modern philosophical style, this amounts to saying:

> *S* knows that *p* if S has a cognitive state having the form *p*, this cognitive state is true, and it is brought about in the right sort of way.

This last formulation in terms of a cognitive state leads me to the third feature I want to draw attention to. Western thought has been torn not only by the conflicting claims of reason and experience, but also at least since Descartes by the dualism of mind and matter, the subjective and the objective. One of the offsprings of the latter distinction is that between the private and the public. In more recent philosophy this has emerged as the problem of psychologism. Epistemology and theory of logic have been haunted by the spectre of psychologism, and have sought to banish all reference to the inner mental states from their discourse. The consequence has been pure objectivism—be it of the Platonic sort or of the physicalist sort. Contrasted with this, the Indian epistemologists made unabashed use of mentalistic discourse, and never really worried about the problems of psychologism, private language, etc. It is possible to accuse them simply of uncritical naïvety. But given the heightened critical acumen which they exhibit, the reasons have to be sought elsewhere. It is well known that, for most Indian philosophers, mind (if that is how *manas* is to be translated) is rather a subtle form of *prakṛti* or matter, a non-conscious inner sense-organ, but not a domain of private

experiences. Cognitions and other experiences belong to the self, *ātman*, and can be 'perceived' only by their owner (if self-manifesting, then so only to the owner). But if *S* alone has an inner perception of his experiences, it does not follow that no one else can know them by any of the *pramāṇas* other than perception. What is more, these episodes, even if belonging to a particular owner, have their ideal intentional contents which numerically distinct episodes, belonging to different owners and occurring at different temporal locations, can have in common. I have shown earlier how, given this conception of 'mental episodes', one is enabled to construct a logic of cognitions with appropriate logical rules of inference. To talk about cognitive events, then, need not arouse the spectre of psychologism.[2]

I referred earlier to the causal story that pervades the Indian epistemologies. It is now possible to look at it closer. Possibly since Kant, it has been usual to distinguish sharply questions of epistemic justification (*quaestio juris*) from questions of causal origin (*quaestio factis*). It is only in more recent times that a causal theory of knowledge has become very much in vogue, but the causal theories of knowledge have to be able to find rooms for justificatory concepts such as logical validity and truth. In this regard, the Indian epistemologies can serve as an useful model. As Matilal has insisted in his recent book on perception, the *pramāṇas* serve both as causes and as justifications of cognitive episodes.[3] It seems to me that this was made possible by first separating out non-controversial instances of true from such instances of non-true cognitions, and then looking for (1) the marks that distinguish the former from the latter, and (2) the distinctive causal conditions which produce the former and not the latter, and, finally, combining (1) and (2) in the definition of *pramāṇa*. In the case of the theories which regard truth as intrinsic (*svataḥ*), the causal conditions producing cognition (of a certain type) and those producing true cognitions (of that type) coincide.

In Western philosophy, causal theories are regarded as being notoriously reductionistic, and therefore suspect for the logician-cum-epistemologist. Not so in the Indian tradition, which regarded them as being descriptive and compatible with the uniqueness of cognitions and their claim to truth. There are two aspects of this liberalism: for one thing, the reductionist causal laws are physicalistic and orientated towards the prevailing physical theory, while

the causal laws used by the Indian epistemologists are formulated in terms of such heterogeneous elements as physical contacts, revived memories, and desires to have a certain sort of knowledge, for example—if necessary, even activation of traces of past *karma* and the ubiquitous passage of time. Secondly, such a causal story is not explanatory but descriptive, for it is formulated in a way that wishes to adapt the story to the intuitive needs of a cognitive event rather than to submit to the constraints of an available physical theory. The general constraints were, rather, those of a large ontological theory.

As regards *pramāṇa theory*, I will make only two more comments before passing on to the *prameya* theory, i.e. ontology. These two remarks will concern *anumāna* (or inference) and *śabda* (word), in that order.

Much has been said in the secondary literature on the fact that the Indian theory of inference is psychologistic (it tells a story about how inferential cognition arises) and non-formal (it requires an instance where the universal major premiss is satisfied). Both characterizations are right, but unless correctly understood are likely to mislead. I have already pointed out in Chapter 4 how psychology and logic were reconciled in Indian thought. The theory of inference is a good illustration of this position. The *rapprochement* between psychology and logic was done by logicizing psychology as well as by psychologizing logic: the former by assuming that the psychological process of reasoning conforms to the logical (any seeming deviance, as in supposedly fallacious reasoning, being due to misconstrual of the premisses); and the latter by making logic a logic of cognitions rather than of propositions. It is not that the Indian theory of inference does not know of formal validity. In fact a formally valid mood can be abstracted from a valid Nyāya inference. But since the interest was in cognitions (and not in either sentences or propositions), and in inference as a *pramāṇa*, as a source of true cognition, the merely formally valid inference, as in *tarka* or reasoning from counterfactuals, was left out of consideration.

This brings me to *śabda* or 'word' as a *pramāṇa*. It is really here that the true foundation and the deeper roots of the Hindu tradition lie. The mere recognition of *śabda* as a means of knowing is itself a novel feature of the Indian epistemologies. The Western epistemologies recognize one or more of the following sorts of

knowledge: perception, reasoning, introspection, and memory. Many, in more recent philosophy, have come to emphasize the decisive role that language plays in shaping our knowledge. But to the best of my knowledge, no one recognizes language—or verbal utterance—as by itself a means of generating knowledge about the world. And yet how much do we know simply by hearing others, by reading books etc? Not to speak of the religious and moral beliefs that we derive from perusal of the scriptures. The Indian epistemologies consequently not only recognize *śabda* (i.e. hearing the utterances of a competent speaker) as a means of knowing, but as the decisive source of our cognitions about all those matters that transcend the limits of possible sensory experience.

While the *pramāṇas* serve both as originating causes of true cognitions and means of critical appraisal of cognitive claims, for almost all Indian philosophers the ultimate ground for all evidence, the source for all 'establishment' (*siddhi*), is consciousnes (*cit*), without which no being or non-being could be asserted or denied and there would be universal darkness (*jagadāndhyaprasaṅga*). However, this consciousness is neutral as against turth (*pramā*) and falsity (*a-pramā*): it establishes both. Thus, though a necessary condition, it is not sufficient for establishing truth (or falsity). For the latter purpose, the Indian Philosophers, in different ways, take recourse to a theory of *pramāṇa*.

To complete this schematic account, I must add a third component (besides the theory of consciousness and the theory of *pramāṇa*)—the theory of action. For all Indian thinkers, cognition issues in practical, actional response (*pravṛtti*), and the ultimate guarantee, for most of them, of the turth of a cognition is practical success. The ultimate limit of scepticism is provided by conflict with practice (*vyāghātavadhirāśaṃkā*). A rational belief, then, is one that is appropriately caused, justified by one or more appropriate *pramāṇas*, and leads to successful practice—all three testified by self-evidencing consciousness.

Prameya

What sort of theories of *prameya*, of possible objects of true knowledge, did the Indian philosopher hold? Given the great variety of ontologies—ranging from the pluralism of Nyāya-

Vaiśeṣika to the monism of Advaita Vedānta—what I can do here is to draw attention to some salient features of those ontologies.

The first thing to be noted is that these ontologies do not countenance any abstract entity of the sorts that ontologies in the West admit. Amongst familiar abstract entities, we have Fregean senses, (e.g. propositions), numbers, and universals. I have already argued that in my view fully fledged Fregean senses are not to be found. Numbers are reduced to properties (*guṇas*) of sets. Universals, although common, are not the sort of rarefied entities amenable only to the grasp of pure reason, which they are taken to be in Western metaphysical tradition. They are, rather, more concrete entities, perceived through the same sense-organ by which their instances are. (If a colour-particular is visually perceived, so also is the colour-universal, e.g. whiteness, inhering in it.) Nor are there pure unactualized possibilities. It is not surprising that these last creatures are absent, for their habitat in the Western metaphysical tradition, God's mind, does not play that role of creating out of nothing. In the absence of possibilia and of abstract entities such as propositions, some standard concepts of necessary truth and its opposite, contingent truth, cannot find any formulation in the Indian systems. Thus we have accounts of what the world does consist in, but not of what might have been or could not possibly not be. Recall that the standard formulation of 'pervasion' (*vyāpti*) is extensional ('It is never the case that in all those loci where smoke is present, fire is absent') but not modal ('It is impossible that . . .').

One reason why, in traditional Western metaphysics, the metaphysical scheme claimed a sort of necessity over against those features of the world which the sciences study is that metaphysics and science have stood sharply separated ever since the beginning of metaphysics in Aristotle. Metaphysics, on this account, is concerned not with beings, but with being *qua* being—the latter, i.e. being *qua* being, being construed in various well-known ways (the highest being; the most general predicates or categories; the meaning of 'being'—to recall a few). For the Indian metaphysicians, science and metaphysics remain continuous: both undertake to understand the structure of the world; they differ only in the order of generality.

If creation out of nothing, and so creation in the strict sense, has no place in Indian thought, that simply is not a marginal

phenomenon for the *darśanas*, but—as I believe can be shown—determines some very central features not only of the Indian cosmologies but also of the metaphysical notions of God, substance, time, and negation. I cannot undertake that task here.

Pramāṇa–Prameya *structure*

I may now make a few remarks on the *pramāṇa–prameya* structure in its entirety, i.e. on the philosophical enterprise as illustrated in the *darśanas*. While engaged in highly sophisticated philosophical activity, the Indian thinkers did not explicitly and self-consciously focus on the nature of their enterprise. It is generally in response to the sceptical challenges of a Mādhyamika that sometimes they would, while defending their enterprise, remark on the nature of what they would be doing. Without going into textual details, let me state some of the main issues.

1. The Mādhyamika critique is not merely a critique of the epistemology but also a critique of the ontology. The critic insists on the mutual dependence of epistemology and ontology. You cannot decide what the means of cognition are unless you have decided what things there are to be known. And you cannot settle this latter question unless you have, at hand, the means of knowing. Where then do you begin? If the circularity cannot be broken, why not give up the entire enterprise?[4]

2. The *pramāṇa-prameya* theorist's response to this challenge has been, in brief, that it presupposes an unnecessarily strong reading of the unity of the two parts of a *darśana*. There is no one-to-one relation between a means of cognition and its object. One and the same thing can be known by more than one means. One and the same system of ontology can be made to go together with different epistemologies: consider the Nyāya and the Vaiśeṣika. The mutual dependence that threatens the relation between cognition in general and object in general is broken by specifying both and establishing a many–one or one–many relation between terms on each side.[5]

3. What (2) entails is that a *darśana* is not a seamless unity such that parts of it cannot be taken out of the context of that system. My interpretation goes against the traditionalists' view of it, which

regards each *darśana* as a unique point of view. Amongst moderns, the Russian emigré David Zilberman (whose untimely death was a serious loss to the cause of Indian philosophy) held this holistic view of a *darśana*[6]—which I reject here.

4. The reflective question what sort of knowledge a philosophical system itself yields (or amounts to) and if it can itself be appropriated into one or more of the *pramāṇas* recognized by the system is not explicitly asked, but the practice suggests that quite often it is the latter alternative that was chosen. The reason—already hinted at earlier—lay in not recognizing that philosophical knowledge is a knowledge that is, *qua* knowledge, distinct from the sorts of knowledge that are thematized within the system. An alternative way out, which would consist in distinguishing between understanding and knowing (such that philosophy yields understanding, but not knowledge) was not open—in view of the purely referential theory of meaning. When the Vedāntin says that knowledge of *brahman* brings about *mokṣa*, this knowledge is such that both the knowledge and the entity of which it is knowledge are thematized within the system. When the *Nyāyasūtra* says that knowledge of the sixteen categories (*padārthas*) brings about the highest good,[7] what sort of cognition is it? Is it by one or more of the *pramāṇas*? The answer seems to be 'yes'.

5. Students of the *darsánas* often wonder from where the early masters—the authors of the *sūtras* and *Bhāṣyas*—derived that framework (the list of *pramāṇas* and *prameyas*) which the later authors went on refining. To say that they elaborated a way of seeing—using the verbal root *drs* (to see)—is not to assuage that anxiety. It is not in any case true that the later authors simply refined and clarified the framework suggested by the founding fathers. They also changed and modified within limits (which also speaks against a strong holistic reading of the *darśanas*). The commoner response was to trace the framework back to the *śruti* (the heard texts with no human author). Consider the intellectual phenomenon that philosophical systems as diverse as Nyāya and Vedānta claimed affiliation to the *śruti*. How then should the nature of *śabdapramāṇa* be construed that this paradoxical situation may be rendered intelligible? I will suggest later in this chapter that for this purpose the nature of *śabdapramāṇa* as applied to *śruti* be construed in a manner that is implicit in the tradition's understanding of itself but not explicitly formulated as

such. And on this point I will differ from the orthodoxy in interpreting the role of *śruti vis-à-vis* the philosophies.

THE FOUNDATIONAL NATURE OF CONSCIOUSNESS

The foundational nature of consciousnes (*cit*) which almost every Indian philosophy (except the *cārvāka*) recognizes concerns its evidential role, but not its alleged constitutive role. This point should be correctly understood, for otherwise a streak of realism that, in various degrees, runs through Indian thought (except Buddhist *vijñānavāda*) would be lost sight of. Consciousness 'manifests', 'reveals', 'shows' all things, it is the ultimate condition of all 'establishment'—as was said earlier in this chapter. None of the *pramāṇas* can do its job without consciousness. In fact, because of this, many Indian philosophers wanted to regard *pramāṇa* itself as a modality of consciousness. How, they asked, could that which is to produce true cognition be other than, in its nature, cognition itself, i.e. other than consciousness? The best example of such a theory is to be met with in Advaita Vedānta theory of knowledge as expounded by Dharmadhvajarindra in his *Vedāntaparibhāṣā*. Such systems as Nyāya and Vaiśeṣika would consider the *pramāṇa* for perceptual knowledge, in the causal sense, to consist in appropriate mode of contact (*sannikarṣa*) of the appropriate sense-organ (*indriya*) with the object perceived. The *Vedāntaparibhāṣā* defines the perceptual *pramāṇa* to be none other than consciousness itself.[8]

This, of course, implies a conception of perceptual knowledge which is an identity, at some level, of the knowing subject (i.e. consciousness as limited, individualized, by 'knowerhood') and the known object (which, again, is consciousness as limited by the object to be known). Such a construction is available because of the large metaphysical theory of Advaita Vedānta that underlying all phenomenal reality there is an ubiquitous spirit whose nature is (pure) consciousness. Without such a metaphysical underpinning independently arrived at, an epistemology of identity is more than what one needs for a theory of knowledge.

I have remarked that consciousness, in the Indian systems, is evidentially primary, but not foundational as the constitutive source of the world. Even Advaita Vedānta, which holds a

universal objectless (*nirviṣaya* = non-intentional), ownerless (*nirāśraya* = non-egological), and determinationless (*nirviśeṣa*) consciousness to be the only reality, does not regard this consciousness to be the constitutive source of the world phenomena and finite individuals, it invokes—as is well known—the principle of ignorance (*avidyā*) for that purpose. On the Advaita view, consciousness does nothing: it simply manifests. A non-intentional, non-temporal, non-actional consciousness cannot constitute. It is the foundation of the world-appearance—but it is not the origin of the world in any sense, theological or phenomenological. Those who rejected the Advaita theory of a non-actional consciousness, and wanted *brahman* to be the source of the world, resorted either to the theory of creation of a sort or to a theory of emanation. This meant construing consciousness as a force or energy, i.e. *cit* as *cit-śakti* (as, for example, in Śaivism and, in modern times, by Sri Aurobindo)—which does inject a certain intentionality into the texture of consciousness, but still stops short of a constitution theory for reasons that lie deep within the structure of Indian thinking. As far as I understand the issues now, these reasons lie in (1) the non-availability of a theory of sense (as distinguished from reference), and (2) an ontologically orientated mode of thinking. Phenomenological constitution is constitution of sense, not constitution of the thing itself (but certainly of the sense 'thing itself'). With a theory of sense not available, theory of constitution would become either a theory of evidence (that is to say, of how things are evidenced, known manifested) or a theory of real origination (that is to say, of how things come into being). The former gives epistemology (i.e. a theory of *pramāṇa*), the latter a causally orientated ontology (i.e. a theory of *prameya*). Phenomenological constitution is a theory of evidence, an account of how senses come to givenness, and through senses things, but this evidencing function is not simply epistemological but also transcendental (in the Kantian sense of being the condition of the possibility of transcendent reference). Consciousness as an absolute domain of being, also as the foundational being, is recognized, but not as the constitutive source of all transcendence.

Thus Indian philosophical literature abounds in a descriptive phenomenology of consciousness (recall the Buddhist classification of cognitions, the Sāṃkhya-Yoga theory of the various kinds

of mental state (*cittavṛtti*), the Vedānta theory of the various (real or apparent) modalities of consciousness) but these do not—save possibly in certain Buddhist theories—amount to transcendental—constitutive phenomenology. They oscillate between descriptive psychology and metaphysics of consciousness.

THE PRIMACY OF PERCEPTION

In the theory of *pramāṇa*, one occupies an undisputed place: perception. Perception is the beginning of cognition; its causes are not epistemic. Other forms of cognition are founded on it. As the Naiyāyika Gaṅgeśa puts it, it is 'not caused by any other cognition' (*jñānākaraṇakaṃ jñānaṃ*),[9] the first in the cognitive hierarchy. Though initially it is sought to be defined in terms of the causality of sense organs (*indriyārthasanikarṣajanyaṃ jñānaṃ*), that definition becomes less and less important. The Jains wanted to characterize perceptual cognition by 'immediacy' and 'clarity' (*vaiśadya*),[10] both these concepts were found to be imprecise. Perception, even if immediate as contrasted with the other forms of cognition, is mediated by relations of varying degrees of complexity (as Uddyotakara first showed).[11] As to 'clarity', it is defined by the Jains as "the manifestation of a thing independent of mediation by another cognition".[2] In a way, this definition comes to the same as that of Gaṅgeśa cited above. In the long run, as Gaṅgeśa says, perception is to be defined as what is known in the reflective cognition 'I am perceiving' (*sākṣātkaromi*).[13] The testimony of one's reflective judgement has to be the final authority.

The peculiar form that discussion of perception assumed in Indian philosophy arose out of a clash between two extreme theories: one defended by Bhartṛhari and the other by the Buddhists. Bhartṛhari's celebrated principle is: "There is no awareness in this world without its being intertwined with the word." Consequently, all perception is linguistic. Vācaspati expounds this view thus:

All things always and everywhere are qualified by names. There is nothing which is sometimes and somewhere dissociated from a name. By this we ascertain the identity of things with [their] names. The things that are

apprehended along with their names are known as having the same locus as the names, as in 'This thing is cow', 'This thing is horse'. This belongingness to the same locus is not possible by the mere relation of instrumentality. One does not say 'This smoke is fire', but rather 'This smoke, because it possesses smokeness, belongs to the same locus as fire'. Even the inferred object for whose inference words are not means is not apprehended apart from its name. Rather, even there the name is present. Since things have their names as a rule, the cognitions by which things are apprehended also apprehend the names of those things. In this sense, all cognitions are linguistic (*śabda*). It is linguistic not because it arises from word as its means, but rather because it arises *in* word. Word is here the cause only *qua* object, because of its identity with the thing.[14]

The Buddhists oppose this with a conception of perception that runs diametrically against it. Beginning with Vasubandhu, who defines perception as the cognition which is caused by its object (*arthādvijñānaṃ*) (whose implication is that the linguistic accompaniments cannot belong to perception, not being generated by the perceived thing), one finds a continuous development through Dignāga, who defines perception as a cognition that is free from name (*nāma*), generic property (*jāti*), etc., up until Dharmakīrti, who, finally and decisively, wanted perceptual cognition to be free from conception (*kalpanā*) and error,[15] meaning by *kalpanā* cognition of whatever is "capable of appearing as related to a linguistic expression".[16] Freed from all that can be named, true perception, or perhaps, pure sensation, one may want to say—according to Dharmakīrti—presents only the bare particular which is 'its own nature' (*svalakṣaṇa*) and which is radically different from that which possesses a nature common to many (*sāmānyalakṣaṇā*).

In view of this radical opposition between Bhartṛhari and the Buddhists, most schools of Hindu philosophy sought to accommodate both by admitting two types, or rather two levels of perception: one non-linguistic and non-conceptual (*nirvikalpaka*) and the other linguistic, conceptual, and so judgemental (*savikalpaka*). If all perception were linguistic, what would it be like—one asks—for a deaf and dumb person to perceive?[17] To say that a name and the named are identical would contradict the testimony of experience: the word 'water' does not do what water does, namely quench one's thirst. A linguistic expression does not belong to a thing (for, if it did, even the inexperienced would use

language much in the same manner as the experienced), nor is it a property of a cognition. A cognition, then, which arises from the 'power' of a thing, should manifest only that thing, not its name.

But, while this is allright, a thing, even a perceived thing, is not necessarily a bare particular. If the thing possesses qualities and exemplifies universals, there is no reason why even when the thing alone produces perceptual cognition, the latter should not apprehend all that is there in the thing—its qualities and actions and universals—without naming them and so without articulating the structure in the thing. This indeed is the Nyāya-Vaiśeṣika idea of the non-linguistic, non-conceptual perception which precedes the linguistic and conceptual cognitions of all sorts.

However the nature of this first-stage, non-linguistic perception may be conceived, all cognition begins here. It is an immediate, though sense-organ-mediated, cognition of the thing itself—which assures the realism of the Nyāya, for in this cognition there is no contribution of the mind, no epistemic entity that could possibly raise the spectre of a purely mind-dependent entity. As perception articulates itself in language, in a sentence, that is to say, there arise structures—the grammatical subject–predicate structure (*uddeśya–vidheya*) and the epistemic qualifier–qualificandum (*prakāratā–viśeṣyatā*) structure—which are at least, in part, cognition-dependent (*jñānīya*).

The thesis of the primacy of perception is to be understood at least in the sense that all *pramāṇas* begin with perception. Whether it should be also understood in the sense that all things whatsoever are, in principle, perceivable is another question. The Buddhists, subscribing as they did to the theory of *pramāṇavyavasthā*, i.e. a settled order of *pramāṇa*—according to which each *pramāṇa* has its own object-type, so that no entity of a certain type can be a possible object of two or more different *pramāṇas*—had to deny the last possibility: what is perceivable is only perceivable, what is inferred cannot be perceived. The bare particular, the proper object of perception as it is, cannot be an object of inferential knowledge, for inference apprehends an entity only as exemplifying a general rule and so not its unique own-nature. Such a theory, by radically sundering perception from all non-perceptual modes of knowing, and the bare particular from all generalities, runs into the obvious quandaries regarding their

rather complicated relationships which ordinary experience does as a matter of fact presuppose.

A more reasonable theory is that more than one *pramāṇa* may together or separately focus on one and the same thing—if only the appropriate circumstances obtain. A thing can be perceived or inferred or made known by the verbal utterances of a competent speaker. Thus it remains open if all things are in principle perceivable. So strong was the temptation to give an affirmative answer that where a thing (such as an atom or the pure self within) seemed to be far beyond the reaches of ordinary perception, a philosopher may be found preserving that possibility by postulating an extraordinary (*alaukika*) perception of which the yogis, having achieved supernormal powers, alone are capable! Positing such a perception is another way of securing and strengthening the basic realism of the ontology and it serves no other purpose than that.

MEMORY (*SMṚTI*) AND HISTORICAL KNOWLEDGE

No Indian philosopher recognized memory as a *pramāṇa*. Is it connected with the refusal (or, possibly insensitiveness) to count historical knowledge as a mode of knowledge *sui generis*? Why is the claim of memory to be a means of knowing set aside? There are two kinds of argument in the literature. One is to appeal to the usage of the word *pramāṇa*: the question whether memory is a proper designatum of the word *pramāṇa* can be decided, we are told, only by men like Gotama and Kaṇāda who use the word with authority.[18] Since they do not apply the word to memory, memory is not a *pramāṇa*. This is clearly a trivial argument; one needs to be able to give a more substantial reason. Is not memory true of its own object, i.e. the past experience? To this, the Prābhākaras reply that truth in the sense of adequacy to its object (i.e. as *yāthārthya*—being as (*yathā*) the object (*artha*)—is) is not the same as *prāmāṇya.*[19] To be a *pramāṇa*, a cognition must be an experience (*anubhūti*).[20] But, again, since *anubhūti* is defined as excluding memory, but including inference, for example, the point is trivial: as before, memory would be excluded by defining *pramāṇa* in a suitable manner.

There are three other ways in which this is done: by requiring

either that a *pramāṇa* must be capable of making its object known independently (*svātantryeṇa*) whereas memory reveals its object only through the awakening of the traces (*saṃskāra*) of the past experience; or by insisting that memory cannot even be true in the standard sense, for its object—namely, the past experience—is no more there; or, finally, by insisting that a *pramāṇa*, worthy of the name, must be capable of making known a hitherto unknown object (*agṛhitagrāhitvaṃ*). (These three of course serve, in fact, to exclude memory from the scope of the word *pramāṇa*—but not by fiat as in the earlier two arguments.) However, none of these is a satisfactory reason for rejecting the claim of memory to be a *pramāṇa*. If one insists upon independence, you do not find it in any of the *pramāṇas*, each of them having to depend upon either non-epistemic or epistemic causes or on both. If what is meant is that memory manifests the object of past experience by first making that past experience its object, then one may reply by pointing out that the object of memory is the past experience itself, and that it is independent with regard to that. As regards the contention that the past experience is no longer there and so its 'manifestation' could not be true, it should be pointed out that memory shows the past experience *as past*, and not as present, so that it is 'faithful' to *its* own object. Does it not make known what is already known, and so is it not merely repetitive? Certainly not, for it apprehends the past experience and its object as past, as then and there, i.e. as qualified by 'thatness' (*tattā*)—which is a new determination. An experience, when it occurs, does not determine its object as that, but as this (*idaṃ*). The point of this reply is that a past time *qua* past is known by memory and *this* is a new object that was not known before.[21] Although the past can be inferred, the past's original grasp must be possible through memory.

In effect, I have argued for the candidacy of memory for the status of a *pramāṇa*. Connected with it is the case of historical knowledge. In this connection, I should briefly like to mention that one kind of cognition that is generally considered in the literature, though almost always set aside, is what is called *aitihya*.

Aitihya or 'tradition' is defined by Vātsyāyana as "This is what *they* have said, the speaker being undetermined—a succession of saying."[22] The word 'they' in the above is explained by Uddyotakara as referring to the elders (*vṛddhāḥ*). Another author further explains the definition as "words whose original speaker is

unknown".[23] From secondary sources we learn that tradition was recognized by the Paurāṇikas as a *pramāṇa*.[24] The Paurāṇikas never gained importance amongst the classical schools, and even the most traditionalist amongst the schools, such as Pūrvamīmāmsā, did not accord that epistemological status to tradition. But this idea of tradition as a *pramāṇa* comes closest to recognizing historical knowledge as being *sui generis*. The general tendency, however, was to subsume this sort of knowledge under *śabda*, i.e. 'word'—as the definitions given above clearly show.

MATHEMATICS

Ever since the ancient Greeks, Western philosophy has been captivated by the model of mathematics. Mathematical knowledge served as paradigmatic for ideal cognition for Plato and Kant. Why is it, one wonders, that the Indian philosophers, despite the contributions of the ancient Hindus to mathematics, never accorded any special status to mathematical knowledge in their theories of *pramāṇa*?

Here again—as in the case of history—it was usual in the literature to consider a kind of knowledge called *sambhava* as a possible candidate for the status of *pramāṇa*, but it was also usual to reject this claim and to subsume the so-called *sambhava* under inference. That *sambhava* included mathematical knowledge is suggested by the examples generally adduced. Vātsyāyana defines it as "the cognition of the existence of one thing on the basis of cognition of the existence of another thing invariably connected with the former".[25] As such this definition would apply to the familiar cases of inference—such as inferring the presence of fire on the ground of presence of smoke. However, the two sorts of example that are given of *sambhava* are: where a larger quantity is present, the smaller must also be present ('If there are 1,000 cows, there must be 100 of them');[26] where a whole is present, its part must be.[27] A curious third example does not go well with the above two: ascertaining the presence of scriptural knowledge (*vidyā*) in a Brahmin. (The last one may be reduced to the same form as the first two by defining Brahminhood in terms of possession of scriptural knowledge.) It would be a mistake to construe these on the pattern of the fire–smoke case, where a prior

determination of the relation of 'pervasion' (*vyāpti*) is needed, i.e. one needs to know that wherever there is smoke, there is fire. In the case of part and whole, or greater and lesser magnitude, such determination is not needed.[28] If that is so, it is surprising that almost all authors agree in subsuming these under *anumāna*.[29] Here we have a set of what come closest to analytic truths, but the tendency to ground these in empirical generalizations bears testimony to the inveterate empiricism of the Indian philosophers—an absence of apriorism even with regard to mathematical knowledge.

This is the occasion to make a few remarks on the nature of ancient Hindu mathematical thinking as throwing some light on the deeper structure of Hindu rationality. These remarks will touch on the concept of number and on the nature of mathematical proof.

The Concept of Number

In the standard categorial framework, numbers—only natural numbers, to be sure—were regarded either as qualities (*guṇas*) or as generic universals, but more often as the former. Let us keep in mind that the Vaiśeṣika guṇas are not all qualities in the standard English, or even standard philosophical, sense if there is any such. (For the Vaiśeṣika list of *guṇas* includes some that one may want to regard as relations. *Guṇas* are also particulars and not universals as some qualities are often taken to be.) Now, on the standard Vaiśeṣika theory, numbers are a particular kind of *guṇas* that simultaneously inhere in, or reside in, more than one entity. The number two, for example, inheres in each of two things simultaneously, and belongs to them, in this manner, only as long as a cognitive act holds them together—much like what Husserl called an act of collective combination.[30] This cognitive act is usually characterized as *apekṣābuddhi*, which corresponds to counting. Also recall the Kantian view that numbers are constituted by counting.

Only the number one, on this theory, belongs to a thing by itself, without depending on the subjective act of counting. All the other numbers, from two onwards, are emergent qualities[31] which owe their being to the act of counting and disappear with the cessation of that act. Number one is purely objective, all the other

numbers are objective qualities that emerge depending upon the subjective act of counting. On this theory, then, one accepts the somewhat strange consequence that the same number, one, is both perishable and imperishable—perishable when it belongs to a perishable substance (e.g. a person) and imperishable when it belongs to an imperishable entity such as a soul. However, all the other numbers are only perishable: they exist as long as the act of counting holds the entities together.

The universals oneness and twoness, however, are, as universals, imperishable. Every number one (or two) exemplifies the universal oneness (or twoness).

The thesis that numbers are qualities or *guṇas* leads to the seemingly unacceptable consequence that we cannot count and so cannot ascribe number to qualities themselves; we cannot say 'This is one quality' and 'These are two qualities'—for on the Vaiśeṣika theory a quality cannot inhere in another quality. This consequence is unacceptable, for it is arbitrary to hold that only substances are countable. Everything whatsoever can be counted.

There are, then, two alternatives: either consider numbers as universals which can inhere in either substances or qualities or actions (on the Nyāya-Vaiśeṣika view), or recognize them as an additional type of entity.[32] Taking them as universals may appear to be simpler (*laghu*), for one admits universal 'twoness' in any case. Why admit, in addition, a perishable particular such as number two? Apart from other technical problems that arise within the system[33] one will be forced—in case one takes numbers to be universals—to recognize number to inhere in sets of universals as well, inasmuch as universals also may be counted ('redness' and 'cowness' are two universals), and recognizing universals as belonging to universals would lead to a vicious infinite regress. The fact is that everything whatsoever can be counted, and it would be better then to recognize numbers as an additional sort of entity that can inhere in any other entity belonging to any other ontological type.

The Nyāya-Vaiśeṣika theory that a number (other than one) inheres in more than one entity at once (that, for example, the number two exists in *both* the sky and the jar taken together, but not in each taken by itself) may appear to be very similar to the modern-day understanding of number in terms of sets. But one should be cautious in pushing such a comparison. The Indian

conception of number was an intentional one, it construed number as a property of a certain kind which, to be sure, inheres in members of a set taken together, i.e. as held together by a cognitive act of counting (*apekṣābuddhi*); it surely does not identify a number with a set (whose members are themselves sets à la Russell). There are obvious limitations of any theory whose concept of number is tied up with the idea of counting. Even if 'zero' and 'one' may be construed as possible answers to the question 'how many?' (the Hindus supposedly discovered zero but the Hindu philosophers did not want to consider zero as a *saṃkhyā*—which is an interesting example of philosophers lagging behind the progress of science!), not all numbers can be taken to be constituted by counting. Only positive natural numbers can be.

Mathematical Proof

An important ingredient of the nature of a mathematical theory is what is to count as a good proof. Although proof theory as a mathematical discipline is new, one can look for, in the present case in Hindu mathematical thinking, what was regarded as a valid proof. I give below two proofs by Kṛṣna as typical and highly instructive examples:[34]

(1) $\vdash o \times a = o = a \times o.$

Proof. As the multiplicand decreases, the product decreases. If the multiplicand decreases in the maximum degree, so does the product. The limit of the former is nothing (or, zero). Therefore, if the multiplicand is zero, the product is also zero. Likewise, as the multiplier decreases, so does the product, and if the multiplier is zero, the product also is zero.

(2) $\vdash \frac{a}{o} =$ an infinite and unlimited quantity.

Proof. As the divisor decreases, the quotient increases. If the divisor decreases to the limit which is zero, the quotient will increase to the utmost, i.e. infinity.

It is clear that as such the proofs are not deductively valid (although if one suitably axiomatizes the theory, they can be made deductively valid). To say that the proofs are not deductively valid is not to say that they are not good as proofs. What we would need is an appropriate proof theory to embed these proofs in. For my

present purpose, it would suffice to point out the nature of these proofs: they are intuitively demonstrative in the sense that they point out, or focus our attention on, a procedure of constructing, or reaching, the desired conclusion. There is an element of 'pointing towards'; we are systematically led to see that the case is such and such. I should therefore say that the proof is intuitive rather than deductive. The fact that it does not confirm to the typical inferential model of Nyāya logic should support my suggestion, made earlier in this work, that mathematical knowledge needs to be recognized as a *pramāṇa sui generis.*

PRAMĀṆAS IN LAW AND MEDICINE

The idea of *pramāṇa* did play important roles in Hindu law and medicine. The inevitable question was: what are the sources of our knowledge in these areas? Thus in medicine, we learn from Dasgupta,[35] four *pramāṇas* were recognized: *āptopadeśa* (teachings by competent persons), *pratyakṣa*, i.e. perception, *anumāna* i.e. inference, and *yukti. Yukti* is not the standard inference, but rather "a series of syllogisms of probability leading to a conclusion"[36] such as obtains in forecasting a good or bad harvest from the conditions of ground, rain, and climate. Under standard inference of *anumāna*, Caraka recognizes, besides inference from cause to effect and that from effect to cause, also a sort of inference in which a disease is inferred form its early symptoms and signs (*pūrva-rūpa*). The role of instruction by competent teachers was of general importance, as in any science: trustworthiness of the authors leads us to accept the validity of the science of medicine, although the truths asserted in that science can also be verified by experience.

With regard to law, Manu lays down the following as sources of our knowledge of law: the Vedas, the *Smṛti* texts (or, possibly, the texts e.g. the *dharmaśāstras* that embody the memory of wise men, i.e. tradition), good custom (*sadācāraḥ*), and one's own self-satisfaction (*svasya ca priyamātmanaḥ*—ot *ātmatuṣṭi*).[37] 'Self-satisfaction' may be construed to mean approval of one's own conscience. Where law texts conflict, reasoning (*nyāya*) should step in.[38] The role of custom (*ācāra*) in law was a matter of considerable discussion. There was a strong tendency to regard the

accepted practices of knowledgeable and virtuous men as an important source of our knowledge of 'law', but where such practices conflict, reasoning has to step in. Kautilya suggests that royal ordinance could supersede custom. Benoy Kumar Sarkar regarded the state as the source of the positive law or *vyavahāra*, whereas the *dharmaśāstras* contested this status of royal ordinance.

One of the things to be noted in the case of law is that here, unlike the general *pramāṇa* theories of Hindu epistemology, a theory of our sources of knowledge of law tended to fall away from a theory of justification, and both again from a theory of application of law to a particular case. The theory of justification is both a theory of interpretation of the law and a theory of evidence. More clearly in law than in any other field the Hindu thinkers squarely faced the problems of hermeneutics. For here it was important to ascertain not merely the meaning and the intention of a particular word, sentence, or passage, but also whether the rule under consideration is to be taken as obligatory or as quasi-obligatory or even as non-obligatory.[39] The obvious principles of interpretation were: when a sentence's meaning is complete and explicit, no attempt may be made to twist it; where the literal and natural meaning does not fit with the context, a technical meaning is to be assigned by taking the external and internal contexts into consideration; rules of grammar are to be invoked to make seemingly unconnected words or sentences into a connected text; where a sentence or a clause has by itself no complete meaning, it has to be read together with some other text with which it agrees and in whose context it may be assigned a complete meaning. As axioms of interpretation, there were two fundamental principles: no word is superfluous, and contradictory texts should be so interpreted that they are made consistent. Further axiomatic principles were: if one rule would suffice, more may not be invoked; a word, once uttered, must have only one meaning; if a subordinate clause conflicts with the principal one, it must be either made to agree with the latter or altogether disregarded; if there is real contradiction between texts, they may be removed by showing either that the texts apply to different cases or that the negative text merely limits the scope of the positive text.

The question of evidence was discussed by listing what sorts of evidence are admissible in a law court, and by ranking evidences in

order of strength. According to a standard list, evidences are either human or divine and human evidences are either witnesses (*sākṣi*) or written documents or inferences. Divine evidences are trial by ordeal or other supernatural signs, but Nārada is clear on the point that where one party relies on the human evidence, and the other on the divine, the king should accept the human, not the divine. Of the three human evidences, witness is superior to inference, and written document is superior to witness[40]—while, in the case of claims to property, undisturbed possession for three generations is superior, as evidence, to all three. Document is superior to witness, for the latter may have defective memory. As Nārada puts it, witnesses are dependable as long as they live, a document is always strong[41] (and possession becomes strong as time passes). A written document is either written in one's own hand or written by another. The former is *pramāṇa* even in the absence of the author, i.e. is not in need of attestation; the latter is *pramāṇa* only when accompanied or attested by a witness.[42] Other qualifications follow: a written document is not a *pramāṇa* if written under compulsion,[43] under fear, if written by a dying person, by a person under intoxication, at night, or by fraud. If there is doubt about a text's authenticity, one needs to take into consideration the handwriting of the alleged author, the signs, circumstantial evidence, and probability of the case.[44]

THE THEORY OF *ŚABDAPRAMĀṆA*

What is, however, the most distinctive feature of Hindu thinking is the thesis of *śabdapramāṇa*. This thesis claims not only that *śabda* or word (or language) is a source of valid knowledge, but also that as a *pramāṇa* it is the strongest of all (at least in certain privileged domains) and cannot be challenged by any other. Since the general theory of meaning (of words and sentences) has been discussed in Chapter 3, I want to pass on immediately to some critical observations on the thesis that word or sentence by itself may, upon being uttered by a competent speaker and heard by a competent auditor, generate in the latter a valid knowledge about a state of affairs.

The issue is: is linguistic understanding (*śābdabodha*) *eo ipso*

also a linguistic knowing, i.e. (*śabdapramā*), or does the former amount to knowing only when certain specifiable conditions are satisfied. If the second alternative is accepted, these additional conditions could not be the same as the familiar conditions of contiguity (*āsatti*), semantic fitness (*yogyatā*), expectancy (*ākāṅkṣā*) and intention (*tātparya*), for these are, on the theory, conditions of linguistic understanding itself. On the first alternative, all linguistic understanding is *pramā*, i.e. is true, so that a false (*a-pramā*) *śābdbodha* would be a contradiction in terms. And yet, in an intuitively clear sense, one does understand a false sentence, so that what hearing a false sentence being uttered by a speaker taken to be competent generates in the hearer could not be knowledge. It can only be understanding of the meaning of the sentence.

In his Commentary on *Nyāyabhāṣya* on *Nyāyasūtra* II. i. 48, Uddyotakara anticipates three objections against the view that *śabda* is a *pramāṇa*. These three are: that *śabda* does not always (e.g. if it is not heard) produce knowledge; that it does not have an object (*viṣayābhāvāt*) which is not presented by either perception or inference; and that, not being of the nature of cognition, it does not, like a jar, inhere in the soul (*ātmani asmavāyāt*). To these three objections, Uddyotakara gives the following replies: *śabda* produces knowledge when experienced or heard; there is no rule that there is no object other than what is known by perception and inference; it is not also necessary that to be a *pramāṇa* something must inhere in the soul. The first and the last are acceptable. It is to the second that we need to attend: what are those objects which are neither possible objects of perception nor possible objects of inference?

Let us not forget that the Nyāya, as also the other schools of philosophy who are committed to *śabdapramāṇa*, do not believe in the thesis that there is a 'fixed arrangement of *pramāṇas*' (*pramāṇavyavasthā*). In other words, they believe that one and the same thing can be known by one or more of the *pramāṇas*. In order to prove, therefore, that *śabda* is a *pramāṇa* it is not necessary to prove that there is some object or some type of object which is known by *śabda* but not by the other *pramāṇas*. But should there be some such object, the case for *śabdapramāṇa* gets an additional support. So I will consider this case in two stages: first by asking when does *śabda* cause us to know something which

we could have possibly known by other means; and then by asking if there is some unique sort of object which can be known only by *śabda*. Now to the first question.

The first question, namely, when does *śabda* cause us to know what could be known otherwise, may itself be dealt with in two stages. We first consider the case of perceptible objects and then consider the (allegedly) supersensible objects (which can be known by inference or by an *arthāpatti* sort of transcendental argument). For the first case, consider the sentence 'Aśvo dhāvati' ('Horse is running'). If this means '*That* horse is running' a demonstrative needs backing by perception. The speaker can point as *that* only to what is being perceived at a distance. The hearer can know *that* horse to be running only if he too perceives, besides understanding the meaning of the utterance. If the Sanskrit sentence means '*A* horse is running', the hearer may be said to know, simply on hearing the utterance, that a horse is running (and need not, for that knowledge, wait for perceptual support). However, there are two things to be noted. In the first place, the hearer must also know that the speaker is *āpta*, i.e. that he knows what he is talking about, and is sincere and reliable, in order to be able to know upon hearing the speaker's utterance. In the second place, he knows, in the case under consideration, not any particular horse to be running, but only that some one horse is running. In other words, his knowledge is not *de re* but *de dicto*: there is no particular horse of which he knows that it is running. Both these points, if closely looked at, will cast doubt upon the claim of *śabda* to be a *pramāṇa*.

The first one suggests a more general question, to which I will return a little later, but let me first address myself to the second issue.

To be able to distinguish between *de re* and *de dicto* knowledge (which, to be sure, is not the same as that between 'knowing' and 'understanding' as I stated it earlier) one needs to be able to distinguish between a proposition and the thing to which the proposition obtains, and one does not have this latter distinction unless one has also a prior distinction of some sort between sense and reference. The Indian philosophers, as we have already noticed, do not have this last distinction, and so cannot distinguish between *de re* and *de dicto* knowledge. All knowledge is *de re*. Upon hearing a competent speaker say 'A horse is running' I am

supposed to know a *res*, a thing being in a state of action, but which thing?

It is here that a familiar strategy of the Indian epistemologist can be introduced. One may want to say that what is known in the case under consideration is not that horse *qua* that horse, i.e. as limited (*avacchinna*) by thisness (*idaṅtva*) and horseness (*aśvatva*), but as limited only by horseness (*aśvatva*). But this won't do, for what establishes the fact that *that* horse is being known even if not *qua* that horse?

The point I am making is that in the case of *laukika śabda* or ordinary 'word' referring to perceptible objects, its knowledge-giving function is parasitical upon perception and inference, and is not an independent one. So when we are reminded, rightly I think, what an enormous amount of knowledge we possess derives from reading books and newspapers amongst others and hearing others taken to be competent say, that fact cannot be used to prove that *śabda* is a *pramāṇa*. In all such cases we are said to know only inasmuch as the possibility of perceptual confirmation or inferential backing is taken for granted.

To turn now to the other point: namely, that *śabda* produces knowledge only when it is uttered by a competent speaker. Apart from the question, if the competency of the speaker must also be known, we need to ask the following questions. Suppose the hearer believes the speaker to be competent, and so *knows* that *p* upon hearing '*p*' being uttered. Suppose also that later on he finds out the speaker was not competent. He still understands the sentence '*p*' although he cannot any longer be said to know that *p*. What sort of understanding is this, that falls short of knowing? To put it in other words, is there linguistic understanding only when the speaker is in fact competent? Does the linguistic understanding change when the speaker, at first taken to be competent, is found not to be so? Many Nyāya authors tend to hold the view that when the speaker is not competent and the sentence is false, there is no such understanding. What seems to be an understanding is some other peculiar mental state. This is an unsatisfactory position: first, it defines 'linguistic understanding' as true cognition so that an understanding of a false sentence is being ruled out by definition. Secondly, it is denying a distinction that obtains in the case of other *pramāṇas*. In the case of perception, an erroneous perception is still perception. In the case of inference, if one ascertains

the presence of a defective mark (*hetu*), the inference is stopped—not as a consequence of the definition of '*anumiti*' but as a matter of psychological fact. In the present case of *linguistic understanding*', however, although one fully understands a false sentence, and even if this understanding is phenomenologically indistinguishable from that of a true sentence, one is *śābdabodha*, the other is not.

What all this amounts to is this: the concept of linguistic understanding (*śābdabodha*) does not yield—as some have wrongly thought it does—a theory of sense. Because of a strictly referential theory of meaning, the Indian epistemologists took *śābdbodha* to be knowledge. My effort, here as elsewhere, has been to suggest that the distinction between *śābdabodha* as linguistic understanding and *śābdabodha* as linguistic knowing is important and should be brought to explicit recognition. That something like this was on the horizon is suggested by the recognition that even if there is doubt about semantical competency (*yogyatā*), *śābdabodha* may occur. This recognition is glossed over by a commentator thus: "*śābdabodha* arises from the cognition of competency. It does not matter if such cognition is assertive or is a case of doubt."[45] There is a serious equivocation here. If there is doubt about competence, there cannot be *śābdabodha* as a true knowledge; but there can be *śābdabodha* as a mode of linguistic understanding. To sum up, then, in the case of indicative sentences about perceptible objects, merely hearing the utterances of a competent speaker can be said to yield knowledge only upon the presumption of verifiability by either perception or inference. *Śabda*, then, in this domain, is not an independent *pramāṇa*. In the case of supersensible realities—such as God or soul—I will defend a similar thesis: *śabda* can generate belief, very strong belief as a matter of fact, but not claim to know unless and until some other *pramāṇa* is brought in support, either inference or some mode of supersensible perception if permissible.

Is the view that we do not have a *śābdabodha* of a false sentence (but only a peculiar mental state) really counter-intuitive? One may reply that it would be so, only if we construe *śābdabodha* as linguistic understanding. It is counter-intuitive to say that we do not understand the meaning of a false sentence. But the view is not counter-intuitive, if by *śābdabodha* is meant linguistic knowledge: we surely cannot be said to know when the sentence heard is false.

As a response to this challenge, let me take it as uncontroversial (1) that we do understand false sentences, but (2) do not have knowledge upon hearing and understanding such a sentence. (1) entails a theory of understanding which the Indian theories do not have. (2) leaves the basic theory of *śābdabodha* intact: *śābdabodha* is intrinsically *pramā* (at least, with regard to its origin, if not with regard to its cognition—i.e. it is true, to begin with, even if it is not known to be so).

But this would be an unsatisfactory solution, for (1) and (2) cannot be held together. A theory of understanding as is implied in (1) requires a theory of meaning—of meaning that is grasped in understanding a sentence, no matter if that sentence is true or false. But such a theory of meaning—which cannot be purely referential, for then (1) will have to be rejected—will undermine the claim made in (2). Nothing less than a purely referential theory can save (2), and yet a purely referential theory will undermine (1). With a purely referential theory of meaning, understanding a false sentence becomes a 'mock-understanding' (as Arindam Chakraborty would have it, using a Fregean locution).

Let me here turn to Arindam Chakraborty's paper 'Understanding Falsehoods: A Note on the Nyāya Concept of Yogyatā',[46] in which he directly confronts the problem. Chakraborty recognizes that on the usual understanding of '*yogtatā* as semantic compatibility or fitness, although sentences such as 'Idleness is green' and 'He is sprinkling with fire' are ruled out from generating *śābdabodha*, a false sentence such as 'The jar is on the floor' is not (when there actually is no jar on the floor referred to in the context of the utterance). Wishing to rule out this possibility, Chakraborty then takes up a suggestion from *Siddhāntamuktāvalī* as implying that a sentence '*a* is *F*' is characterized by fitness (*yogyatā*) only if *a* is *F*—which makes 'fitness' collapse into 'truth'. Only true sentences are fit and so can generate *śābdabodha*. Not only contradictory sentences such as 'The fireless hill has fire', but also consistent but semantically absurd sentences such as 'Idleness is green' and even contingently false sentences such as 'It is raining' (when it in fact is not)—all these cannot generate *śābdabodha*. They may generate a mental state consisting of memories of the referents of the component words, but they cannot generate a relational, qualificative cognition, for there is *ex hypothesi* no such relational entity to know.

Now, on this ingenuous interpretation, 'semantic fitness' (*yogyatā*) is indistinguishable from 'truth'; in fact, it is the same thing. It amounts to ruling out the possibility of understanding false sentences by stipulating by fiat, as it were, that truth is a condition of sentence-understanding. Even if this problem is in some way surmounted, consider this interpretation of 'fitness' together with the position that what is required for *śābdabodha* is not fitness itself but awareness of fitness, then a certain determination of truth is being built into the theory—which is in conflict with the Nyāya thesis of truth as extrinsic. The only way of obviating this is to weaken the sense of 'awareness of fitness (=truth)' to mean 'absence of firm disbelief in absence of fitness (i.e. in untruth)'. But in that case when one believes a sentence (in fact false) to be true (and regards the speaker to be competent, etc.) one must understand it, and since one does not know anything, this understanding has to find a place in a theory of *śābdabodha*. To say that in this and other cases of putative understanding of false sentences what occurs is simple recollection of meanings of the component expressions but no integrated sentence-meaning won't do for four reasons: first to base this claim on the fact that there is no integrated 'featured individual' of the sort is precisely to beg the issue about what one grasps in understanding (as contrasted with knowing); secondly, one cannot distinguish phenomenologically the two experiences (i.e. understanding a false sentence when believed to be true and understanding a true sentence believed to be true); the matter gets—in the third place—more complicated, to the disadvantage of the proposal under consideration, when one considers true sentences taken to be false; and, finally, the way the distinction is sought to be drawn (namely, that in the case of true sentences there is a qualificative cognition whereas in the case of false sentences there is merely memory of unrelated substantial meanings) is compatible with the Prābhākara theory that there is no false cognition rather than with the Nyāya theory that the object of false cognition is real but elsewhere.

Let me now return to a sentence from K. C. Bhattacharya: "The word *directly* refers to the thing, expresses the thing, *touches* it in a sense."[47] Likewise, "The sentence at once refers to an objective relation." There are two things about K. C. Bhattacharya's thesis (or interpretation of *śabdapramāṇa*) which deserve attention. For one thing, in the sentence just preceding

the first-quoted one, he writes that even in the case of a word remembering is not understanding the meaning. This contrasts with the account we examined earlier: in the case of a false sentence, we do understand the meanings of words by way of remembering them, but that does not constitute sentence-understanding. K. C. Bhattacharya is, in fact, distinguishing between (let us not forget, he is interpreting the Vedānta, and not the Nyāya theory) the name, the concept, and the objective reference, for he goes on to write: "The free concept not only requires the name or its support but is identical with it, though transcending it." Then, a little later, he continues: "the same determination of the self gives the name and the concept an identical object-reference". I take 'the free concept' to mean 'meaning' (as distinguished from objective reference). By 'the determination of the self', I take to mean, following the editor's footnote at that place, 'the assertive function of the self'. Read this together with what follows in the next paragraph (and this is the second thing to be attended to): "The primordial objective reference of a judgement is a provisional belief, a belief, it may be, with a certain general cautiousness induced by experience: if it is only *thought*, it is at any rate *continuous* with knowledge." And we are far removed from the Nyāya theory commented upon earlier. It is a theory of direct reference of sentences, mediated by provisional, uncontradicted belief, and also a theory of direct reference of words, again mediated by a concept that is not distinguished from the name. Let us remember that the locutions 'direct' and 'indirect' are ambiguous: one can ask, how direct? how indirect? You may have a concept of mediation by a sense-content (conceived as transparent, objectified only in reflection) which is compatible with a theory of direct reference. This is what I have been intending these critical remarks to point to.

Is there then some unique domain of which *śabda* alone yields knowledge? What other possible object of knowledge could be a candidate for this role, besides sensible and allegedly supersensible realities? The thesis that I wish to defend is this: *śabda* alone gives us knowledge of moral rules, of what one ought to or ought not to do, of *vidhi* and *niṣedha*. I am not only saying that ought-sentences cannot be derived from is-sentences (so that perception and inferences are incapable of yielding knowledge of moral rules), but much more. I am *not* saying that 'one ought to do

Ø,' follows from '*S* (who is a competent speaker) says one ought to do Ø'; for to say that would be to say that moral rules are inferred from the fact that someone has uttered sentences stating those rules. What I am saying, rather, is that we learn the rules only from hearing (or reading) verbal or written instructions. There is no other means of knowing them.

Now, of course, one may come to believe in God as a result of reading scriptures or listening to discourses by competent speakers. But, I would say, such belief, however strong it may be, would not amount to knowledge unless and until it is supported by either perception (supersensible) or valid inference (such as the famed proofs, if they are valid). So, in the case of such things as God, there is a difference between believing (however strongly) and knowing. But in the case of moral rules, there is no meaningful way of drawing this distinction. In other words, there is no other sense of knowing that one ought to do Ø than by imbibing the belief that one ought to do Ø upon hearing 'one ought to do Ø'. (There may be other (additional) conditions to be satisfied, in order to give rise to *śābabodha*, in this case).

Note that if this belief is given up, it is given up by imbibing another such belief acquired similarly (analogously to the way one perceptual error is corrected by another).

Without pausing to defend this thesis any longer, I will, in the rest of this section, turn to an important aspect of the thesis of *śabdapramāṇa*, namely the thesis that the *śruti* texts have no human author.

It is for me too literal an understanding of this thesis to construe it as meaning that the texts are simply not composed by any human author at all, or even that they are not composed at all. It is also totally muddled—and betrays an insensitiveness to the nature of Hindu thought—to say that the *śruti* is *apauruṣeya*, i.e. has no human author in the sense that it contains revealed truths. No less muddled is the cliché that the scriptures express the spiritual experiences of their presumed authors. This last remark needs some comments.

I want to say not only that the scriptures do not express spiritual experiences but much more than that: that a sentence does not express experience in any significant sense of 'expressing'. Positively speaking, what a sentence expresses is a thought. This is not to deny that there are such things as experiences or even

mystic experiences. Only these raw experiences are not expressed in sentences. An experience does not tell its own tale. It is interpreted, transformed into a thought, brought under a conceptual framework, to be put in words. Even poetic language does not express poetic emotions. Poetry is not—contrary to Wordsworth's pronouncement—emotion recollected in tranquility. It is, rather, personal emotion transformed into public concepts, as T. S. Eliot would have it. The *rasa* precisely is this thought-equivalent of private experiences of the poet. When a mystic is reported as having experienced the identity of his self with *Brahman*, it is not the bare experience that is being reported (even by him), but the experience as interpreted by the Upaniṣadic conceptual framework of whatever variety. Even the author interprets himself.

My thesis is: the words do not state, report, convey experiences. The sentence 'That bird is yellow' uttered by me does not state my perceptual experience, but the fact that . . . Likewise, the sentence 'I am experiencing an oceanic feeling' states not my experience, but the fact that I am so experiencing. These facts are constituted by thoughts. Returning to the eminent texts of the *śruti*, I would like to say: those words *qua* words are available to the community, to members of the tradition (itself defined in terms of those words), in terms of which experiences of its members are being interpreted, talked about, and understood. The words are prior to experiences. As made available by the *śruti*, they have defined, demarcated, constituted the horizon within which this tradition has understood itself. (The implication is that the same experiences would be made to tell a different story, in another tradition, where a different set of words fulfil that foundational role.)

But did not someone write these words and through them report his experiences? I have said that in my view the *śruti* texts were composed by human authors, but I have rejected the view that they express their experiences. The notion of 'intention' is more appropriate: didn't they seek to express their intended thoughts? Yes, but saying this is equivalent to saying that they express thoughts. The idea of intention, when rightly located, has a self-effacing character. It recedes into the background, and remains anonymous, pushing the text and its possible interpretations to the front.

The concept of *apauruṣeyatva* (or the property of not having a human author), then, is—as I understand it—the concept of the primacy and autonomy of the eminent text over the subjective intentions of the author. It is also the concept of the role the eminent texts such as the *śruti* play in delimiting the horizon within which our tradition has understood itself and, within the tradition, we have understood ourselves. The words of the *śruti*, available to us in their singular eminence, have been taken up by us, the inheritors of that tradition, to interpret our experiences, and thereby we have also interpreted for ourselves those words themselves. *The more we need to know the author to understand or interpret a text, the less fundamental it is. The less we need to know the author in order to understand or interpret a text, the more foundational it is.* The *śruti* stands at the latter end. In a sense, it is also true of Kalidāsa or Shakespeare. Great poetry—the Hindu epics as much as Homer—define, lay out, set up that *world*,[48] the world of gods, men, heroes, moral and social rules, their infringements and punishment, fulfilments and rewards, within which a tradition begins to think. After the epics, the Hindu world was never the same. A Kalidāsa or a Shakespearean text makes us see the world in a new way. The same is more true, with regard to the Hindu tradition, of the Vedic literature. All enquiry, questioning, self-understanding, understanding of others, of gods, men, and animals, were performed within this newly opened up horizon.

The tradition is not a set of beliefs or truths. You may deny that the *ātman* is identical with *brahman*, and yet may be thinking within that tradition. It is rather that nexus of problems, concerns, and concepts—encapsulated in keywords such as *karma, ātman, mokṣa*—within which thinking of a community moves. What I want to emphasize is that no statement, belief, or thesis is so sacrosanct that it cannot be challenged. But the concerns and fundamental concepts will continue to challenge us. *Śabda's* claim to be a *pramāṇa* may be weakened by my arguments (and limited only to moral rules), but it is restored to its foundational status of defining the parameters of the central core of Indian thinking.

THEORY OF ACTION

Although this volume is primarily about what may be called

theoretical reason—practical reason and aesthetic reason are intended to be dealt with in another volume now under preparation—a brief reference to Hindu theory of action is not, in my view, out of place here. For theory of action not only forms the corner-stone for practical philosophy, but also is the connecting and transitional link between theoretical philosophy and practical philosophy. This is especially so in Indian philosophy where the ultimate criterion of truth was practical success. All cognition leads to appropriate action, which, if the cognition is true, leads to successful action and, if it is false, to failure and frustration. At this point, I will briefly touch upon the general theory of action the Indian philosophers worked with, and upon some general associated concepts such as the ideas of time, rebirth, and freedom. However, I will not undertake a detailed account of the Indian moral philosophies, which, together with aesthetic and religious thinking, will form the subject-matter of another volume.

A theory of action inevitably cuts across psychology, semantics, and ontology before it takes us into practical philosophy. A rather preliminary schematic analysis of an action yields the following factors: agent (*kartā*), knowledge, desire to act (*cikirṣā* or *icchā*) and effort or *pravṛtti*. We can begin by looking at each of these:

1. Agent or *kartā*. Pāṇini defines the (grammatical) agent or *kartā* by the idea of independence. He is independent who is *kriyānukūlakṛtimān*, i.e. possesses *kṛti* or will which is conducive to the action. He is the locus of that will to act (*vyāpāra*) which is the meaning of the verbal root. In the sentences 'the jar rises', 'the jar will be destroyed', the jar is not the primary (*mukhya*) agent even if it is the grammatical subject, for it does not possess independence in the sense defined.

2. The knowledge that is relevant in the context of action theory consists of (*a*) the cognition that something is to be done (*kāryatājnāāna*); (*b*) the cognition that it can be done (*kṛtisādhyatājñāna*); and (*c*) the cognition that some good will come out of doing it (*iṣtasādhanatājñāna*). The cognition is not simple cognition of a fact but rather of an act—not as given but as something to be done.

There is an important difference of opinion with regard to (*c*): the Nyāya emphasizes it while the Prābhākara Mīmāmsakas want to do away with it. The difference is really due to their different views about whether a sense of duty is to be motivated by a desire

for some good consequence or not. On the Nyāya analysis, I do what I do because I recognize that I can do it and that it is the only means to attaining some good. On the Mīmāmsā analysis I do what is enjoined in the moral code (of the scriptures) when I represent the enjoined action as a qualification of myself (i.e. I represent myself as doing it) and I recognize that the said actions are to be done by me. On the Nyāya view, nothing is striven after, desired, save in relation to the agent, and this self-relation is a consciousness of good. On the Mīmāmsā view, self-reference is not necessarily a consciousness of good. We have a sort of distinction between consequentialism and deontologism in moral theory, or rather in action theory in general.

3. Desire to act or *icchā*. One definition of 'desire' (*icchā*) is that it is what is directly conducive to volition (*pravṛtteḥ sākṣādanukūlatvaṃ*). As a rather well-known verse runs:

ātmajanyā bhavedicchā icchājanyā bhavetkṛtiḥ

("Desire is due to the self while volition is due to desire.")

The desire to do leads to:

4. Volition or *kṛti*, which moves the will to put forth actual effort unless there is a powerful counteracting aversion (*dveṣa*). This leads to *yatna* or motor effort, whose general meaning is cessation of passivity (*udāsīnatva-viccheda*). The result of this motor effort is the action itself or *kārya*.

To complete the verse quoted earlier:

kṛtijanyā bhaveccesṭā ceṣṭājanyā bhavet kriyā.

("Effort is due to volition, the action is due to effort.")

To complete this brief sketch, let us recall that the Bhātta Mīmāmsakas distinguished between two kinds of volition (or *pravṛtti*): those that are spontaneous or self-caused (*svarasiki*) and those that are imposed (*prairaṇiki*). The self-caused ones are the ones that are caused by the cognition of what is to be done as conducive to good; the imposed ones are: in ordinary contexts (*loke*), commands of secular authorities such as the king; and in religious contexts (*vede*), the imperative sentences of the scriptures. Those kinds of volition that are caused by the knowledge of conduciveness to a good are hypothetical imperatives, rules of prudence. Those that are imposed by commands of secular authorities (such as the sovereign) are in accordance with law.

Only those that are imposed by the imperatives of the scriptures are strictly speaking ethical.

In the latter two cases, what prompts a person to act is the simple imperative form of the sentence. The imperative sentence or *vidhi* is often defined as the sentence which brings about volition. There is ample discussion in the Mīmāmsā literature about how the grammatical form of an imperative is conducive to volition—into the details of which I need not enter for my present purpose.

In the light of the foregoing, I may say—following Vācaspati—that agency or *kartṛtva* is the co-inherence of cognition, desire, volition, and effort. One who desires and even wills without knowledge of the means adopted and its operations should not be called an agent; nor should one be so called, if he desires, but owing to laziness, makes no effort.

Does this analysis of action—agreed upon in its general outline by the various schools of Indian philosophy—entail freedom of will? The cognition 'I can do', which is a cause of the appropriate desire, may be regarded as psychological evidence for freedom. But at the same time, the desire and the volition are also caused by the cognition of the proposed action's conduciveness to good, or simply by the force of the imperative command of the sovereign or of the scriptures. It is indeed difficult to ascertain whether the Hindu philosophers subscribed to freedom of the will or not. In order to be able to decide this issue, we first have to ascertain whether the Hindu philosophers had the Western concept of will or not. One cannot just assume that this concept was available, that it is a purely phenomenological–descriptive concept without theological–metaphysical and historico-cultural determinations. One thing appears undeniable: the Hindu and the Buddhist philosophers did not have the tripartite faculty of psychology so familiar in classical Western thought. Volition was often a function of *buddhi*, often of *manas* or *antaḥkaraṇa* (the inner sense). If the same concept of will was not available, the problem of freedom could not be the same—also because the problem of freedom arose in Western thinking in the context of the theological idea of divine omnipotence (and foreknowledge).

I may here briefly touch upon the idea of *karma*. It is well known that this idea, with its associated ideas of rebirth and *mokṣa* as deliverance from rebirth, constitutes one of the most distinctive

features of Hindu religious and philosophical thinking. What I am here trying to do is to understand some fragments of this deep conceptual structure, and to interpret its bearing on such familiar concepts as freedom.

Strictly phenomenologically, an action has for its agent what Schutz called 'subjective meaning'. The agent knows what he is doing, what his intention and intended consequences are. He may even have the consciousness of having chosen to do what he does. However, this phenomenological consciousness, though valid within limits—for example, within the 'reduced' domain of how the action is presented to the agent in his consciousness and with the real existential constraints bracketed out—soon comes to grief. Not only does the most rational of agents fail to anticipate—and even retrospectively to reconstruct rationally—all the consequences of his action, but, as Hannah Arendt has insisted, the story cannot be complete before he is dead,[49] and as both Arendt and Hegel realized, his own actions may turn back upon him as an alien power,[50] as destiny in Arendt's case, owing to the complicated web of other people's wills and intentions, in Hegel's case owing to the so-called divine law and the laws of unconscious human nature of which the actor is unaware.[51] The point, however, is that the chain of consequences of an agent's actions recede linearly into the remote horizon never to be recovered by him, in his own lifetime, but also vertically into dimensions from where they can surface recognized only as alien powers.

The Hindus, as also the Buddhists, realized this more clearly than any others. They also realized this situation in its extreme logical consequence, and sought to understand and bear with it in all its fearful and awesome possibilities. We have, however, gone beyond phenomenology into metaphysics.

How do this metaphysics of action and that phenomenology tie together? The connections are not difficult to see. If all action is caused by desire—as our preliminary analysis pointed out, if all desire to act is caused by the belief that it will bring about a satisfying state (*iṣtasādhanatā*), the only consequences that the Hindu thinkers admitted into their theory were states in which desires are either fulfilled or frustrated. All other consequences are reduced to these, not denied. Actions bring about either pleasure (*sukha*) or pain (*duḥkha*). The chain of consequences that recede beyond the reaches of phenomenological inspection

are such states. But such states cannot float in the air, they need a habitat that is capable of conscious experience and one which is, in some sense, identical with the agent.

While such is the connecting link, the conceptual ties are not all that tight. There are indeed loose ends. For example, why assume that all consequences, even those that follow the death of the agent, are of the nature of pleasure (*sukha*) and pain (*duḥkha*) without covertly presupposing that an identical self survives as the habitat of such experiences? But nowhere in the transition from a phenomenology to a metaphysics are the conceptual links that tight—one expects rational intelligibility, but not rational acceptance. The *karma* theory is a metaphysical theory *par excellence*, based upon a phenomenology of action, not following from it deductively. As a metaphysical theory, it is capable of neither empirical confirmation nor empirical disconfirmation. Its appraisal has to be practical: how does the belief transform one's overall view of life, what meaning does it impart to one's vocations, decisions, and choices, to one's rights and obligations and aspirations, to one's relations with others and with the world at large? These are issues into which I cannot enter, but let me take this opportunity to warn against certain hasty and easily available misjudgements.

One such, widely held, view is to the effect that the Hindu theory in some way, and in some sense, involves eternal recurrence, and so, by implication, a conception of cyclic time. Paul Tillich has argued somewhere that with eternal recurrence, there would be no spiritual freedom (*mokṣa*), for the state of *karma* would have to recur—so that all one's efforts at *mokṣa* would be in vain. It would be another story to show how and why certain doctrines in the Hindu philosophies, more so certain themes in the *purāṇas*, got misinterpreted into the so-called cyclic view of time and then contrasted with the Judaeo-Christian linear view of it. That the Hindu view of time was not cyclic has been well documented in a recent study.[52] Connected with this cliché are other clichés regarding the Hindu attitudes towards history and progress. Let us suspend these interpretations.

Another such view, less wide of the mark and understandable in its origin, is that the theory of *karma* involves determinism. If one's actions in the past lives determine one's situation in this, then it may seem as though one is not free to change one's

situation, one is predetermined to be what one is. This, however, is only seemingly so. In truth, what determines one's situation is one's own past actions, and likewise what gives shape to one's future is one's present choices. These latter, however—and this is the truth about the charge of determinism—are not totally free choices as though they are made by a transcendental ego. At any time, my situation, determined by my past choices, has already been carved out, and the present choices are from within this determinate horizon. If I can never be totally free, neither am I totally determined. My life is an interplay of determination and freedom.

Even as I say this, I must add several remarks so that we do not jump to hasty conclusions. In the first place, the standard (Western) deterministic theories have in view such objective impersonal and collective determinants as physical and cultural environments, historical and economic conditions, bodily processes, etc. It is only psychoanalytic determinism which has some inkling of the way one's own past but infantile experiences, operating within one's own psyche, may give shape to one's present mental life, but most philosophers who have thought about it in the context of the problems of freedom and responsibility have statisfied themselves that this sort of determination is compatible with freedom, moral responsibility, and legal culpability. Karmic determinism is along this line, but radicalizes it still further and should be much less repugnant to the ideas of freedom and responsibility.

There is one point, however, with respect to which comparison of karmic with psychoanalytic determinism is misleading. The point of the comparison was that both are internal (i.e. intra-psychic) determinisms. In both cases, it is my past experiences and their traces within my psyche which determine my present. However, while this is clearly true (within limits) of psychoanalytic determinism it is not that clearly true of karmic determinism. For one thing, in the case of karmic determination there is a systematic ambiguity in the applications of the words 'I' and 'my' across different lives. 'I' applies to each member of the series of lives in a unique sense, and there appears to be no one who can call them all 'mine'. If I am J. N. M., and the past life which was mine was K. P. C., I cannot now say that K. P. C. was I in the same sense in which J. N. M. is so; I cannot say K. P. C. was my (past life) in

the same sense in which the infancy of J. N. M. was my infancy. It is only if someone could remember all those past lives as having been his that he would have a sense of I and mine which is different from the way we use those indexicals in sundry mundane applications. If that is so then even if my past life determines my present, that determination is ambiguous as between a purely external determination and a purely intrapsychic determination.

The nature of this determination, the causation involved, is also different from naturalistic causation on the one hand and intentional causation on the other. The Indian theoreticians had to take recourse to the idea of supersensible traces (or *samskāras*) to make sense of translife causality; what is important, then, is to keep in mind that this could not be causal explanation in the sense of a covering law nor could it have been arrived at by an inductive generalization (for ordinary experience could not provide data regarding the causation involved). My purpose is not to make the situation, along with its mystery, any more intelligible than it is; I wish to be able to say how it is not to be understood. There is no karmic science, there is a karmic metaphysical point of view, and this point of view-unless misconstrued as a scientific or pseudo-scientific determinism—is compatible with the introspective sense: I could have done otherwise.

NOTES AND REFERENCES

1. See B. K. Matilal, *Perception: An Essay on Classical Indian Theories of Knowledge* (Oxford: Clarendon Press, 1986), esp. ch. 4, §8.
2. See my 'Psychologism in Indian Logical Theory', in B. K. Matilal and J. L. Shaw (eds.), *Analytical Philosophy in Comparative Perspective* (Dordrecht: Reidel, 1985), 203–11.
3. Matilal, *Perception*, esp. 35, 105, 133.
4. *Nyāyasūtras* II. i. 11, and the *Bhāṣya* and *Vārttika* on them.
5. *Nyāyasūtras* II. i. 16–20, and the *Bhāṣya* and *Vārttika* on them.
6. Zilberman's papers have recently been published under the title *The Birth of Meaning in Hindu Thought*, ed. R. Cohen (Boston and Dordrecht: Reidel, 1988).

7. See *Nyāyasūtra* I. i. 1.
8. "Pratyakṣapramā cātra caitanyameva."
9. *Tattvacintāmaṇi, Pratyakṣakhandaṃ.*
10. "viśadaṃ pratyakṣaṃ" (*Prameyakamalamārtanda* (Bombay: Nirnaya Sagar Press, 1941), 216).
11. "Sannikarṣaḥ punaḥ ṣodhā bhidyate" (*Vārttika*, in A. L. Thakur (ed.), *Nyāyadarśana*, i. (Darbhanga: Mithila Institute, 1967), 199–200).
12. "Avyavadhānena pramāṇāntaranirapekṣatayā pratibhāsanaṃ vastuno'nubhavo vaiśadyaṃ vijñānasya" (*Prameyakamalamārtanda*, 219).
13. *Tattvacintāmaṇi, Pratyakṣakhandaṃ.*
14. *Tātparyaṭīkā* on *Nyāyasūtra* I. i. 4.
15. *Nyāyabindu* i. 4.
16. "Abhilāpasamsargayogyapratibhāsa pratītiḥ kalpanā" (*Nyāyabindu* i. 5).
17. "Yadidaṃ anupayukte śabdārthasambandhe arthajñānaṃ na tat nāmadheyaśabdena vyapadiśyate" (*Bhāṣya* on *Nyāyasūtra* I. i. 4).
18. "Pramāṇābhiyuktānāṃ cākṣacaraṇakaṇabhakṣādīnāṃ smṛtou pramāṇavyavahārābhāvāt" (Vallabhācārya, *Nyāyalīlāvati*, 624).
19. I leave out of consideration here the Prābhākara view that all cognition is true in this sense of being true to its own object.
20. "Na hi yāthārthyaṃ prāmāṇyanimittṃ. Tasya sarvasamvitsādhāraṇatvāt kiṃ tu anubhutitvaṃ" (Rāmānujācārya, *Tantrarahasya*, ed. R. S. Sastry (Baroda: Oriental Institute, 1956), 2).
21. "Kālasya ṣadindriyavedyatvena purvakṣaṇaviśiṣṭaghatasya viṣayikaraṇena tādṛśasyottarajñānaviṣayatayā—nādhigatārtha—viṣayakatvasambhavāt" (Gāgā Bhaṭṭa, *Bhaṭṭacintāmaṇi*, Chowkhamba Edition (Varanasi, 1934), 11).
22. "itihocuḥ iti anirdiṣtapravartakaṃ pravādapāramparyaṃ aitihyaṃ" (*Bhāṣya* on *Nyāyasūtra* II. ii. 1).
23. "ajñātamūlavaktṛkaḥ śabdaḥ" (*Nīlakanthi* on *Vṛtti*).
24. e.g. in *Nyāyasiddhāntamanjariprakāśaḥ*; also see *Nyāyakośa*.
25. "avinābhāvinorthasya sattāgrahaṇādanyasya sattāgrahaṇaṃ" (*Bhāṣya* on *Nyāyasūtra* II. ii. 2).
26. "sambhavati sahaśre sataṃ" (*Vārttika* on *Nyāyasūtra* II. ii. 2).
27. "samudāyasamudāyinoḥ samudāyena itarasya grahaṇaṃ sambhavaḥ" (*Bhāṣya* on *Nyāyasūtra* II. ii. 2).
28. "atra ca vyāptirnāpekṣate" (Visvanātha in *Vṛtti* on *Bhāṣya* on *Nyāyasūtra* II. ii. 2). *Nyāyabhāṣya*, however, considers it as "rooted in *vyāpti*" and explicates the *vyāpti*, in the case of larger and smaller quantities, thus: "mahāparimāṇe avāntaraparimāṇasamāveśo' nubhavasiddhaḥ." (The presence of lesser quantity in the larger is established by experience.)

29. "tapadi anumānameva" (*Bhāṣya* on Nyāyasūtra II. ii. 2).
30. E. Husserl, *Philosophie der Arithmetik*, ed. L. Eley, *Husserliana*, xii (The Hague: Martinus Nijhoff, 1970).
31. Gopinatha Bhattacharya uses this expression in his edition and translation of *Tarkasaṃgraha* (Calcutta: Progressive Publishers, 1976), 128.
32. "Tathā samkhyāpi pṛthaktvāntaraṃ" (*Tantrarahasya*, 20). Bhusaṇakāra is regarded as having held the view that number is a sort of property much like a universal.
33. See Udayana's *Kiraṇāvalī* for this.
34. Both these are taken from B. B. Datta and A. N. Singh, *History of Hindu Mathematics: A Source Book* (Bombay, Calcutta, and New Delhi: Asia Publishing House, 1935, 1962), 243 ff.
35. S. N. Dasgupta, *A History of Indian Philosophy* (Cambridge: Cambridge University Press, 1922), ii. 373–402.
36. Ibid. 373.
37. *Manusamhitā* ii. 12.
38. Thus *Nārada* i. 40: "dharmaśāstravirodhe tu yukti-yuko vidhiḥ smṛtaḥ." Also *Yājñyavalkya* ii. 21: "smṛtyor virodhe nyāyastu balavān vyavahārataḥ."
39. K. L. Sarkar, *The Mīmāmsā Rules of Interpretation as Applied to Hindu Law* (Calcutta: Thacker, Spink, 1909), 4 f.
40. Thus Bṛhaspati's *Vyavahāratattwa*, 350: "anumānādguruḥ sākṣi, sākṣibhya likhitaṃ guruḥ."
41. *Nārada* iv. 175.
42. *Nārada* iv. 135.
43. *Nārada* iv. 137.
44. *Nārada* iv. 143–4.
45. Visvanātha, *Kārikāvali* with Muktāvali, Dinakarī and Rāmarudrī (Bombay: Nirnayasagara Press, 1982), 420–2.
46. *The Journal of the Asiatic Society*, 28 (1986), 10–20.
47. K. C. Bhattacharya, *Studies in Philosophy* (Calcutta: Progressive Publishers, 1956), i. 83 f.
48. I owe this thought to Heidegger's works on art.
49. Hannah Arendt, *The Human Condition* (Chicago: Chicago University Press, 1958), §§ 25–7, pp. 181–98.
50. G. W. F. Hegel, *Phenomenology of Mind*, trans. J. B. Baillie, 2nd edn. (London: Allen & Unwin, 1966), 488.
51. Ibid., ch. 6.
52. A. N. Balslev, *A Study of Time in Indian Philosophy* (Wiesbaden: Otto Harrassowitz, 1983).

9

The Nature of Indian Philosophical Thinking

EMPIRICISM, RATIONALISM, AND ULTIMATE 'GROUNDING'

The preceding chapters must have made it clear that there is a strong empiricist strand in Indian thought. This is testified to by the primacy of perception, by the importance of an 'exemplifying instance' (*dṛṣṭānta*) in the syllogistic theory, and by a conspicuous lack of modal thinking ('possible worlds', 'necessity', etc). However, some of the ruinous consequences of empiricism are avoided by extending the scope of 'perception' to include intuitive grasp of universals and relations (and in some cases to extraordinary (*a-laukika*) perception by the yogis of all time, past, present, and future). As a matter of fact, even if the philosophical positions were never classified as empiricism and rationalism (or their near kin), empiricism has a stronger claim in the Indian philosophical tradition than rationalism has. While the word 'experience' does go over, with some loss of meaning, into *pratyakṣa* (perception), the word 'reason' has no Sanskrit synonym. *Buddhi* may translate into 'intellect', but the principal epistemological and metaphysical associations of 'reason' are missing.

There is, however, an aspect of 'reason' which is especially recognized in modern Western philosophy since Kant. Reason 'constructs' and 'constitutes' the world it also knows. The idea of 'construction' was present in Indian thought in a strand that ran through Yoga philosophy, Buddhism, and Vedānta. The crucial terms were *kalpanā* and *vikalpa*—both meant 'imagination'. By an extension of the meaning in philosophical discourse, they came to mean mental, intellectual, or conceptual construction.

Yogasūtra i. 9 defines *vikalpa* as what "is generated by verbal cognition" but has no real object (*śabdajñānānupāti vastuśūnyo*). Vyāsa's commentary explains it thus: *vikalpa* falls neither within

pramāṇa nor does it belong to the class of false cognitions. Although a *vikalpa* has no real object, yet it is useful owing to the power of verbal cognition. Under *vikalpa* are included not only fictional concepts, but also such a concept as 'time' which, according to the commentary on *Yogasūtra* iii. 52, is "without any real object", which is "a mental construct" (*buddhinirmāṇaḥ*), and "is generated by verbal cognition", and which yet appears to be real to the ordinary mind. *Vikalpa* thus is a peculiar unity of word, thought, and thing—in the case of *pramāṇa*, or even in the case of *a-pramā* the three fall apart. The Yoga *vikalpa* becomes the Buddhists' *kalpanā*, which attaches 'name', 'generic class', 'substance', etc.—as categories—to the instantaneous being, the 'own-nature' (*sva-lakṣaṇa*) that is grasped in (pure) perception. Advaita Vedānta may then be said to regard all objects, and so all differences amongst and within objects, as but verbal constructions (*vācārambhaṇamātraṃ*), due to a beginningless metaphysical ignorance (*avidyā*).

If anything is a priori in the sense of being the non-empirical condition of the possibility of experience—in a large segment of Indian thought—*avidyā* or ignorance may be said to be that. It is non-empirical, for ignorance has—in Buddhism as well as Vedānta—no origin: it is beginningless (*anādi*). It is beginningless, for one thing, because, it does not make sense to ask 'when did you begin to be ignorant of *X*?' and, for another, the tendency to conceptualize, construct, and differentiate is carried over from previous 'births' to the present one and so fundamentally is not learnt (what is learnt is the ability to employ specific empirical concepts, not the highest categories such as 'substance', 'quality', etc). While thus *avidyā* does function as the a priori in those systems, it is different from the a priori in much of Western thinking in so far as (1) it is terminated or rather destroyed by metaphysical knowledge of the nature of things, and (2) what it constructs and thus lets 'be' are, rather, presented false appearances (*mithyā*).

If the idea of a priori is relativized to each system, then, I should think each *darśana's* own *pramāṇa* theory and the list of *prameyas* is an a priori structure that it only elaborates and dialectically defends against the critics. How this theory is arrived at could not, as emphasized by me earlier in this work, be thematized within the

system under consideration. Nor do the philosophers recognize any special mode of reflective knowledge that is involved in the kind of activity that philosophical thinking is: it is the same cognitive tools that the philosopher applies which the layman in everyday life and the scientist also apply. These are the familiar *pramāṇas*: perception, inference, and *śabda*, and there may be a few others that the system may indeed recognize.

What, then, is the ultimate foundation of the *darśanas*? One of the goals which philosophy in the West has set itself is to provide all human experience—cognitive, moral, aesthetic—*and itself* a secure foundation. This traditional foundationalism has come to be suspect, and eventually abandoned, by many contemporary thinkers. But one modern thinker who pursued this foundationalist goal relentlessly was Husserl, and, as before on several occasions, I wish to compare the Indian philosophers' ideal with Husserl's. Indian philosophy shares with Husserl the belief that all evidence, and so the ultimate ground of all establishment (*siddhi*) is consciousness. But Husserl sought a most radical goal—the goal of rationality—that all mundane formations, all scientific and everyday beliefs, for example, can, in principle, be shown to be rooted in the structures of consciousness such that the reflecting philosopher can, within his own ego, bring this rootedness to intuitive clarity. This radical thesis of 'transcendental phenomenology' has never showed up in the Indian thought-world. As emphasized by me earlier, the foundational consciousness, for Indian thought, is an evidencing and/or grounding consciousness, but not quite a universal constituting subjectivity.

Pursuing this question a little further, it appears as though the laying bare of the rationality of our beliefs and cognitions, of moral rules and artistic creations, confronts, in Indian thought, an absolute limit. The *pramāṇas* establish them, consciousness evidences this act of establishment, but the judicative authority of the *pramāṇas* is not, and cannot be, traced back to their origin in the structure of that consciousness. *What then is the source of their authority*? The concept of rationality as operative—even if not thematized—in Indian thought depends upon our answer to this question.

PHILOSOPHY AS INTERPRETATION OF TRADITION: CAN IT ALSO BE A CRITIC?

If *śabda* as the foundation of Indian thinking, especially *śruti* as not composed by any human author (*apauruṣeya*), defines the limits of the tradition, then much of Indian philosophy is an interpretation of that tradition. This might be suspected as undermining the critical nature of the philosophy. At worst, it appears to be a device to justify the scriptures; at best it amounts to stopping the process of critical enquiry by appealing to the competence, and noble intentions, of the divine speaker, or of the divine author. However, that is not a fair estimation of the role of the philosophies *vis-à-vis sábda*.

First, let us bear in mind that the charge of uncritically yielding to testimony is superficial and does not cut deep. The theory of *pramāṇa* provides the critical norms, and the question whether a cognitive claim is valid or not is to be judged in the light of these norms. If *śabda* is a *pramāṇa* (under appropriate conditions), then one cannot challenge word-generated cognition as uncritical; that would amount to importing a critical norm that is not in consonance with those of the theory itself. Thus one cannot prima facie rule out *śabda*, but has to question, from within the tradition of Indian philosophy, if it deserves a place in the list of *pramāṇas*. While the logico-epistemological issue unavoidably is: whether we need to distinguish between sense (which is grasped in mere understanding of a sentence) and reference (which is grasped in knowing), there are domains such as moral rules where it is through interpreting linguistic discourse (and not through any further empirical verification) that one determines what one ought or ought not to do. The point underlying this claim is not that one ought to do Ø because *S* (a competent speaker or text) says one ought to do Ø (for that would be to say that moral rules are inferred from the fact that *S* has uttered sentences embodying those rules). It is rather the point that we learn the rules only from hearing or reading and interpreting verbal or written instructions. Note that if an accepted set of moral rules is given up, it is given up by imbibing another set of moral rules on the basis of another set of verbal or written instructions. In this case, *śabda* corrects *śabda*—as a perceptual error is corrected by another perception. It

is through these accepted texts that a tradition is built up, but the tradition is not a monolithic interpretation of the basic texts but leaves room for interpretive differences as well as for new possibilities for interpretation. Thus although the different schools of Indian philosophy moved within the space opened up by the *śruti* texts, these schools realized quite different interpretive possibilities.

This brings me to the large question of how far or to what extent critical thinking—which is what philosophy is all about—should feel obligated to respect tradition. Here the two extreme attitudes—namely, that philosophy as a critique of tradition shall be outside it, and that philosophy shall state, defend, and disseminate the beliefs constituting tradition—are mistaken. The latter—which I call orthodoxy—is mistaken, for it has no sense of what critical thinking is: it makes philosophy an apologetic, a respecter rather than a critic. The first mistake, though, of orthodoxy lies in understanding a tradition in terms of beliefs and truths. Even in determining these beliefs and truths, orthodoxy does not see the role of interpretation. Orthodoxy claims to have graspsed *the* meaning of the texts, whereas there is no such. Meanings of texts are correlates of acts of interpretation by interpreters. The idea of *the* meaning is misguided as it curtails the possibilities of new interpretations that lie ahead. Interpretation is a historical process by which the efficacy of an eminent text grows.[1] The *śruti* texts are amenable to new interpretations, and our task is to interpret them from our own position, in the light of our problems. One important consequence of the idea of *apauruṣeyatva* as I have construed it is that since the author's intention is irrelevant (not merely because no one can claim to have entered into the author's mind, but for the deeper reason that the author himself is an interpreter of his own text) the text stands on its own, inviting us to interpret it, converse with it, and make it efficacious in shaping our thoughts.

No less one-sided is the votary of critical thinking who, in his pursuit of an ahistorical scientific universality, claims to be able to overcome all traditions, not merely his own. He deceives himself to the point of thinking that in morals as well as in cognition an abstract universality, a complete freedom from all presuppositions, a total transcendence of tradition is both possible and desirable. As against these claims, I want to insist that concrete

universality consists in finding the universal in a concrete historical situation, that one's thinking lives on presuppositions and the best one can do is to bring such presuppositions to explicit self-consciousness, that one can at most seek to criticize one's tradition from another (which is inauthentic) or from within (which assures authenticity).

I can, within the limits of this chapter, best explain the full impact of this thesis by relating it to two different, though allied concerns in moral philosophy. First is the distinction between *Sittlichkeit* and *Moralität* as formulated by Hegel in the course of his critique of Kantian ethics. As I understand it, the point of Hegel's concept of *Sittlichkeit* is that the abstract morality of subjective will is to be sharply distinguished from "the laws existing in and for themselves", the institutions which as the foundations of public freedom, constitute the "fixed basis of state". This given world of laws and institutions is *sittlich* in so far as the individual finds in it the actuality of his action and the goals that move him. The purely inner Kantian freedom is contrasted with the habits and customs, political and social institutions, of which the Greek *polis*, as an 'ethical substance', was, for Hegel, the determining instance.

While this is the truth for conservatism (as opposed to orthodoxy), liberalism rightly sees that some components of that ethical substance may jar with one's own moral intuitions and critical norms, that some individuals may experience the importance of cultivating a purely inner attitude of freedom as contrasted with which the social institutions and notions pale into insignificance. I do not wish to suggest that one can become a mere transcendental ego, and lead a moral life that totally dispenses with the ethical norms of some community or other. We all have to belong to some ethical substance or other and so to some moral tradition. We all have to be critics of our own ethical being from within. This brings me to the second concern in moral philosophy on which I will remark. It should be clear from the foregoing that in my view Habermas was fully justified in objecting to the way Gadamer's thesis (and also mine up to this point) threatens to legitimize all prejudices.[2] The prejudices, prejudgements, and sedimented and anonymous interpretations that constitute my tradition also provide the medium of my moral life and moral growth. But for that reason, to say that I can at most try to

understand it, but can never be a critic, goes against my moral intuitions. As a thinker, I also face the spectre of alternative traditions, of ethical pluralism and relativism. On these rather large and complex issues, I wish to place before you the following few remarks:

In order to be a critic of my tradition, I need, in some measure, to transcend it—while still, as a person, belonging to it. I play the dual role of a person and a transcendental ego. To be critic of my tradition, I need to find an 'Archimedean point' outside it—Gadamer insists in his response to Habermas. My own being as a transcendental ego provides just this Archimedean point. These two roles are open to me. As a member of the community, as participating in its *Sittlichkeit*, i.e. as a person committed to it, I live and breathe within this substance, both nourish and derive nourishment from it. But I can also, from within it, play the role of a critic. I can dispense with either of these two roles only at great cost to my total moral being. Liberalism is wrong in not recognizing the importance of *Sittlichkeit*, conservatism in not seeing the other dimension.

There are two ways a tradition including its *Sittlichkeit* may be sought to be criticized and changed from within. One may point out that a fragment of its *Sittlichkeit* jars with the rest (as, for example, that caste and untouchability jar with the large humanistic core of Hindu morals). Or, one may reinterpret the tradition so as to eliminate the jarring component and re-establish coherence. This is what Gadamer probably meant in his response to Habermas. A classic example of this second path—of seeking to change through reinterpretation—is provided by Gandhi. Committed to the Hindu tradition in general, he reinterpreted the talk of *varna* so as to make it acceptable to his moral sensibility and thereby contributed towards the transformation of the Hindu *Sittlichkeit* into a more coherent ethical substance.

One important difference between *śruti* and *smṛti* (between the Upaniṣads and Manu's law book, for example) is that the former have a plasticity that permits new understanding, the words have a reservoir of meaning, a power of evoking and challenging thought, whereas the words of the *smṛti*, not entirely devoid of hermeneutic possibilites, are relatively fixed in their connotation, and ask you to obey rather than understand. It is no wonder that the former were regarded as *apauruṣeya*, the latter not. This plasticity of *śruti*

keeps open the hermeneutic possibilities. The door to creative criticism through reinterpretation is never closed.

The picture of my tradition as a thinker, that I have drawn above, is, in one respect, simple. Once one provides what it has abstracted from, the search for universality gains an added meaningfulness. My tradition is constituted not by *śruti* alone, but by all those texts with which I think: Plato, Kant, and Hegel, to name a few. Even within Indian thought, texts, not claimed to be *apauruṣeya*, are important links in the chain that bind me to my origin: the Bhāṣyakāras, Vārttikakāras, Tīkākāras, extending—through a line of historical transmission and inheritance—up to my revered preceptor, the late Pandit Ananta Kumar Tarkatīrtha. My tradition, as an Indian philosopher, needs, then, to be represented as a series of concentric circles opening out to many other traditions, to the large conversation of mankind at the outermost fringes. It is only the inner core which would represent *śabda*—in the strict sense. This domain is embedded in a larger background, and transmitted to me through a chain of historical causation and a history of interpretation. This picture rehabilitates my self-understanding as being both an Indian philosopher and a universal thinker.

PHILOSOPHY AS A HISTORICAL INQUIRY AND AS A SCIENCE

In the self-understanding of the Indian thinkers, philosophizing was engaging in an ahistorical inquiry into the nature of things—much in the spirit of doing science. But this was so also with ancient philosophy amongst the Greeks. The idea of the essential historicity of thinking is of modern origin—in the West, it perhaps goes back to Hegel. The Indian philosophers' thinking was untouched by considerations such as the perspectival character of human thinking or by the temporality and situatedness of the thinker. Philosophy was a search for, or perception of, the truth, differing from the empirical sciences only in the order of generality. The role that tradition as defined by the *śruti* played for thinking was not one that could open up a sensitivity to the historicity of thinking; it rather kept alive a sensitivity to rootedness in that tradition. However, as soon as we turn to the

highly differentiated and internally divided world of Indian thought characterized by endless confrontations and mutual *rapprochements* between schools developing in parallel each with its own theory of *pramāṇa*, one cannot but ask a question which the classical philosophers, no matter of which school, never asked: wherefrom does a school, Nyāya or Sāṃkhya or Vedānta or any other, derive its basic concepts, its list of *pramāṇas*, which it so vehemently defends? One cannot trace them back to the *sūtras*, for the *sūtras* only summarized a conceptualization which was already in operation. Perhaps one has to appeal to an anonymous tradition of interpreting the texts! Thus there is an ultimate relativism, an 'either-or', a choice of interpretive tradition. The only absolute behind all this is the tradition with its texts, endowed with a plasticity of meaning which allows such diverse interpretations. This limit to rationality was operative, but never thematized by the philosophers. Now is the occasion to thematize it, and thereby to press relentlessly towards the ground that supports the alternate conceptualizations. I have doubts, however, if this ground would be anything like the Husserlian transcendental subjectivity. I doubt if we can find anything but the text, the words of *apauruṣeyaśruti* (the heard but not composed text), anything but texts behind texts.

METAPHILOSOPHICAL THINKING: THEORY, PRACTICE, AND MYSTICAL EXPERIENCE

One mark of a critical philosophical tradition is not only an ample measure of doing philosophy, but also thinking about what one is doing, i.e. doing what one may call 'metaphilosophy' and relating the philosophical projects to the overall goal of life. Since the Indian thinkers did not clearly separate philosophy from the sciences, their metaphilosophical thought ran the risk of being metascientific thinking. However, we do find thinking that may appropriately be called metaphilosophical. For this, I will consider two interesting examples—situated at two extremes: the Mādhyamika critique of philosophical systems with a view, one may want to say, to 'deconstruct' them, and the Jain theory of *naya*, whose explicit goal was to accommodate all possible systems as so many alternative ways of comprehending reality that has

multiple aspects. If the Mādhyamika considers every philosophical system—realisms as well as idealisms of all sorts—as containing inner contradictions (infinite regresses, vicious circles, etc.) that cannot be resolved, and as making illicit presuppositions that they cannot justify, and so, in a peculiar sense, 'false' (not in the standard sense in which if *A* is false, non-*A* would be true, for both realism and its opposite, both idealism and its opposite, are 'false'), the Jain wants to accord to every possible system its own legitimate point of view, its own legitimacy within its limits. If the Mādhyamika looks upon reality as ineffable, non-conceptual, and essenceless (*śūnya*), and so all conceptualization as missing the mark, incoherent, and self-contradictory, the Jain looks upon reality as having multiple aspects (*anekānta*) and so all systems, all points of view, as having their own basis and legitimacy in so far as each grasps a truth about reality. While the Mādhyamika grants to a conceptual system, to what it calls a *dṛṣṭi*, only relative truth but denies to it unconditional validity, the Jain allows to each *naya* truth within its limits—not, to be sure, a degree of truth—but truth-from-its-own-standpoint. Where, then, a philosophical system goes wrong is in laying claim to be the repository of the sole truth.

The two metaphilosophical theories are based upon—or, perhaps, reflect—two different logical commitments. On the Mādhyamika logical theory, of two judgements *A* and non-*A*, the negation belongs to a higher order of truth than the negated, so does the negation of the conjunction *A* and non-*A* as compared to that conjunction. No eventual synthesis is to capture the last truth, for if such synthesis is an affirmation, its negation would be a still higher truth. The Jain logician developed a more sophisticated logical theory—the so-called *syādvāda*—in which every proposition may be so construed that from a certain perspective it will be true, just as from another it will be false, from still another undecidable. Making combinations of these three primitive values, the Jain recognizes four more (true and false, true and undecidable, false and undecidable, true, false, and undecidable), and comes out, as a result, with a logical theory that recognizes seven truth-values simultaneously for every proposition, relativized to different hypothetical conditions (*syad . . . eva*). In principle, this is an attractive theory exhibiting a liberalism that is exemplary. But it faces two major difficulties. For one thing, it seems

practically impossible to state explicitly (in details) all those sets of conditions under which a given proposition would acquire each of these truth-values. For another, to accommodate all theories—phenomenalism as well as physicalism—within the texture of reality conceived as many-sided is still not to say how conflicting ontological claims are to be reconciled, and, furthermore, it is not to reconcile them within another theory (like the Jain's own) for any theory would have to be *ex hypothesi* true under some condition or other.

I do not intend to choose between these two large metaphilosophical frameworks. Neither of these allows us to pick out some theory as true and the rest as false: all theories have to suffer or enjoy the same fate. Either deconstruct all, or accommodate them all. The choices are ultimate: they concern the nature of philosophical theories as such. Neither is free from large metaphysical-cum-logical assumptions whose justification has to come from a source that is not strictly theoretical. Both are, by virtue of their universality, self-referential. If the Mādhyamika position is true, then it too should be overcome—as Nāgārjuna concedes;[3] if the Jain theory is true, then it too is only conditionally true, as Śaṃkara rightly insists (but mistakenly advances as a criticism of the Jain).[4]

The other kind of metaphilosophical consideration that loomed large in the Hindu and the Buddhist mind is the relation of theoretical thinking to the practical goals of life. Much has been made in textbooks on Indian thought of the so-called practical character of Indian thinking, that is to say, of the subservience of philosophical thinking to the pursuit of spiritual freedom or *mokṣa*. As we approach the end of this study on the nature of theoretical reason in Indian thought, it is time that I briefly reflected on this familiar characterization that sadly enough has turned stale due to unthinking use of clichés. Some philosophical ideas may have their origin in soteriology, some in the very same texts, such as the Upaniṣads, which have continued to guide and determine the spiritual aspirations of the Hindus. In other words, philosophical ideas and spiritual-cum-religious ideas had a common origin. But once philosophical thought achieved a certain degree of sophistication, it also achieved a certain, and increasingly greater, degree of autonomy. The problems acquired a life of their own. Even the 'spiritual' (*ādhyātmika*) philosophies such as

the Vedānta, while preserving that fundamental interest and rootedness in the spiritual ideal, participated in, and contributed to, the developing critical discussion of the problems. I would surmise there was a vague, ill-defined measure to which they sought to conform: any intellectual—logical, epistemological, and metaphysical—hypothesis would be accepted, if it was defensible by the *pramāṇas*, and, as a consequence (for *śabda* was one of the *pramāṇas*), if it did not contradict the texts of the scriptures, and also—this is important—if it did not make the conception of 'spiritual' liberation (*mokṣa*) impossible, either in principle or in practice. For example, if your conception of the metaphysical ignorance (*avidyā*) which makes one see the one reality as if it were many were such that this ignorance is inescapable, then one would commit the (material) fallacy of 'impossibility of *mokṣa*' (*anirmokṣaprasaṅga*). And this is a serious danger to be warded off. In other words, what the philosophies were concerned to demonstrate—and what they could possibly demonstrate—was the possibility of realizing a certain conception of ideal existence. But this was never a serious problem, for that conception of the ideal existence was itself a datum yielded by the scriptual texts, which the system interpreted in its own way so that the possibility of realizing this idea was a consequence of the system. The further question, which of the practical consequences was more desirable, could not be seriously debated; there rhetoric prevailed.[5] The point that I am making is that the task of philosophical thinking was not to bring about the supposed ideal state of existence, but to demonstrate the possibility of—minimally, to make room for—its realization. I am also maintaining that the idea of possibility of the 'spiritual' ideal was counted amongst the theoretical criteria a philosophical system had to satisfy: it falls under the overall rubric of the claim of *śabda* as a *pramāṇa*.

There is, of course, the further claim to contend with: namely, that knowing the philosophical truths, the *tattvas*, would lead to the desired goal of spiritual freedom. Now, I am quite sure, here 'knowing' was used in a rather strong sense that goes beyond philosophical thinking and understanding. Advaita Vedānta, which takes this thesis very seriously, placed at the end of the cognitive process—i.e. after the stages of hearing (*śravaṇa*) and reflective understanding (*manana*)—something called contemplation or meditation (*nididhyāsana*). The task of philosophy ends

with the second phase, which consists in reasoning to convince oneself of the truth of what one has heard and to remove all doubts (*asambhāvanā-buddhi*) about its truth. But the kind of knowledge that is claimed to bring about the spiritual freedom (*mokṣa*) is not this conceptual knowledge that *brahman* is the only reality and that I am *brahman*—as established in the system—but an intuitive knowledge (*aparokṣānubhūti*) of this sole reality which is said to be the consequence of contemplation on the philosophical truth. So I would venture to conclude that philosophical knowledge by itself ends with *manana*; something else, some other sort of cognitive achievement, brings that practical realization, but this sense of 'knowledge' is beyond philosophy, and philosophy is in no interesting sense practical. It does not itself bring about, but only demonstrates the possibility of a practical goal the conception of which is theoretically internal to the system.

Another cliché—perhaps a queer sort of truth made stale by being uttered unthinkingly—is that the texts of the scriptures (which constitute *śabdapramāṇa* in its most significant part) express the spiritual experiences of their authors. I have several serious objections against this way of construing the authority of those texts, (and equally strong objections against construing them as revealed texts). Only the idea of mystic experience is more in consonance with the tradition than is the idea of revelation. First of all, as pointed out earlier, I do not think it right to say that a sentence expresses an experience. The utterance of a sentence may have been occasioned by the utterer's experience, and may announce or intimate or point to such an experience, but what it means, what it expresses, is a thought. (When a speaker says 'I am in pain', he is announcing his pain-experience, but expressing the thought that he is in pain.)[6] I do not intend to deny the possibility of spiritual or even mystic experiences, nor do I want to belittle the importance of such experiences. What really matters in my present context is that those or other experiences are not what are expressed by the sentences of the texts. In the second place, the texts of the *śruti*, in my view, provide us, and have provided the Hindus over centuries, with the sorts of appropriate linguistic and conceptual resources with which to interpret, and then express, their thoughts about their actual experiences as well as their spiritual goals and the means to reach those goals. What I mean is that scriptural sentences such as 'I am He' (*so'ham*), 'you are

brahman', and conceptual frameworks defined by the identity of *ātman* and *brahman*, have determined how members of the communities sharing the tradition whose basic parameters were laid down by the *śruti* texts have, through the ages, understood and interpreted themselves, their world, their gods, and their goals. To put the matter in another way: it is not that people have experiences which they simply express in those sentences, but rather that people interpret their own experiences in the light of the sentences made available by the tradition, and use those sentences to express the thoughts so constituted. If what I say is true, similar experiences may be articulated differently in a different tradition which places at the disposal of the participants of that tradition a different set of sentences.

As I perceive it, the belief of the tradition that the *śruti* is *apauruṣeya*, i.e. is not composed by any human author, should be understood as containing this much of truth that, in the case of *śruti*, the sentences of the text are autonomous, that in order to interpret them no reference to the intentions and experiences of their authors is needed, that it is these texts which have determined the way the tradition has understood itself.

ARE INDIAN AND WESTERN PHILOSOPHIES RADICALLY DIFFERENT?

If this work has laid out the conception of theoretical rationality with which the Indian tradition thought, that overarching structure must be understood as the logical space within which the different philosophies (*darśanas*) moved and carved out their own varieties of theories. But the common critical thinking in which they participated, the common norms that they used and the rhetoric they employed, all suggest and indicate this common space; they all operated within it, but never thematized it. Even the Buddhists, who introduced some radically new modes of thinking, yet succeeded in thinking within that space, so that a fruitful Hindu–Buddhist dialogue could ensue. Wherever there is meaningful conversation, there must be such a common space.

But does this emerging Indian concept of rationality share its major features with that concept of theoretical reason which characterizes Western thought from the Greeks through Kant to

Husserl? This is a large and very difficult question that I did not set out to answer, and it is possible that at the end of the volume to be devoted to morality, art, and religion we may be in a position to speculate on this exciting question. If we can find some general features that the Indian and Western traditions share, we may not have refuted relativism but we may have found an empirical evidence strong enough to render relativism suspect. But that is a task which I did not set out to fulfil in this study.

Let me nevertheless ask: are Indian and Western philosophies radically different? That is to say, are they different as philosophies?

I will begin by recalling three responses to such a question—one more well known than the other two; all three, in a sense, seemingly leading up to the same conclusion, but, as a matter of fact, having very different implications and intentions. In his Vienna Lecture of 1935 entitled 'Philosophy and the Crisis of Humanity', Husserl wrote:

> Today we have a plethora of works about Indian philosophy, Chinese philosophy, etc., in which these are placed on a plane with Greek philosophy and are taken as merely different historical forms under one and the same idea of culture. Naturally, common features are not lacking. Nevertheless, one must not allow the merely morphologically general features to hide the intentional depths so that one becomes blind to the most essential differences of principle.[7]

Husserl then continues to emphasize what he considers these differences to consist in. I quote from him again at length:

> In both cases one may notice a world-encompassing interest that leads on both sides—thus also in Indian, Chinese, and similar 'philosophies'—to universal knowledge of the world, everywhere working itself out as a vocation-like life-interest, leading through understandable motivations to vocational communities in which the general results are propagated or develop from generation to generation. But only in the Greeks do we have a universal ('cosmological') life-interest in the essentially new form of a purely 'theoretical' attitude . . . and the corresponding, essentially new [community] of philosophies, of scientists (mathematicians, astronomers etc.). These are the men who, not in isolation but with one another and for one another i.e. in interpersonally bound communal work, strive for and bring about *theoria* and nothing but *theoria*.[8]

Husserl concludes: 'The theoretical attitude has its historical origin

in the Greeks.' What about Indian thought? It represents the religious-mythical attitude which:

> exists when the world as a totality becomes thematic, but in a practical way; by 'world' we mean here, of course, the world which is concretely, traditionally valid for the civilization in question (a nation, for example), i.e. the world as apperceived mythically.[9]

The interest in this world is practical, "meant to serve man in his human purposes so that he may order his worldly life in the happiest possible way and shield it from disease, from every sort of evil fate, from disaster and death."[10]

The theoretical attitude, as contrasted with this mythical–practical attitude, is characterized by: (1) a turning-away (epoché) from all practical interests, (2) the thinker's becoming a disinterested, non-participating spectator of the world, (3) an awareness of the contrast between world-representation and the actual world, (4) a search for truth that is valid for all, (5) subjecting all truth-claims, even one's own tradition, to universally binding critical norms, and (6) undertaking and disseminating, through education, both an infinite task of achieving the truth, and the progressive though endless pursuit of this task. In the absence of these characteristics, Husserl concludes: "it is a mistake, a falsification of their sense, for those raised in the scientific ways of thinking created in Greece and developed in the modern period to speak of Indian and Chinese philosophy and science (astronomy, mathematics), i.e. to interpret India, Babylonia, China, in a European way."[11]

The prejudgement underlying this reading of Indian thought is only too obvious to need great scholarly efforts in order to be retrieved. It is indeed true that a certain practical interest motivated much of the recorded Indian thought—not the finite interest of shielding life from disease and all evil fate, disaster, and death, as Husserl would have it here, but the infinite interest of freedom from what came to be perceived as the fetters of mundane existence with its 'chain' of rebirth—in other words, the goal of 'liberation'. But it is no less true that philosophical knowledge, in Socratic thinking, was regarded as the means to a good life. It is only we moderns who have divorced theory from practice, and have ascribed that separation, and consequent purity of theory, to the Greeks (and have learned to deny it to the Indians).

The other claim that the one sort of thinking was theoretical, the other mythical, is equally off the mark. Platonic thinking as much moved within the mythical, as did the Upanisadic—in both cases, myths provided the context as well as the content of thinking; in both traditions thought freed itself from the mythical only in stages, as a historical process. In both—as Husserl noted only in the case of the Western tradition—"what is traditionally valid is either completely discarded, or its content is taken over philosophically and thereby formed anew in the spirit of philosophical ideality". A glaring example of this is the history of the concepts of *brahman* and *ātman*. This is not to say that Indian thought did not follow its own unique path, just as to say that it followed its own unique destiny is not to imply that it did not raise, in its own unique manner, those critical questions of validity, grounding, and evidence which, according to Husserl, constitute the hallmark of geniune philosophizing. Within the first two centuries of the Christian era, the theories of *pramāṇa* had raised precisely those questions, and institutionalized that inquiry.

Husserl's judgement is the result of an inadequate factual knowledge, combined with a too hasty 'theoretical' interpretation of the concept of *theoria*, and the all-too-common (in nineteenth-century Europe) romantic view of the oriental mode of thinking. But Husserl's judgement does not presuppose that relativism with regard to reason which arrives at a conclusion similar to his on entirely a priori grounds. For a good example of this, let me now turn to a thesis forcefully presented by Richard Rorty.[12]

The points leading up to this thesis are: (1) what has come to be known as philosophy in the West—the works, for example, of Aristotle, Hume, Husserl, Heidegger, and Quine—has come to be what it is today by self-consciously and successfully distinguishing itself from theology, natural science, and literature; (2) modern Western philosophy is the result of a number of cultural accidents including the departmental structure of the universities; (3) neither (1) nor (2) is true of the so-called Indian philosophies: they had not only quite different histories, they had quite different sorts of histories; (4) to make a comparison between the two traditions, or between anyone picked from the one (e.g. Śaṃkara) and anyone picked from the other (e.g. Bradley) would be (*a*) to impose one's own favoured conceptual scheme on them, (*b*) to overlook the purposes and needs of those authors, and (*c*) to

attribute common needs to them by "a feat of imaginative recontextualization". Consequently, (5) 'comparative philosophy' (not unlike 'comparative literature') is a misleading and pointless discipline. Consequently, (6) what Uddyotakara, Dignāga Nāgārjuna, Śaṃkara, and Gadādhara were doing should not be called philosophy (call it by some other name, if you will), in spite of the intellectual maturity and vigour of their work.

This carefully crafted and persuasively narrated story, in my view, does not succeed in making the case, and completely fails as an argument. First, as regards the allegedly different history and the allegedly different institutional set-up: the 'philosophy' departments in the West go back to the philosophy faculties of the medieval European universities, and no further back than the twelfth century. The Sanskrit intellectual tradition had already by then classified intellectual disciplines into *trayī* (the Vedas), *vārtā* (trade and agriculture), *ānvīkṣikī* and *dandanīti* (science of government). It is also well known that after listing these disciplines, Kautilya in his *Arthaśāstra* (*c.* fourth century BC) continues: "*Ānvīkṣikī* inquires, with reasons (*hetubhi*), what is right and wrong in *tryaī*, what is useful or not in *varta*, and what is proper and improper in *dandanīti*, and the strengths and weaknesses of these three". It is the "source of light of all sciences, the instrument of all actions, and the basis, the foundation, the *āśraya*, of all *dharmas*". I will not enter here into a discussion of what *ānvīkṣikī* is. Wilhelm Halbfass has discussed the texts and the issues in great detail.[13] Whatever it may be, I am not so much concerned with what the first users of the term meant by it, but with how the tradition, as it developed, and its practitioners, perceived themselves. They did perceive themselves as providing the foundation for the other disciplines, even for *trayī*, the discipline whose subject-matter are the three Vedas. It is *pramāṇairarthaparikṣaṇaṃ*, examination by means of *pramāṇas* of all such objects which are known by perception and scriptures. *Ānvīkṣikī*, then, certainly was regarded by its practitioners and intellectuals alike (by Kautilya, for example) as foundational with regard to other disciplines.

What does the point about different histories amount to? It seems to be a contingent fact—if fact it is—that the histories—history of Indian thought and history of Western thought—ran their own courses without having anything to do with each other.

But of what significance has this lack of connection, in so far as what they were doing is concerned? They may still have been doing the same or similar things—if not always or in all respects, certainly sometimes and in some respects. Would the matter change if some historian of ideas made a discovery that there exists a Greek translation of the Upaniṣads, or a Sanskrit text on Aristotle going back to the beginning of the Christian era, or that Hume's library contained a translation of Milindapraśna (with his inscriptions on the margins), or that Kant did indeed read parts of Śaṃkara's *Brahmasūtrabhāṣya* in an as-yet-unknown German translation? Would any such new discovery lead our relativist to revise his view?

Rorty also goes on to speak about 'need'. "Have Asians had any such needs," he asks, "which have led western universities to teach Seneca, Ockham, Hume and Husserl in the same department?" And yet he himself concedes that "Heidegger and Quine, in their professional capacities, felt almost none of the same needs, pursued almost none of the same purposes." But if, then, Heidegger and Quine would still be doing 'philosophy', why not Heidegger and Śaṃkara—even if neither of the three were responding to exactly the same needs. If 'imaginative recontextualization' is needed to compare Śaṃkara and Bradley, the same is also needed to compare Plato and Heidegger, Husserl and Quine.

Moreover, is Hindu mathematics 'mathematic', is Sanskrit grammar (*vyākaraṇa*) 'grammar'? Here Rorty would concede the point of any such comparison, for in these disciplines all are agreed about the point of the inquiry. But there would seem to be no such agreed 'point' of philosophy. I do not wish to press the question whether there is any such point—but if there is no agreed 'point' as between Dignāga and Hume, there is no more agreement in this respect between Heidegger and Carnap. All are in the same boat, and the group does not clearly divide into two groups from the perspective of the point of what they were doing.

Rorty, along with Schneewind and Skinner, writes elsewhere: "The idea of the truth about the past, uncontaminated by present perspectives and concerns . . . is a romantic ideal of purity which has no relation to any actual inquiry."[14] Now, if that be so, our understanding of both Indian thought and Western thought would be contaminated by present perspective and concerns, and such

contamination would not be a fault. Rather, this is as it should be; it couldn't be otherwise. That makes the thesis that Indian philosophy is so utterly different from Western that we should not call it 'philosophy' incoherent, for we in the West can understand Indian thought only from our perspective; such recontextualization would be not a regrettable prejudice but the very condition of our understanding and so perfectly legitimate. It is indeed sickening to find philosophers argue a thesis about a field about which they know almost next to nothing—and so inevitably using arguments that follow a priori from their methodological premisses, expecting that no empirical evidence could show them wrong.

It is only those who know both the traditions from within, who have studied the source material of both, who have learned to think within both traditions, who can judge whether what is being done in the two traditions is similar.

Philosophers who have never undertaken to translate from one language to another are prone to swear by the thesis of the impossibility of translation. Those who are engaged in translating know how difficult their project is, and yet also experience the pleasure of approximating towards success; they learn how to avoid the pitfalls, how to make their choices from amongst competing possibilities. They do not become sceptics.

Another attempt to keep Western thought totally different from non-Western thought in general, and that without appeal to any empirical evidence but rather on the basis of large, global non-empirical claims, is made by Heidegger. Heidegger, in an attempt to think about the totality of Western thought, characterizes it as metaphysical beginning with Plato and culminating in Nietzsche—a tradition which has led, in Heidegger's view, to technology as a way of will to power, of objectifying and calculative thinking. To quote a dear lamented friend, J. L. Mehta, who had a superb understanding of Heidegger:

> Heidegger agrees with Hegel that 'philosophy' is in essence Greek-Western, asserting that there is no other, neither Chinese nor Indian, that the phrase 'Western-European philosophy' is in truth a tautology.[15]

Of course, Heidegger believed that, with the end of modernity, philosophy has come to an end, heralding the need for a new kind of thinking that would not be objectifying or metaphysical.

In a conference at Brock University, Canada, when I pointed

out, contrary to Heidegger's favourite characterization of Western thought as destined to be a metaphysics of subjectivity, that Indian thought since its beginning has been concerned with the twin concepts of *sat* and *cit* (some forms of Vedānta even identifying the two), Gadamer first wondered, then reluctantly conceded, that *cit* should translate to 'consciousness', and, finally suggested that it is only Heidegger who makes us think of Western thought in its totality, and thereby makes it possible for the Western thinker to envisage the possibility of modes of thinking other than the Western.

Mehta draws our attention to Heidegger's view that the East should not interpret its own linguistic and spiritual genius by trying to philosophize in the Western manner and through Western, historically loaded concepts. Mehta rightly recognizes that the Indian tradition was concerned from its early beginnings with the inadequacy of objectifying, representational thought, but also that the extremes of subjectivism and objectivism were not foreign to that tradition. Naturally, he asks: Is Heidegger's characterization of the Western tradition correct? Instead of saying that it simply won't do to draw the line as Heidegger does, Mehta goes on to insist:

> What is important here, it seems to me, is not whether these terms may legitimately be used for the Indian tradition of thought, but to see each tradition in its particularity, that is, in its uniqueness as a historical phenomenon.[16]

In a Heideggerian locution he goes on to ask: "What lies behind the Indian development, what 'destiny of Being'?"

We just cannot accept Heidegger's characterization of Western thought tradition. Leaving aside without fundamental criticism his obfuscating talk about 'destiny of Being', one must question his attempt to give a global characterization of Western thought in its totality, his own claim to have stepped outside it, as heralding the end of that tradition, his interpretive stance applied erratically that the decisive aspect is the unsaid and the unthought, the claim that modern science and technology are grounded in the philosophical thinking initiated by the Greeks, and so on.

If Western philosophical thought has operated with the subject–object distinction, so has a large segment of Indian thought. If Indian thought in some of its decisive moments has sought to

transcend that distinction (as have Vedānta and Mādhyamika with regard to the *pramāṇā–prameya* structure), so also has Western thought (as, for example, in the grand effort, in Hegel's phenomenology, to overcome, through a successive series of 'shapes' of spirit, the subject–object distinction). To be sure, there are deep differences in the motivations and methods in achieving such an overcoming, but it is, in my view, far from the truth to say that Western thought is objectifying while Indian thought is non-objectifying and non-representational.

For one who finds Heidegger's basic reading of Western thought deeply unsatisfactory, his way of drawing the limit has simply to be rejected.

Stereotypes and clichés have long prevailed over writings on Eastern thought. When it comes to clichés, the Indian side is no freer from them, no less guilty of illicit generalization. Writings in English coming out of India abound in claims to the effect that while Western thinking is intellectual, logical, discursive (and, even, materialistic), Indian philosophy is intuitive, mystic, experimental, and spiritual. It is surprising that these clichés have survived at least a century of intellectual contact with the West, when it should have been clear to scholars on one side having some acquaintance with the other that these are just not true, that neither is Indian *darśana* based on intuition, nor is Western thinking 'materialistic', that the Indian logical theories were no less 'logical', and epistemological theories no less 'analytical' than their counterparts in the Western tradition, that the Indian ontological theories were no more or no less secular than the Western. (For two other such stereotypes, think of the claim that the Indians held a cyclic view of time, as opposed to the linear view of time of the Judaeo-Christian West, or the claim that the Indians did not accept the law of non-contradiction.)

I have often wondered how Uddyotakara, Vācaspati, Udayana, Dignāga, Ratnakīrti, and Gadādhara would have taken these clichés. What would they have understood when told that their thinking—for they are the Indian philosophers *par excellence*, counterparts of Hume, Kant, or Husserl—was fundamentally intuitive, spiritual, mystic? Not unconnected with this question is the question I ask myself: what is the Sanskrit word that captures these adjectives, especially the word 'spiritual', which abounds in modern Indian discourse? As far as I can see, there were two

interests which may be said to be spiritual—making allowance for the fact that the word 'spirit' is deeply Judaeo-Christian. One of these two interests is the *ātman*. A philosophy whose purpose is to determine the nature of *ātma* (as distinguished from body) is *ādhyātmika* (whose contrasts are *ādhidaivika* and *ādhibhautika*). The other, of, course, is the notorious instrumentality of thinking for the goal of *mokṣa* or *nirvāṇa*.

I will briefly comment on this last point, as well as on the much abused contrast between intellect and intuition, and finally revert to the question, has Indian thought developed a standard of critical rationality?

Let me begin with the concept of intuition. As illustrations of contemporary Hindu self-understanding, let me quote a couple of passages from Sarvepalli Radhakrishnan. In his Hibbert Lectures, he writes:

> The Western mind lays great stress on science, logic and humanism. . . . For the Hindus a system of philosophy is an insight, a *darśana*. It is the vision of truth and not a matter of logical argument and proof.[17]

A little later, in the same context, he continues:

> The acceptance of the authority of the Vedas by the different systems of Hindu thought is an admission that intuitive insight is a greater light in the abstruse problems of philosophy than logical understanding.[18]

It is indeed interesting that in pressing this point about intuition Radhakrishnan discusses a whole list of intuitionists from the West: Bradley, Bergson, Croce, not to speak of Plato, Aristotle, Descartes, Spinoza, and Pascal. The only Indian philosopher he discusses, in this context, is Śaṃkara.

Radhakrishnan, however, saw more correctly that that distinction is not to be pressed beyond a point: the distinction was one of degree. There are Indian *tārkikas*, just as there are Western intuitionists. Thus Radhakrishnan writes much later:

> Logical method knows no frontiers. The law of contradiction obtains in both East and West. Even in the East no one can hold at the same time the two principles of the reality of God and His unreality. The acceptance of one requires the rejection of the other.[19]

In this connection, I will briefly comment on the following issues (1) the primacy of the logical in Western thought; (2) the

primacy of intuition in Indian philosophy; (3) the distinction between intellect and intuition; (4) the role of intuition in philosophy; (5) where really does the difference between Western philosophy and Indian philosophy lie?

The Alleged Primacy of the Logical in Western Thought

For my purpose here, I need not recall the historical genesis of Western logic as a science from the Platonic dialectic. What is important is to bear in mind the role that logic comes to play in theoretical and scientific thinking, and that is best expressed thus: 'Science in the Platonic sense intends to be no longer a merely naïve activity prompted by a purely theoretical interest. Every step that it takes, it also demands to justify as genuine, as necessarily valid, according to principles.'[20] In this originally instituted sense of scientificity, there was the idea of 'justification according to principles', but also the idea of 'logical insight into the validity of each step taken': this inevitably implied the idea of an intellectual intuition into each step of one's deduction—an idea that continues until the time of Descartes, eventually to be displaced by Kant. What, however, does determine the large and variegated fortunes of Western thought is a theory of concept originating with the Socratic striving towards a precise definition. Detached from the idea of intellectual intuition (Descartes's 'clearness and distinctness'), it becomes eventually the Kantian concept as a rule of synthesis—and the intuitive understanding (of Plato and Descartes) becomes the discursive understanding whose performance consists in synthesizing sensible data by a priori or empirical rules. The human mind, in its cognitive enterprise, becomes the constitutive source of the world that it purports to know.

The Platonic idea of scientificity continues through the mathematization of the sciences, and by a parallel development through the mathematization of logic itself.

While thus logical-deductive reason plays a dominant role in shaping Western thought, is it true that logical reason has an unquestioned primacy? An affirmative answer has to take note of the following historical features: throughout the history of the way logical activity of the understanding was conceived, an intuitive component (insight, evidence, clarity/distinctness, mathematical construction) was a candidate for recognition, so that the

intellect and intuition were taken as belonging together. In the second place, there was a continuous attempt to limit the reaches of intellect, on the one hand, by the way sensory experience presents data for the intellect to organize (Kant called this intuition) and, on the other, by that highly dubious, but never quite overcome, claim of 'intellectual intuition'. Kant meant by it one thing when he rejected it; Fichte and Schelling meant by it something else when they reintroduced it. Modern Western thinking has been deeply transcendental, returning always to the structure of human subjectivity—and even when this structure was conceived as 'logical' (as with Kant) the return was by a method of reflection which—and this was the point Fichte made so obscurely—claimed to bring to clarity what was all along being obscurely lived through. Western thought thus constantly sought to go beyond logic to the foundations of logic in the structure of subjectivity that itself is only reflectively accessible.

The Alleged Primacy of Intuition in Indian Philosophy

Thinking about the alleged primacy of intuition in Indian philosophy is hard, and inevitably goes with thinking about the role of critical thinking in Indian philosophy. A first and inevitable step is to the simple, but often neglected, questions: How is 'intuition' to be translated in Sanskrit? Do we have a Sanskrit word for it? Do we have a near synonym in the Sanskrit philosophical vocabulary? (The same questions also apply to 'critical reason'.) For intuition, the commonly cited equivalents are: *prajñā, pratibhā, ārṣajñāna, yogipratyakṣa, samyagjñāna, anubhava, aparokṣānubhūti.* Of these clearly, *anubhava* or *anubhūti* are used sometimes as synonyms for 'knowledge' other than memory, sometimes for cognition other than memory, inference, and *śabda* (i.e. for perception, *pratykṣa*). What must be said about *anubhūti* such that it would amount to intuition? The two *ārṣajñāna* or *yogipratyakṣa* mean not so much intuition in the sense in which it is of importance in philosophy, as extraordinary perception (of things too far or too small or not mediated by sensory apparatus), which only *ṛṣis* or yogis could have. Its objects are by and large things in principle perceptible though not perceptible by any ordinary man under (such and such) ordinary circumstances. (Its object, for example, is not *brahman* or *ātman*).

The word *pratibhā*, as used in Yogasūtra III. iii. 2, means the yogi's ability to know what is in future. *Samādhi* is a state of being free, rather than knowing anything. Discriminating knowledge (*viveka-jñāna*) is the cognition that two things—in this case, the *puruṣa* and the *prakṛti*—are different, and such a cognition, obviously, is relational and mediated. In Vedānta, one finds use of '*aparokṣā-nubhūti*': an immediate experience of the identity of *ātman* and *brahman*. It certainly comes close to what one may call an intuitive awareness of the truth about the self. This may be taken to be 'higher' intuition of the metaphysical truth. But what role do these concepts play in the *darśanas*? I wish to suggest that the *darśanas* themselves did not make use of these notions. In providing or establishing their respective metaphysical theses, the *darśanas* used the *pramāṇas*; the *pramāṇas* were also to demonstrate the possibility of such experience as their theory demanded. To the list of *pramāṇas* belonged one or other of the following: perception (*pratyakṣa*), inference (*anumāna*), word (*śabda*), comparison (*upamāna*), postulation (*arthāpatti*), non-perception (*anupala-bodhi*), possibility (*sambhava*), tradition (*aitihya*). Where are intuitive experience and mystic experience? They are not *pramā-ṇas*: they are experiences.

To recall an example discussed earlier: the Advaita Vedānta placed at the end of the cognitive process—i.e. after the stages of *śravaṇa* (hearing) and *manana* (reflecting), something called *nididhyāsana* or contemplation. In my view, the task of philosophy ends with reflection. Something else, generally known as *sādhanā* or spiritual practice, brings about that experience which supposedly brings about or itself is *mokṣa*. Reflection by itself does not lead to immediate experience of the truth, i.e. to *aparokṣānubhūti*, not to speak of including it. Philosophy only demonstrates the possibility of achieving a goal, the conception of which—be it noted—is theoretically internal to the system. What I am contending, then, is this: the Indian philosopher *qua* philosopher exercises intuitive grasp and achieves intuitive experience no more and no less than his Western counterpart. What he does is no less critical thinking. The *pramāṇas* are the norms of critical assessment.

Let me then summarize: it is an essential component of Indian culture to believe that it is possible for individuals, given suitable effort, discipline, and, perhaps, past *karma*, to achieve

experiences—intuitive, if that word is to have any sense—that free them from pain of bondage due to the cycle of rebirth, but the philosophies do not make any direct use of such experiences (in fact, they just cannot), nor did the philosophers, *qua* philosophers, have any access to such experiences.

The Distinction between Intellect and Intuition

Our thoughts about this distinction are not coherent. Does intellect analyse a given whole into parts, or does it also synthesize parts into wholes? Or does it do both? Does intuition grasp an individual in its uniqueness (not as instantiating a universal), or does it grasp an undifferentiated whole? Or does, after all, intuition grasp anything (for does not the metaphor of 'grasping' imply the subject–object distinction), or does it amount to being identical with what is allegedly known? Is intuition operative only in artistic creation (as well as artistic enjoyment) or also in mathematical proofs, scientific discoveries, and theory-building? Also in religious experience and in spiritual self-knowledge? Could all these be intuitions in the same sense, or are there, rather, radically different senses of 'intuition'? How are these respectable senses connected with the alleged supernormal, extra-sensory perceptions of distant and not-yet-actual events, the sort of intellectual intuition Kant derided in his 'Dreams of a Spirit-Seer'? Granted all these, one cannot but ask: is philosophical cognition 'intuition' in some other sense? Or, rather, is there any need for the philosopher to develop this special sort of intuition? Before returning to this last question, let me cast doubt on a familar way of drawing the distinction, i.e. in terms of mediacy and immediacy. Is ordinary sense-perception immediate or mediate? It is not inferential, hence immediate, but it is mediated by the sense-organs (as well as by past cognition), hence mediate. Ferhaps, one is looking for a cognition that is absolutely unmediated. Is there any such? Please note that I have no qualms about conceding that there are such unmediated experiences. What I am at great odds with is the claim that there are such unmediated cognitions. It is also often said that intuitive knowledge is self-manifesting (*svayaṃprakāśa*). This must be so in some sense other than that in which the issues have been debated in Indian thought, for both the self-manifesting and the self-validity

theories regard all cognitions, including the inferential, as being so.

It must be clear that I do not wish to deny that there is some interesting distinction between intellect and intuition. I wish only to say that the distinction is far from being clearly and coherently drawn. Besides, in some complex manner, the two sorts of cognition must involve each other.

The Role of Intuition in Philosophy

Granted that, in some as yet unclear sense, intuitions of various types are operative in pre-philosophical life, it does not follow that philosophy itself, trying to comprehend life and experience in all their modalities, is in need of any special sort of intuition. Philosophy of perception is not perceptual; philosophy of mathematics is not mathematical.

The only view about the role of intuition in philosophy—not in religion, art, or elsewhere—that I know of, is to be found in Fichte: since Fichte wanted philosophy to be a systematic science, it needed a starting-point—which was, for him, the intellectual intuition of the ego of its own activities.

Note that Indian philosophy does not need such an absolute starting-point: a *darśana* is not a logically deductive system; the *Ātman-Brahman*, even for Vedānta, is not such an axiomatic first principle.

At the beginning of a *darśana* there is no intuited first principle (the etymology of 'seeing' here is misleading). There is, rather, a point of view as encapsulated in the texts. There are texts behind texts.

What about the alleged lack of critical reason in the Indian *darśanas*? A system of philosophy has not merely to put forward a theory of reality, of man and his relation to the world, of experience and cognition, it has also to ground, validate, and legitimize its theory. Philosophers have never agreed about the norms, the criteria, and the sources of such validation. In general, Western philosophers have, for this purpose, appealed to several such: if empiricists, they have fallen back on sensory experience as the ultimate court of appeal; if rationalists, they have appealed either to logico-mathematical reason, or as with Descartes and the German Idealists, to the principle of reflective self-consciousness;

or, as with the phenomenologists, to the data of eidetic intuition. The Indian *darśanas*, early in their lives, developed the theory of *pramāṇas* which were both the orginating conditions of true cognition and the normative principles of their validation. There are several interesting features of this theory, to which I have drawn attention earlier. There is one particular feature to which I will draw attention now—this is the theory of *śabda* as a *pramāṇa*. It is this particular feature which has been criticized as having excluded from the reaches of the Indian thinker a truly critical spirit. I myself used to think so. Reading Gadamer's *Truth and Method* made me see that while, in many details, my criticism was valid, I had not perceived the true nature of *śabda vis-à-vis* critical reason. If Gadamer is right, authentic thinking takes place from within a tradition. The theory of *śabdapramāṇa* raises this insight into a self-conscious epistemological theory.

In the long run, coming from the Western intellectual tradition as also from the tradition of Indological studies, the crucial question remains: can the chapters spread out over the Sanskrit texts of the *darśanas* on perception (*pratyakṣa*), inference (*anumāna*), sentential understanding (*śābdabodha*), truth (*prāmāṇya*), to name only a few—can these chapters, topics, disputations, be separated from the supposedly fundamentally soteriological, theological, and ritualistic thinking of that tradition, and be elevated to the status of an intellectual discipline to rank with those of a Plato, Kant, or Husserl? I wish to emphasize that not only can they be so separated, but the tradition itself achieved the necessary idealization. It is also true, in my view, that the same process happened in Western thought. (Recall the process of secularization that went on even after Descartes. Both Nicolai Hartmann and Heidegger continued to look upon the Kantian Transcendental unity of apperception, the Hegelian *Geist*, the Fichtean Ego as but secularized versions of deeply theological notions. Not surprisingly, Heidegger characterized Western metaphysics as onto-theological.) Recall Śaṃkara's refusal, at the beginning of his *Brahmasūtrabhāṣyam*, to regard the *jñānakānda*, i.e. the chapters on knowledge, and *karmakānda*, i.e. the chapters on action, as forming two parts of the same book, and to sharply separate knowledge (*jñāna*) from action (*dharma*).

The crucial question is not, are the *darśanas* philosophies? The latter doubt, when it is verbal and trivial, questions the justifica-

tion of applying a word, instituted first by the Greeks, to a different tradition. This anxiety, even if justified, is not of much worth if it concerns the word, for then the same sort of anxiety would haunt the purist if he heard of Hindu 'mathematics'. The really substantive concern would be not about the word but about the concept. Does the Indian *darśana*, by virtue of its subject-matter, its concerns, its methodology come under the purview of the concept 'philosophy'?

Let us remember, however, that nothing depends upon what you decide. It is as though some Sanskrit pundits in Benares decided not to dignify the philosophies of a Kant or of a Husserl as a *darśana* because they lack some feature that they thought a *darśana* properly so-called should have.

We need to avoid two extreme views in this context: one relativistic, the other essentialistic. The relativist holds that the Indian concepts of philosophy (of rationality, truth) are not only different, but radically different from the Western; that the Indian and the Western philosophies are not only different, but are, as philosophies, so different that one ought not to apply the term 'philosophy' in the Indian context. (Rorty holds such a view. I believe Heidegger would have assented.) The essentialist holds that philosophy is a rational enterprise, that rationality has no geographical or cultural variations, that in their essence, stripped of the cultural externalities, they come out as the same sort of enterprise.

I believe that both are mistaken. The relativist is wrong in arguing, almost a priori, that the two could not be generically identical. Show him that a particular thesis or a particular argument or a particular concern in Indian thought is just about the same as one in Western thought, and he would say: it is you who have so abstracted the phenomenon under consideration from its context that you have made it appear in that way. In other words, your interpretation has created that semblance of identity. This is an a priori argument; how can you refute it? What is suspicious is that the essentialist also uses a similar argument. Show the essentialist that two nearly identical theses, concepts, or concerns differ in important respects, and he will respond by saying: those differences are extrinsic, context-sensitive, and so inessential elements.

I believe that there are enough similarities between Indian

darśanas and the Western philosophies to justify translating *darśana* as 'philosophy'—enough differences erupting precisely where similarities first showed themselves to justify talk of *Indian* philosophy. 'Philosophy' is a concrete universal in the Hegelian sense, not an abstract identity. The universality of rational thinking transcends and yet comprehends local differences; it lives in and through such differences.

NOTES AND REFERENCES

1. It should be obvious that I am indebted to H. G. Gadamer's thoughts for interpretation of *śabdapramāṇa*, 'tradition' and 'interpretation'. For a systematic working out of the concept of interpretation, see my *Transcendental Phenomenology: An Analytic Account* (Oxford: Blackwell, 1989), ch. 1, § 1.8.
2. See J. Habermas, 'Der Universalitätsanspruch der Hermeneutik' in K. -O. Apel, (ed.), *Hermeneutik und Ideologiekritik* (Frankfurt: Suhrkamp, 1971).
3. 'Evam madiyamapi vacanaṃ pratītyasamutpannatvāt niḥsvabhāvaṃ niḥsvabhāvatvāt śūnyamityupapannaṃ' (Nāgārjuna in *Vigrahavyāvartani*).
4. See Śaṃkara's commentary on *Brahmasūtra* II. ii. 33.
5. An example of such rhetoric is to be found in the theist *Kṛṣṇa*-worshippers' claim that it is better to be a jackal (*śrugāla*) in Vṛndāban (the home of Kṛṣṇa) than to be 'free' or liberated in the sense of the Naiyāyika!
6. For the distinction between announcing and expressing, see Husserl, *Logical Investigations*, ed. and trans. J. N. Findlay (New York: Humanities Press, 1970), vol. i, Inv. I, §§ 6–8.
7. E. Husserl, *The Crisis of European Sciences and Transcendental Phenomenology*, ed. and trans. David Carr (Evanston, iii.: Northwestern University Press, 1970), 280.
8. Ibid. 280.
9. Ibid. 283.
10. Ibid. 284.
11. Ibid. 284–5.
12. Review of G. J. Larson and E. Deutsch (eds.), *Interpreting across Boundaries: New Essays in Comparative Philosophy*, *Philosophy East and West*, 39 (1989), 332–7.

13. W. Halbfass, *Indien und Europa* (Basle and Stuttgart: Schwabe, 1981), 296 ff.
14. R. Rorty, J. B. Schneewind, and Q. Skinner (eds.), *Philosophy in History* (Cambridge: Cambridge University Press, 1985), 8.
15. J. L. Mehta, *Philosophy and Religion: Essays in Interpretation* (New Delhi: Indian Council of Philosophical Research, 1990), 13.
16. Ibid. 16.
17. S. Radhakrishnan, *An Idealist View of Life* (London: Allen & Unwin, 1932), 127.
18. Ibid. 128.
19. P. A. Schilpp (ed.), *The Philosophy of Sarvepalli Radhakrishnan* (New York: Tudor Publishing Co., 1952), 826.
20. E. Husserl, *Formal and Transcendental Logic*, ed. and trans. D. Cairns (The Hague: Martinus Nijhoff, 1969), 1.

INDEX

abhidhā 77, 96
abhihitānvayavāda 70–81
abstract entity 233
action 14, 23, 31–2, 41–2, 140–4, 196–8, 232, 259–66
aitihya 188, 242–3
akhanda-vākya-vāda 67
ākānkṣā 73, 77, 92, 250
Annaṃbhaṭṭa 98
anuvyavasāya 145
ānvīkṣikī 286
anvitābhidhānavāda 70–81
anyāpoha 54, 60–2, 93, 159, 167
apauruṣeyatva 257–9, 273, 275–6, 282
Āraṇyaka, Hariharānanda 98
Arendt, Hannah 263
artha 57, 62–3
arthakriyākāritva 158
arthāpatti 251
āsatti 73, 77, 150
astitā 153–5
atomism 205–6, 209, 219–21
avayavin 208, 215–19
avidyā 164, 182, 237, 270

Barua, B. M. 226
Basham, A. L. 224
being 5, 150–69, 178, 233, 289
belief 136
Bergson, H. 291
Bhartṛhari 54, 60, 67, 94, 99, 238
Bhattacharya, K. C. 147, 149, 203–4, 211, 224, 255–6
bhāvanā 85
Bhave, Vinoba 195, 224
body 23, 28, 204
Bradley, F. H. 44, 163, 285, 291
Brahmānanda 147
Brentano, F. 107, 114

Caraka 247
Cārvāka 27, 28, 29
Category 152, 235
Causality 218–19, 226 n., 229
  causal theories of knowledge 230–1
  historical 276
  karmic 266
Chakraborty, A. 254
cognition 19–20, 130–1, 134–5, 136, 172–3, 174–5, 228–9, 230–1, 234
consciousness 5, 23, 26–40, 41–2, 42–6, 50
  as constitutive 236–7, 271
  as force or energy 237
  as foundational 236–8, 271
  historicity of 190–1
  as impartial spectator 51
  and metaphysics of presence 201
  pure 42–6, 50–1
  reality, 163–4
  as representational 201–2
  as self-manifesting, 46–7, 51, 163
  temporality of 191
  transcendental 50–1, 191
content 108–10, 165
  real and intentional 40, 148
construction 269–70
creation 18, 233, 237
critical thinking 52, 273–5, 277, 285, 293
criticism 8, 11, 13, 15, 16, 181, 234–5, 272–3
Croce, B. 291
Custom 247–8

darśana 8–10, 14–17, 23, 170, 227
Dasgupta, S. N. 147
Davis, Lawrence 117, 132, 183
Dayānanda 10
definition 19
demonstrative ('This') 125
Derrida, J. 60
Descartes, R. 199, 291, 292, 297
description 177–8
desire 42, 196–7
  to act 261

De Smet, R. V. 182
dharma-dharmi 122–3
Dharmakīrti 90, 99, 120, 149, 239
Dharmottara 141, 142, 149
Dignāga 37, 52 n., 90, 142, 239, 286
doubt (*saṁśaya*) 20
dṛṣṭānta (example) 117–18
Dummett, M. E. 65, 80, 99

Eliade, M. 187
Eliot, T. S. 259
empiricism 269
essentialism 221
eternal recurrence 264
experience 227–8, 269, 294–5
  spiritual 281–2
extensionalism 19, 21–2, 125–9, 131, 298
Evans, G. 67, 88, 99

Fichte, J. C. 293, 297
form (*ākāra*) 33–40, 135, 174, 180, 221
formed (*sākāra*) 33 ff.
formless (*nirākāra*) 33–5, 40, 51, 108, 135, 174, 180
formal validity 116 ff., 131
foundationalism 271
Frauwallner, E. 212, 226
Frege, G. 19, 54, 55, 57, 59, 60, 62, 64, 65, 67, 69, 70, 78, 79, 80, 81, 82, 83, 88, 97, 99, 107, 108, 114, 115, 125, 233, 254
Funke, G. 224

Gadādhara 286, 290
Gadamer H. G. 24 n., 274, 275, 289
Gāgā Bhaṭṭa 267
Galileo 221
Gandhi, M. K. 275
Gaṅgeśa 140, 145, 146, 148, 238
Gārgya 87
Gautama, 14
God (*Iśvara*), 221, 233, 257
Guha, D. C. 25 n.
guṇa 14, 41–2, 209–12, 219, 244
Gotama 170–1
grammarians 56, 57, 84, 85, 86, 87, 172

Habermas, J. 25, 274–5, 299
Halbfass, W. 181 n.
Hartmann, N. 152, 297
Hattori, M. 52 n.
Hegel (-ian) 122, 165, 181 n., 190, 215, 263, 274, 276, 290, 297
Heidegger, M. 152, 199, 285, 287, 288–90, 297
Heisenberg, W. 226
Henle, M. 114, 132
hermeneutics, in Hindu Law 248
Herzberger, H. 98
hetvābhāsa 112–13, 137
Hintikka, J. 118, 132
Hiriyanna, M. 212–13
historical knowledge 188–9
historicism 4, 18, 221
history 21, 25 n., 187–92, 214
Hume, D. 118, 285, 287, 290
Husserl, E. 6, 10, 24, 25, 55, 62, 63, 92, 98, 107, 115, 119, 130–1, 132, 147, 182 n., 192, 200–1, 203, 226, 244, 271, 277, 283, 284, 285, 287, 290, 298
holism 80

'I' 26–9, 30–1, 43, 164, 176
idealism 173
identity 166–7, 177, 236
  sentences 95–7
ignorance 164, 176, 237, 270, 280
inference (*anumāna*) 100, 228, 231
  process of 101–3
  structure of 103–6
Ingalls, D. H. 182
interpretation 5, 23, 272, 273, 276
intensionalism 19, 21, 22, 125–6, 127, 128, 129, 131
intention, speaker's 55, 77, 90, 91
  meaning-intention 89–92, 258–9
intentionality 38, 42–6, 50–1, 164 202–3, 204, 237
intuition 125, 281
  in Indian philosophy, 293–5
  and intellect 291–6
  in philosophy 296–9

Jainism 90, 143, 238
theory of *naya* 277–8
syādvāda 278–9
Jayanta 76, 92, 142, 149
jñāna 33, 134–5

Kahn, C. 181 n.
Kalhaṇa 189, 223
Kaṇāda 155
Kant, I. 39, 44, 50, 53 n., 118, 125, 197, 199, 224, 243, 244, 274, 276, 287, 290, 292, 293, 295, 298
karma 23, 191, 213, 262–6, 265–6
Kātyāyana 87
Kautilya 188, 286
knowledge 32–3, 37, 39, 50, 79, 80, 89, 140–2, 147, 174–5, 195–6, 197
de re and *de dicto* 251–2
as a *guṇa* 42
as intentional 42
metaphysical theory of 41–2
of moral rules 256–7
philosophical 235
scriptural 143
knownness (*jñātatā*) 41
Kripke, S. 65, 92

lakṣaṇā 77, 81, 86, 96
language learning 68–9, 75–7
law 219–20
evidence in 248–9
pramāṇas in 247–9
problems of interpretation in 248
life world 16, 22
logic 13, 15, 16, 19, 20, 23, 106, 109, 114
of cognitions 130–1
Indian 100–32, 231; in Western philosophy 292–3
and ontology 101
and reality 122–5
and theory of knowledge 101
logicism 20, 22, 137

McDowell, J. 67, 68
Madhūsadana Saraswati 147
Majumdar, R. C. 189, 223
man 192 f
Manorathanandi 90, 99
Manu 247
mathematics 21, 243–7
mathematical truths 137
mathematization of nature 221
Matilal, B. K. 83, 84, 99, 120, 127, 129, 132, 168, 181 n., 183, 230, 266
māyā 198
meaning 19
denotative theory of 58, 60, 77
Platonic theory of 60
sentential 67–83
word-meaning 54–67, 138
mechanism 212–15
Mehta, J. L. 288, 289
memory 21, 30, 146–7, 241–3
mental 107–9, 119
Merleau-Ponty, M. 203
Metaphilosophy 277 ff.
Metaphysics 150–3
mind (*manas*) 202, 229
mithyā 270
modalities 2, 126, 128, 129, 131
modernity 11, 12, 16, 22
mokṣa 14, 191, 214–15, 264, 279–80, 281, 291, 294
Mookerjee, S. 182
Moore, G. E. 35, 36, 38, 52
Moralität 274
Mukhopadhyaya, P. K. 52, 181, 182
Murti, T. R. V. 207, 208

Nāgārjuna 14, 163, 286
Nageśa 62, 98
Nārada 249
nature 205–21
necessity 118–19, 120, 126, 127, 128, 131
negation 163–4, 233, 278
Nietzsche, F. 288
nirākāra 36, 108
nirvikalpa 239–40
non-attachment 197
Notturno, M. 132 n.

object 108 ff.
object-in-general 51

ontology 150–1, 152, 166 ff., 170, 171, 172, 173, 174, 178, 179, 180, 181, 184, 216–19, 232–4
orthodoxy 11, 273

padārtha 10, 78
pakṣatā 102
Pāṇini, 54, 57, 97, 98
Pappu, S. S. Rama Rao 52 n.
paraprakāśa 34
paryāpti 21, 25 n.
Pascal 291
Patanjali 54, 55, 62, 87, 95, 98
perception (*pratyakṣa*) 100, 167–8, 177, 178, 179, 217–19, 228, 236, 238–41, 251, 269
person 4, 31, 32, 50, 194, 195–205, 222
phala 141, 142–3
phenomenology 6, 22, 44, 108, 164, 177, 180–1, 187, 203, 237, 263, 271
Philips, C. H. 188, 189, 223
philosophy 7, 8, 9, 15, 16, 17, 18, 22, 43, 150–1, 172, 177, 180–1, 215–16, 222, 227, 234, 235, 260, 270–1, 272–3, 276–7, 277–99
Plato 221, 243, 276, 288, 292
platonism 107, 131
pluralism 166, 168, 172, 210
possibility 19, 20, 233
Potter. K. 132, 226 n.
Prabhācandra 90, 99
prakāra, (qualifier) 40, 51, 84, 123,
prakāratā 67, 88, 123, 168
prakṛti 14, 205, 208–12
pramāṇa 5, 8, 10, 16, 21, 22, 37, 52, 66, 79, 101, 116, 170, 171, 179, 180, 227–32, 235, 236, 240–1, 241–3, 243–44, 247–59, 270, 271, 272–3, 277, 280–1, 285, 294
  vyavasthā 240–1
prameya 8, 170–1, 232–4
pratibhā 68
pratyaya 57, 63–4
pravṛtti 138–9, 171, 196–7, 212
principle of excluded middle 120–1
principle of non-contradiction 120–1
proof, mathematical 246–7
proposition 109–10, 114, 119, 122, 124–5, 126, 130–1, 134, 136, 233
psychoanalysis 46
psychologism 20, 22, 106–7, 112–13, 114, 115, 131, 137, 211, 229, 230
Pusalkar, A. D. 188, 223
Pythagoras 221

quality (*guṇa*) 40, 84
quasi-*Sinn* 83, 88, 89
Quine, W. V. O. 127, 129, 285, 287

Radhakrishnan, S. 291
Raghunātha Śiromaṇi 14, 66, 146, 157, 158, 165, 181
Raja, K. Kunjunni 98
Rāmānuja 45, 53 n., 11, 97, 99, 190, 202,
Rāmānujācārya 267
Ramsey, F. P. 83
rasa 258
rationalism 269–70
rationality 2, 3, 7, 8, 113–14, 227, 277, 282
Ratnakīrti 290
realism 36, 38, 40, 41, 108, 172–3, 174–5, 180, 203, 218, 240–1
reason 227–8, 269
reference 55, 69, 70, 78–9, 80–2, 88, 91, 96–7, 160
representationism 36, 38, 201
revelation 281
Rorty, R. 285, 287
Russell, B. 107, 125, 148, 158–9, 182, 246

śābdabodha 57, 66–7, 83–9, 249–50
śabdapramāṇa 11, 21–3, 59, 80, 231–2, 235, 249–59, 272–3, 299
Śaivism, Kashmir 51, 237
Sakatāyana 87
Śālikanātha 182
sāmānādhikaraṇya 95, 97
samavāya 154, 166, 176, 218
sambhava 21, 243–4
Śaṃkara 27, 31, 43, 44, 45, 52 n.,

53 n., 95, 97, 149, 162, 163, 166, 182, 193, 207, 214, 226, 279, 285, 286, 287, 291, 297
samsargatā 168
Sartre, J-P. 53 n., 169
sat, sattā 153–4, 155, 156, 157, 160, 161 ff.
Sautrantika 36, 61
Saussure, F. de 60, 62
Sayana 10
scepticism 20, 138, 142, 171, 172, 232
Schelling, F. W. J. 293
scripture 13, 14, 22, 43, 143, 170, 178–9, 235, 257
Seal, B. N. 210
Sen, P. K. 99
sense (*Sinn*) 55, 59, 60, 61, 62, 64, 65, 67, 69, 70, 78, 79, 81, 82, 83, 88, 91, 95, 114, 135, 233, 237, 272
sentence 67–83, 114–15, 134
Shaw, J. L. 98, 132
Shusterman, R. 226
Sibajiban (Bhattacharya) 120, 131, 132, 148, 149
Siderits, M. 60, 61, 98
similarity (*sādṛśya*) 121
singular terms 125
Sittlichkeit 274–5
Sivaraman, K. 53 n.
Spencer, H. 209
sphoṭa 57, 62–3
Spinoza 291
spiritual 17, 290–1
Sri Aurobindo 10, 203, 224, 237
Śrīharṣa 157, 182
Staal, J. F. 98, 132
Stcherbatsky, T. 182, 183
subject 4, 31, 50, 166, 195–6
  as transcendental 196
  object distinction 289–90;
    predicate distinction 122–4,
    primacy of 197–8
subjectivity 199, 201, 202, 203, 204
substance (*dravya*) 41
suffering 211–2, 214–15
sva-lakṣaṇa 93, 159, 239
svaprakāśa 34, 44, 49, 295
svataḥprāmāṇya 140–1, 230

tādātmya 166–7, 176
tarka 20, 116, 117, 231
tātparya 81, 96, 250
  śakti 77
teleology 212–15, 221
theoretical 17, 284, 285; mythical 283, 285
  practical 279 ff., 281, 283–4
thought 66, 281
Tillich, P. 264
time 18, 19, 25 n., 157–8, 165, 184–7, 214, 234, 264, 270
tradition 9, 10, 11, 12, 13, 14, 15, 16, 17, 21, 22, 23, 24, 188, 242–3, 259, 272, 274–5, 281–2
transcendental:
  argument 44, 50, 170, 179
  consciousness 42, 50–1
  constitution 237
  ego 200–1
  in modern Western philosophy 293
  observer 201, 203, 205
  person 204
  point of view 41
  question 36
  structure 51
  subjectivity 199–201, 202–3, 204, 277
  truths 138
  unity of apperception 199–200

Udayana 120, 121, 138, 140, 141, 142, 146, 149, 172, 290
uddeśya 123
Uddyotakara 226, 238, 242, 250, 286, 290
understanding 66, 74, 75, 79, 83, 89, 249–50, 252–5
universals 233

Vācaspati 14, 90, 138, 140, 142, 146, 149, 157, 158, 159, 162, 182, 238, 262, 290
Vaiśeṣika 5, 14, 150, 152, 154, 155, 170, 176
Vallabhācārya 52 n., 267
Varadarāja 117
Vardhamāna 66, 172

Vārsyāyaṇi 154
Vasubandhu 158, 239
Vātsyāyana 138, 171, 184, 226, 243
vidheya 123
vidhi 262
Vijñānabhikṣu 14
vikalpa 64, 159, 269–70
viṣayatā 83, 88, 89, 148, 168
viśeṣa 207
viśeṣyatā 88, 123
Visvanātha 267
volition (*kṛti*) 261
vyāpti 25, 124, 126–7, 136–7, 233

Vyāsa 269

whole (and part) 215–19
will, freedom of 262
word, 87
  meaning 55–67

Yāska 87, 154
yoga 23, 43, 46, 56, 60, 64
yogācāra 35, 36, 38
yogyatā 73, 77, 250, 253, 254

Zilberman, D. 235, 266

Printed in the United States
711100001B

REASON AND TRADITION IN INDIAN THOUGHT